The Reconstruction of
White Southern Womanhood
1865–1895

THE RECONSTRUCTION OF
WHITE SOUTHERN WOMANHOOD 1865–1895

JANE TURNER CENSER

LOUISIANA STATE UNIVERSITY PRESS

BATON ROUGE

Copyright © 2003 by Louisiana State University Press

All rights reserved

Manufactured in the United States of America

First printing

cloth

12   11   10   09   08   07   06   05   04   03

5   4   3   2   1

paper

12   11   10   09   08   07   06   05   04   03

5   4   3   2   1

Designer: Melanie O'Quinn Samaha
Typeface: A Garamond, Trajan
Typesetter: Coghill Composition Co., Inc.
Printer and binder: Thomson-Shore, Inc.

Library of Congress Cataloging-in-Publication Data:

Censer, Jane Turner, 1951–
    The reconstruction of White Southern womanhood, 1865–1895 / Jane
Turner Censer.
        p.   cm.
Includes bibliographical references and index.
    ISBN 0-8071-2907-0 (alk. paper) — ISBN 0-8071-2921-6 (pbk. : alk.
paper)
    1. Women—Southern States—Social conditions—19th century.   2. White
women—Southern States—History—19th century.   3. Upper class
women—Southern States—History—19th century.   4. Sex role—Southern
States—History—19th century.   5. Women—Southern States—History—19th
century.   6. Southern States—History—1865–   I. Title.

    HQ1438.S63C45   2003
    305.42′0975—dc21

                                                                2003006660

For Jack

CONTENTS

ILLUSTRATIONS

Following page 90

Southern Female Institute, 1870s

Nannie Tunstall

Katherine Waller Barrett

Amélie Rives

Castle Hill

Mary Ellet Cabell

Eliza Lord DeRosset

Frances Christine Fisher

Mary Bayard Devereux Clarke

Julia Magruder

M. G. McClelland

ACKNOWLEDGMENTS

This is not the book I intended to write. Female writers and schoolteachers played no part in my thinking when I considered pursuing the postwar experiences of planter families. Yet as I delved deeper into my research, the women of the old elite grabbed my attention and would not let go. Not only were they an especially vital and fascinating part of the story, but I became convinced that they were an important part of the late nineteenth-century South. In that way, schoolteachers, authors, and their stay-at-home sisters forced their way into my consciousness and eventually hijacked my project. And in some ways perhaps it was only fitting that I should make this exploration, for the southern female schoolteachers who followed the pioneering generation that I chronicle here played a vital part in my family and even in my own career. My beloved aunt, the late Elizabeth Turner, passed on a legacy that she received from my great-aunt, Ethel Hays, both of them former schoolteachers, to help me begin my graduate studies in history. I am grateful to both of them. I also fondly remember other schoolteachers in the family—my aunt, Mabel Turner Smith, and my grandmother, Flora Phelps Embry. My sister-in-law, Rhonda Cole Turner, continues this commendable tradition.

I owe thanks to many, many people and institutions for various kinds of assistance with this project. Fellowships from the National Humanities Center and the American Council of Learned Societies funded the research into southern planter families that began this project. A Mellon Research Stipend from the Virginia Historical Society supported research in their rich collections. A Fellowship for College Teachers from the National Endowment for the Humanities allowed me time to complete a draft of the entire manuscript. My home institution, George Mason University, has supported this undertaking in a multitude of ways: course reductions, research assistance, a summer stipend, and study leaves. I am also grateful to the History and Art History department for underwriting the purchase of and permissions for illustrations for this book.

My researches have been made enormously easier by the knowledgeable and helpful staffs I encountered at the Southern Historical Collection, Wilson Library, University of North Carolina at Chapel Hill; the Virginia Historical Society; the Special Collections Department, University of Virginia Library; the Library of Virginia; the Duke University Rare Book, Manuscript, and Special Collections Library; the Library of Congress, the North Carolina Division of Archives and History; and the Fauquier County Circuit Court's Hall of Records. I owe special thanks to Frances Pollard at the Virginia Historical Society and to Sandra Gioia Treadway, Sara Bearss, and John Kneebone at the Library of Virginia. Brent Tarter at the Library of Virginia has helped me with more research problems than either he or I care to recall. I was very fortunate to have George Oberle as a research assistant; his careful combing of the records and his superb bibliographical skills greatly enriched my study. For lodging and great companionship on research trips I am grateful to John and Cheryl Lang in Raleigh, North Carolina, and my cousins, Jane and Paul Kingston, in Charlottesville, Virginia.

Many friends have assisted this project over the years. My colleagues at George Mason University have been a constant source of good cheer and encouragement. In particular, Michael O'Malley, Roy Rosenzweig, Jeffrey C. Stewart, and Rosemarie Zagarri read parts of this work and offered invaluable suggestions. When I presented papers on this research at the History Graduate Colloquium at George Mason, the Washington Seminar on American History and Culture, and the annual meeting of the Organization of American Historians, I received numerous helpful criticisms and suggestions. Anne Firor Scott and Joel Williamson have been steadfast supporters; I have enjoyed my discussions with them and I appreciate the many ways in which they have aided this project. Vernon and Georgeanne Burton, John Inscoe, John David Smith, James C. Turner, David Schuyler, Elizabeth Varon, and LeeAnn Whites have all read and commented on various versions of this research. I am particularly indebted to J. William Harris for his careful annotation of the entire manuscript. Bill rescued me from numerous missteps and an enormous number of infelicities; he also gave me new ideas about how the parts could all fit together.

As I have been turning my manuscript into a book, I have relied on many people. Stephanie Jacobe at the Virginia Historical Society helped me find images in their large collection. At the University of Virginia, Michael F. Plunkett, Margaret D. Hrabe, and Rey A. Antonio all were extremely helpful. Audrey C. Johnson of the Library of Virginia was indefatigable in helping me obtain pictures of female writers. I would like to acknowledge the permission of *Southern Cultures* and the *North Carolina Historical Review* to use materials from articles published in them. I also am grateful to Anne Carter at the *North Carolina Historical Review* for allowing me to use illustrations that appeared with my article. I appreciate the enthusiasm with which Maureen Hewitt and Sylvia Frank Rodrigue have promoted this book. As my editor, George Roupe has patiently helped me manage a million details. I am also grateful to Alisa Plant for saving my prose from its worst excesses while allowing me to tell this story my way.

My family has played a special part in the long process of researching and writing this book. My husband, Jack Censer, has read and discussed with me the many drafts of every chapter. Even when I rejected his suggestions, his searching criticisms have helped me strengthen the book's organization and argument. He has also put up with the relocations and dislocations of research with good humor. Marjorie and Joel continue to remind me of both the complexities and joys of life. Any errors of interpretation or fact that remain are mine alone.

ABBREVIATIONS

CWF   Colonial Williamsburg Foundation

Duke   Rare Book, Manuscript, and Special Collections Library, Perkins
          Library, Duke University, Durham, N.C.

FCCC   Hall of Records, Fauquier County Circuit Court, Warrenton, Va.

JSH   *Journal of Southern History*

LC   Library of Congress, Washington, D.C.

NCDAH   North Carolina Division of Archives and History, Raleigh

NCHR   *North Carolina Historical Review*

SHC   Southern Historical Collection, Wilson Library, University of
          North Carolina, Chapel Hill

UVA   Special Collections Department, University of Virginia Library,
          Charlottesville

VHS   Virginia Historical Society, Richmond

VC   *Virginia Cavalcade*

VMHB   *Virginia Magazine of History and Biography*

The Reconstruction of
White Southern Womanhood
1865–1895

INTRODUCTION

The changes brought to the South by war and emancipation have fascinated observers for now over a century, yet for no period of southern history have white women been so little studied as for those years immediately following the Civil War. This seems particularly ironic, since elite white women's activities during the heyday of plantation society and the Civil War inspired a host of studies. Indeed, it was those women writing their memoirs of the Civil War at the century's end who helped to spark their inclusion in histories. As scholars in the 1960s began to turn their focus more broadly on women, Anne Firor Scott wrote the definitive story of this transformation in her book, *The Southern Lady*.[1]

For over thirty years, Scott's book has stood as the major interpretation of elite southern women's position in the nineteenth century. Asserting that the war helped to emancipate women, Scott argued that postwar women altered gender roles and took on new activities, such as operating plantations. Yet because she was surveying elite women over a century's time throughout the South, Scott devoted only a short section of her book to the late nineteenth century. In recent years, scholars such as Jonathan Wiener, Suzanne Lebsock, George Rable, Drew Gilpin Faust, and LeeAnn Whites have disputed Scott's findings. Wiener, after surveying households in the 1870 U.S. census, has argued that Scott overestimated the extent of women's plantation management, while Lebsock has speculated that women's access to land and other property decreased after the war. Although Rable, Faust, and Whites have posited changes in gender roles during the Civil War, they have tended to see the postwar period as a return to old practices. Faust has asserted that slaveholding women were most reluctant to change. Both she and Whites believe postwar white women to have been so deeply involved in bolstering the manhood of the defeated Confederate soldiers that they neither agitated for nor even sought alterations in their status. Yet only

---

1. Anne Firor Scott, *The Southern Lady: From Pedestal to Politics, 1830–1930* (Chicago, 1970).

Whites has undertaken detailed postbellum research, and her studies have focused more on non-elite women and later periods.[2]

In the years since Anne Scott wrote *The Southern Lady*, a generation of scholarship has grown up about black and white women in the Old South. While Scott pointed out discrepancies between the image of the leisured southern lady and the actual life of the busy plantation mistress, a host of other scholars have added to those findings. Lebsock's work on Petersburg, Virginia, has shown a town full of women active in the public sphere—whether as property owners, businesswomen, or civic-minded workers for benevolent causes. Despite all the rhetoric about a married woman's legal existence being subsumed in her husband's, Lebsock discovered the existence of separate estates—that is, property held in trust for married women—and passed on by them to children, friends, and relatives. Christie Farnham in *The Education of the Southern Belle* has pointed out the intellectual content of the education that many elite southern women received, even as southern spokesmen denounced strong-minded women and women's rights agitators.[3]

Although scholars agree that the nineteenth-century South was never a hotbed of advanced ideas about woman's place, a debate of sorts has raged among the historians of the Old South about the extent of patriarchy in that society. Many scholars continue to argue that the South was peculiarly repressive for white women. Some, like Elizabeth Fox-Genovese, have held that elite white women themselves preferred a hierarchical society in which they were subordinated, if that was the price for slavery and its exploitation of poorer classes. Others (such as Lebsock) believe that these white women, rather than being alone and repressed, aided one another in a community of women whose values and actions often differed from those of the men around them. These conflicting interpretations agree that the antebellum South was a place of nuances and complexity. In the daily life of the rural South, brimming with face-to-face interac-

2. Jonathan Wiener, "Female Planters and Planters' Wives in Civil War and Reconstruction: Alabama, 1850–1870," *Alabama Review* 30 (April 1977): 135–49; Suzanne Lebsock, *The Free Women of Petersburg: Status and Culture in a Southern Town, 1784–1860* (New York, 1984); George Rable, *Civil Wars: Women and the Crisis of Southern Nationalism* (Urbana, Ill.,1989), ch. 13; Drew Gilpin Faust, *Mothers of Invention: Women of the Slaveholding South in the American Civil War* (Chapel Hill, N.C., 1996), 247–57; LeeAnn Whites, *The Civil War as a Crisis in Gender: Augusta, Georgia, 1860–1890* (Athens, Ga., 1995), 160–208. See also LeeAnn Whites, "The Charitable and the Poor: The Emergence of Domestic Politics in Augusta, Georgia, 1860–1880," *Journal of Social History* 17 (1984): 601–13; idem, "The Degraffenried Controversy: Race, Class, and Gender in the New South," *JSH* 54 (Aug. 1988): 449–78.

3. Lebsock, *Free Women of Petersburg*; Christie Ann Farnham, *The Education of the Southern Belle: Higher Education and Student Socialization in the Antebellum South* (New York, 1994).

tions, room clearly existed for individual variations—whether it was the local judge who kept a "shadow family" with his African American housekeeper/mistress or the widow who operated a plantation.[4]

Yet our image of women in the South immediately after the war has changed relatively little. Because of the prevalent notion that the poverty of the postwar South offered only hard work and bitterness even to elite women, relatively few studies have explored their lives. To be sure, Edward Ayers's massive tome about life after Reconstruction evokes a changing womanhood in a fluid South, while Laura Edwards's cameo of Granville County, North Carolina, suggests that black and white men and women were working out new understandings of old themes. Although a number of excellent monographs have focused on women's civic activities, primarily in various urban areas of the New South, no study combining research on a variety of subjects with a broad perspective on women has been undertaken to revise or enhance Scott's arguments about postwar women.[5]

This book focuses on privileged white women, not because their experience was more valuable, but because their education and status gave them chances

4. Elizabeth Fox-Genovese, *Within the Plantation Household: Black and White Women of the Old South* (Chapel Hill, N.C., 1988); Jean E. Friedman, *The Enclosed Garden: Women and Community in the Evangelical South, 1830–1900* (Chapel Hill, N.C., 1985); Adele Logan Alexander, *Ambiguous Lives: Free Women of Color in Rural Georgia, 1789–1879* (Fayetteville, Ark., 1991); Allie Bayne Windham Webb, *Mistress of Evergreen Plantation: Rachel O'Connor's Legacy of Letters, 1823–1845* (Albany, N.Y., 1983). Most recently, Joan Cashin has sought to bridge some of these divergent interpretations by arguing that even though southern women forged a community of support for one another, their dominant ethos was a "culture of resignation" in which they used evasions, denial, and Christian submission in response to the violence and inequalities that confronted them. See "Introduction: Culture of Resignation," *Our Common Affairs: Texts from Women in the Old South,* ed. Joan Cashin (Baltimore, 1996), 1–41.

5. Edward L. Ayers, *The Promise of the New South: Life After Reconstruction* (New York, 1992); Laura F. Edwards, *Gendered Strife and Confusion: The Political Culture of Reconstruction* (Urbana, Ill., 1997). Edwards's more recent work, *Scarlett Doesn't Live Here Anymore: Southern Women in the Civil War Era* (Urbana, Ill., 2000), and Alexis Girardin Brown's article, "The Women Left Behind: Transformation of the Southern Belle, 1840–1880," *The Historian* (summer 2000): 759–78, each devotes less than one-third of the text to the postwar period. On urban women, see Elizabeth Hayes Turner, *Women, Culture, and Community: Religion and Reform in Galveston, 1880–1920* (New York, 1997); Anastatia Sims, *The Power of Femininity in the New South: Women's Organizations and Politics in North Carolina, 1880–1930* (Columbia, S.C., 1997); Sandra Gioia Treadway, *Women of Mark: A History of the Woman's Club of Richmond, Virginia, 1894–1994* (Richmond, Va., 1995); Marsha Wedell, *Elite Women and the Reform Impulse in Memphis, 1875–1915* (Knoxville, Tenn., 1991); Elizabeth Enstam, *Women and the Creation of Urban Life: Dallas, Texas, 1843–1920* (College Station, Tex., 1998); and Judith N. McArthur, *Creating the New Woman: The Rise of Southern Women's Progressive Culture in Texas, 1893–1918* (Urbana, Ill., 1998).

denied to others. I have looked at women from the old elite, both within the household and in the larger world, exploring how they understood themselves and their world and how they responded to the chances it offered them as well as those it held out of reach. The topics examined here flow from these possibilities for change, which occurred even in a setting of economic deprivation and social dislocation. Women's letters, diaries, and published writings, and those of their male relatives and friends, reveal both female activities and the mindset that lay behind them.[6]

Any history must have a geographical as well as a chronological focus. Mine is the Upper South of North Carolina and Virginia, two neighboring though quite different South Atlantic states. Virginia had been the cradle both of presidents and of an aristocracy wealthier and more self-conscious than that of the persistently rural state to its south. Moreover, as the Tidewater's plantation economy sagged in the nineteenth century, Virginia moved more quickly into the industrializing world. Richmond was larger and more cosmopolitan than any of North Carolina's cities. Although both states only reluctantly seceded from the Union, their Civil War experiences differed. North Carolina contributed its sons to the war; its per capita casualties exceeded any other state's. Virginia was the capital and heart of the Confederacy; only the vast swath of destruction in Georgia could begin to rival the devastation wrought by battles and invasion in the Shenandoah Valley and to the east, from Northern Virginia to Petersburg. The experiences of elite white Carolina and Virginia women provide an entry point for surveying the changes and continuities of life after 1865.[7]

In the research I tried to cast a wide net, drawing in families from the western areas as well as Tidewater and Piedmont locales. At times, to understand the families I encountered, I felt that I needed information beyond that usually provided by collections of personal papers. For these close-ups I looked primarily to three locales: coastal Craven County, North Carolina, with its cotton economy; New Hanover County, North Carolina, home to rice plantations; and

6. I have defined "privileged" or "genteel" women loosely as those belonging to families whose parents or grandparents owned more than fifteen slaves in the antebellum period. Many of the women who appear in this study are from families that owned more than fifty slaves. I use the term "old elite" to apply to all these former slaveholding families, even though the property losses of war and emancipation changed the economic situation of many of these families after 1865. Thus, my definition includes women who came from a privileged background but no longer lived in luxury or even comfort. Yet much of this deprivation was relative, and many in this "old elite" continued throughout the nineteenth century to wield considerable economic and political power.

7. Marie Tyler McGraw, *At the Falls: Richmond, Virginia, and Its People* (Chapel Hill, N.C., 1994).

Fauquier County, Virginia, with its mixed farming. In these areas I consulted county records and newspaper accounts to gain a local view of the former privileged families. In particular, I traced a number of women and their families over time through the census in Fauquier County to gather more systematic quantitative evidence about household arrangements and property holding.

Fauquier is an area of rolling hills, forests, and red clay soil. While no single county can be fully representative of Virginia and North Carolina's many agricultural regions, the county shared many characteristics common to plantation locales. Fauquier was fully integrated into the slave economy. In the postwar period it supported both a grazing culture and the cultivation of important grain crops, namely, corn, wheat, and oats. In the nineteenth century, slaveholding was widespread in Fauquier; fourteen separate households owned fifty or more slaves. At that time the premier family in the county had long been the Marshalls, descendants of Chief Justice John Marshall and his brother James. Along with their brother-in-law, financier Robert Morris, the Marshall brothers had purchased huge tracts of land in Fauquier and nearby Clarke County at the end of the Revolutionary period. The Marshalls, while intermarried with families from other parts of Virginia, were deeply enmeshed with members of the Fauquier gentry, such as the Clarksons, Striblings, and Amblers. Although the Marshalls were among the landholders who owned the northern half of Fauquier County, others—such as the Beales in southern Fauquier and the Dulanys near the Loudon border—held significant chunks of real estate. These families' provisions for their daughters and wives provide a window into women's experiences elsewhere in the state and in the South.[8]

In addition to using close-ups of certain counties to give greater detail to my work, I also read widely in primary sources, published and unpublished, about these two states during the late nineteenth century. Because these accounts touched on, often in incomplete fashion, many individual women from different families, I found it impossible to quantify these experiences. I did try to evaluate what proportion of women were involved; this results in expressions such as "some" and "most." To understand these women, I also delved into the letters, diaries, and writings of other southern white women of the period. I have included some of the best of these parallel examples.

As I sought patterns among many experiences that I discovered, a generational perspective became helpful in explaining some of the differences among

8. On Fauquier County, see Fauquier County Bicentennial Committee, *Fauquier County, Virginia, 1759–1959* (Warrenton, Va., 1959); Emily Ramey and John K. Gott, eds., *The Years of Anguish: Fauquier County, Virginia, 1861–1865* (Warrenton, Va., 1965).

elite women. While allowing for individual differences, I divide the women into three groups: (1) the older generation born before 1820; (2) those born between 1820 and 1849; and (3) young women born between 1850 and 1869. The evidence makes apparent that it was the two younger generations that largely sought to redefine women's sphere and influence after the war, often by linking domestic competence and control with a public persona in print or in the schoolhouse. Yet these two younger generations had different experiences as well. Women of the second generation had adult memories of the war; they also remembered the different social world it engendered. Moreover, their educational and work experiences differed from those of their daughters and nieces.[9]

Such a generational interpretation promises to resolve some of the current disagreements over the extent of change experienced by postwar women. My study's emphasis on change among younger women and greater continuity among older women points toward a new synthesis of the period based on the rich detail of primary sources. Perhaps it can reconcile the works of Scott and her critics, whose differences may be explained by the varying mixes of women they examine. In the end, however, my study most agrees with Scott, as the younger women tended to exhibit behaviors and attitudes similar to those she documented.

By focusing both on women's private and published writings, I have discovered postwar women involved in rethinking and rebuilding themselves, their families, and their region. Notions of proper behavior and the characteristics of the ideal woman were in flux after the war. Some southern white women in the 1870s and 1880s forged identities that challenged the notion of the "southern belle," the version of femininity that stressed power through "fascination" and romantic appeal. Although during the antebellum period the perfect belle had been at heart a modest creature, content to enjoy her brief moment in the sun in the few years between school and marriage, this ideal was changing after the war. Some belles had become more heedless, and poverty might have added a harder edge to their quest for the good marriage. At the same time, the intense piety of the period set other women to rebellion in various other ways. During

9. For a discussion of generations, consult Howard Schuman and Jacqueline Scott, "Generations and Collective Memories," *American Sociological Review* 54 (June 1989): 359–81. Some will notice that my generations are not completely parallel; the middle generation encompasses a longer timespan. In this, I have been influenced by Robert Wohl, *The Generation of 1914* (Cambridge, Mass., 1979), 203–37, who argues that a cataclysmic event may have a different impact on different age groups. My definition sees the Civil War as a formative experience, differentiating those who were adolescents and young adults from children. I would not, however, argue that these nineteenth-century people self-consciously thought of themselves as part of a particular generation.

the 1870s and 1880s, many southern women promulgated an ethic that emphasized "nondependence" in domestic or other roles. This ideal, which included self-reliance and female capability, can be found not only in private writings but also in the fictional heroines created by southern women.

The reconstruction undertaken by southern women also took place at home. The immediate postwar period was one of domestic upheaval in the southern household, as elite women were forced to negotiate new relationships with former slaves and new ways of dealing with housework. While scholars have documented the changes that emancipation brought to white households, they generally have chronicled only the closing days of the war and its immediate aftermath. In actuality, the new relationships with free servants evolved over many years in a gradual process, as African Americans emptied out of white households. In this new world where servants could quit, even privileged white women had to increase their knowledge of domestic affairs. Ironically, greater capabilities among the young were also part of a more thorough "domestication" of southern white women, as many elite women came to define their achievements in terms of the homes over which they presided. The staff of live-in servants became far smaller over these decades. The white family continued to take in relatives, but co-residence with them became increasingly uncomfortable for many. Building upon their religious beliefs, women sought increased moral influence on the household, with varying results.

While the elite household was reconstituted with a different membership, women continued to play an important role in property owning and transmission. Although some historians have speculated that women's access to property diminished in the impoverished postwar South, this does not seem to have been the case for North Carolinian, and especially Virginian, women. In keeping with a major change that had begun before the war, unmarried women, even those highly unlikely ever to marry, increasingly shared in the family lands and other property. Women from the old elite were rarely entrepreneurial; instead they saw themselves as conservators of family wealth. By the end of the nineteenth century, some of them would see themselves as conservators of family lands as well.[10]

Tending to prefer residence in towns and cities, women, especially the unmarried or widowed, turned to paid work, especially teaching and clerical positions. Teaching for many remained merely a means to an end, and large numbers of women taught only for a few years. Most of them seem to have seen teaching as a way to support themselves and aid their families. By the 1870s and 1880s,

10. Lebsock, *Free Women of Petersburg,* 244–49.

some women began to make teaching a long-term occupation of a sort largely unknown earlier in the South. Some teachers, especially those at residential schools, found the world of school to be an alternative community, a way to live with books, flowers, and other things of beauty. Still others saw it as a platform for influence in the community and among youth. Paid employment moved some women into the public sphere outside the home, but others found an arena for action in their churches and other benevolent activities. The late nineteenth century gave rise to a plethora of organizations, and women, even some rural ones, took an active role in them.

Many southern women found their voice in organizations, but others looked to publishing to spread their ideas. Some sought celebrity, achievement, or careers in the literary world; others seem merely to have wished to tell stories. Driven by these various purposes, women wrote not only for local and regional publications but for a national audience. Although now little-known, these authors published with prominent New York publishing houses and achieved fame in their day.

In their fictional works, southern female authors—such as Frances Christine Fisher Tiernan, M. G. McClelland, Amélie Rives, Henrietta Hardy Hammond, and Julia Magruder—presented southern women who were intellectually astute and domestically skilled. Their heroines neither sought nor enjoyed belledom but instead searched for fulfilling, useful lives, preferably including marriage to a supportive, understanding man. These authors, a significant minority of whom themselves never married, depicted the single state as preferable to loveless marriages for money or position. Rather than merely writing neo-Confederate paeans, they experimented with gender conventions, delineating strong-willed women and a range of romantic heroes, from wealthy, charismatic northerners to those sensitive southern men. They were less successful in their attempts to write about those of other racial and class backgrounds, but a few did try to bridge class and racial divides.

In many ways, the chronicle of privileged white women after the war is a success story. A host of women tried their hands at new activities—domestic, educational, and literary—and individually they could count many triumphs. Numerous women resisted the pressure to marry simply for a home or status and found another way to live. Many teachers and other working women among this group educated sons, daughters, siblings, or nieces and nephews and managed to fashion lives of which they could be proud. Yet there were also drawbacks. In the reorganization of the household, white women still demanded black workers but became all the more contemptuous of them. As African Americans built their separate institutions and lives, fears and prejudice flourished among white men and women. As some white families of the old elite retained their lands or regained their prosperity, they acknowledged neither the contributions of their womenfolk nor the tribulations of those less fortunate.

This account of the new activities and views of postwar white women both echoes and expands Edward Ayers's view of the possibilities of change that existed in the postwar South. For well over a decade after the end of Reconstruction, some privileged white women critiqued their own society and looked to northern models of men, manners, and mores. Such a vantage point increasingly came under attack in the 1890s, as more virulent strains of racism and Confederate celebrations took a new, aggressively martial form.

Even as white women from elite backgrounds experimented with different notions of women's proper role—notions that validated womanly independence and achievement—external forces and the contradictions within their position were making these notions untenable. Pressures for a solid South were brought to bear on these women as well as other dissenters. In this world, elite southern women would become increasingly polarized between a revived image of the "southern belle" and that of the emancipated new woman. To be sure, the belle emerging in the 1880s was far less demure than her grandmother had been in antebellum days. Even white women who argued for traditional female roles at the same time claimed new, prominent positions for themselves in hereditary and memorial societies, while others turned toward women's rights and more political forms of activism.

1

CHANGING VISIONS OF

WOMANHOOD

Few in Richmond doubted during the winter of 1873 that Mary Howard was a belle. Among those who danced attendance upon her was Albert Bruce, son of the wealthy Charlotte County family. Yet for all her powers of fascination, Mary Howard was a belle of a new stripe—when not charming young men on the dance floor, she taught school. That this young Richmond woman could command both admiration and a schoolhouse illustrates the changing nature of ideals of womanhood in the postwar period.[1]

Few myths have been as durable as that of the southern belle. Any observer of the social life of either the nineteenth- or twentieth-century South might expect at least one southern belle to make her appearance. A creature of elegant evening events, the belle always commanded a host of male admirers. A belle was the cynosure of all beauty, the center of admiration. And in the parlance of the day, a belle trailed in her wake a gaggle of smitten suitors, each of whom offered undying devotion and marriage. Coquettish and fickle belles could rule capriciously, rejecting suitors right and left and breaking numerous hearts. Yet despite the ubiquity of the concept, the belle and her attributes have a history; they varied a great deal according to the period. Over time both men and women altered the definition of the belle's charm and style as surely as they did their notions of fashion and beauty. Contemporary writings in the late nineteenth century suggest that the belle was merely one persona of the new woman emerging at a time when elite southern whites were rethinking notions of womanhood and proper female roles.[2]

---

1. Sallie Bruce to Morelle Bruce, Dec. 22, 1873, Bruce Family Papers, VHS.

2. On the ideals that guided white southerners in regard to women, see Anne Firor Scott, *The Southern Lady: From Pedestal to Politics, 1830–1930* (Chicago, 1970); Catherine Clinton, *The Plantation Mistress: Woman's World in the Old South* (New York, 1982); Elizabeth Fox-Genovese, *Inside the Plantation Household: Black and White Women of the Old South* (Chapel Hill, N.C., 1988), 192–289; Jean Friedman, *The Enclosed Garden: Women and Community in the Evangelical*

Although the imagery of belledom looms especially large in writings about the antebellum South, the actual ideal for women even then had been much more complex and divided. Through the early part of the nineteenth century, the celebration of the belle had conflicted to some extent with the other pervasive ideal of modest, retiring womanhood. Belledom was simply the best-known phase in a life that otherwise was supposed to be largely oriented to self-abnegation and service. Historian Christie Farnham has commented on the ideals of self-control that from earliest childhood were drilled into girls in the select boarding schools that so many among the privileged attended. As adults, they should be modest, gentle, kind, quiet, industrious, and naturally innocent and pious in thought. At the same time, girls were occasionally allowed to be lively and, within the confines of school, competitive. Even the world of courtship and belledom had its competitive element.[3]

Antebellum manuals and parents alike censured the conduct of some belles. Beauty and captivating charm were admirable only when used unconsciously. A belle who self-consciously played on her attractiveness was regarded as a schemer whose arts and wiles might well create disgust and revulsion in her audience. Moreover, the queen of beauty who reigned too long risked losing her appeal, which was based on a mixture of loveliness, pleasing manners, and unavailability. As her hold over the hearts of men weakened, her vulnerability to criticism became all the greater. Admiration and popularity were commodities to be traded for a good marriage when their value stood at the zenith; once a belle's stock began to drop, she had to use caution and sell quickly. In the 1830s, young Penelope Skinner showed how even belles knew some of this language of the market when she assured her brother that although she had as many admirers as any other belle in North Carolina, she also "wanted some of the old stock off the carpet, myself included."[4]

South, 1830–1900 (Chapel Hill, N.C., 1985), 1–38; Suzanne Lebsock, The Free Women of Petersburg: Status and Culture in a Southern Town, 1784–1860 (New York, 1984), 15–37, 230–35. For American ideals of female appearance and behavior in the late nineteenth century, see Martha Banta, Imaging American Women: Idea and Ideals in Cultural History (New York, 1987), 46–51. Among the three major types Banta describes is the "Beautiful Charmer," who is pretty and candid but also willful and spoiled.

3. Scott, Southern Lady, 23–28; Steven Stowe, Intimacy and Power in the Old South: Ritual in the Lives of the Planters (Baltimore, 1987), 50–121; Jane Turner Censer, North Carolina Planters and Their Children (Baton Rouge, La., 1984), 65–83; Christie Farnham, The Education of the Southern Belle: Higher Education and Student Socialization in the Antebellum South (New York, 1994), 120–45, 168–80.

4. Penelope Skinner to Tristram Skinner, April 22, 1839, Skinner Family Papers, SHC. See also Stowe, Intimacy and Power, 109–14, for a detailed analysis of her courtships.

When the Civil War burst on the world of the southern belle, its impact on these contradictory notions of womanhood was immediate and long-lasting. In particular, the demure image that so many parents and teachers had earlier sought to foster lost much of its appeal for young women. The war and the numerous soldiers it brought into southern parlors made courtship more frenetic, flirtatious, and bold. In the longer run, the war also promulgated images of heroines and heroic women who spied, nursed wounded soldiers, or valiantly protected hearth and home. Like the Joans of Arc and Deborahs of old, modern-day heroines now seemed close at hand. The ideal of womanhood, along with traditional values of self-sacrifice and duty, had come to include a more active, outspoken, and courageous aspect. This female self-reliance could be channeled into different forms of usefulness—benevolent and politically and socially conservative activities, as well as reforming ones—but the genie of engaged womanhood could never again be wholly bottled up.[5]

One excellent vantage point for observing the older generations' prescriptions for proper womanhood in the late nineteenth century is in the sorts of upbringing they wished for their daughters and granddaughters. Both the virtues they espoused and the educations they sought for young women reveal their perspectives on these issues. Their views of courtship and women's proper roles are evident in numerous discussions that also illustrate the outlook of younger women. Further evidence of beliefs about women's ideal traits of character, abilities, and behavior can be found in the sorts of heroines created by southern women novelists of varying ages.

The kinds of education available to young women reveal some of the contradictions and ambiguities of their parents' goals for them. For much of the nineteenth century, education had not proceeded in linear fashion at one school for either boys and girls. Rather, it was a patchwork construction, combining maternal instruction or that given by other close relatives with schooling by governesses and tutors, local schools, and boarding schools in larger towns. The war and later the straitened financial position of many old elite parents helped to perpetuate this pattern of haphazard schooling. Moreover, some parents feared that schooling would affect the health of their "nervous" or "delicate" daughters. Shortly before vivacious seventeen-year-old Sue Hubard was to leave for school in Baltimore, she became ill. The doctors decided that the "attack was from too

5. Anne Sarah Rubin, "Redefining the South: Confederates, Southerners, and Americans, 1863–1868" (Ph.D. diss., University of Virginia, 1999), 151–67, indicates encomiums for women's bravery as well for their self-sacrificing and dutiful work. See also Augusta J. Evans's novel, *Macaria, or Altars of Sacrifice,* ed. Drew Gilpin Faust (1864; reprint, Baton Rouge, La., 1992).

much excitement" and not only advised against her attending school, but even against reading and writing.[6]

Despite the reduced circumstances of many among the old elite, most continued to pay for educations for young women that far exceeded mere literacy. While parents believed the education of sons was vital, many of them also valued the training of daughters. To be sure, the level and seriousness of the education differed according to the intellectual pretensions of the family. While the Carter family farmed historic Shirley plantation, the two daughters, Alice and Marion, were taught at home. Reminiscing decades later, Marion Carter Oliver claimed that their education by five different governesses had been a money-saving measure. Marion spent one year away at school, her sister none. Although the Carters economized on schooling, they nonetheless wanted educational opportunities for their daughters.[7]

Whether parents employed private teachers or sent their daughters to schools, members of the old elite worried about their daughters' training. Discussing the education of her nephew's daughters, Emily Dupuy declared that she fully agreed with the "opinion that a good education is a better fortune than gold & silver." She rather tartly added, "As there seems at present but little prospect of many having this last to give, it seems more desirable than ever that our children should be well educated." For many years the old elite had been urging daughters to study hard and make the most of their educational opportunities. These injunctions might have gained added weight when family "belt tightening" and sacrifice was necessary to pay for schooling. In 1879, William R. Aylett, who prided himself on being a descendant of Patrick Henry, brought up the question of education when he and his wife Alice were calculating whether she could afford a visit to friends and relatives. William assured Alice that she could use part of the eighty dollars recently deposited in the Planters National Bank, but he cautioned that she should not tap the Union Bank account. It must be retained for their daughter Pattie's education, or she would not have the advantages her older sister Sallie had enjoyed. That Pattie might not receive as good an education as her sister was a prospect, according to William, "which would grieve me." Yet he thought that this was the best time for Alice's trip, since "our large & growing family of children will hereafter require every personal sacrifice at our hands."[8]

6. Farnham, *Education of the Southern Belle,* 68–93, and Censer, *North Carolina Planters,* 42–64, comment on the haphazard nature of schooling for many women. Sue Hubard to [unknown], April 3, 1869, Hubard Family Papers, SHC.

7. Marion Carter Oliver, "Reminiscence" [c. 1937], Shirley Plantation Papers, CWF.

8. Emily Dupuy to William Purnell Dickinson, Jan. 4, 1869, Emily Dupuy Papers, VHS; William R. Aylett to Alice Aylett, May 27, 1879, Aylett Family Papers, VHS.

Some mothers and even a few fathers taught their own daughters and sons. In Virginia at war's end, Martha Clarke instructed her daughter, Mary Lyle Clarke, and two nieces. According to Martha, "The three little girls have a fine time together, and also have a very fine effect upon each other, in the study line in stimulating each other to do well in their books, which Mary Lyle needed badly, as I had great difficulty in making her study." Sally Manning, Martha's sister-in-law and a "fine French scholar," taught the girls that language. In other cases, as in Charles and Carey Pettigrew's large family, older daughters who recently had left school served as instructors. Jane Pettigrew, in particular, much preferred remaining at her boarding school to teaching her siblings, but acquiesced in the latter as part of her duty to her parents: "Of course I know I ought to go and teach the little ones at home, but I do wish I was young enough to come back here next year." Virginia Hankins, a schoolteacher herself, at times supervised the education of her younger sister, Mary. In February 1883, Virginia reported about Mary: "I have put her hard to work again, at her books."[9]

Some old elite families who had fallen on hard times took advantage of the newly created free schools. In Virginia, Martha and William Ambler enrolled their daughter Nannie in the "public free school four miles off," although a few months later they decided that it was "not a good one, the female employed not being a good teacher." The next year they found a school near their Louisa County home for Nannie, but sent her to board because the round-trip ride would have been ten miles each day. In Wilmington, North Carolina, northern reformer Amy Bradley, who had worked for the U.S. Sanitary Commission (the Civil War forerunner of the Red Cross), opened Tileston Institute, a school she intended for the education of poor white children. But her school's reputation soon stood so high that members of the old elite were also enrolling their offspring there. John DeRosset, a physician and member of a wealthy planting and professional family, profusely thanked her in 1877 for educating his children: "In my opinion Wilmington has *never* possessed an institution where order, discipline and effective methods of instruction have been carried to such an excellent degree as in that under your charge. I can never forget my own obligation to you." In 1875, while a student at Tileston Institute, John's niece, Adelaide Meares, called it a "splendid school," and added, "So far, I am perfectly delighted with it."[10]

9. Martha M. Clarke to Phebe Bailey, Feb. 15, 1866, Bailey Family Papers, VHS; Jane N. Pettigrew to William Pettigrew, May 15, 1873, Pettigrew Family Papers, SHC; Virginia Hankins to Louis Hankins, Feb. 4, 1883, Hankins Family Papers, VHS.

10. Martha E. Ambler to Phebe Bailey, Dec. 9, 1874, March 22, 1875, and Oct. 11, 1875, Bailey Family Papers, VHS; M. John DeRosset to Amy Bradley, Oct. 15, 1877, Amy Bradley Pa-

Although Leila Madison Dabney was married to a prestigious lawyer and judge in Powhatan County, Virginia, the family struggled financially during the postwar years. At one point the Dabneys so worried about their children's training that Leila begged her wealthy elderly aunt, Phebe Bailey, for assistance. Leila justified her request: "I ask you because I know how kind you have always been to me, and it goes to my very soul to see my children growing up in ignorance around me. I have taught them as far as I can, but you know I cannot teach music." It is unclear whether Phebe Bailey responded to this request, but two months later Leila reported that her husband had taken a case that would pay one hundred dollars and had immediately hired a music teacher for their daughters. Describing the woman as a "fine music teacher, but poor in other respects," Leila quickly added, "We were glad to get her as I can teach every thing but music myself."[11]

This emphasis on music leads to the question of the curriculum studied by young women. The patchwork-quilt nature of women's education, even among those who spent considerable time at school, meant that their instruction was far from standardized. In addition to subjects such as English grammar and composition, history, natural sciences, mathematics, and moral philosophy, antebellum female schools had taught the "ornamental arts": music, embroidery, and more esoteric arts and crafts, such as netting, china painting, and the like. By the 1850s, many female schools, especially those that styled themselves academies, seminaries, or colleges, had created intellectually demanding curricula. In 1868, Maria Louisa Carrington reported that her youngest daughter's Richmond school offered music (both instrumental and vocal), French, Latin, natural philosophy, and algebra. Sue Hubard, at age sixteen, when her education was still unfinished, wrote, "I understand French and Latin tolerably well, and have studied the usual English branches taught now except Arithmetic of which I know very little. I have always disliked it & being an only daughter & much indulged have never studied [it] as I should."[12]

In addition to literacy and general knowledge, the elegant young lady was supposed to possess a host of accomplishments, foremost among which were

pers, Duke; Adelaide Meares to "Dear Miss Mary," c. Oct. 11, 1875, Adelaide Savage Meares Papers, Duke. See also Mrs. J. E. Lippitt to Amy M. Bradley, Oct. 4, 1877, Bradley Papers, Duke.

11. Leila M. Dabney to Phebe Bailey, Sept. 4 and Nov. 7, 1877, both in Bailey Family Papers, VHS.

12. Farnham, *Education of the Southern Belle*, 50–93; Maria L. Carrington to Eliza Dabney, Oct. 11, 1868, Saunders Family Papers, VHS; Sue Hubard to Augusta Evans, Aug. 21, 1867, Hubard Family Papers, SHC.

music, art, and foreign languages. Parents and grandparents alike pushed young women to practice their playing or singing. Elizabeth Horner, for example, congratulated her granddaughters on improving in their music. Parents and daughters alike testified to the high regard in which these accomplishments were held. One young woman, Sallie Aylett, proudly informed her parents that she would be singing second soprano in the Christmas soirée at her school in Staunton. (Music particularly occupied the Aylett family. When William R. Aylett, Sallie's father, had drawn up his will several years earlier, he bequeathed a piano each to three of his daughters, while the fourth received the family pipe organ.)[13]

The aim of education broadly defined was to provide, in addition to academic knowledge, the marks of a thoroughly finished young lady. These included a number of skills, such as writing without mistakes or blots in the graceful, spidery handwriting of the day. R. H. Dulany admonished his daughters to improve their penmanship and told his daughter Fannie, "Both Mary and you are improving in your writing as well as in your composition. Continue to take pains and you will find but little trouble in writing a good hand." Charlotte Carrington, while teaching her daughters, considered the possible educational influence of a flower garden: "I want to interest myself with establishing a flower garden, for my little girls this spring, they all love flowers. And I think it is a beautiful taste which should be cultivated." Here, parents of the old elite were continuing an earlier kind of training, as all these arts and graces had long been a valued part of a young lady's education.[14]

On its surface, this education seems composed of impossibly contradictory elements. Why were parents combining such different kinds of courses as Latin and the ornamentals? If they wanted their daughters well educated, why the emphasis on music and art? If female education were to be limited to what today might seem a frivolous display of upper-class notions, why had Latin, German, algebra, and the like wormed their way into the curriculum? To a large extent, this unlikely combination flowed historically from the more rigorous antebellum female academies, which had simply expanded their curricula, retaining the ornamental subjects while incorporating elements of the general humanistic education that young males received. Once accepted, this vision of education for females continued into the postwar period with the addition of more demanding

13. Elizabeth Welsh Horner to Josephine and Mary Eppes, March 12, [1867], Eppes Family Papers, VHS; Sarah Aylett to Alice Aylett, Dec. 14, 1878, and Will of William R. Aylett (written 1872, probated 1900), both in Aylett Family Papers, VHS.

14. Margaret Ann Vogtsberger, *The Dulanys of Welbourne: A Family in Mosby's Confederacy* (Berryville, Va., 1995), 88; Charlotte Carrington to Eliza Dabney, March 24, 1880, Saunders Family Papers, VHS.

coursework. Peter Evans Smith captured this uneasy pairing of knowledge and "polish" when he told his daughter that his design for her had always been for her to be an "accomplished and fine Lady." Other postwar southern parents wanted this somewhat contradictory amalgam of well-educated daughters who also possessed "womanly" accomplishments. Moreover, as historian Christie Farnham has pointed out in her survey of antebellum southern women's education, training in music and art need not necessarily be frivolous. Music lessons could prepare the recipient to perform well, in addition to rounding out an aesthetic education.[15]

In the estimation of late-nineteenth-century parents, music and, to a lesser extent, art could have a decidedly practical aspect. Leila Dabney had been careful to mention her practical goals to her aunt when she sought Phebe Bailey's financial assistance: "I wish my girls to learn music so that they may be able to teach some day themselves." In the meantime she wanted them to be able to instruct their youngest sister. Widowed Maria Louisa Carrington, who taught school herself, explicitly indicated the larger purpose of the education of her two daughters, Willie and Bessie, while discussing Willie's curriculum: "I hope she will lay in such a fund of learning, that she will be able to support herself, by teaching, and not be dependant on any one. I know I have tried to instil into both her, and Bessie a feeling of independence, and I think they have it." Several years later, Maria Louisa praised Willie's aptitude for drawing: "I feel that every accomplishment she can learn, will add to her power of self support, if she has to lean on herself." Carey Pettigrew of North Carolina expressed similar sentiments about the importance of education: "I dread any more debt, tho' if I had the opportunity of borrowing the money to educate my children I certainly would, as that would make them independent and able to support themselves." Thus, even as some mothers emphasized the graceful ornamental arts and accomplishments that would make their daughters admired members of society, they also wished to give young women some means of self-support. Formal education would make it possible for women to earn wages and ensure, if necessary, an independent existence. This indicates an important change of attitude from the antebellum period, when southern elite whites did not expect education to prepare women for paid employment, in part because higher education remained so exclusively the province of the wealthy.[16]

15. Peter E. Smith to Lena Smith, Feb. 5, 1875, Peter E. Smith Papers, SHC; Farnham, *Education of the Southern Belle,* 86–89.
16. Leila Dabney to Phebe Bailey, Sept. 4, 1877, Bailey Family Papers, VHS; Maria Louisa Carrington to Eliza Dabney, Oct. 11, 1868, and Jan. 29, 1870, Saunders Family Papers, VHS; Carey Pettigrew to William S. Pettigrew, July 1, 1879, Pettigrew Family Papers, SHC. Compare these attitudes to Farnham's discussion in *Education of the Southern Belle,* 18–32.

While some of the emphasis that both schools and parents placed on music and French sprang from practical reasons, these adults also wanted education to reinforce class distinctions. Some parents were motivated in part by fear of falling into the lower orders. In a moment of brooding over her children, Leila Dabney despaired about their futures: "I sometimes wish all mine, were laid low in their graves . . . , for it is a keen pang to see them suffer, and grow up like the lower class around us." In Virginia Hankins's measured approval of her brother's fiancée in 1888 lurked a similar foreboding: "She is very nice and is a lady with refined ways—she will make the best poor man's wife I know of. She knows how to work, and how to be poor and not lower herself. Johnny's poverty and being cut off from all society was beginning to make him lower himself, in dress—in manners, after a while it would have had its effect on his principles and morals. She will I believe, keep him up for she has a great deal of the right kind of pride." These were difficult days, as the women of old elite had to improvise ways to advertise and retain some distinction in society.[17]

Parents tried to make clear the sorts of virtues as well as school lessons that they wished young women to learn as they moved toward adulthood. E. D. F. Worthington thought her daughter Lizzie embodied these desirable traits:

> Very fair, light hair . . . quite tall and slender. I cant say she is a beauty, but she is far from homely. Above all, she is a thoughtful, considerate daughter, a noble minded girl. A good student while at school, stood well in her classes, very often taking the mark of honor. Not so quick to learn as L. Badham but studious habits & *application* made up for it. Does not talk a great deal, yet one everybody likes for her modest manners & fine traits of character.

Parents and other relatives still preached the importance of piety and religious feeling, but they also included such virtues as devotion to duty and industriousness. In 1867, Sarah Carraway lectured her nineteen-year-old niece about her role in life; in the current "dreaded . . . hard times" it would be necessary to "give yourself to the conflict, and be the comfort of your parents, not in your own strength can you do this my dear child, but God will give you grace equal to our trials and duties if we ask him."[18]

Young women frequently heard that usefulness should be their part in life.

17. Leila Dabney to Phebe Bailey, Sept. 4, 1877, Bailey Family Papers, VHS; Virginia Hankins to Louis Hankins, March 10, 1888, Hankins Family Papers, VHS.

18. E. D. F. Worthington to Emily Haywood, Aug. 6, 1888, Benbury-Haywood Papers, SHC; Sarah F. Carraway to Rosa Biddle, Nov. 13, 1867, Samuel S. Biddle Papers, Duke (emphasis in original).

Lena Smith's grandmother congratulated her in 1875 on excellent exams as providing "encouragement for the future. A life usefully employed brings you more
real pleasure and interest than all the praise and flattery the world could bestow."
At another point, the elderly lady lectured Lena that "God's blessing is promised
to those who steadily pursue the path of duty[.] I feel assured it will reward you
dear child for your unselfishness in trying to do all you can to assist your parents.
. . . it will be such a real pleasure in after life to know you did all you could for
their ease and pleasure."[19]

Some parents found galling the contrast between the life that they had expected to give their children and their postwar poverty. Peter Evans Smith poignantly expressed this feeling in a long, sad letter that he wrote his eldest
daughter, Lena, on her twenty-first birthday. He evoked the time "twenty one
years ago this night" when she was born, "and I held you in my arms picturing
to myself what I intended to do with you. I dreamt and fancied that I would
raise and educate you to be an accomplished and fine Lady—and that when you
were 21 years of age, I would give you a handsome entertainment and a present
of $10,000." Smith had had reason to be optimistic. Both he and his wife be-
longed to North Carolina's wealthiest planter families, and, as he put it, "I had
the brightest prospects before me, kind friends, good health, an affectionate
wife, and plenty of property for a young man." But the war was followed by the
"dreadful crash and loss of property. I lost all, and the bright visions of your
happy future vanished like the dew before the morning sun." He ruefully
summed up his state in 1875: "I am not able to give you 10 cents, instead of
$10,000, I could weep tears of blood if it would avail anything."[20]

Virginia Hankins sought a good education for her younger sister Mary, but
also wanted Mary to have an active social life. As Virginia reminisced to a
brother about her own prewar life: "I remembered my own girlish days, dear
Louis, ah! what a happy merry girl I was! and how much Father and Mother did
to make me happy. . . . I want Mary to be bright and happy too." Accepting an
invitation for Mary to visit with the Lanier family, Virginia saw the event not
only as entertainment but as a chance for social growth and advancement: "I
want her to realize that she is a young lady, that she must be interested in people—courteous and kind to all and learn to talk, without feeling it to be an
effort."[21]

While the older generations expected young women to be dutiful and yet

19. Grandma to Lena Smith, July 18 and May 12, 1875, Peter E. Smith Papers, SHC.
20. Peter E. Smith to Lena Smith, Feb. 5, 1875, Peter E. Smith Papers, SHC.
21. Virginia Hankins to Louis Hankins, Dec. 3, 1883, Hankins Family Papers, VHS.

enjoy social occasions, the entertainments in the postwar years sometimes seemed racier than the elders would have preferred. In particular, some young ladies seemed bolder. Some were less careful about obtaining the necessary chaperonage and remaining out of the public eye, both of which were rules urged on them by the older generation. Chaperonage had two quite different aspects. One was the escort of males for females of virtually any age when traveling; the other involved adults overseeing places and scenes of courtship. Both forms of chaperonage had been considerably stronger in the antebellum South than elsewhere in America, but were somewhat on the wane during the postwar period.[22]

Some young women of the third generation made it clear not only that they would choose the places they visited but also that they considered male escorts unnecessary. Sue Hubard's independent actions sometimes became a point of contention between her and her parents. Sue seems to have arranged the itinerary of her expeditions to Baltimore, Richmond, and Washington to please herself. As a twenty-two-year-old, she traveled to Richmond and decided on the spur of the moment to accompany a friend's family to Washington. She told her father that it had been a "great relief" to find that he did not object to her visit, because "the fear that you might not approve it was the only thing wh[ich] at all marred my pleasure." Nonetheless, before he had even had a chance to object, Sue was on her way to Washington. Three years earlier, when she relayed her plans to go from Washington to Leesburg on her own, without an escort, her mother violently opposed the trip, arguing, "It is painful enough when forced by necessity to *bear the ills of life alone.*" In any difficulty, her mother warned, "A young & unprotected female would not find it very *pleasant.*" Sarah Hubard's conflation of chaperonage with male "protection" shows parents' continuing desire to control the movements of young women, much as had been the case in the antebellum period. This parental desire might have been further strengthened by the fear and hostility that southern whites in the 1870s and 1880s exhibited toward African American men. Yet when it pleased them, other young women overlooked or ignored the older generation's notions of chaperonage. In 1874, seventeen-year-old Mary Henderson wrote her mother that she intended coming home from Raleigh: "If brother John is busy he need not come after me as I can drift along with the crowd and have not a doubt I will arrive at Home safely." While Mary might accept an escort, she did not think her brother's care necessary.[23]

22. Clinton, *Plantation Mistress,* 62–65, 175–79.

23. Sue Hubard to E. W. Hubard, March 23, [1873], and Sarah. A. Hubard to Sue Hubard, April 5, 1870, both in Hubard Family Papers, SHC; Mary Henderson to Mary S. Henderson, May 5, 1874, John S. Henderson Papers, SHC.

To be sure, having a male escort provided practical advantages. Twenty-seven-year-old Louise Holladay, on a visit to relatives in Kentucky, considered her options for returning home to Spotsylvania County, Virginia. If she waited until March, she could be accompanied to Charlottesville by a friend's husband. Louise wrote that "it might be better to wait & have his escort as I was such a coward about traveling alone & having no one to see to my baggage." The baggage seems to have concerned Louise more than the male escort. In an earlier letter, she had written that if she traveled alone, she planned to board a through train from Frankfort to Charlottesville so she would not have to supervise its transfer.[24]

While almost all genteel antebellum southern women had traveled only with male escorts, the postwar practice was confined mainly to young unmarried women. A rather carefree young matron like Eleanor Kearney Carr, then in her early thirties, spent her time in a barroom waiting for the train at Weldon, North Carolina, in 1871. Yet even less adventurous women were able to navigate the trains quite well. Nannie Tunstall's trip to Europe in 1884 sheds further light on the question of escorts and chaperonage. Unmarried at age thirty-four, Nannie retained the panache that had marked her seasons as a belle and that made her a favorite companion of the elderly banker W. W. Corcoran. When she considered spending several months on the Continent and in England, Nannie turned to her cousin, Virginia Tunstall Clay, widow of Senator Clement Clay of Alabama. Virginia Clay had shone as one of the brightest social lights on the prewar Washington scene. Nannie broached the project with her cousin in September 1883, asking:

Why can we not go to Europe together? Traveling there is rather expensive. But continual residence is not, and after a summer of junketing we might settle down for a month of content in one of the chateau cities, or in southern France where we could enjoy existence and forget the cares and denials of life. . . . I think if we arranged to go next spring there would [be] no scarcity of escorts, the one thing needful will be a Chaperone—for my mother will not consent to go, and they say that I am not old eno' or plain *eno'* to go alone! Now my cousin why not you?

As the two women discussed the trip over the next few months, a male escort receded in importance. "We ought to have an escort," Nannie opined, "but *oughts* & *cans* seldom agree in this world—and so far as I am concerned, I should not hesitate on that score." She then planned the trip, depending on Cook's

24. Louise Holladay to J. M. and Lucy Holladay, Feb. 1, 1889, and Oct. 26, 1888, Holladay Family Papers, VHS.

travel service for the continental itinerary: "As to our getting to London sans escort, that is nothing & after that we will not need any but what Cook provides." When Nannie Tunstall made her trip to Europe in the summer and fall of 1884, the middle-aged and ever-exuberant Virginia Clay accompanied her as a "chaperone," but the ladies traveled without any male "protector."[25]

As some elite women became bolder about traveling alone, the old strictures about women's invisibility from the public gaze were lessening as well. To be sure, a woman like Virginia Hankins, who was already concerned about her family's possible social slippage, continued to observe the traditional proprieties. Virginia reproached her brother about encouraging a younger sister to form a chapter of a literary group popular at his school: "By the way I don't fancy Mary's forming a Chapter of the Society, so you see, a girl's name had better never be spoken in public among boys. It is probable being a member the boys might talk about her. So if you hav'n't done any thing more, you had better let the matter drop." Yet if Virginia hewed to the old standards for her sister, other young women were more interested in participating in public events. Part of this might have come about through the increasing penetration of drama into recreation.[26]

The courtship of the antebellum period—especially at balls, with their highly stylized behavior—might be viewed as a form of dramatic performance, but such traditional activities were being eclipsed in the postwar period by more stylized and more scripted dramatic performances, whether expressed in tableaux, play presentations, or tournaments. These activities had begun to gain acceptance during the Civil War. To be sure, some resisted. Out in the Shenandoah Valley, Lucy Breckinridge and her friend Page Saunders refused to act in a set of tableaux for soldiers because "we declined showing ourselves to the public." But in Richmond, elite youth partly replaced balls with Starvation Parties (with no refreshments) that featured plays and charades. According to Sallie Brock, these parties included music and dancing, but on occasion "were varied . . . by the performance of plays and tableaux vivants, in which considerable talent was exhibited in the histrionic art by some of the quickly created actors and actresses. This introduction of plays and tableaux added an exquisitely charming variety to the winter's social enjoyment." In all of these performing activities, much greater visibility for young women, either through the semipublic nature of the

25. Lala Carr Steelman, "The Life-Style of an Eastern North Carolina Planter: Elias Carr of Bracebridge Hall," *NCHR* 57 (winter 1980): 32–33; Nannie Tunstall to Virginia Clay, Sept. 23, 1883, and March 21, 1884, Clement C. Clay Papers, Duke (emphasis in original).

26. Virginia Hankins to Louis Hankins, June 4, 1881, Hankins Family Papers, VHS.

event or through newspaper coverage, was accepted and thus was becoming acceptable.[27]

Perhaps the most socially conservative form of these semipublic performances was the tableau, a genre growing in popularity. Most often the tableau was a staged representation of an historic or fictional scene. Young Pattie Aylett described a fundraising evening of tableaux in her King William County, Virginia, town in 1879: "Our tableaux went off very well. I think they made over $100. Fannie was in three tableaux and I, in one." More ambitious were the amateur theatricals just beginning to appear. Edward Alfriend tried to convince Sue Hubard to appear in a Richmond production of "The Rivals," telling her that she was the unanimous choice of "our dramatic club" as Julia. He assured her, "I have great confidence in your ability in the histrionic art." When Sue rejected his request, Edward renewed his pleas, sending her a copy of the play and reassuring her that she would not be the "only lady" making her first appearance onstage. Yet if Sue Hubard had any compunctions about appearing onstage, she did not even mention them in her reply. Instead she insisted that her social schedule could not accommodate the scheduled date, and she did not appear in the play.[28]

Tournaments, fancy-dress balls, and theatricals not only put young women on display, but at times brought them into notice in the local papers. In tests of horsemanship at local tournaments, young women provided the ornamentation, as one of their number was crowned a queen of the entertainment. The *Warrenton (Va.) True Index,* in a long piece on a recent dance at the local watering hole, chose an arch tone to describe many of the costumes: "Miss Nattie Horner, the Queen of Hearts, exercised a sweet and gentle control over subjects, whilst Miss Fannie Horner as the Belle of '76 acknowledged no improvement in modern times in the witcheries of the conquering sex." An article one week earlier had appended a postscript that "there were many fair ones present not in costume, and perhaps others who were, whose names may have been omitted but without intention." Clearly, the "fair ones" now expected to see their names in print, especially if they had contrived a costume. At that town some twenty years later, an amateur troupe presented two short plays, with an interlude of vocal music.

<hr>

27. Mary D. Robertson, ed., *Lucy Breckinridge of Grove Hill: The Journal of a Virginia Girl, 1862–1864* (Columbia, S.C., 1994), 144, 152; Sallie Brock, *Richmond during the War: Four Years of Personal Observation* (1867; reprint, Lincoln, Neb., 1996), 270; C. Vann Woodward, ed., *Mary Chesnut's Civil War* (New Haven, 1981), 497, 528–33.

28. Pattie Aylett to Alice Aylett, June 1, [1879], Aylett Family Papers, VHS; Edward M. Alfriend to Sue Hubard, April 7 and 17, [c. 1872–73], Hubard Family Papers, SHC.

All these presentations eroded the antebellum notion that young ladies must be shielded from the public eye.[29]

The prominent place of theatricals, tableaux, and tournaments in the fictional worlds that young women encountered in their novel-reading also promoted greater acceptance of the public display of young women. In *Left to Herself,* a long, convoluted, 1871 novel written by Jane Lathrop Stabler of Lynchburg, numerous young men and women amuse themselves with tableaux, in which even her pious heroine Florence participates. These amateur productions provided the backdrop for a major courtship scene. Still, Stabler sharply distinguished between them and professional theatrical appearances by creating an antiheroine who recklessly attempts to find fame on the public stage before attempting murder and committing suicide.[30]

Even when parents cautioned modesty, they could be ambivalent or divided in their counsels. Some, in their lectures about propriety, harkened nostalgically back to the prewar scene of belles and beaux. Edmund W. Hubard, a former Virginia congressman, resorted to old adages in a long harangue of a letter to his daughter Sue, then age twenty-one, about her visit in Richmond. While Edmund preached the virtues of feminine modesty, his aim for his daughter was belledom. He cautioned her to "let strick [*sic*] *propriety* mark" both her bearing and conversation. "You can't be too circumspect," he continued, "good taste—caution—prudence, & propriety should ever characterize all you say or do." She must avoid using slang and a "slapdash" manner, and she should appear unconcerned about her appearance and self-presentation. Ironically, the ultimate aim of all this modesty and reserve was to gain wide acclaim. "The *Ladylike* is more captivating. Much talent & beauty draped with the veil of *modesty* is at all times most lovely," Edmund concluded. "The highest compliment a Lady can win is to be universally reported lovely—May you wear this Coronet by general Consent adorned with virtues clustering & sparkling as dew drops on spring Flowers." While Edmund sought to mold Sue's behavior, his wife Sarah worried about Sue's wardrobe. Three years earlier, Sarah had tried to obtain the money to buy Sue a new silk dress for a visit to Richmond. "I know you are just as anxious about Sue's appearance as I am," Sarah confided to her husband, "so whatever you think right, I shall be perfectly satisfied with." Sarah Hubard's letters to her daughter consistently echoed this concern for elegant attire. As she put it in 1873, "I dislike for you to be in Richmond with a used up wardrobe."[31]

29. *Warrenton (Va.) True Index,* Aug. 31, 1867, Aug. 24, 1867, and Dec. 1, 1894.

30. Jane Lathrop Stabler [pseud. Jennie Woodville], *Left to Herself* (Philadelphia, 1871), 73–74, 179, 296–97.

31. Edmund W. Hubard to Sue Hubard, April 12, 1872, Sarah A. Hubard to E. W. Hubard, March 2, 1869, and Sarah A. Hubard to Sue Hubard, April 7, 1873. See also Sarah A. Hubard to Sue Hubard, May 20, 1870. All in Hubard Family Papers, SHC.

Yet another trope appearing in the writings of many of the old elite was the depressed nature of the social scene. In 1886, Nannie Tunstall reported about Lynchburg: "There seems to be little doings in town. The paper says there are no 'belles' as there are no beaux." Sallie Bruce of Staunton Hill had been a noted belle during the antebellum period; apart from her wish for her sons and daughters to shine, she retained a keen interest in the courtship scene. In 1872, she commented upon the lack of interest her two older sons showed in the social scene, writing, "If all the other beaux in the State hold the same opinions as they do, the race of Native Virginians (of their class) will die out."[32]

In fact, the world of belles and beaux did not disappear in the 1870s and 1880s, though the difficult financial circumstances of much of the old elite gave a new cast to their rituals of courtship. In the cities and large towns, especially Richmond, many events celebrating courtship regularly took place. Yet the old world had been shattered and could not be fully reconstituted. The example of Mary Howard that opened this chapter indicates that some postwar belles were working women, most often schoolteachers. In 1873, Sallie Bruce was amazed that Mary was a "great belle in R[ichmond]—notwithstanding her poverty obliges her to keep school, so you can imagine what her attractions must be."[33]

On the whole, Sallie Bruce found the new world of courtship rather appalling. Mary Howard soon became her least favorite daughter-in-law, and Sallie found particularly unsettling the excellent marriage made by Mary's sister. How, Sallie marveled, could such a homely girl have snagged a well-to-do northerner? Especially rankling was the vision of this young woman married and on a bridal trip to Europe, where she could spend the five hundred dollars that her father-in-law had given her for a trousseau. "Think of this change to a girl who never before had $5 at her command!" Sallie complained, "Mary made a splendid stroke when she sent this ugly sister to Vassar." In Sallie Bruce's view, such a lack of beauty and family wealth should never have gained a prosperous husband.[34]

Despite the admonitions and oversight of parents like E. W. Hubard and Sallie Bruce, the younger generation of men and women after the war seem to have put their own interpretations on proper courtship and belledom. Richmond remained a center of activities for young people. Some of their writings positively bubble over with their enjoyment of life; they wanted to have fun. Pearl Tyler, daughter of the former president, found Richmond a bit stuffy, but that did not depress her. "This old City is certainly a funny old place," she

32. Nannie Tunstall to Virginia Clay, Dec. 12, 1886, Clay Papers, Duke; Sallie Bruce to Morelle Bruce, Nov. 22, 1872, Bruce Family Papers, VHS.
33. Sallie Bruce to Morelle Bruce, Dec. 22, 1873, Bruce Family Papers, VHS.
34. Sallie Bruce to Morelle Bruce, July 4, 1889, Bruce Family Papers, VHS.

mused. "As for the few girls (& gracious knows I wouldn't meet any more) they are as stiff as barn doors, plague it—they are crazy but I will 'be just as stiff.'" If Pearl were, in fact, as stiff as a barn door, she had a peculiar way of proving it. Six weeks later she gushed to her mother about the "beautiful drive I had Monday with a Mr Lee." In her account, "About six o'clock up drove a spirited black horse, & a high buggy, it was a dashing 'turn-out,' and the best of all, I took the ribbons, & you know I was delighted. We drove up Grove road, & actually flew. Ah! such a fine animal, so fast, still sound as even you could wish." Young ladies like Pearl Tyler, with her adventurous drives, were often not particularly careful about remaining out of the public eye and about the necessary chaperonage urged on them by the older generation. In 1874, Sarah Hubard reminded her daughter Sue (then twenty-three and visiting a West Virginia spa), "As soon as your plans are definitely formed let us know as we feel worried & anxious about your being properly chaperoned—*it is everything.*"[35]

Even when young women complied with chaperonage rules, they complained. In 1892, Alice Saunders's friends planned a trip that would involve six young men and women hiking in the North Carolina mountains. Decrying the difficulties of finding married women capable of the physical exertion involved, Carolina Davis sighed, "It would be so much more fun without an older person who would have to be taken care of."[36]

The behavior of some rebellious daughters severely tried their parents. In 1887, May Bondurant, already known for high spirits and "nervousness," briefly attended school in Knoxville, Tennessee. Her unmarried aunt, Harriet Morrison, found the social discipline far too lax, telling May's pious Presbyterian parents, "She is not thrown with the boys yet she is liable to see them and be seen and when winter sets in it will be worse. She has not such surroundings as I think will be good for her." In this case, May Bondurant returned to Virginia, where she spent several years battling nervous problems and occasional "fits." Only a long stay at a Pennsylvania water cure establishment brought May to the desired demureness.[37]

In other cases parents may have been more tolerant of dancing and frolicsome behavior. For over a decade beginning in 1869, Sue Hubard sent enthusiastic accounts to relatives and friends of the parties and gatherings that she attended, primarily in Richmond, Baltimore, and Washington, D.C. Aged eighteen, she

35. Pearl Tyler to Julia Tyler, April 25 and June 2, 1880, both in Julia Tyler Papers, VHS; Sarah A. Hubard to Sue Hubard, July 24, 1874, Hubard Family Papers, SHC.

36. Carolina Davis to Alice Saunders, July 18, 1892, Saunders Family Papers, VHS.

37. Harriet Morrison to Emily and Alexander J. Bondurant, Nov. 27, 1887, Bondurant-Morrison Family Papers, UVA.

enjoyed a trip to Richmond in the spring of 1869 which included a soirée with "edibles of all description, wine and cordials for the ladies and liquors for the men." Later that year she visited the fair in Richmond, where she also intended to attend a masquerade ball. She asked her friends for aid in conceiving a striking costume, confiding, "I don't like anything of the pastoral style, i.e. flower girls, etc." Three years later Sue Hubard recounted her adventures, which in the meantime had become more elaborate, to her mother. After an evening at the theater Sue had feasted on hot oysters, cold turkey, and champagne. She closed her letter, "I want to see you all very much but I tell you I feel in my proper element down here, & I expect to have a great deal of fun." Her mother's reply came laced with the caution about such festivities that often characterized the older generations. Assuring Sue that she did not need to hurry home if she was having a good time, Sarah Hubard added a thinly veiled criticism, conveniently attributed to an aunt. "E says I must tell Jinnie & yourself that she fears you are treated too much to *Champagne* & eatables, for the beaux to consider you angels."[38]

Although Sue Hubard seems never to have acted onstage, she managed her love life as if it were a production—though whether a drama or a romantic comedy is not always clear. She very much aspired to be a writer, but her social goals also loomed large. Even more important than enjoying herself was making her mark; and in her estimation, a brilliant marriage would be such an achievement. At first, her letters focused on clothes. In 1870, she wrote from Baltimore, "My new velvet suit has created a decided sensation." In 1872, emphasizing the importance of the men whom she had met, she excitedly related the evening spent with "an English widower staying here worth 50 *millions*." Indeed, the millions so impressed Sue that she double-underlined them.[39]

Over the course of the next eight years, the term "distinguished" became one of Sue Hubard's favorite descriptions of her potential "catches." She had settled on the type of suitor she preferred: a middle-aged or older man, often a widower, who could count wealth, political prominence, or both among his attractions. She showed little interest in men of her own age, perhaps because so many of them were struggling financially. In 1873, when she was twenty-one, Sue met A. B. Steinberger, a northern widower who greatly impressed her. She told her brother that "it was a case of love at first sight." Describing Steinberger to her

38. Sue H. Hubard to "My dear Friend," June 19, 1869, Sue Hubard to George, Oct. 13, 1869, Sue Hubard to Sarah A. Hubard, Feb. 2, 1872, and Sarah A. Hubard to Sue Hubard, April 1, 1872, all in Hubard Family Papers, SHC.

39. Sue Hubard to Sarah A. Hubard, March 14, 1870, and Sue Hubard to Edmund W. Hubard, Feb. 2, 1872, Hubard Family Papers, SHC.

father as almost the only man of her acquaintance whom she wished him to meet, Sue promised that he would deem Steinberger "quite the proper person for such an extremely aspiring young lady as Miss S. H.," that is, herself.[40]

That spring marked the beginning of Sue's love affair with, and eventual engagement to, Steinberger. Even though less than a decade had elapsed since the end of the Civil War, Sue worried little about her suitor's northern origins, which she succinctly described as "old Knickerbocker stock." Her letters to her family concentrated on his wealth and charm:

> He is a very brilliant conversationalist and very intellectual & elegant but nevertheless has had a very hard life, and very little to make him happy except money. I think I wrote you that he was a widower. His wife was a millionairess and made his life so miserable that he says the wonder is that he did not commit suicide. . . . I think he is very much devoted to me. Why I can't see, but chiefly I expect because I am exactly the opposite of all the fashionables he knows. He acted in the most honorable and generous way. Said while telling me the State of his own feeling that he did not ask any pledges or even acknowledgements from me as he was on the eve of a journey as hazardous as it would be long.

It turned out that Steinberger was a political and military adventurer intent on joining western Samoa to the United States, a futile endeavor that occupied several years. By May 1873 Steinberger was sending Sue Hubard beautiful embroidered gloves from Salt Lake City as he traveled westward.[41]

During most of an engagement that lasted several years, Sue Hubard and Steinberger were separated. As she pursued her interest in writing fiction, Sue drafted elaborate, highly emotional love letters. As she wrote one January, "I am expecting you now my dearest every day. You cannot come too soon. I sometimes think that I, above all other women, have known 'the heartsickness of hope deferred.' Oh when—when will it end?" The finale came when Steinberger stopped replying to her letters and Sue broke the engagement.[42]

By 1877, Sue Hubard, at twenty-six, was involved with a middle-aged congressman, Milton Sayler, a Democrat from Cincinnati, Ohio. In a long letter to her mother, Sue pointed out that "he compliments me for everything and blushes like a girl when they tease him." Although one of her friends thought

---

40. Sue Hubard to Edmund Hubard Jr., March 15, [1873], and Sue Hubard to Edmund W. Hubard, March 23, [1873], both in Hubard Family Papers, SHC.

41. Sue Hubard to Edmund W. Hubard, March 23, [1873], and Sarah A. Hubard to Eddie Hubard, May 29, [1873], both in Hubard Family Papers, SHC.

42. Draft letter, Sue Hubard to A. B. Steinberger, Jan. 28, n.d., Hubard Family Papers, SHC.

an engagement to be a "settled thing," Sue was more hesitant in her own assessment of the romance, though warm in her appreciation of her suitor: "Now honestly I don't know. I don't think it is very deep yet, but he is struck, and as he is not a ladies man[,] any attention from him means a good deal. *He is the most brilliant catch in the house*—rich, the finest scholar in Congress & very fine looking blonde but slightly bald—is 45—I w[oul]d be a proud gal to bring such a fellow to V[irgini]a."[43]

Two years later, the Sayler affair had come to naught, and Sue was carrying on flirtations with recently widowed North Carolina senator Zebulon Vance and Congressman Martin Clardy, whom she believed to be the richest member of the Missouri delegation. According to Sue, she and Clardy were "having a very heavy flirtation & they all here think it is serious on his part. I don't know yet. He has asked me to let him go to V[irgini]a with me & of course I am willing but whether he will or not remains to be seen."[44]

Sue's terminology about her adventures in the Washington marriage market reveals how thoroughly she viewed them as business ventures. "I think I have done pretty well on a small capital," she boasted to her mother. "Don't you think so? There are not many girls in the City who have a member & senator both in their train." Evaluating Clardy as a "better chance" as he was "younger & richer & no children to bother," Sue warily added, "It is time enough to decide when I am asked." Her declaration that such a match would be a "great thing" for her brothers provides yet another hint of the role that financial considerations played in her decisions. A year and a half later, Sue's romantic adventures ended rather anticlimactically when she became the third wife of the elderly editor of the *Baltimore Sun,* who died within a few months of their wedding. Sue herself died the following year at age thirty-one.[45]

Although Sue Hubard surely had numerous counterparts who played the marriage market, some women remained censorious toward belledom and its artificialities. During the Civil War, when a friend accused Virginia Hankins, then twenty years old, of becoming more flirtatious, Virginia devoted an angry entry in her diary to the question:

> I am sure she is wrong. Society (the little I may have seen that could be called polite) and the utter nonchalance with which I regard the greater portion, know-

43. Sue Hubard to Sarah A. Hubard, Feb. 26, [1877], Hubard Family Papers, SHC.

44. Sue Hubard to Sarah A. Hubard, June 2, [1879], Hubard Family Papers, SHC.

45. Ibid. Sue Hubard married John Taylor Crow of the *Baltimore Sun,* who was almost sixty years old, early in 1881. He died in March of that year. Edmund Hubard Jr. to Sue Crow, Feb. 4, 1881; newspaper clipping, "Obituary of John T. Crow," Hubard Family Papers, SHC.

ing my own superiority to its babbling, gossiping views has perhaps given me more ease of manner which she calls 'polish'. The accusation which she brings against me of becoming a coquette I treat with supreme contempt. The thing is so foreign to my nature even were I able to do it and the deception falseness and affectation which are the tools of flirts I would regard as ignoble and far beneath the dignity and purity of a true woman.

No doubt, other young women—especially pious ones—shared Virginia's sentiments.[46]

In fact, the belle's round of parties and flirtations formed a small part of life for most young women reaching maturity. A social scene that centered on the wooing of belles tended to be possible only in larger towns and cities. Elsewhere life moved more slowly. Sue Hubard contemptuously called life in rural Buckingham County, Virginia, a perpetual Lent, and other less exuberant young women also recorded many uneventful days. Bessie Cain of Piedmont North Carolina described her life to a suitor as the "same unvarying round of reading sewing and visiting." Even their parents realized that such a life might be boring. Richard Eppes reported his older daughters' schedule to their younger sister: "Sister Josie & Mary spend their mornings sewing in mother's chamber, in the afternoons sister Josie goes out visiting & Mary reads. . . . So you see our life is quite a monotonous one."[47]

Even while some, like Sue Hubard, pursued belledom and a brilliant match, marriage as the ultimate aim of life was quietly being reevaluated. In the South, as elsewhere in the United States, religious authorities and popular culture continued to tout marriage as the most appropriate station for women and the goal to which they should aspire, but even some of these tributes to the institution may have strengthened doubts about it. For example, a squib in the *Warrenton (Va.) True Index* in 1867 entitled "Marriage" seems at first glance to be yet another encomium to wedded bliss. Yet the little piece, written from the woman's point of view, was far more ambiguous. First, it presented marriage as stripping away all of a young woman's supports and happiness, even as it promised future ones: "Marriage is, to a woman, at once the happiest and saddest event of her life; it is the promise of future bliss, raised on the death of present enjoyment. She quits her home—her parents—her companions—her amusement— everything on which she has hitherto depended for comfort, for affection, for kindness and for pleasure." According to the column, "Every former tie is loos-

46. Virginia Hankins diary, June 18, [1863], Hankins Family Papers, VHS.

47. Bessie Cain to John S. Henderson, March 4, 1878, John S. Henderson Papers, SHC; Richard Eppes to Emily Eppes, Feb. 9, 1882, Eppes Family Papers, VHS.

ened, the spring of every action is changed; and she flies with joy into the un-trodden paths before her." After a brief glance at that marital bliss, the piece winds up to its tragic climax: "*Then woe to the man who can blight such fair hopes!* Who can treacherously lure such a heart from its peaceful enjoyment and watchful protection of home—who can coward-like, break the illusions which have won her and destroy the confidence which love had inspired." Obviously the article merely meant to strike a cautionary note, yet it far exceeded its aim. "The death of present enjoyments" seemed all the more concrete when con-trasted to the mere "promise" of future bliss. The overall tone glorified the pro-tection afforded by one's birthplace over the threatening allure of a new relationship.[48]

By the 1860s, the world of marriage and family had been slowly shifting for some time for young women of privileged families in the South. Before 1830, it was unusual when a woman from a privileged background did not marry. Al-though small circles of spinsters existed among wealthy merchant families in Charleston and Savannah, relatively few people seem to have challenged the ideal of marriage as woman's highest, best, and almost only destiny. Historian Anya Jabour has chronicled the unhappiness that Laura Wirt, daughter of Attor-ney General William Wirt and his Virginian wife, Elizabeth Gamble Wirt, expe-rienced over the question of courtship and marriage. Well-educated and uninterested in domestic affairs, Laura Wirt suffered through several depressions in the 1820s as her well-meaning parents propelled her toward marriage. Al-though Laura was happy teaching her younger siblings, her parents saw other-wise. Laura herself leaned toward the single life but had no means or vision to carry out that inclination. When she wed a Maryland lawyer and moved to Flor-ida, a brief and unhappy marriage resulted. After three children in as many years, Laura died.[49]

In the years leading up to the Civil War, southern women had begun to mount a critique of male power in marriage, a critique that would in time be directed at marriage itself. Autograph albums belonging to young Virginia women testify to the support of female friends, but the verses in these albums also included gloomy predictions that "recorded their anxiety about a future that could mean separation from female friends, a lifelong union with an uncaring

48. *Warrenton (Va.) True Index,* March 16, 1867 (emphasis in original).

49. Anya Jabour, "'It Will Never Do for Me to Be Married': The Life of Laura Wirt Randall, 1803–1833," *Journal of the Early Republic* 17 (summer 1997): 193–236; Christine Jacobson Car-ter, "Indispensable Spinsters: Maiden Aunts in the Elite Families of Savannah and Charleston," in *Negotiating Boundaries of Southern Womanhood: Dealing with the Powers That Be,* ed. Janet L. Cory-ell et al. (Columbia, Mo., 2000), 110–34.

husband, frequent and dangerous pregnancies, and even premature death." In their diaries, women like Elizabeth Ruffin in the 1830s and Lucy Breckinridge in the 1860s wrote sarcastically about the institution of marriage; yet they, like other young women, eventually wed. The companionate ideal of marriage remained strong among southern women who looked for a helpmate who would love and cherish them. Yet, as Suzanne Lebsock has so well put it, because of the disparities in legal status and power, a marriage need be only "as companionate as the husband allowed it to be." This poor fit between the ideal and the actual state of marriage left some antebellum southern women unsatisfied with their choices but with little ability to find acceptable alternatives.[50]

While increasing numbers of marriageable women seem not to have made it to the altar in the 1850s, most likely the Civil War constituted a watershed. Although some scholars have questioned whether any change occurred in the proportions of women marrying in the postwar years, a cursory examination of privileged postwar families suggests that a considerable number of women from this class never wed. Some historians might view this simply as a demographic event; the wartime loss of a huge number of men born between 1830 and 1850 made it more difficult for women to marry. In fact, a recent profile of Virginia Civil War widows shows that while a majority of those under age thirty in 1865 remarried, most over that age did not. And most of the widows—who were contemporaries of the second generation described here—tended to marry men either much older or somewhat younger than they. This disparity of ages would not have been acceptable before the war and suggests that women were settling for marriages that they would not earlier have thought desirable. Fanny Andrews, a thirty-one-year-old privileged woman from Georgia who never married, was faced with such a situation in 1871 when a local man, aged at least fifty, became a suitor. Calling him the "old gentleman," Fanny Andrews mused, "I don't pretend to say that I haven't my price, but old Sam Wynn, with all his money, isn't rich enough to pay it. . . . I wish I was like other girls—willing to marry anybody and be done with it." According to Fanny, her twenty-five-year-old sister Metta "has been trying for six months to make up her mind to take old Hobbs, but then he is a far worse case than old Sam, though he has got

50. Anya Jabour, "Albums of Affection: Female Friendship and Coming of Age in Antebellum Virginia," *VMHB* 107 (spring 1999): 158; "The Journal of Elizabeth Ruffin," in *An Evening When Alone: Four Journals of Single Women in the South, 1827–1867,* ed. Michael O'Brien (Charlottesville, Va., 1993), 57–106; Robertson, ed., *Lucy Breckinridge of Grove Hill,* 167, 170, 180, 208–10; Lebsock, *Free Women of Petersburg,* 35. See also Anya Jabour, *Marriage in the Early Republic: Elizabeth and William Wirt and the Companionate Ideal* (Baltimore, 1998) for the case of a couple who sought companionate marriage but found their other goals thwarted it.

more money." Although Metta Andrews later married, it was not to this ancient swain.[51]

Personal choice seems to have played a role for women and men alike. Historian Howard Chudacoff's survey of bachelorhood suggests that the number of young unmarried men was on the rise by 1880, especially among white native-born men. While the deaths of so many single men in war might have put marriage out of reach for some women, for others it impelled them toward a life they might have already been considering. In some women's behavior, as well as in their comments, marriage came into question as the goal of their life. John Rice Andrew, writing about his childhood in late-nineteenth-century South Carolina, declared that after women took charge during the Civil War, the war of the sexes began in earnest. In his view, the war produced hard-edged females: "Four years had fixed the habit of command, which, when I first began to know them, thirty had not broken, nor could they forget how pleasant life had been when all the men were gone." With some hyperbole, Andrew declared that the war merely had given numerous southern women an excuse for being single. As he wrote, "In the South of my childhood an old maid was respected; somewhere toward the North, beneath the sod of Gettysburg or Appomattox lay a gray-clad lover, real or imagined." In this scenario, the dead soldier was simply the window dressing, not the reason that a woman remained single.[52]

Some women suggested that marriage was unnecessary and even unwise. Although Louise Holladay would herself later marry, she criticized an engaged cousin and intimated that marriage was inappropriate for some who should not leave their families: "I have been expecting to hear that Nora Johnston contemplated matrimony, as I had heard she had a good many beaux & was quite a belle. Of course it is no *business of mine* but I think she will be doing *a very foolish thing* to leave her Mother & home as she is *delicate*. It is *so unnecessary* for so many persons to marry."[53]

51. Orville Vernon Burton, "On the Confederate Home Front: The Transformation of Values from Community to Nation in Edgefield, South Carolina" (unpub. paper, Woodrow Wilson International Center for Scholars, 1989) argues from a large database that the proportions of women marrying did not greatly change. Robert Kenzer, " 'The Uncertainty of Life': A Profile of Virginia's Civil War Widows," in *The War Was You and Me: Civilians in the American Civil War*, ed. Joan E. Cashin (Princeton, 2002), 112–35; Eliza Frances Andrews, *Journal of a Georgia Woman, 1870–1872*, ed. S. Kittrell Rushing (Knoxville, Tenn., 2002), 35, 36.

52. Howard P. Chudacoff, *The Age of the Bachelor: Creating an American Subculture* (Princeton, 1999), 47–79; John Andrew Rice, *I Came Out of the Eighteenth Century* (New York, 1942), 116–17.

53. Louise Holladay to James M. and Lucy Holladay, Oct. 26, 1888, Holladay Papers, VHS (emphasis in original).

In some cases, the closeness of the Victorian family impeded marriage. Some daughters became devoted to their parents, especially their mothers, and did not want to make other attachments. The intense emotional engagement in such families made it difficult for young women to break free, even in families in which daughters eventually married. Jeannie Meares confided to her fiancé, "I have been the oldest unmarried daughter for so long now, that the thought of giving up my place to another and going out from under my Mother's care causes a quick throb of pain sometimes." Rosa Biddle, who married at age thirty-one, found it hard both to leave her family and to visualize happiness in marriage. "You can't imagine how sad it makes me to say 'good bye' to my dear old home," she told her fiancé. "I know my dear mother finds it a heavy burden of sadness tho' she esteems you highly & believes as we all do that you will make me happy if it is in the power of man to do so." Her adolescent sister Lizzie Biddle reacted even more strongly to Rosa's wedding: "I certainly do hate for her to get married, for I don't know how I should do without her, it seems almost as if she is going to die, for I know I shall not see much more of her than if she were dead. . . . I nearly cry every time I think of it."[54]

It was among schoolgirls like Lizzie Biddle that one first finds a deep unwillingness to separate from parents. In 1874, Mary Ferrand Henderson wrote her mother from boarding school, "I like to go to school here very well but don't like to be separated from you all. I don't see why children and their parents should have to be separated. I would just like to stay at home all the time. I think an education is dearly bought even excepting the money cost." Lizzie Biddle, who so resented her sister Rosa's marriage, sought to reassure her mother that "my schooldays will soon be over and then I can stay with my Mama." Even though Dabney Bondurant as a collegian was popular and had, according to her sister, a number of beaux, she still closed her letter to her mother, "Goodnight my sweetheart, I will never love anyone like I do you."[55]

While some young women outgrew or overcame these feelings, other daughters did not. Historian Carol Bleser has described the conflicted impulses of Harry Hammond's two daughters, who found it so difficult to leave their parents that one never did. Similar in the intensity of her devotion was Ella Seddon,

54. Jeannie Meares to William A. Williams, Aug. 26, 1881, John and William A. Williams Papers, SHC; Rosa Biddle to S. P. Smith, Dec. 15, 1879, and Lizzie Biddle to Mary E. Biddle, Nov. 29, 1879, both in Samuel S. Biddle Papers, Duke.

55. Mary Ferrand Henderson to Mary S. Henderson, Feb. 11, 1874, John S. Henderson Papers, SHC; Lizzie Biddle to Mary E. Biddle, Nov. 29, 1879, Samuel S. Biddle Papers, Duke; Dabney Bondurant to Emily Bondurant, Dec. 12, 1899, and Lula Harrison to Alexander J. Bondurant, Jan. 8, 1896, both in Bondurant-Morrison Family Papers, UVA.

daughter of Sarah and James Seddon of Virginia. Sarah Bruce Seddon had been an enormously popular belle in the 1850s, her husband had been Secretary of War for the Confederacy, and they remained highly sociable. During the 1870s they hosted dancing lessons for their youngsters and their Bruce cousins, and Sarah's sister-in-law, Sallie Bruce, marveled that the Seddons frequently entertained more than twenty people at dinner. But in the midst of all this gaiety, their eldest daughter, Elvira, known as Ella, remained a homebody. Several relatives remarked on Ella's attachment to her parents. When James Seddon died, a cousin noted, "Ella was the last person he spoke to or recognized. She, poor child, would have died, I think under the weight of such a blow, but for the immediate care her mother needs so much." Sarah Seddon's last illness called forth similar devotion from Ella. For almost two months she watched by the bedside and "never allowed any one to take her place." Only during the last week of her mother's life did Ella leave her post, when the doctor feared that her "anxiety and distress" might threaten the older woman's recovery. After Sarah Seddon's death, Rosa Rutherfoord, Ella's younger sister, worried, "My poor sister! My heart aches for her, for she feels that her *all* has been taken from her." Rosa could foresee little happiness for Ella: "She can never be otherwise than sad, but I hope she will take an interest in my little baby, who is her God child." Rosa's pessimism appears prescient; Ella Seddon survived her mother by less than a year.[56]

Even women who married sometimes resented the wedge that, in their eyes, marriage drove between the bride and her family of origin. As a widowed mother, Maria Louisa Carrington had taught school to support her two daughters, Bessie and Willie, and one would thus expect her relatives to have rejoiced in a daughter's wedding. Yet Bessie's marriage in 1876 prompted Betty Saunders, Maria's sister and close companion, to write a letter of sympathy rather than congratulation to Maria and Willie. Betty Saunders believed, as she told another relative in funereal tones, that Maria's and Willie's "loss is greatest." Betty continued, "Even though they may look forward to the pleasure and comfort of having her always near them, the companionship and intercourse can never be the same." Marriage was coming to be seen as detaching women from their families, while its glories were muted.[57]

While some women preferred their families to marriage, others might have

56. Carol K. Rothrock Bleser, ed., *The Hammonds of Redcliffe* (New York, 1981), 216, 232–36; Anne Seddon Smith Carrington to Maria Louisa Carrington, Aug. 25, 1880, and Rosa Rutherfoord to Maria Carrington, April 27, n.d., both in Saunders Family Papers, VHS.

57. Betty Saunders to Eliza Dabney, March 24, 1876, Saunders Family Papers, VHS.

felt little attraction toward men in the first place, or at least toward the men available to them. Nannie Tunstall snidely reported about an unmarried acquaintance: "She seems to be on bad terms with everybody! Why I wonder? I suppose she is still *hating* men & beaux as much as ever!" Twenty-five-year-old Frances Christine Fisher criticized the available men at White Sulphur Springs in the summer of 1871, saying, "To the fascinations of the young gentlemen I was most shockingly insensible." Arguing that her "many seasons in society (more than I like to count!)" had given her an appreciation of a "thorough gentleman," she declared that such a man was not to be found at the Springs. Fisher concluded her indictment by quoting a visiting Englishman who had commented "how very far inferior the men are to the women." Although she had disputed his remark, "Deny it I could not. It was too deeply branded on my soul by days and nights of such boredom as I shudder even yet to recall."[58]

Other women concentrated more on male behavior as a problem. Heavy drinking had long been a male prerogative in southern society, and wartime traumas and peacetime dislocations might have even increased alcohol consumption during the years immediately following the war. Certainly, it was a problem that stared many in the face, as inebriation and emotional upheavals landed men in trouble and sometimes in jail or the asylum. "[His] career of dissipation and ungoverned passions has come to a sad end indeed," Kate Meares, a young widow who never remarried, uncharitably remarked about an acquaintance from a wealthy Wilmington, North Carolina, family who had recently been institutionalized as mentally ill. In Charlotte County, Virginia, a veritable rash of alcoholism and suicides among young men depressed old and young women alike. Scholar Barbara Sicherman has suggested that the widespread reading among late-nineteenth-century young women might have encouraged a discontent with the men they knew, as the heroes of Victorian literature seemed far "nobler" than their flesh-and-blood counterparts. This contrast might have been even more pronounced in the South, where both young and middle-aged men struggled with an unfriendly economic environment and fell prey to many weaknesses of the flesh.[59]

In such cases men's behavior might well have encouraged young women to

58. Nannie Tunstall to Virginia Clay, Nov. 22, 1885, Clement C. Clay Papers, Duke; Frances C. Fisher to Paul H. Hayne, Sept. 15, 1871, Paul H. Hayne Papers, Duke.

59. Kate Meares to Louis H. Meares, April 15, 1878, Meares Family Papers, SHC; Sallie Bruce to Morelle Bruce, Oct. 4, 1872, Jan. 28, 1874, and Jan. 29, 1883, Bruce Family Papers, VHS; Barbara Sicherman, "Sense and Sensibility: A Case Study of Women's Reading in Late-Victorian America," in *Reading in America: Literature and Social History,* ed. Cathy N. Davidson (Baltimore, 1989), 201–25.

lengthen engagements and delay marriage. Mary Lord, a schoolteacher from Wilmington, provides one example. In 1875, her cousin believed that Mary would marry at the end of the month: "She runs a fearful risk but being 30 years old & after 6 years consideration will put her foot into it." Despite her long deliberation, Mary did not put her foot into it—a decision which her female kin might have influenced. The following year Mary's relatives were still complaining about her fiancé: "Poor Mary Lord I feel very much for her—I wrote her a long letter some time ago, told her I was glad she was spared the mortification of hearing at home of that wretch being carried home beastly drunk, he has been turned out of employment and of course has gone to the dogs ere this." Another fifteen years passed before Mary married, and then, not surprisingly, it was to another man. Similarly, family gossip held that Lena Smith's courtship with an Englishman named Wilkinson ended after the drunken suitor sat on a stove during a boating party on the Roanoke River.[60]

The prospect of sexual activity and childbirth frightened some young women during this time of Victorian respectability. Marietta Minnigerode, who had watched a long procession of younger siblings arrive even as her father's business failed and his drinking increased, spoke for those who preferred to postpone their initiation into sexuality. At sixteen she attracted a suitor. While she enjoyed the "theater tickets and ice cream and flowers and candy galore," she was otherwise uninterested in him. Looking back on the event forty years later, she reminisced, "Mother was very fearful lest the oldest and least pretty of her girls should miss a good match. . . . My reluctance was not to him but to the connubial state on principle. It did not appeal to me. The more I thought of the inevitable climax the more repugnant the whole idea of marriage became. There is a time for all things. The time for this surely had not come. My mother and I disagreed." Much of Marietta's distaste seems to have been fueled by the birth of her twin sisters, one of whom died immediately, the other a few days later in her arms. She mused about this tiny sister's death: "Was it *Love* that produced this imperfect thing, this little weary body and fleeting spirit? . . . There was no beauty to me then, in Love or Death."[61]

In this case, the engagement ended. According to Marietta, "Father did not often run counter to Mother in any matter, but here he came to my rescue and urged her to let me alone as to this marriage." In the confidential discussion that

60. Kate Meares to Richard A. Meares, June 3, 1875, and Eliza J. DeRosset to Kate Meares, Feb. 6, 1876, both in Meares-DeRosset Papers, SHC; Claiborne Thweatt Smith Jr., *Smith of Scotland Neck: Planters on the Roanoke* (Baltimore, 1976), 121.

61. Marietta Minnigerode Andrews, *Memoirs of a Poor Relation: Being the Story of a Post-war Southern Girl and Her Battle with Destiny* (New York, 1927), 256, 258.

ensued, Marietta's mother related "how a woman feels when she wants to be the wife of a man—she told me of the moods of which I read, of palpitating hearts and throbbing pulses—(so all this was real)." When Marietta admitted that she did not feel that way, her mother responded that "she supposed she had made a mistake, and I was at liberty to break the engagement." Relieved, Marietta turned back to art, noting, "I felt I should probably never marry now and yet I was happier than for many a day." In fact, after a succession of suitors and earning a living as an artist and art teacher, Marietta eventually did marry. Other privileged southern women, however, did not outgrow their distaste for childbearing and children. After a grueling week nursing the sick children of her local minister, Fanny Andrews grimly joked to her diary that she might as well get married, writing, "My main reason for staying single, was to get rid of being bothered with children, but I believe the only difference is that now I have the care of other people's instead of my own."[62]

While some women worried about male conduct or sexual relations, in other cases men seemed unsuitable because of their class position or lack of education and breeding. Widowed Carey Pettigrew so strongly disapproved of a proposal that her daughter Annie received that even though Annie showed no interest in the affair, Carey sent her away to visit relatives in South Carolina. Apparently objecting to the suitor's plebeian origins, Carey Pettigrew indignantly described the incident:

> After two positive refusals and declaring then he *would* never mention the subject again, he protested his feelings were too much for him and even at Church took an opportunity of speaking to her! She passed him by without a word—a day or two after they left, he called to see me to ask my permission to write to her!! I took the opportunity which I had not had before of speaking most frankly to him. I know I spoke strongly and well, for I was excited, but I did not insult the man—he promised his attentions should cease, that he *would* give up, tho' "he never *could* marry &c &c."[63]

Similarly Esther Meares of Piedmont North Carolina was singularly unimpressed with the suitors she attracted. In 1877, twenty-three-year-old Esther rather laughingly recounted a recent tiff: "My Country beaux have all deserted me, Mr Spain says he does not intend to call on 'flirts.' I am very glad they have all stopped coming, for you know they are very tiresome." Only a month earlier Esther had flippantly described a Sunday evening that Frank Smith spent at her

62. Ibid., 267, 269; Andrews, *Journal of a Georgia Woman*, 37.
63. Carey Pettigrew to William S. Pettigrew, July 31, 1877, Pettigrew Family Papers, SHC.

house: "He talked a great deal about matrimony. I tried to hush him up by telling him I would never marry anyone unless they were in every way my superior. He said of course I meant in the way of trade, and that he thought he was as good a trader as there was in the country. Some men are so conceited." If Esther were in fact waiting for such a "superior," she apparently never found him. Three years later, when Mr. Murdock "courted her again," Esther rejected his proposal with the comment that "she would not live in Salisbury with any man." Esther seemed more to disdain the men who wooed her than to dislike the institution of marriage, but she did not reveal any interest in the latter either. Whether her notion of a husband as a necessary "superior" was unfulfilled idealism or a simple rationalization of her situation cannot be determined. Nor can it be known if she found men as a group unappealing. But clearly she was dismissive of the possibilities that presented themselves. Her comments reveal a signal unconcern with her increasing age and offer intriguing suggestions into why she never married.[64]

Existing alongside these critiques of individual men, and equally important, was a skepticism that marriage would somehow better a woman's lot in life. In 1877, Carey Pettigrew wrote about her eldest daughter's courtship: "I do not think Jane has quite made up her mind, but he is very devoted, and so highly spoken of by all who know him, that if she marries at all, I doubt any one making her happier." In the prewar period such a devoted mother would barely have entertained the notion voiced in the doubt "if she marries at all." In this case, Jane Pettigrew did accept the proposal. Even then, although Carey approved of the engagement, her enthusiasm was muted: "I feel this is a most serious thing, the most momentous step in a woman's life, but I think she has decided wisely." Other women sometimes echoed a similar wistfulness about whether marriage and any man could make them happy.[65]

In some cases, what first emerged as a decision not to marry the particular suitors who offered themselves seemed to harden over time into a general determination not to marry. Virginia Hankins's wartime diary, begun when she was twenty years old, reveals a fascination with the poet Sidney Lanier and his brother Clifford, but it is difficult to determine whether she suffered from unrequited love or merely reveled in their company. The following year she rejected the proposal of a young man from her area who had begged her to let him know

64. Essie Meares to Louis H. Meares, April 15, 1877, and March 25, 1877, Meares-DeRosset Papers, SHC; Mary T. Meares to Fred Meares, Nov. 20, 1882, William B. Meares Papers, SHC.
65. Carey Pettigrew to William S. Pettigrew, July 31 and Nov. 22, 1877, both in Pettigrew Family Papers, SHC.

what he could do to make her love him, since the "love I feel for you is not prompted or fed by passion but is the mature and well ripened fruit of a long & devoted friendship." Virginia seems to have given him no encouragement. Fifteen months later, after the war had ended, he again renewed his offer of marriage, and once again she rejected him.[66]

By this time, Virginia apparently had begun to think that she might remain unmarried. A year earlier she had broached the subject of spinsterhood with a friend, who replied, "I hope dear friend you will come to see me many times before you are an old maid, tho I do not agree with you that you will be one." By 1880, when Virginia was thirty-seven, she authoritatively instructed her brother to deny any reports that she might marry: "Who in the world did you hear I was going to marry? Whenever you hear anything of the kind please say 'I know it is a mistake.' For I have never had the least intention of marrying."[67]

Nannie Tunstall of Lynchburg lightheartedly reported an encounter with an old beau in Washington "accidentally on the street. He was there on a visit. Our meeting was brief and ceremonious. He has I suppose never forgiven me for my bad conduct towards him & is now paying court to Miss Frelinghuysen. Well, I'd like to have a Cottage at Newport & all that, but I want to choose the householder also!" A year and a half later, when her family responsibilities seemed especially onerous, Nannie wrote more despairingly to her cousin and worried that her decision not to marry reflected badly on her family. As Nannie saw it, the marriages she might have made would not have been personally fulfilling, but any union might have better satisfied her mother. "It is very hard to tell what to do, & how to act to be the greatest advantage to your home people," she mused. "Sometimes I regret bitterly that I did not marry—not that I cared eno' for any of the men for it to make my happiness, but perhaps had I so allied from prudential motives as so many of my friends have done—things w'd have been better at home. It must be a terrible incubus and grief & mortification to have an old-maid daughter! It is too late to mend matters now. An old maid I am and so I must remain, to the end of the chapter."[68]

To be sure, some women who decided never to marry did not necessarily advocate the single state for others. When unmarried schoolteacher Virginia Hankins sent her younger sister off for a visit, she told a brother, "I was not

66. John H. Willcox to Virginia Hankins, Dec. 2, 1864, and March 29, 1866, Hankins Family Papers, VHS.

67. Nannie [Smith?] to Jennie Hankins, June 9, 1865, and Virginia Hankins to Louis Hankins, May 1, 1880, both in Hankins Family Papers, VHS.

68. Nannie Tunstall to Virginia Clay, April 21, 1884, and Sept. 18, 1885, Clement C. Clay Papers, Duke.

willing that Mary should spend her youth without ever having any brightness, and grow to be a gloomy nervous, sour old maid. I thank God for all the happiness I have ever had." While marriage might be a tenuous and even dangerous bargain, some single women hesitated to advocate their state as a positive general condition for others.[69]

Even though women did not necessarily prize the unmarried state, some explicitly suggested that they did not welcome the constraints of marriage on their autonomy. As Jeannie Meares told her fiancé of one week's standing, "Yes, it is hard to give up one's name and independence," although she assured him that she was "confident that mine will be entrusted to a very kind & loving heart." Other women more vehemently insisted that they despised dependence. After being asked by an aunt to teach at a cousin's house, Fanny Dabney sought to clarify her position within that household. Did in fact her cousins intend to employ her? As the time passed and they said nothing, Fanny set out her questions in writing. Avowing her attachment to her cousins—"you know I do love you all dearly, and if I could feel satisfied on this subject would rather live with you than anyone else"—she set out her ideal of self-support: "I should never expect to become as much attached to any other family, or to feel as much at home as I did at Bleak Hill, but the idea of being dependent is so dreadful to me, that I could never be happy in that position as long as I had strength to work; if I had not, then I should try to be contented, knowing that it was the will of God."[70]

The range of strictures and praise for differing behaviors we have seen thus far provide glimpses of various notions of female character; they also show how the younger generations rebelled against and sometimes reshaped these ideals through discussion and their own conduct. Other sources, particularly fictional depictions of women, can supplement these visions of ideal behavior and traits. Particularly helpful in this respect are the many heroines of novels written by elite women in the South. These characters at times reflected prescriptive ideals, but they also had to be appealing enough that readers would want to learn about them; they served as fantasies of how southern white women wished to appear

69. Virginia Hankins to Louis Hankins, Dec. 3, 1883, Hankins Family Papers, VHS.

70. Jeannie Meares to W. A. Williams, c. June 1881, John and William A. Williams Papers, SHC; Frances Beverley Dabney to Betty Saunders, Aug. 26, 1867; see also Julia Myers to Kate Dabney, April 6, 1870, and Williamine Cabell Carrington to Betty Saunders, Nov. 23, [c. 1868–70], all in Saunders Family Papers, VHS. See also Friedman, *Enclosed Garden*, 39–49, for the example of Anna Maria Akehurst, who thought herself blessed that she had "employment which keep[s] me from being beholden to either friend, relative, or kin." Friedman, however, considers Akehurst anomalous.

and behave. That they were constructed by white southern women of the old elite might have given them a particular appeal. Fictional heroines' daily routines and dialogues mimicked, while improving upon, reality, and the novels' richness of detail surpasses that for even the best documented of historical personages.

The 1870s were a transitional period for the heroines in novels, as can be seen in the work in Frances Christine Fisher, who wrote under the pen name Christian Reid. She published extensively in the 1870s and 1880s, and southern women's diaries and writings are replete with references to her books. Like the heroines of antebellum romances, most of Fisher's maidens are heavily idealized. Scholar Martha Banta has noted that antebellum characters generally were small, dainty, and delicate young women. Fisher's heroines follow a similar mold; even if not beautiful, virtually all are "graceful," "dainty," and pleasing in appearance. Many young women are characterized as flowers of one sort or another. In *A Daughter of Bohemia,* for example, Leslie Grahame starts out as a rose but soon turns into a lily. Many of these novels utilize double heroines, often of different social classes, but both showing character and breeding. In *Morton House,* Katharine Tresham is a "stately creature," while Irene Vernon is a "beautiful, golden-haired vision." Norah Desmond of *A Daughter of Bohemia* boasts "regular clearly-cut features, the skin white as milk and smooth as marble, the scarlet lips so proudly curved and firmly closed, the rich masses of hair, chestnut in the shade, spun gold in the sun, . . . large full eyes." Norah also possesses a sort of "magnetism," while her half-sister Leslie Grahame is "slender, graceful" with a "fair highbred face."[71]

Frances Christine Fisher created a wide range of female characters, from the frothy belle to the thoughtful, hardworking governess, the foreign heiress, and even the fortune hunter. Over time, her heroines became more serious, though not necessarily more intellectual. *Mabel Lee,* one of the author's very early novels and the first to win a wide readership, featured a beautiful blond heroine who finds Robert Browning's poetry overly difficult. Compared to a fairy princess

---

71. Banta, *Imaging American Women,* 514. Illustrative of the popularity of Fisher's novels, Louise Humphreys Carter's teenaged daughters read Fisher's *Valerie Aylmer* aloud to her while she sewed; a few weeks later she read *Morton House.* Louise Humphreys Carter diary, Nov. 29 and Dec. 20, 1871, Shirley Plantation Papers, CWF.

Although her books are catalogued under the last name "Tiernan," I refer to Frances Fisher by her birth name because the novels I use were written before her marriage. Frances Christine Fisher Tiernan [pseud. Christian Reid], *A Daughter of Bohemia: A Novel* (New York, 1874), 5, 25, 28, 136–37; idem, *Morton House: A Novel* (New York, 1872), 1, 49. Mary Hiatt, *Style and the "Scribbling Women": An Empirical Analysis of Nineteenth-Century American Fiction* (Westport, Conn., 1993), 82–86, finds that both male and female authors in her sample from the period 1860 to 1880 frequently used such adjectives as "adorable, charming, dainty, delicate" to describe women.

because of her wealth of golden hair, Mabel is abducted by Ralph Ainslie, a jealous suitor. Earlier, in passages full of sexually charged imagery, Ainslie had tried to hypnotize or mesmerize her. Showing herself to be perhaps the ideal belle or the ideal fantasy for would-be belles, Mabel displays some steel in her ability to defend her virtue and resist the mesmerizing villain. From her first meeting, Mabel dislikes him; that night all her dreams are of snakes, every one of which "had his eyes." On his deathbed, the villain Ainslie confesses, "I loved her—and she was the first—who ever resisted my power—to attract." Mabel's successful resistance to the kidnapping (and implicitly to sexual attack) literally drives her insane. After her rescue, the death of the villain, and a year spent recuperating in Europe, Mabel regains her memory and reason, and the ending looks toward her happy marriage with the young scion who had won her heart.[72]

After this story, first published in 1870, Frances Christine Fisher moved on to heroines with greater talents and considerably more presence of mind than poor Mabel. Whether Ermine St. Amand, a Charleston beauty pressured to marry her cousin, or Nina Dalzell, a young flirt who comes to rue her engagement, these female leads are often grappling with their uncertain futures. The author never seems completely sanguine about the outcome. In one particularly telling passage, a would-be suitor, Mr. Martindale, tells nineteen-year-old Nina Dalzell, "Our lives are what we make them." Nina's reply is far more fatalistic and cryptic: "If it is true at all, it is true only of men—never of women. Circumstances make us." Ironically enough, Nina engineers a pyrrhic triumph over circumstances. In this case, Nina defeats Martindale's attempt to murder her fiancé, whom she does not love, but the victory comes only at the cost of her own life. In a similar scene in *Hearts and Hands,* a romance primarily set at a nineteenth-century southern spa, a suitor tells Sybil Courtenay that he hopes she does not plan to settle down into domesticity. "'I don't know what I shall do,' she answers a little petulantly. 'How absurd it is to ask a woman such a question! We can't make our own lives—they are made for us, and not always agreeably I fancy.'" The question of women's ability to control their lives runs through Fisher's many novels and stories. Despite the protestations of these heroines, she allowed many of them to make active decisions about their lives. Taking control of their destinies, however, did not always lead to happy endings or consummated romances.[73]

<hr />

72. Frances Christine Fisher Tiernan [pseud. Christian Reid], *Mabel Lee* (New York, 1872), 22, 152, 64, 160.

73. Frances Christine Fisher Tiernan [pseud. Christian Reid], *Ebb Tide and Other Stories* (New York, 1872); idem, *Nina's Atonement and Other Stories* (New York, 1873), 7; idem, *Hearts and Hands: A Story in Sixteen Chapters* (New York, 1875), 30.

Frances Christine Fisher, who herself married only in her forties after two decades of authorship, tentatively explored in some of her stories the part that marriage should play in women's life. Most of her heroines were able to find love and marriage with a devoted suitor, but Fisher clearly believed that a woman should not accept a proposal, even from a wealthy suitor, against her own inclinations. In novels and stories, the author wrestled with the problem of what belledom meant and whether marriage was permissible for any reason other than love. Katharine Tresham, the governess in *Morton House* (Fisher's own favorite among her novels), and Norah Desmond of *A Daughter of Bohemia,* both spunky young women, reject men whom they do not love and are ultimately rewarded for their independence of mind and heart. *Morton House* features two young women, governess Katharine Tresham and Irene Vernon, the belle, who turn down several proposals of marriage. At one point, Katharine Tresham in a single day rejects two suitors, one of whom is very handsome and wealthy: "For the second time that day Katharine deliberately put aside the love and protection which two different men, each well worthy of trust, had offered her, and with the blind, heedless, yet sometimes divine impulse of youth, turned from the golden gifts of life, those gifts for which some wretched women are willing to sell themselves into legal bondage, and went her way alone." These proposals are set up as trials; they indicate the integrity of the heroines, and each eventually marries a worthy man she loves. Irene's belledom is also used to comedic effect; she rejects one particularly persistent admirer every six months.[74]

While Frances Fisher's novels of the 1870s criticized women who married for money or material gain, *After Many Days,* an 1877 novel, provided two different interpretations of the marriage of convenience. In this story, the heroine, Amy Reynolds, is the talented daughter of a poverty-stricken music teacher. When diphtheria kills her favorite brother and father and destroys her voice, making a stage career impossible, Amy marries an elderly merchant who promises to care for her orphaned brothers and sisters. "If he had asked her for love," Fisher writes, "she would have turned away from him; but he had not done so, and she felt an instinctive sense that she could trust him not to demand more than she could give." Yet earlier in the story, Amy is wooed by Brian Marchmont, who seeks her affection while simultaneously attempting to marry Beatrix Waldron, a wealthy heiress. When Beatrix discovers his perfidy, she not only rejects him but enlightens Amy about his conduct, administering a tongue-lashing to him in Amy's presence. Marrying to provide a home for one's siblings might be per-

74. Tiernan, *Morton House,* 227, 211.

missible, but a marriage for social position under the guise of love was, in this formulation, heartless self-seeking.[75]

Fisher's short stories made marriage less central to the plot. When Ermine St. Amand believes her ship captain lover is lost at sea, she turns down the marriage her mother has planned for her and, after giving her fortune to a cousin, goes to Europe to paint. Her lover finds Ermine only when she is on her deathbed. In another story, Powell Vardray, a young Georgia teacher, is romanced in Jamaica by a British army officer, Major Romeyne. They declare their love for one another during the course of a long, secluded ride together, but Romeyne is seriously injured in a fall from his horse. Powell vows to remain with him. After they finally are rescued, the machinations of a jealous woman sends the unconscious Romeyne back to England, but his ship sinks in transit. "The good ship went down, the ocean-tides swept over the heart that might have been so true, and yet again might have been so false; and all love, all hope, all suffering was at an end forever," Fisher concludes. For Powell Vardray, life is never quite the same: "In all the years of her existence she never lived again. Yet these years were quiet enough and in one sense—the sense of duty fulfilled and work performed—even happy." Here the author is ambiguous; although Powell's romantic life has ended, she still has a short, contented life of service. It is enough that Powell has experienced romance. Her tombstone, written after her heroic death while nursing victims of a yellow fever epidemic, reads in German, "I have lived and loved."[76]

In short stories, then, Frances Christine Fisher sometimes suggested that romances could fail and heroines could live unmarried lives. Some of these stories were cautionary about the necessity of a good character. One heroine loses her fiancé when he discovers that she has dishonestly claimed another's rightful inheritance. In "The Story of a Scar," a middle-aged woman identified only as "Miss Stuart" narrates the tale of how she came to bear a scar on her hand. As a "heartless coquette," she became enthralled by new neighbors and soon became "outrageously fast," despite a cousin's attempts to warn her that one of them was a professional gambler. When her father stored precious gems at their estate and was detained in town by a storm, thieves attempted to break into the house. Miss Stuart barricaded herself in a room with the jewels and shot one of the

75. Frances Christine Fisher Tiernan [pseud. Christian Reid], *After Many Days: A Novel* (New York, 1877).

76. Tiernan, *Morton House;* idem, *Daughter of Bohemia,* 49, 115, 120; idem, *Ebb Tide and Other Stories;* idem, "Powell Vardray's Life," in *Nina's Atonement and Other Stories,* 129–40.

intruders, only to discover that this would-be jewel thief was the neighbor who had been wooing her. She never marries.[77]

In the 1880s, other white southern women writers created more intelligent and determined heroines than Fisher's serious but marriageable young maidens of the 1870s. In these later novels, the fascination of southern women was as likely to stem from their intellect and strength of character as from their beauty. Some of these 1880s heroines more actively dominated the plots, and female authors became more insistent about their spunkiness. Thus Nannie Tunstall's heroine, Janet Brown, spends much of her vacation reading, and M. G. McClelland's Pocahontas Mason amuses herself by perusing a volume of Ralph Waldo Emerson one hot summer day. In a similar vein, novelist Julia Magruder assured her readers that her heroine was no lightweight but had undertaken "varied and miscellaneous reading."[78]

In these novels, presence of mind and decisiveness matter more to character than modesty, chastity, or pliability of temper. Margaret Trevennon, the heroine of Julia Magruder's *Across the Chasm,* typifies these young women, whose strength of character gives them a certain self-possession. Although only nineteen, Margaret has definite opinions on politics, work ethics, and proper social behavior. Baring for her readers the scaffolding of romantic novels, the author divides heroines into two categories, the "maiden in the first flush of youth, who is so immaculately lovely as to be extremely improbable and the maturer female, who is so strong-minded as to be wholly ineligible to romantic situations." The novelist then places Margaret Trevennon with the former, but with a caveat: "It must be said, on the other hand, that the term 'strong-minded' was one which had been more than once applied to her by those who should have known her best." Similarly, M. G. McClelland uses the appearance of her heroine of *Princess,* Pocahontas Mason, to indicate her determination: Pocahontas's "well-cut chin, . . . spoke eloquently of breadth of character and strength of will." Pocahontas's mother, of all people, describes marriage as being a "terrible risk for a girl like her" because she "is too straightforward, too uncompromisingly intolerant of everyday littleness, to have a very peaceful life. . . . She is largehearted and has great capacity for affection, but she is self-willed and she could be hard upon occasion."[79]

77. Tiernan, "My Story," in *Nina's Atonement and Other Stories,* 81–103; idem, "The Story of a Scar," in *Ebb Tide and Other Stories.*

78. [Nannie Whitmell Tunstall], *"No. 40": A Romance of Fortress Monroe and the Hygeia,* 2nd ed. (Richmond, Va., 1884), 8, 41, 71; M. G. McClelland, *Princess* (New York, 1886), 46–47; Julia Magruder, *Across the Chasm* (New York, 1885), 3.

79. Magruder, *Across the Chasm,* 1–2; McClelland, *Princess,* 25, 41.

Some of these 1880s novels by southern white women celebrate the determined self-sufficiency of heroines who either own property or support themselves. Nannie Tunstall's Janet Brown has no father or brothers, but retains her family lands and tells a suitor, "I could manage to live upon my rent if I had not such luxurious tastes. In order to gratify them, ultimately, I mean to go out teaching for a few years." Here, a possible occupation is introduced in the most matter-of-fact manner. Barbara Pomfret, the heroine in two novels by Amélie Rives, apparently owns a plantation, Rosemary.[80]

Several self-possessed and self-supporting heroines appear in stories and novels that Henrietta Hardy Hammond wrote before her untimely death in 1883. Unlike most other southern white women novelists, Hammond was vague on the question of whether her heroines hailed from North or South. Their self-confidence, however, was not in doubt. In "A Love Story," the young artist Lois Holme finds Mary Silverthorn, an artist and old friend of her mother, a mentor and role model of sorts. Mary Silverthorn never regrets her failure to marry, and she contrasts the happiness of her single life to the trials of Lois's mother, Bessie Holme, "who instead of becoming an independent being like myself, elected to marry Ned Holme, have her heart broken, and be left . . . a widow with a son who promises to follow in his father's steps." In a long impassioned tirade, Mary Silverthorn entreats Lois to choose art over marriage:

> An artist, Lois, should never marry. You may be simply a woman, bearing the lot of womanhood and wifehood, all its joys and sufferings; or an artist, with all the intellectual pleasures, the freedom, the charm of that life your own. It is time for you to choose. Can you merge all your loves and ambitions and interests into this better, happier life—I honestly believe it so—and keep your freedom and cultivate your gift? What is marriage in the end? Think of the fearful risk; think of its horrible, prosaic cares and bonds, and resolve not to be tempted by its pleasant preliminaries, the pretty fooleries that turn girls' heads. Choose the free life and use the power living in you.

In the course of the story, Lois sees the man she loves marry another, and she herself receives and rebuffs a proposal from a young professor, even though her family's financial problems are great and she has sold only a few pictures. "Because she was in trouble, that was no reason for marrying," Lois reassures herself, "to a generous soul it was reason not to marry." Instead her solution is a stoic independence: "Perhaps life was not to be made very easy for her; certainly it must not be made easy for her by another's laying of his life beneath her feet.

80. Tunstall, "No. 40," 48; Amélie Rives, The Quick or the Dead?: A Study (Philadelphia, 1888).

She must bear and endure and live alone such a life as was altogether honest and was given." The story's end depicts the unhappiness of Lois's former lover and the woman who had married him largely for financial reasons. In Hammond's last book, *A Fair Philosopher* (1883), the heroine is a young woman who writes to support her father and sister and also organizes a reading group to discuss philosophers and philosophical ideals. In this case, unlike in "A Love Story," the heroine eventually weds, but the emphasis remains on her willingness and ability to support herself financially, emotionally, and intellectually.[81]

Although these white southern female authors produced heroines brimming with self-confidence and possessing the requisite skills for financial independence, some of these fictionalized young women also tended to be adept in traditional arts of housewifery. This appears to be part of an attempt at a complex depiction of southern women in regard to models of traditional womanhood and domesticity. Southern women's housekeeping abilities, rather than implying any traditional submissiveness, simply demonstrate one aspect of their general competence. M. G. McClelland's heroine, Pocahontas Mason, competently arranges a room for a meal, cleans and reorganizes the library, tends turkeys and chickens. Yet these are never her primary interests; they simply show a range of talents among her many abilities.[82]

By the 1880s, southern women's fiction had seen some marked changes in its heroines. In Frances Fisher's early novels, heroines might be accused of being bohemian and even "fast," but they remained stalwartly high-minded and proper, even when they led somewhat unconventional lives. By the 1880s, sexual experience and female sexual feeling was beginning to make its appearance in romantic novels written by southern women. This may simply indicate the influence of French writers, or even popular English writers such as Ouida (Maria Louise de la Ramé), author of the enormously successful *Under Two Flags* (1867) and *Moths* (1880). In her most intriguing novel, *The Georgians,* Henrietta Hardy Hammond presents a love affair between Félise Orlanoff, a Frenchwoman who is estranged from her husband and has inherited an estate in Georgia, and Marcus Laurens, a young southern lawyer who had been a Unionist during the war. In this case, it is the hero who has been living a "secluded, religious, chaste, and manly life" as a devout Methodist. A tragic sexual intimacy develops, as the discovery of this illicit love literally shocks into illness Kate Laurens, the hero's young sister. Kate dies of scarlet fever while estranged from her heretofore be-

81. Henrietta Hardy, "A Love Story," *Southern Magazine* 17 (July–Dec. 1875), 108, 644; Henrietta Hardy Hammond [pseud. Henri Daugé], *A Fair Philosopher* (New York, 1882).
82. McClelland, *Princess,* 20, 75–78.

loved brother. The sexual magnetism between Marcus and Félise makes *The Georgians* differ from many sentimental novels of its day. Even after their fatal assignation, the two assure each other of their love, Marcus telling Félise, "We were not to blame if nature conquered conventionality." Although the timely death of Count Orlanoff frees Marcus and Félise to wed, their indiscretion has destroyed their love. As the novel ends, an observer comments that theirs is a failed marriage because of mutual distrust. The author thus punishes her guilty lovers, yet the impression that lingers is of the strength of their sexual attraction.[83]

Henrietta Hardy Hammond limited such sexuality to a non-southern heroine, but by the end of the 1880s, Amélie Rives led the way in presenting more sexually aware southern women. Her early magazine novella, "The Quick or The Dead?" (1888) became an immediate sensation and later a bestselling book. Perhaps its most famous scene was a dialogue between the young widow Barbara Pomfret and her suitor, in which she constantly interrupted him with "Kiss me." Virginia readers wondered about the relationship the story's heroine bore to its twenty-three-year-old author. Years later Marietta Minnigerode Andrews vividly recalled a discussion among the older women in her family over the "novels of a young Virginian [Rives] which I gathered were full of suggestions that little girls can't understand." In her family, the scene that had left the greatest impression was one in which Barbara "sank into the arms which he held out for her, and, pressing down the collar of his silk shirt, rested her wordless lips in the hollow at the base of his strong throat." Marietta described her own reaction to her female relatives' description: "One of the ladies in the book had pulled down the collar of one of the gentlemen and had kissed him in the hollow of his throat. Well, what was there in that to make such a fuss over? That was not hard to understand. Grandma said no lady would do such a thing; Aunt Ida said the authoress certainly had a vivid imagination. My mother flatly declared that in addition to a vivid imagination the authoress had had some considerable experience." The reactions of these older women to Rives's book exposes the compet-

---

83. Dee Garrison has described the work of sixteen female authors that a survey of librarians in the American Library Association in 1881 found "sensational or immoral." According to Garrison, it was the rebelliousness of some of the authors' female characters that most offended the librarians. Dee Garrison, "Immoral Fiction in the Late Victorian Library," in *Victorian America,* ed. Daniel Walker Howe (Philadelphia, 1976), 142–59. Anne Goodwyn Jones has argued that the concept of desire made its way into women's novels by 1899, but versions of it existed at least a decade earlier. Anne Goodwyn Jones, "The Work of Gender in the Southern Renaissance," in *Southern Writers and Their Worlds,* ed. Christopher Morris and Steven G. Reinhardt (College Station, Tex., 1996), 41–56; [Henrietta Hardy Hammond], *The Georgians* (Boston, 1881), 305.

ing ideals of womanhood in the turn-of-the-century South. While Amélie Rives's Barbara Pomfret did not necessarily replace more conventionally demure heroines as an ideal for young women, her vibrant sexuality offered a different model for elite women, especially since a marriage proposal rewarded this sexy heroine. Barbara Pomfret and other less sexual, but nonetheless assertive, heroines opened up to southern female readers a host of new possibilities.[84]

In the late nineteenth century, ideals of female behavior and character were in flux. The education of privileged young women had come to incorporate many academically challenging subjects. Even though it continued to include ornamental skills, such as music, art, and other "womanly accomplishments," some of these had been turned to new, more practical ends. Young white southern women, like their Victorian peers, received strong calls to fulfill their duty to family and religion, but notions of courtship and marriage were changing. Some women chafed against rules of propriety and chaperonage. The continued idealization of marriage made some proposals, at least those offered by patently flawed males, less than compelling. Some women of the old elite did not wish to leave beloved parents; others simply did not find enough love or even companionship in the possible marriages they contemplated. At the same time, the social world of privileged southern youth in the postwar period was populated by working women (such as teachers), and the notion of the belle was shifting to incorporate greater sexual appeal and a more active female sexuality. The intelligence and assertiveness of the southern heroines emerging in novels of the 1880s written by female southern novelists both reflected and encouraged the wishes and fantasies of a generation of privileged southern women. First among their fields of activity and action would be that of home and family.

84. Rives, *Quick or the Dead?*, 433, 510–11, 513; Andrews, *Memoirs of a Poor Relation*, 99–100.

2

WOMEN AND THE NEW DOMESTICITY

As female aspirations and self-definitions were changing in the wake of the Civil War, elite white women put such concepts to work in their households and families. These households were in flux, for the war had rearranged combinations of those living together. The loss of fathers, brothers, husbands, suitors, and friends created temporary alterations, some of which became permanent. Shifts in position and wealth also made a difference in the kinds of kin and non-kin who resided and visited in the white household. Even southern women from privileged families found the postwar household filled with different responsibilities and challenges. Like wealthy northern households, antebellum southern establishments had included servants along with the nuclear family, but most southern servants were enslaved African Americans. Emancipation allowed these freed people to leave the white household and, as a result, new relationships arose between white mistresses and their servants. This chapter chronicles changes in the household and its workers, black and white, as white women reconfigured their domestic space. In the wake of the demise of "domestic slavery," southern white women would themselves become more adept but also more "domesticated."

The well-known picture of the privileged white family as multigenerational might actually have become more common after the war than earlier. Little has been written about the structure of the postwar elite white family, but some scholarly debate has focused on the nature of that family in the antebellum period. Most scholars have tended to see the common stereotype of generations of the white planter family living together in the great house primarily as a popular myth. In contrast, historian Joan Cashin has argued that a significant minority of planter households included additional kin and non-kin members. Nonetheless, her argument about the importance of extended kin depends less on coresidence than on attitudes about kin, especially the significance of cousinhood. Other scholars have posited the primacy and pervasiveness of the nuclear family ideal. Yet even those, like Orville Vernon Burton, who stress the nuclear structure of southern families have shown that significant deviations from it did exist.[1]

In Virginia and North Carolina, elite families that varied from the nuclear structure most commonly were augmented by kin from a fractured family or by young couples who did not yet have their own household. Some augmented families took in orphan nieces or nephews or homeless cousins. In other cases, a young married couple lived with the widowed parent of the husband or wife. For example, in 1860, Eliza L. S. Marshall, a sixty-two-year-old widow, numbered among her Fauquier County, Virginia, household her unmarried adult daughter, Mildred, as well as her son Jacquelin, his wife, and their two infant children. That same year Henry and Ida Dulany, who had three young children, housed Ida's widowed mother and two unmarried sisters at their Fauquier plantation, Oakley. Planter families expanded from time to time to incorporate such unmarried or widowed kin, orphans, and poor relations.[2]

In the Civil War, both forced and voluntary relocations often reconfigured household arrangements, even those of the privileged, temporarily creating what historian Drew Faust has characterized as households of women and children. Sometimes these arrangements continued beyond the war, as one family in Fauquier illustrates. At the outbreak of the Civil War, elderly Ann Dulany headed a rarity, a four-generation household that contained her unmarried son William, her widowed daughter Elizabeth Payne, and Elizabeth's teenaged sons and married daughter, Alberna, along with Alberna's husband, Austin Jennings, and their two infant children. The war, William Dulany's death, and the maturing of the young men emptied most of the males out of this household; in the early 1870s, only Elizabeth Payne and the Jennings family remained with nonagenarian Ann Dulany. While Dulany's arrangement was unusual, elite families after the war were more apt to vary from the nuclear norm.[3]

1. Joan Cashin, "The Structure of Planter Families: 'The Ties that Bound Us Was Strong,'" *JSH* 56 (Jan. 1990): 55–70. Compare to Orville Vernon Burton, *In My Father's House Are Many Mansions: Family and Community in Edgefield, South Carolina* (Chapel Hill, N.C., 1985), 109–14; Jane Turner Censer, *North Carolina Planters and Their Children* (Baton Rouge, La., 1984), 20–25, 103–4.

2. MS Census of 1860, Virginia, Fauquier County, sch. 1, pp. 249, 25; Marietta Minnigerode Andrews, *Memoirs of a Poor Relation: Being the Story of a Post-war Southern Girl and Her Battle with Destiny* (New York, 1927), 62.

3. Drew Gilpin Faust, *Mothers of Invention: Women of the Slaveholding South in the American Civil War* (Chapel Hill, N.C., 1996), 30–45; MS Census of 1860, Virginia, Fauquier County, sch. 1, p. 279; MS Census of 1870, Virginia, Fauquier County, sch. 1, p. 497. On women's experi-

First, the coresidence of adult siblings appears to have become more common. Widowed Ann Miller described such a situation among her siblings soon after the war: her sister Jane lived with sister Mary, her sister Kate with brother Fred Davis, and her never-married sister Rebecca Davis "of course" with Ann herself. Ann recounted a scene shortly before her husband's death in the summer of 1865, when "he begged Bec always to live with us, told her as long as he had a crust of bread or house over his head he wanted her to share it with us." Before the war, however, Ann's family had been a nuclear one, and Rebecca Davis had resided with her widowed father.[4]

In Virginia, other adult siblings turned to coresident arrangements after the war. For example, in 1860 Eliza and Hannah Beale lived with their aged widower father, who died during the war. In 1870 they shared a home with their brother-in-law and sister, Charles and Mary C. Gordon; their unmarried brother, William Beale, lived nearby. Although Eliza and Hannah had inherited not only land but also the "mansion house" of their father, it is not clear whether they were residing there or in a house that belonged to the Gordons. Their other brother, the younger John G. Beale, had also died during the Civil War; his adult children, Mary Aurelton, Ludwell, John, and John's wife, Susan Beale, shared a household in 1870, perhaps in another "mansion house" that Mary Aurelton Beale had inherited from her grandfather. In 1866, Martha Clarke reported an arrangement in which she and her husband Lyle lived with his widowed mother. Lyle's married sister, Sally Manning, and her children temporarily resided with them; a widowed sister-in-law and her child divided their time between the Clarke household and her mother's in Hanover County, Virginia.[5]

While the evidence does not suggest that the Beales were financially hardpressed, the financial aftershocks of the war drove other siblings to share housing. Alethea Warren of Edenton, North Carolina, faced with the loss of much of her property, at one point resided with her sister in Alabama. Her nephew

---

ences as war refugees, see Joan Cashin, "Into the Trackless Wilderness: The Refugee Experience in the Civil War," in *A Woman's War: Southern Women, Civil War, and the Confederate Legacy*, ed. Edward D. C. Campbell Jr. and Kym S. Rice (Richmond, Va., 1996), 29–53.

4. Ann Miller to Kate Kennedy, Aug. 17, 1865, DeRosset Family Papers, SHC; MS Census of 1860, N.C., New Hanover County, sch. 1, p. 405; MS Census of 1850, N.C., New Hanover County, sch. 1, p. 334.

5. MS Census of 1860, Virginia, Fauquier County, sch. 1, pp. 146–47; MS Census of 1870, Virginia, Fauquier County, sch. 1, pp. 490, 503; Commissioners to William Beale et al., March 10, 1866, Fauquier County Deeds, vol. 60, pp. 253–56, and Division of Property, June 28, 1869, Fauquier County Deeds, vol. 61, pp. 369–70, in Records Hall, FCCC; Martha Clarke to Phebe Bailey, Feb. 15, 1866, Bailey Family Papers, VHS.

Arthur asked her to live with him at Weston, his plantation in Chowan County, and she accepted that offer.[6]

While the coresidence of siblings, even married ones, seems to have become more frequent after the war, the more common extended household of adult children living with parents also continued. The DeRosset family of Wilmington, North Carolina, experienced both arrangements. Elderly Armand and Eliza DeRosset remained in their large house in town; at times they endured, at other times welcomed, additions to their household. In 1868, Armand's widowed sister, Kate Kennedy, and another unmarried sister divided the basement. While Kate Kennedy's stepdaughter and another relative camped out in the old nursery, Armand and Eliza's widowed daughter claimed two rooms in another wing. Although the DeRossets expressed neither satisfaction nor dismay about so many lodgers, they actively encouraged their adult offspring—both married and widowed—to live with them. In the antebellum period, adult children sometimes had stayed with parents during transitional periods—as newlyweds, or when either they or a parent had been recently widowed—but in the postwar South, straitened finances seemed to encourage others at least to contemplate such a household arrangement. Only a few weeks before his sisters moved in, Armand DeRosset seemed dismayed that he had been unable to convince a daughter and son-in-law to join his household, saying that he had hoped to have all his married daughters live with him.[7]

Even without their married daughters' company, a constant stream of kin surrounded the DeRossets. In 1873, Eliza DeRosset's mother, Eliza Lord, who oversaw her widowed son's large family, moved next door to the DeRossets after her own house burned. In 1875, when Armand and Eliza DeRosset's son Louis died, leaving a young widow and two infants, the elder DeRossets successfully campaigned for her and the children to live with them.[8]

Not all elite families appreciated coresidence. In 1866, Hill Carter, an elderly widower, convinced his son Robert to manage Shirley, the family plantation, and to bring his wife and children to live there. Louise Humphreys Carter, Robert's wife, voiced her objections to her father-in-law's behavior in her diary, where she relived many of the family rows. In November 1870, she recorded a recent scene at the breakfast table during which her father-in-law had thrown a basket of rolls. Almost a year later Louise referred to another family spat that

6. Alethea Collins Warren to Sallie Collins, April 21, 1879, Collins Papers, SHC.
7. Cattie Kennedy to Kate Kennedy, Sept. 19, 1868, and A. J. DeRosset to Kate Meares, Sept. 11, 1868, both in DeRosset Family Papers, SHC.
8. Kate Meares to Louis H. Meares, Jan. 5, 1873, and Kate Meares to Richard Meares, Dec. 8, 1875, both in Meares-DeRosset Papers, SHC.

seems to have arisen from her father-in-law's opposition to his granddaughter's suitor. The upshot of it was a sick headache for Louise, who considered such quarrels all too frequent.[9]

Other testimony suggests that the coresidence of kin became less accepted during the closing decades of the nineteenth century. Sallie Bruce considered it an enormous burden to her son Albert and his wife, Mary Howard Bruce, when sporadically they housed Mary's father and her unmarried sisters. In Sallie Bruce's unflinching estimation, Mr. Howard had been "ruined by the War & could not adapt himself to the changed conditions of things." In 1884, Sallie confided to another son: "Mary wrote me recently that Addie was to live with her which I can't help regretting as I think she is fully able to support herself & I do so want Albert to be freed from the constant calls made on him by his wife's family." When Mr. Howard died in 1887, Sallie believed that "his death will certainly take a burden from Albert's life." She then hoped that Albert would "stand firm" and not assume the care of Ellen, yet another of Mary's unmarried sisters. What is remarkable here is that such a traditional "great lady" as Sallie Bruce did not consider the housing of family members, especially young unmarried women, to be incumbent on Mary and Albert. Instead it was a burden that could and should be avoided, since the sisters, as trained teachers, could be expected to support themselves.[10]

Some households sheltered, even if they did not welcome, more distant relatives. Notions of kinship and obligation at times ensured a home—or at least temporary housing—for many whose presence was more suffered than desired. In such cases, tensions and anxieties could run quite high. Thirty-five-year-old Nannie Tunstall found herself dealing with her alcoholic cousin, Emmet, who resided with her and her widowed mother: "He stays out occasionally until a late hour, and sometimes when he comes in, requires aid to get to bed! . . . it is *I* who always deal with him. On these occasions, my presence is to my mother like a shield & buckles—she hides behind my strength, . . . I feel sometimes that if Emmet sh'd continue to take his drink, it will be a burden almost beyond even my endurance." These sprees particularly worried Nannie because Emmet's

9. Louise Humphreys Carter diary, Nov. 18, 1870, and Oct. 5, 1871, Shirley Plantation Papers, CWF.

10. Albert and Mary Howard Bruce seem to have left no direct testimony about their own attitudes about Mary's relatives living with them. Sallie Bruce to Morelle Bruce, April 8, 1887, and July 28, 1884, Bruce Family Papers, VHS. Joan Cashin suggests that by the 1850s, yeoman families in the South Atlantic were unwilling to take in extended kin. See Joan E. Cashin, "Households, Kinfolk, and Absent Teenagers: The Demographic Transition in the Old South," *Journal of Family History* 25 (April 2000): 141–57.

father in later life had become extremely difficult with "violent hysteria" when-ever he drank liquor. Nannie's forebodings seemed justified when, a year and a half later, the situation worsened. While she had been away touring Europe with two female relatives, Emmet's behavior had deteriorated:

> When Em is excited with liquor he is sometimes wild, and even dangerous. He cuts & slashes things generally, and threatens death & destruction to everybody. It is actually *perilous* to contradict him as to try and persuade him, and Mama is powerless to do anything. Thus far I have had as much or more influence over him than anyone else—but lately I have not been physically strong enough to cope with him—for while his want of nervous energy makes him ordinarily slug-gish, when he has the stimulus of intoxication given to him, his large *bulk* becomes a burden to drag around & to try to prevail over.

According to Nannie's analysis, Emmet lived with them because he could not get work: "Emmet is unhappily not capable of steady employment—nobody cares to be bothered with him, naturally—he has no mental resources." Yet she did not find his behavior outrageous enough either to involve her brother in regulating it or to expel Emmet from her household: "Emmet has too much sense, to be adjudged a lunatic, and he is scarcely yet a fit subject for an inebriate asylum. So I feel that nothing can be done but to endure it as it is." The bonds of kinship meant that she and her mother had to continue to tolerate a some-times violent resident. Still, she carefully hid all knives, swords, pistols, and the like.[11]

In addition to coresident kin, elite households often faced large numbers of relatives who came for extended visits. Such visiting had long been a favorite southern practice. This was especially the case for women of the gentry, many of whom disliked or were ill at ease mingling socially with people from lower classes. At the war's end, some women testified to the importance of visiting, even as they came to realize that it multiplied chores that earlier had been per-formed by slaves. In October 1865, M. E. Hill bravely announced to her cousin: "There is no use in our giving up one another if we are poverty stricken, we must visit each other, and help cook, clean up the house, &c when we are there." Yet others hesitated to schedule lengthy visits if the mistress of the household did not have what she considered to be sufficient household help. Rebecca Gra-ham wanted to accompany her legislator husband to Raleigh but worried that they would be a burden to her aunt, Margaret Cameron Mordecai. Her solution

---

11. Nannie Tunstall to Virginia Clay, March 21, 1884, and Sept. 18, 1885, Clement Clay Papers, Duke.

was to wait for an invitation: "I could nor would not like to stay anywhere but with our aunts, for many reasons, & and during Aunt Milly's sickness and the uncertainty about servants, I do not think of it for a moment unless I should be specially invited."[12]

While Louise Carter seems to have enjoyed many of her visitors—even those like Markie Williams, who she had to nurse through an illness—she barely tolerated at least a few who made extended sojourns. In February 1870, Bernard, who seems to have been a distant relation, came to visit the Carters, telling them that he had a job that would begin March 1. From the beginning, Louise was skeptical that the visit would be short. As Bernard's visit unfolded, she found him to be a pest. The hour she spent one day sitting with him she thought was a trial, and one night in late February his incessant coughing kept her awake. Louise's prediction that Bernard would not leave in March was all too prescient; it was April before he departed for Baltimore. Although nearly all old elite households struggled economically in the postwar South, many still were asked to house their unemployable male relatives and impoverished women and children.[13]

In the summers, spacious plantation houses were sometimes pressed into service to provide a respite for urban relatives, especially those no longer able to finance visits to the mountains or beaches. Henry and Ida Dulany's Oakley plantation became an important summer retreat after the war, as Ida's married sister, with children in tow, made long visits each summer there and to relatives at Oatlands in Loudon County. Some single women, like Mildred and Mary Lee, daughters of Robert E. Lee, financed their extensive travels in part by long visits to relatives, sometimes rather distant ones. According to Marietta Minnigerode, her cousin Mary's annual visit was distinctly a mixed blessing: "On her visits in New Orleans cousin Mary honored my father's house for weeks and weeks, her presence greatly flattering to him as a Confederate soldier, but rather difficult to mother who found that cousin Mary's arbitrary ways and luxurious and irregular habits made the household arrangements difficult. The entertaining necessary for so distinguished a guest and the numerous calls to be received, added quite a little to mother's responsibilities."[14]

While extended visiting might appear similar in antebellum and postwar

12. M. E. Hill to [Harriet Benbury], Oct. 28, 1865, Benbury-Haywood Family Papers, SHC; Rebecca Graham to Anne Collins, Nov. 8, 1868, Collins Papers, SHC.

13. Louise Humphreys Carter diary, Feb. 7, 14, and 22, March 8, and April 2, 1870, Shirley Plantation Papers, CWF.

14. Since the Minnigerodes then lived in New Orleans, these were winter visits. Andrews, *Memoirs of a Poor Relation,* 194.

South, it was in fact changing in function and meaning for these old elite families. In the antebellum period, visiting largely served to maintain family connections and provide companionship. In postwar America, when places of entertainment proliferated, family visits became a less expensive alternative to summers spent at spas or beaches. In some cases it replaced the multiple households that privileged antebellum families had maintained—not only in town and countryside, but also at the beach or mountains—in order to make the sticky southern summers more bearable.

Predictably, vacation areas became all the more appealing to the old elite, even though many could no longer afford them. The Masonboro Sound remained a place of recreation for many of Wilmington's old families. In both the 1870s and 1880s, Kate Meares recorded the movements of her siblings and cousins as they whiled away the months of July through September and even into October at the Sound. Other eastern and Piedmont Carolinians continued to visit Nag's Head, where numerous summer cottages had sprung up during the prewar period. Yet these vacationers now had to be more careful. When Carey Pettigrew noted that her son and two daughters had spent a week at Nag's Head, she emphasized its moderate prices. In Tidewater Virginia, Old Point with its Hygeia Hotel was a seaside resort that still beckoned to Virginians able to afford it. Perhaps not surprisingly, Nannie Tunstall set her fictional romance between a middle-aged northern general and a lovely southern girl at the Hygeia, a place she herself enjoyed. After a visit to that hotel in the same year she published her novel, she declared that "extravagant charges" kept out most fellow southerners. "There must be 1000 people in the hotel, not a vacant room," she marveled, but knowingly noted that they were "nearly all northern & Western people." Nonetheless, Nannie found "several old friends." For others with limited resources, local spas and watering holes figured as affordable alternatives to the best-known beach resorts.[15]

Mountain resorts in western North Carolina and West Virginia continued to attract elite southerners, although they too sported a smaller southern clientele than in the past. When Samuel Biddle journeyed to White Sulphur Springs in 1870, it was his first visit there in fifteen years and one that he took alone, proba-

15. Kate Meares to Louis H. Meares, Sept. 9, 1872, and Kate Meares to Louis H. and Richard A. Meares, Oct. 10, 1882, Meares-DeRosset Papers, SHC; Kate Meares to Louis H. DeRosset, July 21, 1870, DeRosset Family Papers, SHC; Carey Pettigrew to William Pettigrew, Aug. 12, 1875, Pettigrew Family Papers, SHC; [Nannie Whitmell Tunstall], *"No. 40.": A Romance of Fortress Monroe and the Hygeia,* 2nd ed. (Richmond, Va., 1884); Nannie Tunstall to Virginia Clay, April 3, 1884, Clay Papers, Duke. On Hygeia Hotel, see William M. E. Rachal, "Walled Fortress and Resort Hotels," *VC* 2 (summer 1952): 20–27.

bly because of finances and his wife's health. The mountain resorts also continued to serve as centers for courtship. Frances Christine Fisher, writing as
Christian Reid, set one of her frothier romances, *Hearts and Hands,* at the West
Virginia watering holes and populated the novel with both northern and southern characters. In another book, *The Land of the Sky,* she more self-consciously
touted the recreational beauties of her native North Carolina. The travelogue of
an extended family's rambles among the picturesque mountains and streams of
western Carolina tended to overshadow the romantic action.[16]

Even though extended family visits were the only recreational destination for
those who could not afford vacation trips, visiting itself gradually fell somewhat
into disrepute and ultimately disuse. Writing in 1897, Jennie Friend Stephenson
remembered visiting and the "hospitality" that it demanded as a "side of southern life that has passed away as surely as the institution of slavery, and because
of its abolishment." The stays of weeks and months, in her view, had been made
possible by the hostess's large staff: "For hadn't she the trained cook, who stood
in the kitchen with a half grown under her to do her biddy; and were there
not house maids to dress, if need be, the visitor, or to do any service for their
comfort."[17]

While the number of kin living in and visiting old elite households might
have been on the upswing immediately after the Civil War, other alterations in
the household occurred as well. Perhaps the most important single change was
the necessarily restructured relationships between elite whites and their former
slaves. For many families, the war itself had begun the reconfiguration of relationships between servant and mistress, as the proximity of battles or the Union
army had destabilized such relationships. Planter families suddenly came to believe that they did not know some of their most trusted servants, as enslaved
men and women absconded or became surly and less communicative. In 1865,
African Americans figured more prominently in the letters and diaries of elite
women than ever before or perhaps ever again, and almost all of the white
women were distinctly unsympathetic to blacks' hopes and aspirations.

A common complaint in the months after emancipation was that various
slaves were insupportable or "unbearable," as Columbia Lord referred to a servant in August. Other white women viewed the possibility of valued ex-slaves

16. Samuel S. Biddle to Mary E. Biddle, Aug. 28, 1870, Samuel S. Biddle Papers, Duke;
Frances Christine Fisher Tiernan [pseud. Christian Reid], *Hearts and Hands: A Story in Sixteen
Chapters* (New York, 1875), and idem, *"The Land of the Sky"; or, Adventures in Mountain By-Ways*
(1875; reprint, New York, 1891).

17. Jennie F. Stephenson, "My Father and His Household, before, during, and after the War"
(unpub. typescript, April 22, 1897), p. 9, Blanton Family Papers, VHS.

leaving for new jobs or locales as a dereliction of duty. In 1866, Sallie Collins railed about how Emily, a trusted servant of her mother-in-law, had left "tho' she knew Mama's utter dependence on her and what trying times we were coming to here. . . . I think Emily's case little short of desertion." Elite white women experienced the free-labor system in a variety of ways, but rarely did they enjoy any of these experiences.[18]

Older women—who at the outbreak of war in 1861 were forty years of age or already had adult children—seem to have found the new labor regime most onerous. In the immediate postwar period, domestic chores seemed so burdensome that some middle-aged and older women felt almost overcome. Forty-year-old Rebecca Davis described her state of mind, which modern psychologists might well term depression: "I believe I have been so overpowered that I cannot feel much, I am sure I feel no wounded pride. I could do anything of which I am capable and do sweep and dust and carry baskets and bundles with pleasure, but I feel neither acute pain or vivid pleasure." Finding emancipation a heavy blow, these women adjusted poorly to losing their slaves; some probably never adjusted at all. In 1865 the mood was generally grim, but two years later an elderly Warrenton, North Carolina, matron was still "very low" in spirits because she could not "stand the great change, which has been introduced into our social system." Others were hardly reconciled to the new order. Such white ladies could not imagine life without servants, yet they were not usually pleased with those they could hire. In 1881, as sixty-seven-year-old Sarah Harvie summed up the problem: "The servant question is troubling me now. Our two are the most indifferent we ever had & yet they are better than none."[19]

A close examination of several matrons' postwar household management reveals that the difficulty adjusting to free labor experienced by most older elite women was no passing problem for that generation. Eliza DeRosset, a Wilmington resident in her fifties at the war's end, provides a revealing case study of how sullenly matrons continued to respond to the new organization of household service. DeRosset's story of "servant problems" began in August 1865, when she fumed that John, then their only servant, was "very insolent" and stayed only

18. Eliza J. DeRosset to Kate Meares, Aug. 18, 1865, DeRosset Family Papers, SHC; Sallie Collins to Anne Collins, March 15, 1866, Collins Papers, SHC. For a view of white southern households in the late nineteenth century that emphasizes their movement toward the middle-class "home," see Grace Elizabeth Hale, *Making Whiteness: The Culture of Segregation in the South, 1890–1940* (New York, 1998), ch. 3.

19. Rebecca Davis to Kate Kennedy, Nov. 7, 1865, DeRosset Family Papers, SHC; Peter R. Davis to Bettie Amis, March 25, 1867, Elizabeth Amis Cameron (Hooper) Blanchard Papers, SHC; Sarah Harvie to Charles Olds Harvie, Dec. 19, 1881, Harvie Family Papers, VHS.

because his wife had not yet returned to Wilmington. In the following June she only had four servants, Maumee, Louisa, Swann and a yardman, and she reported them "quite enough to take ill looks from."[20]

Eliza DeRosset's anger, while not dissipating, tended over time to resolve into a frantic pursuit of servants who either were or somehow resembled her lost slaves. Two years after the end of slavery, she still sought relationships that recalled it. In 1867, she mused that Maria Swann "is a great comfort to me, Maumee too, I do not know what I would do without her, and John brought me his second daughter 10 years old and begged I would take her just as tho' she belonged to me." At that point DeRosset rather proudly reported that she had only one "strange" servant, that is, one who had not been earlier owned by the family—a very efficient dining room "girl." Such a situation—servants who had once been family slaves, an ex-slave bringing his daughter to live in the former master's family—immensely pleased DeRosset, perhaps because it seemed to show a dependence that recalled the old days of slavery. But such a comfortable state of affairs for her lasted only a short time. Six months later, convinced that Maria Swann had stolen some of her china, Eliza DeRosset brought in the authorities. Yet she found that the case did not yield a satisfactory outcome: Maria was fined one dollar and costs. DeRosset had hoped for a sentence to the workhouse—a punishment that had been common in the days of slavery and recalled its compulsions. In her eyes, such leniency actually punished her: "It makes my blood boil to think of the indignities we are obliged to submit to from even our former servants."[21]

Although Eliza DeRosset's relationship with her servants remained rocky, it remained no less necessary to her, and the saga continued. To be sure, she continued to supervise servants, and her elderly husband did the marketing, although he considered it his "great cross." Decrying her "wretched country" in May 1868, DeRosset wished herself instead in England with her son, where she believed that the class system had virtually enslaved poor white people. For her, the major problem was the freed people. As she wrote, "The negroes are getting past bearing—every day they are worse and worse. I cannot get a cook now."[22]

In 1876, shortly before her death, Eliza DeRosset employed only two servants. She explicitly noted that although her widowed daughter-in-law had joined the household, the grandchildren's elderly nurse did not figure in that

20. Eliza J. DeRosset to Louis H. DeRosset, Aug. 6, 1865, June 17, 1866, DeRosset Family Papers, SHC.

21. Eliza J. DeRosset to Louis H. DeRosset, April 8 and Nov. 24, 1867, and Jan. 12, 1868, DeRosset Family Papers, SHC.

22. Armand J. DeRosset to Kate Meares, Sept. 11, 1868, and Eliza J. DeRosset to Louis H. DeRosset, May 24, 1868, both in DeRosset Family Papers, SHC.

tally. Over ten years after slavery's demise, DeRosset still relied on a possessive vocabulary for servants; she recorded that "Maumee is given to [my daughter-in-law] Jennie—and I am very scrupulous in not calling upon her."[23]

While Eliza DeRosset's experiences illustrate how one middle-aged towns-woman coped with the turnover in servants, the situation was somewhat different for ladies overseeing plantation households. Susan Bullock, a sixty-three-year-old widow living in Granville County, North Carolina, frequently chronicled in her diary her struggles with household help. On January 24, 1867, Matilda, the cook, left. By February 5, Bullock had hired a new cook, in addition to three plantation workers and two other female house servants. The new cook, like one of the laborers, soon departed, and Bullock grimly recorded, "We are having trouble with the darkies."[24]

After her son consulted a "Yankey" (probably an official of the Freedmen's Bureau posted in a neighboring town), Susan Bullock reported the result, using the old vocabulary of slavery: "The Yankey ordered the return of our runaway servants." Bullock viewed a servant who left "without an excuse" as analogous to a slave who stole him- or herself; the language of free labor and contract had not conquered this elderly widow. In her diary she perhaps unconsciously continued her antebellum practice of using no surnames for the servants.[25]

Some elderly plantation mistresses seem to have fared better than their town counterparts because of the range of their past experience. Certainly Judith Page Rives, of Albemarle County, Virginia, initially seemed more comfortable than many of her peers in managing free labor. Reporting in November 1865 on the seven hundred gallons of molasses that had been produced, with yet another hundred to go, she told her son: "I have done, and am doing all I can to assist in re-organizing our dilapidated affairs. You would have thought me quite energetic about the sorghum, taking a hand when one was wanting, superintending the rest, . . . carrying on, spinning and weaving, with other duties too numerous to mention." Nine months later she was planning a busy routine of preserving damsons and drying tomatoes, lima beans, and corn, which she considered a "resource" during the "scarce season in winter and the early spring." Yet on closer examination, even as energetic a woman as Judith Page Rives still depended on a considerable staff. As she considered her expenses almost ten years later, she vowed, "I shall balance receipts and expenditures, and if it must be,

23. Eliza J. DeRosset to Kate Meares, April 9, 1876, Meares-DeRosset Papers, SHC.

24. Susan Bullock diary, Jan. 24 and 30, Feb. 5 and 18, 1867, Charles E. Hamilton-John Bullock Papers, SHC.

25. Ibid., Jan. 24 and 30, Feb. 5, 18, and 19, 1867.

will part with my house servants, the only household expenditure of a serious nature." Six weeks later she explained the situation more thoroughly: "My current expenses . . . are very small except the servants wages: these at $50 per month for all my household (three men and three women) would seem very little at the north, where a good coachman or cook can command $1200 pr annum, but it comes so heavily to me, that I have several times been on the point of breaking up my household, and doing without servants." Amazingly, a decade after emancipation, Judith Page Rives still oversaw a force of six household servants; other plantation mistresses in Virginia also commanded considerable staffs.[26]

Sallie Bruce, the mistress of Staunton Hill plantation in Charlotte County, Virginia, apparently wished to run her postwar household in much the same manner as she had done before the war. One of her sons later remembered her declaring that "good servants are three-fourths of the happiness of life." The introduction of free labor allowed her husband, Charles Bruce, to discharge workers he believed to be dishonest, but Sallie Bruce sometimes regretted this remedy. In 1872 she complained about parting with Henry Clay, her gardener, who had been fired for stealing from the smokehouse. In her view, Clay "certainly suited me better than anyone I have had on the grounds since Ned's death—in fact I have had no trouble & everything has been kept in the most beautiful order." Sallie, who valued the condition of her home and gardens more highly than the virtue of her subordinates, concluded her account, "I had no idea he was such a daring rogue! but I confess I miss him dreadfully he was so quick and handy." A decade later, she faced a similar situation when the dismissal of Henry, a stableman, for malfeasance would mean that his wife, Viney, a house servant, would quit. Although earlier expressing the hope that another servant, Hannah, could be taught to fill Viney's place, in December 1886 Sallie lamented to her son, "It was a hard struggle to me to part with Viney." While Charles Bruce used his ability to fire workers as a way to enforce moral standards, Sallie Bruce preferred the smooth operation of her household.[27]

Other older matrons similarly valued a high level of personal service. In Piedmont Virginia, Ann Hairston, then in her late sixties, confided that she disliked answering her own doorbell and that she greatly missed having a servant to run interference between her and her guests, whether welcome or unwanted: "As

26. Judith Page Rives to William C. Rives Jr., Nov. 14, 1865, Aug. 15 and Sept. 28, 1875, Judith Page Rives to Sadie C. Rives, Aug. 24, 1866, all in William C. Rives Papers, LC.

27. Quoted in Nelson D. Lankford, *The Last American Aristocrat: The Biography of David K. E. Bruce, 1898–1977* (Boston, 1996), 10; Sallie Bruce to Morelle Bruce, Aug. 16, 1872, Nov. 27 and Dec. 11, 1886, all in Bruce Family Papers, VHS.

much experience as I have housekeeping I never can bear to open doors[.] should the knocker be a friend and acquaintance I don't like to do it and we might run the risk opening to an intoxicated straggler, pedlar, beggar or someone you would not like to admit. I always like to have some one about to open and report before I make my appearance."[28]

With her old regime ideals and her proven ability to enforce them, Sallie Bruce was contemptuous of the problems that one of her daughters-in-law faced in housekeeping. In 1884, shortly after a visit to the young couple, she complained that their household was "as usual in a state of disorganization as regards servants—having only one inexperienced girl about the house." A manservant had departed for railroad work, which Sallie regarded as arising out of her daughter-in-law's incompetence. "It is a pity that such a pretty cottage cannot be kept in good order but some people have no system naturally & cannot understand the benefit to be derived from it."[29]

Although Sallie Bruce's domestic problems stemmed largely from her husband's standards, many Virginia old elite families probably found that their straitened finances made it harder to obtain and hold domestic servants. In 1870, after Mary departed, Sarah Hubard could depend only on one remaining servant, Eliza. Other families encountered similar problems. Maria Louisa Carrington reported that her parents, the Dabneys, "have no servant, at all about the house but Ceasar, and as you may know they have tough times during this cold weather. I am glad to tell you that Ma has a right good cook." Maria Louisa even blamed the family's illness on housework: "For nearly a month before Xmas, after old Eleyce left them, the white family had to do most of the cooking, no doubt that was what made them all sick."[30]

Younger matrons took a different approach than their elders. They seem to have spent less time worrying about procuring and keeping servants, electing instead to do some of the work themselves. Although these elite women generally had even less experience than their mothers and aunts with domestic management and household chores, they proved more psychologically and somewhat more physically adept at facing such challenges. To be sure, the initial adjustments sat badly on them as well. In the fall of 1865, M. E. Hill complained of too many servants rather than too few, but cynically observed, "I expect about Christmas it will be impossible to get them to do anything." In what might have

28. Ann H. Hairston to Bettie Hairston, Dec. 8, 1869, Hairston-Wilson Papers, SHC.
29. Sallie Bruce to Morelle Bruce, April 19, 1884, Bruce Family Papers, VHS.
30. Sarah A. Hubard to Sue Hubard, March 22, 1870, Hubard Family Papers, SHC; Maria Louisa Carrington to Betty Saunders, Feb. 2, 1868, Saunders Family Papers, VHS.

been a burst of bravado, she asserted that she could keep her most important servant as well as the others: "I do not think she has any idea of leaving me, she has behaved very well all the time—in fact all mine have done well, I tell them they can leave whenever they find any one they like better than they do me[.] I do not wish them, that I can get a plenty to wait on me."[31]

Despite such brave talk, some younger women found themselves doing more of the work. In 1866, young matron Lucy Holladay, whose Spotsylvania County household included her five unmarried sisters-in-law, coped with only a part-time cook and washerwoman and an eleven-year-old nursemaid for her two young children. One of her sisters-in-law remarked on the situation, telling a relative, "Lucy has no dining room servant or housemaid; she sets the table herself, and often does all the cooking for dinner on washing days." Thirty-five-year-old Ann Pope unleashed a diatribe about the freed people leaving and otherwise "doing very badly here." "I live in dirt, eat, and sleep in it," she angrily complained. "I want the power of annihilation. I get so mad that I don't know what to do—but I grin and endure it." Yet almost in the same breath, Ann looked to the future, telling her teenaged niece, "I have got Donum cooking for me, but I intend getting a stove and doing my own cooking so you had better come down and pay me a visit and I will give you some lessons."[32]

Such general housekeeping skills came hard to elite white women, who only slowly expanded their domestic competence. Even six years after the war, Kate Meares suffered in Wilmington, North Carolina, when she had no servant: "For several days we had to do all our cooking & cleaning up—because we could not get a servant, but today we succeeded in getting one. You would have laughed to see Cousin Rosa & me trying to cook some biscuits & make some coffee for breakfast." The following year, when Kate again lacked any domestic help for over two months, she and her son sometimes had only bread and milk for breakfast "when we could get the cow milked." Yet she had learned to accomplish heavy household work, reporting, "Yesterday I was washing windows & the consequence is, I am so stiff & sore today that I can hardly move." In a similar vein, her sister-in-law Jane Meares told her daughter, "I can assure [you] I have my hands ful[l], with an inefficient house servant and the little girls at school."[33]

Generally women of this second generation (born between 1820 and 1850) were able to trim their household staffs more quickly, though perhaps only a

31. M. E. Hill to [Harriet Benbury], Oct. 28, 1865, Benbury-Haywood Family Papers, SHC.
32. F. A. Holladay to Bet Lewis, March 2, 1866, Holladay Family Papers, VHS; Ann J. Pope to Rosa Biddle, n.d., 1865, Biddle Papers, Duke.
33. Kate Meares to L. H. Meares, Oct. 24, 1871, and Sept. 9, 1872, Meares-DeRosset Papers, SHC; Jane Meares to Jennie Meares, Nov. 11, 1875, William A. Williams Papers, SHC.

little less painfully, than the grande dames of the old regime. Late in 1865, Lucy P. Wickham reported, "I hope we will be more comfortable after Xmas as re-gards house servants—we having done without a cook or dining room servant for 18 months, which is enough to try the temper of an angel. There is a little Boy in the dining room, and we scuffle along." Mary Friend of Prince George's County saw her household staff reduced from twelve in 1860 to three in 1865. In 1869, twenty-six-year-old Virginia Hankins, who was running her father's household, worried when her principal servant, Lina, was married. Virginia told her brother, "I am very sorry she should have married and expect she will not be as useful as she used to be. I don't know what I shall do in keeping house, if she leaves me. I never will be able to leave home or keep things clean & nice." The experience of losing Lina to her wedding celebrations had been unpleasant for Virginia. Her father had been ill, and, as she wrote, "I had to do everything, so I feel right tired to day. I got up at sunrise, to get out breakfast, and then took a walk over the field to the mill road." And some elite women, no matter how hard they tried, found it difficult to cultivate domestic skills. In 1877, six-teen years after her marriage, Mary Bernard Guest complained, "I've had a hard time lately with servants or rather *without* them—have just gotten two new ones." She then retailed a recent experience when she spent an entire day making preserved foods, only to see them turn out abject failures, "the jelly like molas-ses & the pickle I tried to make also spoilt." She concluded that she "had far rather sweep the streets than keep house, for I never succeed in my undertak-ings."[34]

Even as these second-generation matrons coped, they also fondly recalled the prewar period, which they remembered as a time when housekeeping meant overseeing a staff of dependable, properly submissive servants. Their standards for the well-conducted household, much like their ideal of relations among the races, harkened back to the old slavery regime. For some mistresses, it was a matter of keeping the upper hand in the relationship with domestics. Anne Cameron Collins signaled that desire when she sold some of her old clothes to obtain money to pay her maid because she "could not bear to be owing servants for their services." Anne's sister-in-law, Sallie Collins, could still recognize rem-nants of the old regime, as when she described Henrietta Page's establishment

34. Lucy P. Wickham to Bessie Shields, Dec. 20, 1865, Wickham Family Papers, VHS; Ste-phenson, "My Father and His Household," p. 42, Blanton Family Papers, VHS; Virginia Hankins to Willie Hankins, Oct. 1, 1869, Hankins Family Papers, VHS; Mary Bernard Guest to "Cousin Maria," Sept. 18, [1877], Guest Family Papers, VHS.

in Edenton, North Carolina: "Aunt Hennie's house servants are like old times, more than any body else's in the state, I suppose."[35]

To be sure, some younger wives took advantage of economic prosperity as an opportunity to set up a full domestic establishment. When Charles Myers's business flourished immediately after the war, his wife Lossie entertained extensively. She hired two adult nursemaids for her children and four other servants, as well as sending out the laundry. Still, these younger women did not exhibit the same obsession about procuring servants that seemed to preoccupy the Eliza DeRossets of the old regime, and even extravagant Lossie Myers later adapted to more straitened circumstances. In 1872, when she had a new baby, her sister stayed with her a week because she had no servants. Eventually this second generation made its peace with the new system of free labor; in 1885, Kate Meares philosophically remarked to her son in South Carolina about a shortage of servants, "It is too bad things should be in such a condition—but it isn't peculiar to your part of the country."[36]

It was the youngest generation—the young unmarried schoolgirls of the war period and their even younger siblings—that proved relatively unfazed by domestic chores. The dislocations of the war introduced the older members of this group to responsibility at an early age. Eliza Lord, part of a large family whose mother became increasingly incapacitated before her early death, learned about household activities during wartime. In 1863, while her mother was giving birth to her last child, Eliza kept house, and her grandmother declared, "She is certainly the most practical useful child of her age I ever saw." Such experience probably paid off ten years later, when the newlywed Eliza did all her own housework. Other young women stepped into the breach when servants left. When Bella, the family cook, resigned in 1875, it was twenty-year-old Annis Meares, rather than her mother, Mary Exum Meares, who took over the kitchen. Annis later turned it over to her sister Esther.[37]

This younger group, both as daughters and wives, undertook housework with

35. Anne Collins to George Collins, Feb. 8, 1867, and Sallie Collins to Anne Collins, Jan. 1, 1866, both in Collins Papers, SHC.

36. Eliza J. DeRosset to Louis H. DeRosset, June 17, 1866, DeRosset Family Papers, SHC; Kate Meares to Louis H. Meares, July 4, 1872, and Kate Meares to Richard A. Meares, Sept. 2, 1885, both in Meares-DeRosset Papers, SHC.

37. Eliza Lord to Kate Meares, Lossie Myers, and Alice Daves, Sept. 19, 1863, DeRosset Family Papers, SHC; Kate Meares to Richard A. Meares, Sept. 2, 1885, Meares-DeRosset Papers, SHC; Mary T. Meares to Frederick Meares, March 20, 1875, William B. Meares Papers, SHC; Esther Meares to Louis H. Meares, Nov. 7, 1877, Meares-DeRosset Papers, SHC.

an equanimity the older two generations never approached. Yet their comments suggest that they more often merely accepted rather than enthusiastically embraced such chores. Before her marriage, Rosa Biddle matter-of-factly included churning among her day's duties; perhaps such past work led her after marriage to comment complacently on her good health "notwithstanding the hard work & cooking." In 1883, young matron Mary Cameron declared that her health was so much better that she could do her own housework and underscored her point by alluding to the servants she was willingly foregoing: "We have had nine applications from different parties to come live with us, but I do not intend to get anyone, at least yet awhile." Annie Tucker Tyler, then living in Richmond, replied to her mother-in-law's question about the dismissal of a servant: "You ask why we dismissed Mary, for economy, & really we do better without her, Louis paid her and let her go." In Lynchburg, Nannie Tunstall indicated both her racism and her disdain of servants in her description of her household arrangements: "This past week, we had nobody but Edmund, but an old nigger set in last night to cook. . . . There is so little regular work to do in keeping this house in order that I prefer to do it myself. It gives me exercise and occupation. By 10 A.M. all is done, and if the bell rings the cook can go to the door."[38]

Not surprisingly, some among the younger generation proved more loathe to embrace domestic industry. When Jennie Cowan DeRosset's husband died, she moved in with her parents-in-law, who provided a nurse for her two children. Relieved of having to oversee an urban household, Jennie slipped into a leisured existence. Eliza DeRosset, her mother-in-law, deemed Jennie insufficiently grief-stricken over her husband's death and insufficiently domestic, "the same Jennie as of old—reading novels most of the time, goes to ride with her Mother daily."[39]

Thus many younger white women, especially those of the third generation, came to play a more physically active role in their households. While straitened circumstances and the attenuation of bonds with the African American community might have compelled some of this adaptation, these women so ably coped

38. Rosa Biddle to Samuel P. Smith, July 26, 1879, and Rosa Biddle Smith to Mary E. Biddle, Oct. 6, 1886, both in Biddle Papers, Duke; Mary Cameron to "My dear Cam," Feb. 24, 1883, Bailey Family Papers, VHS; Annie Tucker Tyler to Julia Tyler, Aug. 9, 1884, Julia Tyler Papers, VHS; Nannie Tunstall to Virginia Clay, Nov. 22, 1885, Clay Papers, Duke. Some of these changes can be seen in George C. Rable, *Civil Wars: Women and the Crisis of Southern Nationalism* (Urbana, Ill., 1989), 253–64.

39. Eliza J. DeRosset to Kate Meares, Jan. 24, 1876 (misdated 1875), Meares-DeRosset Papers, SHC.

with far fewer servants and a life that their grandmothers would have considered drudgery that some willingness on their part also seems involved. Obviously this new capability had its elements of irony. At the same time as white women were becoming more practiced in the domestic arts, they were exchanging the managerial functions held by their grandmothers for actual physical labor. More skillful, younger women were also more domesticated. Young Pauline Cameron explained to her brother-in-law that she was not attending a commencement ceremony at Chapel Hill because the "trip is fatiguing and then too having so much nursing and housekeeping constantly tires me out and unfits me for effort of any kind."[40]

While privileged white women coped to a greater or lesser extent with a reconfigured household, they all dealt with servants who were renegotiating their terms of service during the immediate postwar years. Almost from the moment of emancipation, former slaveowning women were debating how the household could function with free labor and what would be the new relationship with their African American servants. Both employee and employer, black and white, played a part in recasting these relationships. In addition to the issue of work, there was also that of coresidence. Over time the "bleaching" of the southern white household became apparent, as blacks looked for separate living arrangements with their own families. Moreover, some employers sought and were at times able to obtain white domestic servants.

After the war, as relationships with servants became more tenuous, white women of the old elite, much like their menfolk, looked to non-African American workers as a possible solution for their domestic troubles. The experiments of planters in hiring European and even Asian workers for their plantations are well known and have been closely documented. Yet privileged white southerners' desire to replace black workers with other supposedly more docile and more productive workers had a parallel in the household as well as the field.[41]

Relying on white domestics was largely uncharted ground to privileged women. In the antebellum South, white women occasionally accepted jobs as housekeepers, but for the most part domestic work had come to be racially defined as the province of African Americans. It was unusual enough to excite comment when Varina Davis, as first lady of the Confederacy, chose a white woman as the nursemaid for her young children. Nonetheless, as members of the old elite pondered emancipation, they considered the possibility of using

40. Pauline Cameron to George P. Collins, May 8, 1876, Collins Papers, SHC.
41. See Lucy Cohen, *Chinese in the Post–Civil War South: A People without a History* (Baton Rouge, La., 1984).

white domestic labor. In part this search for new sources of labor was a reaction to the former slaves' economic demands, but it also sprang from white fears that blacks would not work without the compulsion of slavery. In May 1865, Kate Meares reported in Wilmington that although blacks seemed to want overly high wages, "very few white girls are willing to go out at all." In contrast, the following year in Richmond, Sadie Rives told her mother-in-law about the search for a "parlor girl" or parlormaid: "I was told today at the Intelligencer office that there were a good many girls (American) who had been reduced in circumstances within the past few years, & who were very anxious to find employment." Elite families, both in Piedmont and coastal North Carolina and Virginia, soon began experimenting with white domestic labor much as they had with white farm labor. In a letter to his older sister, young Bennehan Cameron remarked, "I wish you could hear mama's dutch boy talk[,] you would die laughing. He calls Papa and Mama master and mistress of his own accord."[42]

Despite this fascination with white domestic labor, most experiments with it did not work out. Impressed with the devotion but dismayed by the bad temper of a relative's Irish nursemaid, Lucy P. Wickham mused, "Still for all that I have changed my mind & I like our old coloured nurses the best—tho Aunt Betsy does put as much covering on in August as January. She was *such a faithful kind friend to the children.* She died this fall, it was a satisfaction to me that she had everything she wanted & I hope & believe she is in Heaven."[43]

Though Lucy Wickham seems to have reached her conclusions through observation, it took actual experience for others to give up on white servants. Sallie Collins's experiences on the family plantation, Somerset Place, in coastal North Carolina, shows how one family pursued white domestic labor. In 1866, she reported, "We are scouting the country for a white cook, we have already two white 'helps,' one assists Maria in the dining room, and makes bread, and the other cleans the rooms up, and washes for the family. We only got them yesterday and up to that time, Mamma and I were worked almost to death!" Not

42. On Varina Davis's nursemaid, see Beth G. Crabtree and James W. Patton, eds., *"Journal of a Secesh Lady": The Diary of Catherine Ann Devereux Edmondston, 1860–1866* (Raleigh, N.C., 1979), 180. Kate Meares to M. John DeRosset, May 10, 1865, DeRosset Family Papers, SHC; Sadie C. Rives to Judith Page Rives, May 14, 1866, Rives Papers, LC; Bennehan Cameron to Anne Collins, March 11, 1866, Collins Papers, SHC. For the general fascination and later disillusionment with white workers, see Leon F. Litwack, *Been in the Storm So Long: The Aftermath of Slavery* (New York, 1980), 351–55.

43. Lucy P. Wickham to Bessie Shields, Dec. 20, 1865, Wickham Family Papers, VHS. Sadie Rives also considered hiring a white nurse and consulted her mother-in-law, who declared it the "nicest of plans, provided you can find a neat quiet amiable girl." See Judith Rives to Sadie Rives, Dec. 21, 1865, Rives Papers, LC.

surprisingly, given such high hopes, disillusionment soon set in. A month later Sallie considered one "white help," Caroline, a *"perfect treasure,"* making delicious bread and turning "her hand to everything," but she vehemently criticized the other two. Sallie confessed her "exceeding joy" when the unsatisfactory duo quit their positions, for "they did nothing but eat." While fewer references to white servants can be found after this early postwar period, other sources suggest that some households employed them. In 1870 in Fauquier County, Virginia, not only William Horner but also his sister, Janet Horner Weaver, had white servants working in their households. In that same county ten years later, Mary Skinker Goldsmith's live-in white cook was only twenty years old. Nonetheless, domestic work remained largely the province of African Americans.[44]

After the war fewer white households relied on coresident African American servants. In Fauquier County, Virginia, roughly 28 percent of former large slaveholding families had no live-in servants by 1870; a decade later the proportion had risen to 50 percent of those white families. In some Virginia households the loss of live-in help occurred relatively quickly, as Ann Hairston's experiences illustrate. In December 1865, while her husband was in Mississippi, she reported having no live-in help at her plantation house, "not even a servant in the house. I have got up to open doors in the morning just about light every morning since you left. Esther does her business very satisfactorily indeed, but I never keep her in the house after the business of the house is finished." As Ann Hairston's experience shows, not having live-in servants did not mean that the white family had no servants; it instead indicates that their numbers were fewer and separate households were emerging.[45]

The flight of African American servants from the white household came about for a combination of reasons. In part, servants were enjoying their freedom to leave unsatisfactory situations and to strike better bargains with employers. Some African Americans, much like their white neighbors, found that isolated plantations held little appeal and abandoned them to live in towns or cities. In 1883, when Emily Bondurant of Buckingham County, Virginia, hired

44. Sallie Collins to Anne Collins, March 13 and April 15, 1866, Collins Papers, SHC; MS Census of 1870, Virginia, Fauquier County, sch. 1, pp. 443, 448; MS Census of 1880, sch. 1, p. 74. For the complicated relationship between race and domestic work from the early nineteenth century, consult David Roediger, *The Wages of Whiteness: Race and the Making of the American Working Class* (London, 1991), esp. ch. 3.

45. This evidence on servants was drawn from a group of Fauquier households owning fifty or more slaves in 1860. These slaveowners and their children were traced through the two succeeding censuses of 1870 and 1880. Ann H. Hairston to Bettie Hairston, Dec. 19, 1865, Hairston-Wilson Papers, SHC.

a new cook, she complained about the difficulty of procuring servants in the countryside, adding emphasis to what she saw as the two major problems involved: "Darkies are much harder to get around here than on the river; they are *such ladies & so full of going to cities.*" Bondurant was remarking on a process that had been going on for almost two decades. Soon after the Civil War some black families signaled an unwillingness to remain in rural areas, particularly if whites would not rent or sell land to them. Privileged white women, despite their lack of sympathy for African American aspirations, were well aware of these objections. In January 1866, Sallie Collins reported that their only black servant at Somerset Place, located in a particularly remote section of eastern North Carolina, was the cook, Willis. Sallie conflated two different aspects of African Americans' search for autonomy in her description of the problem of retaining servants: she claimed that the blacks were all wanting to be "near a city to *educate* their children and all thinking themselves badly treated in not being allowed to rent the lands."[46]

Freedmen and women frequently exercised their newfound right of mobility, but even those who remained in the areas where they had been slaves realized that they now could quit one employer for another. According to Jennie Friend's later reminiscence, "Our own servants were never in our employ after the surrender, save one, who rented a house of my Father's in Blandford and paid the rent in the family laundrying." This occurred in the Friend family even with the most esteemed family servant, Amy, who had protected furniture and valuables in the family's Petersburg house from federal troops. After the war, Amy never worked for the Friend family again. Jennie simply reported that "Amy made a good living until her death, nursing for ladies in Petersburg." Obviously, Amy preferred not to resume a position with the people who had owned her.[47]

High turnover in servants continued to disturb white matrons. Lucy Patterson thought it a matter for congratulations when her aunt, Mary Friend, was able to continue to employ the "good servants you had in the house." Lucy typified those white women who refused to see any logic in servants' behavior when she disparagingly compared their changing employers to a children's game: "It reminds me of 'Puss in the corner' the way they change places at the end of each year[.] this one particularly[,] all seemed to think they needed an airing." Here, a privileged woman refused to see that domestic servants could be justifiably

46. Emily Morrison Bondurant to Alexander J. Bondurant, April 3, 1883, Bondurant-Morrison Family Papers, UVA (emphasis in original); Sallie Collins to Anne Collins, Jan. 30, 1866, Collins Papers, SHC. See Litwack, *Been in the Storm So Long,* 294–96, 312–16.

47. Stephenson, "My Father and His Household," pp. 39, 42, Blanton Family Papers, VHS.

unhappy with their wages and working conditions; instead, she labeled their actions as childish and irrational. A few matrons among old elite tried to accommodate themselves to their servants' wishes and aspirations. In Danville, Virginia, elderly Emily Dupuy noted in 1883, "Our housegirl Mary goes to school, only works morning & night, so we have rather more to do, attend to the dining room, wash dishes, &c. But [I] don't mind it at all, rather do it, than to bring another servant to the house." After Fanny Hairston returned to run Cooleemee plantation in the late 1880s, she paid for her young butler to attend Livingston College, a college for African Americans in Salisbury, North Carolina. But such mistresses were rare indeed.[48]

Calculating the number and proportions of house servants who remained with the same family over time is not possible, but census enumerations provide a snapshot of live-in servants in 1870 and 1880 in approximately twenty households of Fauquier County's former elite. With the 1870 census, many African American servants, who had worked in nameless numbers under slavery and whose presence as live-in domestics went unnoticed, suddenly became visible to the government. Only one of these households, that of Henry and Ida Dulany, contained domestics who were working there ten years later. Two middle-aged black domestics, Kitty Sydney and Robert Buckner, lived in the Dulanys' household in both 1870 and 1880. Ida Dulany's niece, Marietta Minnigerode, identified them as "Aunt Kitty," the cook, and "Uncle Robert," who waited on the table. Their supporting cast changed during that decade as a new housemaid and coachman joined them.[49]

Over time, elite women came to be more vocal about their distrust and fear of African American servants. In August 1868, Susan Bullock's shocked tones indicated her distress about a fire at her cousin John Bullock's house: "His house was burnt Wednesday night, supposed to have been set on fire by the cook and other servants[.] these are awful times[,] may the Lord deliver us from our troubles." Susan's unease may have been compounded by a suspicion that her house

48. Tera Hunter, *To 'Joy My Freedom: Southern Black Women's Lives and Labors after the Civil War* (Cambridge, Mass., 1997), 29–31; Rable, *Civil Wars,* 254–62; Lucy Patterson to Mary Friend, Jan. 17, 1871, Blanton Family Papers, VHS; Emily Dupuy to Emmie Watkins, Jan. 18, 1883, Emily Dupuy Papers, VHS; Henry Wiencek, *The Hairstons: An American Family in Black and White* (New York, 1999), 284–85.

49. Because of deaths, marriages, and outmigration, households during these decades were in the process of formation, disintegration, and re-formation. Thus, there are few households among these families that are strictly comparable from 1870 to 1880. MS Census of 1870, Virginia, Fauquier County, sch. 1, p. 647, MS Census of 1880, Virginia, Fauquier County, sch. 1, p. 100; Andrews, *Memoirs of a Poor Relation,* 63.

servants, as well as her farm workers, were stealing corn. While such activities had occurred under slavery, white men and women from the old elite now reinterpreted them as part and parcel of a threatening behavior.[50]

Southern elite women and men alike were quick to label African American servants as untrustworthy and larcenous. In Lynchburg in 1885, Nannie Tunstall declared that "I have vetoed the luxury of any more housegirls. As soon as you teach them they leave[,] either sent away, or of their own sweet will, & you run the risk of thievery with all. . . . The darkeys in Ly[nchburg] are the most indifferent I have ever seen, & they are growing worse day by day." Similarly, in Patrick County, Virginia, in 1879, Daniel Staples, detailing the activities of the household one sleepy Sunday afternoon, described the practice of cooks being allowed to carry home leftovers as a kind of wholesale robbery. According to Daniel, the cook was "stealing her pro rata share of a Sundays dinner fixed for the preacher from which there was left twelve basketsfull."[51]

In addition to possible thefts, other behaviors of servants began to appear more menacing. Some matrons, like Susan Bullock, worried about cooks who might set the house on fire, while others increasingly feared servants as carriers of disease. Ann Hairston cautioned her daughter to "be very guarded to avoid having any about that may be diseased." In Wilmington, the DeRossets charged that "Delia the dirty creature" might well have brought smallpox into the family. Here they were participating in a widespread paranoia about African Americans that was on the increase among white Americans. Historian Lawrence J. Friedman has suggested that this myth about African Americans as carriers of contagion became more common by the late 1880s.[52]

Many domestic servants might have dealt with such white alarm by leaving the worst domestic situations, but at least a few apparently adopted the excessively deferential demeanor that many former slaveowners desired. Such performances could deflect abuse and even allow the servant to dodge or otherwise subvert impossibly high standards. In 1869, when Lucy Taylor pronounced her

50. Susan Bullock diary, Aug. 8, 1868, Feb. 23, 1868, Hamilton-Bullock Papers, SHC.

51. Nannie Tunstall to Virginia Clay, Nov. 22, 1885, Clay Papers, Duke; Daniel Staples to Mate Waugh, Sept. 21, 1879, Staples-Persinger Family Papers, UVA.

52. Eliza J. DeRosset to Kate Meares, Jan. 16, 1876 (misdated 1875), Meares-DeRosset Papers, SHC; Ann Hairston to Bettie Hairston, Dec. 19, 1865, Hairston-Wilson Papers, SHC; Eliza J. DeRosset to Kate Meares, Feb. 27, 1876 (misdated 1875), Meares-DeRosset Papers, SHC. See Lawrence J. Friedman, *The White Savage: Racial Fantasies in the Postbellum South* (Englewood Cliffs, N.J., 1970), 123, and Hunter, *To 'Joy My Freedom*, 191–203, on whites' fears beginning in the 1880s of blacks as possible carriers of diseases such as tuberculosis.

family "blessed in our servants," she also observed that "Ellen though she is careless and ignorant about many things, is so humble that we like her."[53]

These varied examples fit a gradually emerging pattern of the old elite's increasing distance from and distaste for African Americans in the postwar period. Over time, southern white women would mix these fears with hazy memories to create the myth of the harmonious antebellum household containing perfect servants. Such fantasies, beginning in the late nineteenth century, perhaps reached their apogee in the figure of Mammy in both the written and screen versions of *Gone With the Wind*. Yet in fact, privileged women did not lead the way in inventing these devoted slaves of the past. It was Thomas Nelson Page, rather than his female counterparts, who limned the description of the old servant who was so devoted to his master that he too reminisced about the good old days and the grandeur of the planter family. At least through the 1880s, most privileged women focused on the present in their writings, daily or fictional, rather than attempting to recreate an idyllic plantation past peopled by fawning slaves.[54]

Among the Fauquier County old elite, the staffs of live-in domestic servants, primarily blacks and a few whites, had become quite small by 1870. Most of the live-in domestics were either mature women with children or young people in their teens. Silve Halestalk, a thirty-year-old African American servant who lived with her eight-year-old son and five-year-old daughter in Ann Dulany's household, typifies this first group, more common in 1870 than 1880. Some white employers preferred childless women. When Maria Louisa Carrington opened her girls' school in Richmond in 1871, she immediately hired two servants, "a very good cook, without husband, or children, and a chamber maid in the same happy state." Yet the status of these women was uncommon enough for Maria Louisa to remark upon it and exult in her good fortune.[55]

The most striking characteristic of the other group of domestic servants was their youthfulness. For example, in 1870, widowed Harriet Ward could count three adolescents, fourteen-year-old Sarah Bryan and two youths of twelve and fourteen respectively, among her four resident servants. That same year Henry and Ida Dulany employed an eight-year-old, Mary Hunter. Martha Clarke in

53. Lucy Taylor to Mary Dabney, Feb. 12, 1869, Saunders Family Papers, VHS.

54. See, for example, Thomas Nelson Page, *In Ole Virginia, or Marse Chan and Other Stories* (New York, 1887), and idem, *Bred in the Bone* (New York, 1904). See Chapter Seven for a more thorough description.

55. MS Census of 1870, Virginia, Fauquier County, sch. 1, p. 497; Maria Louisa Carrington to Eliza Dabney, Sept. 3, 1871, Saunders Family Papers, VHS.

1866 reported that a "smart little boy of ten years old," with the assistance of the family's former nurse, did "all the work of the dining room." This ten-year-old boy was the son of another servant, and his mother's annual wages of forty dollars plus room and board covered his services as well.[56]

Most scholars have overlooked the flight from domestic service of African American men, who during slavery had served wealthy white households as waiters, butlers, valets, carriage drivers, and gardeners.[57] Even in the early days of emancipation, one can find examples of men, especially the younger ones, leaving domestic service. The lack of a male domestic was news in itself, as Martha Clarke reported early in 1866: "We have no man servant in the house." That same year a vacationing Judith Page Rives was appalled when her manservant, Henry, announced his intention to leave, and she begged her son to inquire into his wage demands and "advise us as to what we should offer to induce Henry to remain with us." By the 1870s and 1880s, African American men rarely figured in the references to domestic servants. While in the 1880s, Nannie Tunstall of Lynchburg employed Edmund as the only servant who slept on her premises, it was also clear from her references to him as an "old darkey" that he was quite elderly. African American males living in white Fauquier households in 1870 tended to be either very old, very young, or employed as laborers rather than domestics. The 1880 households included one twenty-six-year-old black male cook and one twenty-three-year-old coachman, but all other young adult African American males were laborers.[58]

Most likely the demographic profile of live-in servants and the turnover in servants were related. African Americans' desire for control over their personal and family lives limited the number of them willing to work and live in whites' homes. While poor economic prospects kept many African American women in domestic servitude, white mistresses found that for live-in positions, they had to choose between women burdened with children or inexperienced youths. Domestic workers typically faced poor pay, hard labor, or onerous working condi-

56. MS Census of 1870, Virginia, Fauquier County, sch. 1, p. 647; Martha Clarke to Phebe Bailey, Feb. 15, 1866, Bailey Family Papers, VHS.

57. William Dusinberre, *Them Dark Days: Slavery in the American Rice Swamps* (1996; reprint, Athens, Ga., 2000), 347–49, points out men's importance as house servants and indicates that many black men took service positions in the public sector in the postwar period.

58. Martha Clarke to Phebe Bailey, Feb. 15, 1866, Bailey Family Papers, VHS; Judith Page Rives to Sadie C. Rives, Aug. 24, 1866, Rives Papers, LC; Nannie Tunstall to Virginia Clay, March 21, 1884, and Sept. 18, 1885, Clay Papers, Duke. For example, in 1880 Jacquelin Marshall Jr. housed his twenty-seven-year-old cook and her husband, a thirty-year-old laborer, as well as three black males who were laborers on the farm. MS Census of 1880, Virginia, Fauquier County, sch. 1, pp. 21, 100.

tions. Living in the white household often meant longer hours, little privacy, and the threat of unwelcome sexual advances. Over time, domestic servants increasingly sought and successfully demanded day work rather than a live-in position in an employer's household.[59]

After emancipation, few African American men, other than those too old to learn new skills, were willing to make a career of domestic service. Young African American males who did housework generally left service as they reached maturity. We have little direct testimony from either African Americans or whites about this phenomenon, but it might have been fueled by ideals and prejudices. Some historians have pointed out that after the war, black men wished to exert their masculinity and take control of their own households. Live-in domestic service provided little of the autonomy that these men wanted. Their desires for independence, at least in their own home life, were more easily satisfied by manual labor or by service in public institutions such as hotels and restaurants, rather than by remaining at the beck and call of a white family. Given that white women of the old elite spent much of their time in the household, the departure of black men and women meant lessened interaction between these privileged white women and African Americans.[60]

The household had long been southern women's domain, but elite women had expected to manage the work and workers rather than actually perform it themselves. While plantation mistresses continued to oversee a wide variety of tasks, younger matrons who lived in town or in extended households often had more limited managerial skills. Now that many women from the old elite had to undertake part or all of the manual labor, the difficulty of running a household in a grand manner quickly became apparent. For some plantation mistresses, the amount of labor was far greater than they had ever tackled, and they struggled to produce households that ran smoothly despite the challenges offered by domestic servants whose new freedom made them both able to renegotiate their terms of service and unwilling to bear the earlier onerous conditions of unrelieved work. Having grown up with numerous servants, elite white women after emancipation found that they were expected to work miracles—or at least

59. Hunter, *To 'Joy My Freedom*, 2–43. Elizabeth Clark-Lewis, *Living In, Living Out: African American Domestics in Washington, D.C., 1910–1940* (Washington, D.C., 1994) deals with the question of "living in" for a later time period.

60. Laura Edwards, *Gendered Strife and Confusion: The Political Culture of Reconstruction* (Urbana, Ill., 1997), 92–106, 161–77. That Sarah Maza's *Servants and Masters in Eighteenth-Century France: The Uses of Loyalty* (Princeton, 1983) finds that large numbers of French men left domestic service in the eighteenth century because they were unwilling to bear the connotations of their dependence suggests that these constructions of masculinity had a long history.

create a comfortable home—with far fewer resources at their disposal. Some continued to see domestic chores as labor for black women. M. E. Hill, a young widow gossiping about another plantation mistress's loss of her major household worker, revealed a common attitude: "I was astonished to hear that Amey left Meeta, and has since died, they say Meeta works herself nearly to death, well I don't mean to do that while there are a plenty of lazy negroes standing around, if they stay around me they shall wait on me." Yet others, like Meeta Capehart, concentrated on producing the pleasant surroundings (complete with well-reared children) that exemplified the domestic ideal.[61]

The struggle with domestic workers was ongoing, as limited economic opportunities made many black women dependent on wages. In truth, domestic work in the Upper South, while still grossly underpaid, was becoming more comparable throughout the nation. The tone of the dialogue between mistress and servant varied among different households. Some southern white women, like their counterparts elsewhere in the United States, looked to structural and technological change to solve their problems. Ironically, in the course of bringing new innovations into the household, southern elite women would more thoroughly join in their own domestication. They would become the mistresses of machines as well as of servants.

Most important among these changes, yet most difficult to chart, were the alterations in southern kitchens. Traditionally, southern plantation kitchens had been outbuildings. Such an arrangement, while often resulting in cold food at the table, kept the heat and odors of the kitchen separated from the main house and reduced the possibility of fire. Some historians have speculated that this distance removed the kitchen from the white mistress's sphere of influence and allowed servants, especially the cook, to dominate there. Certainly, while privileged women hated and feared laundry and ironing above all, cooking seems to have been the other task that they tried to avoid; such ladies might have wished to have a mastery of cooking, but rarely did they glory in carrying it out themselves. Maria Dupuy Anderson, for example, was proud of having trained her young cook, writing, "I am getting my little cook into the traces now and am not nearly so closely confined as at first. She can now get a right good plain meal without any assistance and is learning her place a little better than at first." Virginia novelist Mary Tucker Magill captured the ideal of these women in her 1870 novel, *Women,* in which the heroine attempts to make bread but the faithful family cook rescues her from a possible culinary disaster.[62]

---

61. M. E. Hill to [Harriet Benbury], Oct. 28, 1865, Benbury-Haywood Family Papers, SHC.
62. Maria Anderson to Mary Watkins, Nov. 25, 1878, Emily Dupuy Papers, VHS; Elizabeth Fox-Genovese, *Within the Plantation Household: Black and White Women of the Old South* (Chapel Hill, N.C., 1988), 98–99; Mary Tucker Magill, *Women, or Chronicles of the Late War* (Baltimore, 1871).

After emancipation, white women looked to rearrange their kitchens and exert their own presence there. Even older women shared in the general movement toward a new household that included appliances in order to lessen their need for human workers. One young widow in eastern North Carolina described the change in two households: "Mrs. Hunter and Mother have both bought new cooking stoves. Mrs. Hunter's has come, she has it put up in a room adjoining the house, and is arranging things very conveniently around her, for doing her own work if she has it to do, says she has no idea of being caught unprepared. Mother is looking every day for her stove, will put it up I expect in the room next to the kitchen, but I tell her when we have to cook it must be put in the dining room or pantry." As these and other comments indicate, southern women were rethinking the layout of their houses. In the postwar period, the kitchen was slowly but surely migrating into the house—even if, as in the preceding example, the kitchen merely tagged along after the stove. This process probably occurred sooner in towns than on plantations, but everywhere the house was being rearranged.[63]

The major technological change in the kitchen was the advent of the cast-iron stove. A fixture in northern kitchens for over two decades, the stove appeared in many southern kitchens only after the Civil War, when it displaced the huge fireplaces that had earlier cooked the food. Jennie Friend Stephenson recalled that her mother had attempted to introduce the stove into the kitchen before the war, but "it was the cause of much disgruntlement" because the cook, Aunt Betty, objected. Aunt Betty cooked in a huge old-fashioned fireplace and baked in "ovens with close fitting lids" that were "set at the corners of the big, wide hearth." The slowness of southern households, even wealthy ones, to adopt the stove might have sprung at least in part from prewar stoves being designed as much for heat as for cooking. Historian Priscilla Brewer has noted that after 1850, manufacturers tended to advertise the "ease of use and convenience" of their models rather than their fuel-saving features. Moreover, among the numerous options available to the postwar consumer were small models suitable for parlors. Sue Hubard noted in 1866 that her mother was sending her father advertisements for cooking stoves. By 1869, Sarah Hubard was concerned with improving the stove with a pair of waffle irons. She reminded her husband that "all four of the circular tops are cracked and broken so as hardly to keep in the heat. The name of the Stove is Banner Stove No. 5."[64]

63. M. E. Hill to [Harriet Benbury], Oct. 28, 1865, Benbury-Haywood Family Papers, SHC; Mary T. Meares to Fred Meares, Nov. 20, 1880, William B. Meares Papers, SHC.

64. On the introduction of the cast-iron stove in nineteenth-century households, see Ruth Schwartz Cowan, *More Work for Mother: The Ironies of Household Technology from the Open Hearth to the Microwave* (New York, 1983), 53–62; Susan Strasser, *Never Done: A History of American Housework* (1982; reprint, New York, 2000), 32–49; Priscilla Brewer, "Home Fires: Cultural Re-

Along with stoves, elite women sought to replace human with machine labor through sewing and washing machines. When Rebecca Anderson visited the plantation belonging to her grandfather, Thomas Ruffin, in Alamance County, she noted the presence of a new washing machine, along with familiar African Americans working as the cook and house servants. At Prospect Hill in Spotsylvania County, the Holladay women—Lucy Holladay and her unmarried sisters-in-law—became very interested in technological innovation. In 1866, Frances Holladay informed a relative about the new stove. The money that Lucy had saved to buy a new stove had been needed for taxes, but James, "resolved that Lucy should not be disappointed in getting a stove," had traded a cow and twenty-five dollars to procure a used one for her. Pronouncing it a "very nice good stove," Frances noted:

> It is set up in the dining room for the present and Lucy got dinner and supper herself yesterday, as Martha her cook was sick. I never examined a cooking stove before, and like it so much. It is so much less trouble, and labour to cook on than a fireplace. . . . It does not smoke at all here and draws finely. Many of the housekeepers about here are supplied with cooking stoves, and many are having wells dug. When we can get money enough, we wish to get one of the improved washing machines, and then we will feel quite independent.

Frances did not further elaborate on the meaning of "independence" and most likely did not see the irony that the new stove meant more cooking by Lucy herself. Apparently such white women from the old elite believed that they were freeing themselves from a dependence on African American workers and thought little about the new domestic tasks they had more thoroughly assumed.[65]

While matrons of the older generations, especially those worried about retaining a cook, initiated the purchase of cookstoves, the two younger generations found sewing machines most appealing and became their most frequent operators. Alfred Rives jokingly noted the importance of a sewing machine to his wife: "Sadie now has a piano & first class sewing machine, so that she has the elements of constant occupation, the great source of contentment, if not happiness." But

sponses to the Introduction of the Cookstove, 1815–1900" (Ph.D. diss., Brown University, 1987), 71–113, 116; Stephenson, "My Father and His Household," p. 15, Blanton Family Papers, VHS; Sue Hubard to Edmund W. Hubard, Feb. 1866, and Sarah A. Hubard to Edmund W. Hubard, March 2, 1869, both in Hubard Family Papers, SHC.

65. Rebecca Anderson to Anne Collins, March 10, 1866, Collins Papers, SHC; F. A. Holladay to Bet Lewis, March 2, 1866, Holladay Family Papers, VHS.

rather than young matrons like Sadie Rives, it was the unmarried women of the second and third generation who actually showed the most excitement about this machine's potential. In Baltimore in 1870, twenty-one-year-old Sue Hubard proudly informed her mother about successful shopping expeditions for bargains in dry goods and extolled her newfound ability to use the sewing machine: "I . . . expect to make both y[ou]r dress and mine except the body of yrs. Kitty says & in fact everybody in the house that the rapidity with wh[ich] I have learned to manage the machine would be perfectly marvellous in any body else but as it is I[,] the wonder ceases."[66]

The speed of the sewing machine in manufacturing clothing led some young women to spend long hours refurbishing their own and their friends' and relatives' wardrobes. One doctor, worried about too many hours at the sewing machine, forbade young widow Rebecca Anderson from using it until her health improved. In reporting the doctor's proscription, Rebecca's young unmarried sister, Maggie Cameron, declared, "The sewing machine is a great comfort to me. . . . I expect to make three dresses this week, two for Becca and one for myself." According to Maggie, the life of the Cameron women centered about the machine: "Our sewing parties are so pleasant, Mother, Becca and myself seat ourselves in the passage after breakfast [8:30] . . . there we sit until dinner." When Jeannie Meares's fiancé commented on her attachment to the machine, she in turn chided him that she had heard of "lovers wishing to be all things[,] butterflies flowers even mosquitos but never a 'sewing machine.'" In the Meares household, the use of the sewing machine became so common that Jeannie's cousin, Essie Meares, paid a visit just to make a calico dress on it. Young matron Maria Dupuy Anderson's gushing comments about her sewing machine could have been used, unedited as advertising copy: "I have exchanged my old Singer Machine for a new Domestic and like it very much—the new one is a much handsomer machine and runs so easily that I sew for pleasure now, as well as necessity." Elsewhere in the South, other women shared the excitement. In Georgia in 1871, Fanny Andrews used her first payments from teaching school to buy a sewing machine.[67]

Sewing had been a staple of women's work for years, but the sewing on ma-

66. Alfred L. Rives to Will Rives Jr., June 12, 1873, Rives Papers, LC; Sue Hubard to Sarah Hubard, March 21, [c. 1870?], Hubard Family Papers, SHC.

67. Maggie Cameron to Anne Cameron Collins, May 3, 1868, Collins Papers, SHC; Jeannie Meares to Will Williams, [c. 1881], Jane Meares to Jeannie Meares, Aug. 31, 1875, and see also Jane Meares to Jeannie Meares, Dec. 26, 1876, all in John and William A. Williams Papers, SHC; Maria Anderson to Mary Watkins, Nov. 25, 1878, Emily Dupuy Papers, VHS; Eliza Frances Andrews, *Journal of a Georgia Woman, 1870–1872*, ed. S. Kittrell Rushing (Knoxville, 2002), 50–51.

chines had a different purpose and seemed part of a different kind of work. Although antebellum elite women's diaries reveal numerous days engrossed by plain and fancy needlework, these handworkers had most often been married women constructing and mending clothing for babies and children. Such sewing was a traditional chore; in contrast, the use of the sewing machine to knock out a new wardrobe for oneself seemed innovative to young white women. At the same time as the sewing machine was outfitting them, it was being marketed, as one historian has noted, as a "symbol of a family's middle-class respectability" and even as an "agent of civilization." Young women could concentrate on a domestic chore that was sometimes intended to increase their own attractiveness and still be swathed in an aura of virtue and high-mindedness.[68]

Thus, after 1865 southern privileged women began to fit themselves ever more firmly into the culture of domesticity then resurgent in America. Sallie Collins summed up some of this education: "I found I have to give my mind to it, to master the science of housekeeping myself before I could teach another. I now find myself a good deal mistress of the situation but it keeps me going from morning till night." According to Sallie's niece, housekeeping was the "saving of Aunt Sal . . . she is very fond of it and is so energetic and thorough that I expect to hear of her being quite distinguished in that line." Industriousness, long touted for nineteenth-century women, was receiving new encomiums. Jeannie Meares wrote her fiancé when she was home alone, "I do not however feel lonely, because I am busy, and to speak truly, I do not believe I *ever am* lonely, for which I am very thankful."[69]

Some women came to judge themselves by the surroundings they created, often with their own hands. Unmarried Nannie Tunstall detailed the changes that she had made in her Lynchburg home: "Our new carpets are down & some of the new curtains are up & the house looks handsomer than it ever did. I have to work like a Trojan to make it so, but it is so central to me to have pleasant surroundings & as I have to live indoors all the time I have exerted myself to make it attractive." She went on to describe the new curtains, carpet, and "odds and ends" that had made her own bedroom lovely.[70]

68. Ava Baron and Susan E. Klepp, "'If I Didn't Have My Sewing Machine . . .': Women and Sewing Machine Technology," in *A Needle, a Bobbin, a Strike: Women Needleworkers in America,* ed. Joan M. Jensen and Sue Davidson (Philadelphia, 1984), 37. Baron and Klepp also indicate the skyrocketing sales of sewing machines between 1868 and 1875.

69. Sallie Collins to Anne Collins, Feb. 31 [*sic*], 1869, and Lizzie Jones to Anne Collins, March 2, 1869, both in Collins Papers, SHC; Jeannie Meares to William A. Williams, July 16, 1881, John and William A. Williams Papers, SHC.

70. Nannie Tunstall to Virginia Clay, Nov. 14, [1886], Clay Papers, Duke.

The domestication of elite southern women did not proceed without some questioning on the parts of various participants. Samuel Biddle told his seventeen-year-old daughter in 1865 that he thought more horseback exercise and less "needlework"—a term that could cover embroidery as well as sewing—would be "of service" to her. Although Biddle probably was referring to her health, he might well have been thinking of lifting her spirits.[71]

While some of their new chores probably made southern white women feel more capable, others experienced nagging doubts. Bluntly chronicling the weariness caused by nursing her invalid mother, Nannie Tunstall chose language that, while crudely racist, also indicated how hard she believed that she was working: "You will believe that I do not exaggerate when I tell you that there is not one hour in the day I can command. . . . She takes strong medicines every six hours—at 9, 3, 9, 3 o'clk—so that I am up & down with her during the night—but like the other niggers I have developed a faculty for sleeping the instant my head touches the pillow." The way that elite women described some activities clearly suggests that they worried about work often carried out by African Americans turning them into something approaching that "other."[72]

Women who quilted were prey to similar anxieties. Quilting had been a craft primarily of slave and yeoman white women; antebellum planter wives and daughters sewed, embroidered, and even knitted, but almost never quilted. When Jane Alston began fashioning a quilt after the war, she told her daughter Lucy, "Well my quilt is in the frame, and Ella and I are putting some regular darkey quilting on it."[73]

Postwar women's greater domestic capabilities and aspirations for domestic perfection are apparent, but the actual power they wielded within the household remains difficult to measure. Here one must distinguish among decisions made in different contexts. Did they concern the mundane aspects of life or major issues? Moral influence or family obligations? In terms of household expenses, wives' power and knowledge varied a great deal. Some women undertook much of the decision-making in business. Ida Dulany, according to her niece, "managed the estate in all particulars and with the greatest serenity." In this case the household and plantation seemed practically indivisible, and both were Ida Dulany's realm. In the household of young lawyer Daniel Staples, the division of responsibilities is more difficult to pin down. When he returned home after caring for an elderly uncle for four months, he praised his wife's direction of affairs:

71. Samuel S. Biddle to Rosa Biddle, Sept 12, 1865, Biddle Papers, Duke.
72. Nannie Tunstall to Virginia Clay, Aug. 3, 1886, Clay Papers, Duke.
73. Jane Alston to Lucy Alston Williams, [c. 1890], Lucy Williams Papers, SHC.

"You have gotten along much better than if I was at home. You have had your own family with you and more money than I am able to give you when I am at the Office, although the amount you have had was little enough the Lord knows and not half what you rightly deserved and you managed much better than I do." As the following chapter demonstrates, some married women from the old elite owned property that they could direct and control. In other cases, women oversaw the disposition of funds that their husbands provided. Yet the reduced circumstances that many elite families endured after the war caused considerable tension. In Buckingham County, Virginia, a constant tug-of-war occurred between Emily Morrison Bondurant and her husband, Alexander, over what was truly essential. He complained to an adult son, "I am all the time so pressed for money, that I can not do for my children what I want to, & it grieves me near unto death that your Ma can not realize my poverty & will take no excuse from me when money is wanted."[74]

Women wanted and expected a greater influence in the household. While they read about and heard abundant testimony to their high moral status, their actual power had its limits in both moral and mundane matters. In 1868, Prudence Person discoursed in a school essay on a woman's right during wartime to be a "ministering angel" and her right to "brighten the fireside." Prudence was advocating a form of separate spheres, in which the "provinces" of men and women were "distinct." Most of all, she asserted, "The Right of Woman is to elevate man's moral nature and to be to him in the language of [Alexander] Pope 'God's last best gift.'" Prudence's writings no doubt reflected the teachings of her instructors and parents, but others among her generation of young privileged women took such roles quite seriously. Perhaps prompted by the suicides, financial failures, and heavy drinking of the men around them, these young women believed they needed to uplift the male sex rather than mankind in its more generic sense.[75]

Women's attempts at moral reform can be found in the regular religious observances of some elite postwar families. When Robert B. Herbert spent time with his Beverley grandparents at Avenel plantation in Fauquier County, Virginia, his grandmother, Jane Carter Beverley, led family prayers every morning. Herbert's reminiscence suggests the male response such activities evoked: his

74. Andrews, *Memoirs of a Poor Relation,* 63; Daniel Staples to Mate Staples, n.d., Staples-Persinger Family Papers, UVA; Alexander J. Bondurant to Alexander L. Bondurant, Nov. 9, 1890, Bondurant-Morrison Family Papers, UVA.

75. Prudence Person, "Woman's Rights" (unpub. school essay, 1868), Presley C. Person Papers, Duke.

grandfather, Robert Beverley, would become restless if the prayers lasted overly long.[76]

To be sure, genteel southern white women had long been fighting a battle for moral influence, a battle that had become heated even back in the 1850s. Generations of mothers among the old elite begged their sons not to drink and to keep themselves sexually pure. While these warnings had not gone totally unheeded, they had produced neither upright, virtuous men nor wholesale reformation among the rakes. Something of the uphill battle that mothers faced can be seen in Ann George's admonition to her son, Samuel Hairston: "I hope my child you are trying to do what is right. Always try to find out what is right to do and pursue it at all events. I hope you will never follow Will's footsteps. One dissipated son is enough to break any mother's heart."[77]

By the late nineteenth century, privileged women were trying to increase further the impact of their moral admonitions. Mothers hoping to rear upright sons tried from the earliest years to evangelize and train them in religion and virtue. By a boy's adolescence, a mother was vying with a host of other influences, but she then could call on other girls and women to reinforce her teachings. In the family, sisters tried to influence their brothers' conduct. Virginia Hankins devoted herself to her younger brothers and financially aided them through her teaching stipends. When her brother Louis, then away at school, took up chewing tobacco, Virginia begged him to quit, giving a whole host of reasons: "It is nothing but a self-indulgent habit. It is a false stimulus and bad for your health." She urged him to rely on his self-control: "I am sure if you chose to use sufficient self-control you could conquer the habit, and it will be better for your health & your nerves & by the time you are an old man save you hundreds of dollars. Now do try my dear brother to give it up. Keep on trying until you do." Virginia was especially proud that Louis was a church member. At another point, when she feared that Louis was quarreling with an older brother, she counseled self-abnegation and forgiveness: "You must be sweet & forgiving and try to show him that being a member of the Church is something more than a mere form." Later in life, when Louis Hankins thanked his sister for her financial support of his education, he was equally effusive about the pious Christianity that had marked her life and character, crediting her "prayers to our Heavenly Father" with helping him and his brothers make their way in life.[78]

76. Robert Beverley Herbert, *Life on a Virginia Farm: Stories and Recollections of Fauquier County* (Warrenton, Va., 1968), 44–45.

77. Ann George to Samuel Hairston, Oct. 29, 1884, George Hairston Papers, SHC.

78. Virginia Hankins to Louis Hankins, Jan. 25, 1880, and Sept. 25, 1881, and Louis Hankins to Virginia Hankins, Dec. 19, 1888, all in Hankins Family Papers, VHS.

Concerned sisters offered advice on many issues. Hodgie Pender wrote her brother, "Baldy" Williams, on the eve of his marriage, cautioning patience and forbearance with his wife-to-be and adding an impassioned plea against excessive drinking, which was a "weakness to which too many of our relatives are addicted." Calling drink a "viper" that would destroy the happiness of his home, she continued, "If your wife ever beholds your manly form converted into that of a brute or its equivalent by the degrading influence of liquor, her respect for you will cease. There must be something in a husband to command respect." Instead, she commanded, "Spend your spare moments reading something beneficial. You have a mind as well as a farm & both will be overgrown with weeds or thistles without cultivation." Even middle-aged women, faced with brothers whose lives scarcely mirrored the virtues preached to them, continued to press for restraint and self-abnegation. Saidie Mason, then in her fifties, admonished her elder brother to "do take good care of yourself," and scolded him, "Don't go to that dreadful grog shop or have anything to do with those that drink. Above all you cannot stand drink and it distresses us & keeps us anxious about you."[79]

Affianced and recent brides also marked out areas in which they and their suitors wished and expected women to have power. The trope of women redeeming young males had become so thoroughly accepted that many suitors presented themselves as possible projects for reform. One of Rosa Biddle's cousins unsuccessfully wooed her, promising reformation but at the same time throwing the responsibility for his conduct onto her: "When I get a nice little home of my own, will *you* come . . . and in reality be *my own Rosa?* Please say yes I will be a 'good boy'—and you will make me a good man." When John Willcox renewed his futile courtship of Virginia Hankins, he admitted that he had been "imprudent some times" and thus not "what the world calls a very steady man." Yet he argued that she, as the right woman, could alter all this: "I *truly* believe that if I ever marry a woman that I *really* love & she exerts the proper influence over me, that my habits would entirely change." Promising that his chief object would be to make her happy, John closed with the declaration that "if you consent to marry me your influence will so strengthen my good resolutions, that I will eventually become a good man & I hope one worthy even of you." Even suitors whose staid lives and few wild oats would seem to have left them with no necessity for apologies deferred to their fiancées' moral guidance. Daniel Staples of Patrick County, Virginia, wooed his future wife by

79. Hodgie Pender to Archibald Williams, July 30, 1890, Lucy Alston Williams Papers, SHC; Saidie Mason to Lewis Mason, May 14, n.d., Mason Family Papers, VHS.

sketching a picture of their future life. "Your influence over me," he wrote, "wrought by your nobility and purity of character will bring about a radical change in a rather harum skarum fellow who hitherto has found very little to live for but the enjoyment of the present moments and the pleasures which the present moments gives, a restless fleeting pleasure that brings no contentment."[80]

Society at large and young women themselves expected that they would not only reform their fiancés but also inspire religious conversion, or at least more devout religious feelings, in their future husbands. Rosa Biddle entreated her fiancé, "Please don't think like so many husbands that the wife must have all the religion in the family. I shall insist on your doing many pious things whether you wish to or not. So be getting yourself in a 'pious frame of mind.'" Jeannie Meares praised William A. Williams when during their courtship he reminded her about his regular attendance at the local Episcopal church. Jeannie seems to have taken her role as moral compass quite seriously; at one point she told William that she felt her responsibilities were greatly increased because earlier her actions had affected only her family but his entire life might be changed by her example. Similarly, Hodgie Pender assured her brother that he "must encourage, uphold & cherish the refining & elevating influence" that his wife would "shed around you." Women had gained additional powers as the arbiters of conduct and correct deportment. Not only William Williams's morality but his social deportment came under fire, as Jeannie criticized his writing to her on "horrid old blue business paper" and warned him against the impropriety of slang.[81]

Despite these protestations of female influence, women were well aware of the bounded nature of their power. A fiancée might ask for or even demand reformation, but as a married woman, she had fewer weapons at her disposal. Given the stereotype of the nagging wife, some elite women, especially those of the older two generations, seem to have retreated to the pedestal. There they tried to set an excellent example and ignore the problems before them, foremost among which was excessive drinking. Describing how her father's descent into alcoholism caused her mother to treat him as an invalid, Marietta Minnigerode succinctly labeled her mother's behavior as part of a more general response: "All of the women of our connection have spoiled their husbands." Such a refusal to acknowledge men's alcoholism and irresponsible behavior meant that someone

80. Walter Duffy to Rosa Biddle, Jan. 10, 1876, Biddle Papers, Duke (emphasis in original); John V. Willcox to Virginia Hankins, March 29, 1866, Hankins Family Papers, VHS (emphasis in original); Daniel Staples to Mate Waugh, Aug. 21, 1879, Staples-Persinger Family Papers, UVA.

81. Rosa Biddle to Samuel P. Smith, May 18, 1879, Biddle Papers, Duke; Jeannie Meares to William A. Williams, Aug. 26, Aug. 12, and Aug. 23, 1881, John and William A. Williams Papers, SHC; Hodgie Pender to Archibald Williams, July 30, 1890, Lucy Alston Williams Papers, SHC.

else had to assume increased responsibility for the family's well-being. In Mariet-ta's case, the older daughters became the family mainstays. In other cases, wives themselves took increased responsibility and wielded greater influence in the home. This oblique approach empowered individual women but did little to justify a greater authority for them more generally.[82]

Women had long had considerable authority over child-rearing and childcare, and some husbands in the postwar period were obviously willing to entrust wives with important decisions in this area. When the parents of Freda Eppes deter-mined to have a Philadelphia specialist examine her leg, it was Freda's mother who accompanied her there to make the decision whether to operate. Yet many women expected to exercise much of their authority by influence and indirec-tion, as men still expected to carry certain weight as the head of the household. For example, Carey Pettigrew commented that her son-in-law, even while defer-ring to his wife's wishes, had named the new baby: "Of course he knew that Jane wished to name him for her father but it was very pleasantly done as his act."[83]

The extent to which southern elite women participated in the reduction of family size that marked American life in the late nineteenth century has received little attention. Historians of antebellum gentry women in both Virginia and Alabama have suggested that they exerted a primitive control over their fertility and were consciously limiting their family size. Planter women in South Atlantic areas might have succeeded by the 1850s in increasing the intervals between childbirths, but their families still averaged six children.[84] After the war, Virginia and North Carolina elite women left little testimony about their power in this

82. Andrews, *Memoirs of a Poor Relation,* 238.

83. Richard Eppes to Emily Eppes, Feb. 9, 1882, Eppes Family Papers, VHS; Carey Pettigrew to William Pettigrew, Nov. 2, 1881, Pettigrew Family Papers, SHC.

84. Jan Lewis and Kenneth A. Lockridge, "'Sally Has Been Sick': Pregnancy and Family Limi-tation among Virginia Gentry Women, 1780–1830" *Journal of Social History* 22 (1988): 5–20; Ann Williams Boucher, "The Plantation Mistress: A Perspective on Antebellum Alabama," *Step-ping Out of the Shadows: Alabama Women, 1819–1990,* ed. Mary Martha Thomas (Tuscaloosa, Ala., 1995), 34–38. For planter women's possible limitation of family size by the 1850s, see Ca-shin, "Households, Kinfolk, and Absent Teenagers," 151.

For the late nineteenth century, Daniel Scott Smith has hypothesized that women's desire for smaller families carried the day with those couples who, despite rudimentary family planning mea-sures, bore fewer children. Yet other studies on contraception have suggested that access to informa-tion about family planning—particularly about efficacious uses of douching—decreased under the Comstock law, which banned birth control information and devices as well as pornography. See Daniel Scott Smith, "Family Limitation, Sexual Control, and Domestic Feminism in Victorian America," *Feminist Studies* 1 (winter–spring 1972): 40–57; Janet Farrell Brodie, *Contraception and Abortion in Nineteenth-Century America* (Ithaca, N.Y., 1994).

respect, although some dropped hints that they considered smaller families acceptable or even desirable. George Collins's letter to his wife in 1874 suggested that they had wished to avoid her current pregnancy. Assuring her that he "would do anything than scold you in your present condition," he confessed that "I only felt a little hurt that you had not intimated sooner, the suspicion you speak of. I thought and hoped for your sake [it] had passed by." Young matron Mary Welby Beverley wrote about pregnancy and childbearing to her sister in the most veiled of terms: "'F. B.' will have her 'Tea Party'—in Sept. so she told Ma, & 'Sadie' will be in 'Dec.'—so my dear child you have plenty of company even if I cant keep up with you young people. I may come 'aplodding' along after a while." Even as Mary's euphemisms and jokes would seem to indicate her embarrassment about the subject and her belief in its unpredictability, she ended her letter with a bitter blast about the women's lack of control over fertility: "You know if we are not having children we are either in bad health or talked about & it all goes to make up a life time—we are all *poor wretches 'females' I mean.*" Rosa Biddle Smith, after noting that a forty-year-old neighbor had just had a baby, even though her other child was nine years old, observed, "I hope I will not follow her example."[85]

Louise Humphreys Carter obliquely dealt with the question of family size in a diary entry penned on her eighteenth anniversary, in which she referred to her husband as wishing they still had small children. In this period, women showed little faith in their ability to control their fertility, even if some of them had achieved small families through various stratagems. Smaller families were in evidence here and there, but little information exists about how men and women attained them.[86]

In the end, women from elite families had become far more domesticated by the turn of the century than their grandmothers had been before the Civil War. Economic problems encouraged conglomerate households, but these lost many of their domestic servants. In particular, African American men rejected domestic work, and African American female servants were increasingly unwilling to live with the families they served. Live-in servants tended to be either quite young or old, and turnover was frequent. It was the youngest generation of white women from the old elite who adapted best to this situation; they did so, however, by becoming far more domestically talented themselves. Many of these

85. Mary Welby Beverley to Detta Beverley, [c. 1880s], Beverley Family Papers, VHS; George P. Collins to Anne Cameron Collins, Collins Papers, SHC; Rosa Smith to Mary E. Biddle, Oct. 6, 1886, Biddle Papers, Duke.

86. Louise Humphreys Carter diary, Jan. 6, 1870, Shirley Plantation Papers, CWF.

elite women looked to stoves and sewing machines to help with domestic labor. At the same time, they claimed the beauty and cleanliness of a house to be all the more their own achievement.

In the more intangible area of the extent of the authority women exercised in these new households, a great deal of variation occurred, depending on the energy, tenacity, and general management skills of the woman involved. In many families, women seem to have controlled the domestic economy, making decisions about childrearing and domestic spending. In other areas, their authority was more ambiguous. Were women self-consciously limiting the size of their families? They testified to their husbands' appreciation of large families, but they were more discreet about their own practices and goals. Given the general agreement about the higher nature of women and the moral authority they could exert, some women might have lessened fertility simply by limiting sexual encounters. But such behavior likely affected the marriage and might have increased husbands' interest in extramarital affairs. It was clear, however, that many people agreed that genteel women should exercise moral leadership in the family, not only over sons and daughters but over husbands as well. Here we encounter something of a culture war between pious churchgoing wives and the rowdier side of male culture. Some women sought to make such behavior off limits to husbands as well as sons. Though the double standard still prevailed in many households, women had gained the authority to criticize, even if not to prohibit.

To modern observers, elite women's entanglement with domesticity might seem to contradict the independence that they were trying to construct. Yet if one surveys the situation from the contemporary point of view, it becomes apparent that these white women, faced by war's ravages and poverty, made an aggressive effort to respond to their new and often unfamiliar way of life. When domestic chores increasingly fell to them, many women transformed themselves to meet this challenge. Others, resentful of their former slaves' defection, hurled epithets after them. In their households, women sought a new mastery. White women of the old elite tried to become the creators and guardians of clean, beautiful homes that housed upright men and well-brought-up children. In this way, they contributed to the propagation of Victorian domestic ideals in the South and helped to define the permutations of middle-class respectability not only in their surroundings but in the behavior of their family members.

Southern Female Institute, 1870s
Courtesy Virginia Historical Society

Nannie Tunstall
Courtesy Virginia Historical Society

Katherine Waller Barrett
Courtesy Virginia Historical Society

Amélie Rives
Courtesy Virginia Historical Society

Castle Hill

Courtesy Special Collections Department, University of Virginia

Mary Ellet Cabell

Courtesy Special Collections Department, University of Virginia

Eliza Lord DeRosset

Courtesy *North Carolina Historical Review*

Frances Christine Fisher
Courtesy *North Carolina Historical Review*

Mary Bayard Devereux Clarke
Courtesy *North Carolina Historical Review*

Julia Magruder
Courtesy Library of Virginia

M. G. McClelland
Courtesy Library of Virginia

3

"WHAT WILL BE MY OWN": WOMEN

AND PROPERTY OWNERSHIP

Virginia jurist Wood Bouldin faced a difficult case in 1875, when his niece Mary Ellet Cabell sought his advice in a delicate situation. Should she rescue Norwood High School, owned by her heavily indebted husband, William Daniel Cabell, by purchasing it with her own funds? Would it be "prudent and practicable," Mary asked, for her to own the grounds and building of the school as her own personal property, known then as her "separate estate"? Bouldin seems to have believed he had two major points to address. The first was the legal issues involved if Mary Cabell purchased the property; the second, even more important, was what this purchase would mean financially for her. In his long, carefully worded reply, Bouldin assured his niece that "there is no reason why you should not purchase and hold the property as your exclusive separate estate, *provided always* you are properly and amply protected from the claims of your husband and *his* creditors, past present and future." The jurist advised Mary that while it would be "eminently wifely and wise" for her to save her husband's school, she should do so only if her husband would accept his "proper relation" to it.[1]

The rub lay in the phrase "proper relation." Relying on the concept of the inviolability of women's separate estates, Bouldin argued that a husband should respect his wife's right to her property as being "as absolute, as high, and as holy certainly, as a mere stranger's or the rights of an associate in business." Yet even

1. Wood Bouldin to Mary E. V. Cabell, July 20, 1875, Cabell-Ellet Family Papers, UVA (emphasis in original). Although there were two Wood Bouldins, both of whom were lawyers and judges, Mary Cabell most likely sought advice from the elder, who was her uncle, given her husband's comment that she was seeking the advice of "Uncle Wood." William D. Cabell to Mary Ellet Cabell, July 16, 1875, Cabell-Ellet Family Papers, UVA. For biographies of Mary Cabell and Wood Bouldin, consult John Kneebone et al., *Dictionary of Virginia Biography* (Richmond, Va., 1998), 2: 122–24, 490–91.

while Bouldin expounded this point in law, he realized that it was far from universally respected in practice. "I know Mary," he told his niece, "that it is extremely difficult to make any husband understand, especially one with the temperament of *your* husband, that as to his wife's separate estate, he is no longer husband with any of the ordinary rights of husband, that such estate, if any way it come to his hands, should be as absolutely sacred from any use, pledge or promise on his part for any debt of *his* or any purpose of *his,* as would be the funds of a Bank of which he perchance be the cashier." Bouldin pointed out that he was emphasizing a "proper understanding and appreciation by an involved husband of his wife's rights and his own duties in relation to his wife's separate estate" because he knew that some of Mary's property had already been lost through what he euphemistically called the "disastrous consequences of an innocent forgetfulness or disregard of these principles."[2]

Mary Ellet Cabell's interchange with her uncle illustrates the complex nature of privileged women's property rights and activities in the postwar period. In Virginia, even before a married women's property bill was finally passed in 1877, women's ownership of property through the separate estate had become accepted in law and practice. The above correspondence shows that a conservative man like Bouldin, who as a member of Virginia's Supreme Court of Appeals in 1872 argued that the state was legally bound to pay its prewar state debt, also upheld a married woman's rights to property. Yet, as in the Cabell case, complicated family interactions constantly impinged on women's property transactions, making women's property rights contingent on their support by male relatives. The post–Civil War period produced no revolution in property rights for even the most privileged southern women, but neither did it mark a retreat in those rights, as some scholars have believed.

Until the last two decades, historians generally assumed that nineteenth-century southern women, even those from well-to-do families, seldom owned property or took part in the world of business. Pathbreaking work by Mary Beard on equity law notwithstanding, scholars considered most nineteenth-century women to be "covert," that is, covered by the marriage relationship and thus sheltered from economic relationships. Over time, however, this picture has changed. Although coverture—which vested control of property in the husband at marriage—in theory barred most adult women from the world of business, this prohibition was neither complete nor permanent. Moreover, unmarried women who acquired property by inheritance or their own efforts did not face

2. Ibid.

the same legal disabilities as married women. In wealthy families, widowhood often made women property owners and economic actors.[3]

Recent research has suggested that the economic experiences of women among the elite varied during the antebellum period. Many women took little interest in financial affairs, leaving them to male relatives, but others actively ran businesses or oversaw the operations of plantations. In Petersburg, Virginia, privileged women had access to and often control over significant amounts of property. The emergence of the separate estate or trust estate, protecting women's property from their husbands (or more often, from their husband's debtors) meant that married women could, in effect, continue to own property. Although their actual control over that property might be limited to receiving the benefit of its revenues or profits, some trusts allowed women actively to manage the property and to dispose of it by will or deed. These separate estates allowed even married women to participate in business dealings.[4]

Despite this picture of women's activity in business affairs during the antebellum period, scholars have been far more pessimistic about the postwar period. They suggest that the loss of property or diminution of its value pushed most women out of the economic arena. In this view, more outlined than fully explored, women's autonomy and independence suffered in the postwar world. Thus, scholars currently present elite white women as far more empowered under the slave regime than after emancipation in the postwar South.[5]

Women's relationship to property can be determined through ascertaining their access to land and other forms of wealth during the different phases of life—as single women, wives, and widows—and their management, sale, or other dispositions of it. Women's business ventures and moneymaking activities outside and within the household also are germane. To explore in greater detail privileged women's financial affairs, I systematically examined the property transactions of several generations of the wealthiest slaveholding families in Fauquier County, Virginia. Information on property transfers in other wealthy Virginia and North Carolina families then allowed me to check the applicability of the Fauquier patterns. My research paid close attention to women's age, marital

3. Mary Beard, *Woman as Force in History: A Study in Traditions and Realities* (New York, 1946).

4. Suzanne Lebsock, *The Free Women of Petersburg: Status and Culture in a Southern Town, 1784–1860* (New York, 1984), chs. 2 and 6. The most thorough survey of women's legal status in a single Texas county is Angela Boswell, *Her Act and Deed: Women's Lives in a Rural Southern County, 1837–1873* (College Station, Tex., 2001).

5. Lebsock, *Free Women of Petersburg*, 237–49; George Rable, *Civil Wars: Women and the Crisis of Southern Nationalism* (Urbana, Ill., 1989), ch. 13.

status, and kinship ties. The role that women played in these transactions suggests the contours of both their economic position and their attitudes toward property. Particularly significant were the roles that women played in overseeing the disposition of their own or their husbands' wealth. The frequency with which privileged white women served as executors of their husbands' estates is one indication of women's financial responsibilities. All in all, elite women's financial transactions show a continuity with the antebellum years, rather than a disruption, and a modest postwar increase in their relative access to various forms of wealth.[6]

A very common way in which numerous married women from the old elite came to own or control property was through the settlement of their late husbands' estates. Large numbers of widows were involved in overseeing the division of property, and some were their husbands' principal legatees. Historians have tended to view both the exercise of executorship and the inheritance of property as empowering for widows. In the postwar period, these were overlapping rather than mutually inclusive or exclusive categories, as most elite Carolina and Virginia men designated their wives as executors to see that their wills were carried into effect. A will's executor was responsible for paying off all debts of an estate, making any necessary sales of property, and generally squaring all accounts before the final payment of legacies. For performing this service, the executor received a commission on the funds received and disbursed.

During and after the Civil War, the majority of Fauquier County's wealthiest men (with living wives) who wrote wills named their wives as their executors. Like their contemporaries in a rural Texas county, Virginia widows were active in settling their husbands' estates. James Keith Marshall, son of Chief Justice John Marshall, provides an example of a man designating his wife as his executor. As he divided up the property, he not only selected his "much beloved wife" as his executor, but also bequeathed her the 350-acre farm known as "Little Farm." Along with this, James included the household and kitchen furniture, carriages, and horses, and a life estate in the remainder of the property not already parceled out to their ten surviving children.[7]

6. The sample group for Fauquier County were the families of the fourteen men and women owning fifty or more slaves in 1860.

7. The nineteenth-century term for a female executor is executrice, but I have simply referred to the women as executors. Carole Shammas, Marylynn Salmon, and Michel Dahlin, *Inheritance in America: From Colonial Times to the Present* (New Brunswick, N.J., 1987), 112–19, find a late-nineteenth-century resurgence of wives as executors but argue that adult sons were still favored as executors. Boswell, *Her Act and Deed,* 119–22. Compare to Lebsock's finding that during the antebellum period, the wealthiest men in Petersburg were least likely to designate their widows as executors of the estate, both because of the complexity of the business matters involved and their

In North Carolina, most planters also looked to their wives to administer their estates. William K. Kearney of Warren County, who died in 1869, left a bevy of adult children but designated his wife as his sole executor. Wealthy Josiah Collins named his wife executor and guardian of their children. Both Collins and Kearney not only designated their wives as sole executor of their estates but also bequeathed them all their property with complete powers to dispose of it. To be sure, Collins, after giving Mary Collins "my entire estate of every kind and description, with full and absolute power and authority to her, to use, occupy, possess and manage the same, without being accountable to any person or persons whatever," also made provisions for the property in case she did not draw up a will. In contrast, Kearney simply wrote that his "beloved wife Maria A. Kearney" should receive all of his estate in "fee simple forever."[8]

For some women untutored in the world of business, the responsibilities of executor and woman of affairs posed a new challenge. Ann Davis Miller, who had grown up on a rice plantation and married a successful lawyer-planter, recorded her response to her husband's designation of her as his executor. Although local gossip held that Thomas Miller had died in another woman's bed, his wife stressed to female relatives, in language typical of the day, how her husband had been her "idol" and had shielded her from "all trouble or care." Because her father and husband had died within several months of each other in 1865, Ann Miller bemoaned these deaths as depriving her of her advisers. "All upon whom I have been in the habit of looking up to and leaning on," she wrote, "are gone!" Despite Ann's lifetime of dependence, her husband named her, rather than their adult sons, his sole heir. It was with obvious pride that she repeated her husband's "strictest injunctions" that she retain "entire control of everything." She explained how, in tidying up his business affairs, he had discussed the issues and possible courses of action with her—a discussion that she perceived as "so thoughtful of me in everything" and indicating "such confidence he had in me." This interaction can be read in several ways. Perhaps Thomas Miller believed his wife to have innate abilities in this area that simply needed development, or perhaps he hoped to make her a surrogate to carry out his wishes beyond the grave. At the very least, his choice indicates a change in direction for both Thomas and Ann Miller. While he "sheltered" her earlier in

---

notions of the proper duties of women. Lebsock, *Free Women of Petersburg,* 116–28. Will of James Keith Marshall (probated 1865), Fauquier County Wills, vol. 30, pp. 8–10, FCCC.

8. Will of Josiah Collins (probated 1866), Josiah Collins Papers, NCDAH; Will of William K. Kearney (probated 1869), Warren County Wills, NCDAH.

their marriage, he wanted her to take control of the property after his death. Ann Miller herself seemed quite willing to plunge into the world of business affairs; she viewed her role as executor as a special honor—an indication of her husband's affection and confidence in her judgment.[9]

Although Thomas Miller did not give his sons a role in administering his estate, other men designated adult sons to serve as executors along with the widow, since they could be useful surrogates in the business world. The example of Robert M. Stribling well illustrates this point, because he amended a will, drawn up in 1846, over a fifteen-year period. In 1846, he appointed his wife Caroline and his friend Thomas M. Ambler as executors, asking her to employ two of their sons, then in their twenties, to collect debts. Over the succeeding years Stribling added various codicils to this will, allowing sons as they reached adulthood to join his wife as executors. In the end, when Robert Stribling died in 1865, Robert Jr. settled the estate. At that point, Caroline Stribling apparently did not think it necessary to renounce the executorship, though Ambler and Robert Jr.'s brothers did.

Robert Stribling's will, with its updates over a fifteen-year period, provides snapshots of his changing perceptions of his family's needs. When he first drew up his will, he was concerned about the possibility that Caroline Stribling, then aged forty-six, might remarry. Although he gave her a life estate in all his property, he specified that it would last only during her widowhood and would be replaced by her legal share should she remarry. In that event he also stipulated that Ambler would act as guardian for the minor children. As his sons grew to adulthood, Robert first visualized their simply aiding Caroline in the numerous duties of executorship by running errands for her. Finally, as they proved themselves reliable householders, he allowed them to join her as executors of the will.[10]

Robert Stribling's many emendations of his will show how numerous decisions about an estate might relate to a wife's age, capabilities, and willingness to accept responsibilities, rather than simply her gender. If a wife were still youthful, the husband might worry about her marrying again and control of the property passing out of her hands. As she aged, the numerous business concerns might prove more a burden than an emblem of responsibility. Those husbands who passed over their wives in choosing an executor usually called on male rela-

9. Annie W. Miller to Kate Kennedy, Aug. 17, 1865, DeRosset Family Papers, SHC.

10. Will of Robert M. Stribling (probated 1865), Fauquier County Wills, vol. 29, pp. 420–23, FCCC.

tives (such as sons, brothers, or brothers-in-law), or respected friends and law-yers. In a will made in 1897, for example, James Skinker designated his two sons rather than his elderly wife as the executors of his estate.[11]

The business of administering an estate, especially an indebted one, was not an easy matter, and some husbands might have wished not to inflict such a chore on their wives. This possibly was the case with Isaac Carrington of Charlotte County, Virginia, who before his death in 1887 designated as his executor a local lawyer, Mr. Darby, allegedly chosen for his reputation for honesty. Isaac's elderly aunt, Elizabeth Cabell Daniel, assessed quite highly the managerial abilities of Isaac's widow, Nannie Seddon Smith Carrington: "I have no fears about Nannie. . . . I think when thrown on her own responsibility[,] self reliance will come; she has good practical sense—industry—power of managing—determination, which I think will enable her to carry on her household with less means than some others would require. I may be mistaken but this is my esti-mate of her capabilities."[12]

By the second half of the nineteenth century, many men had come to share the opinion that some women, especially enterprising widows, could carry out certain activities in the public sphere. The judgment about executorship weighed business sense, honesty, and reliability; obviously in many men's eyes some women, usually their wives, qualified on all three counts. Other mature women also seemed able to assume such responsibilities. In 1873, widowed John D. Flanner of New Bern, North Carolina, chose his sixty-year-old mother-in-law, Eliza Dean, to serve as executor and guardian for his five young children.[13]

Moreover, widows continued to inherit substantial amounts of property from their deceased husbands. Many legacies were lifetime estates, while others were fee simple, in which the widow had the right to dispose of the property. Claudia Marshall, Mary Collins, and Maria Kearney all inherited all their husband's property in fee simple, even though they had children who could have been the legatees. More often, wealthy Upper South planters tended to set up fee-simple arrangements for their widows when the couple was childless or when the widow was a second or third wife.

Childless widows inherited some, often much, of a husband's property with

11. Will of James K. Skinker (probated 1900), Fauquier County Wills, vol. 45, pp. 90–92, FCCC.

12. Elizabeth Cabell Daniel to Emma Cabell Carrington, Feb. 9, 1887, Carrington Family Papers, VHS.

13. Will of John D. Flanner (probated 1873), Craven County Wills, vol. E, pp. 79–80, NCDAH.

no strings attached. In 1867, for example, Colin Clark, a wealthy Halifax County planter, bequeathed the "whole property & estate of which I shall die seized or possessed, consisting of Real, personal & mixed property to my beloved wife Eliza L. Clark and her heirs in fee simple forever." Such postwar wills became much shorter and more to the point than antebellum wills. While the abolition of property in slaves and the diminution of other wealth contributed to this brevity, it also suggests a growing confidence in the ability of widows to take care of themselves. William Chambers, an antebellum planter who in 1847 left property to his wife Ann, had appointed male executors and had given them detailed instructions about the sale of property, but twenty years later Colin Clark made no such stipulations.[14]

The second set of widows who often received property in fee simple were women who were second or even third wives, especially those who were not the mothers of their husband's surviving legitimate offspring. William Eaton, a wealthy planter living in Warren County, North Carolina, just by the Southside border, bequeathed his third wife Martha in fee simple his carriage and carriage horses, one year's provisions, and his land on the north side of Roanoke River, along with its horses, cattle, hogs, sheep, and plantation tools. He also gave her a life estate in his house in Warrenton and a nearby tract, dividing the rest of his property among his four surviving children. A granddaughter, the daughter of Eaton's deceased son from his first marriage, challenged her exclusion from the will, alleging that her elderly grandfather had been mentally incompetent and unduly influenced by his wife. In the trial that followed, numerous family members and friends testified to William Eaton's strength of mind and his intentions in regard to the disposition of his property. Eaton's family physician testified, "I have heard Mr Eaton a great many times speak of his property, and said he intended to leave his wife abundantly provided for." When questioned about Eaton's reasons for doing so, Dr. Powell replied, "I don't recollect, except he said at that time she was the best woman in the world, that he had the best wife in the world. I have heard him say so frequently." While Dr. Powell agreed that Martha Eaton was a lady of "strong mind and strong will," he also claimed that "she and all the other men and women in the country could not sway [Eaton] from what he wanted to do. If what his wife wanted him to do was agreeable to him, it was all right, otherwise I have seen him curse right out and go his own way." The will was upheld in 1875. Giving some property in fee

14. Will of Colin Clark (probated 1868), Halifax County Wills, and Will of William Chambers (probated 1847), Rowan County Wills, both in NCDAH.

simple to a second or later wife was an attempt to sort out and defuse family tensions although, as the Eaton case illustrates, it did not necessarily work.[15]

Other widows of the old elite received a life estate in their husband's property, while some who were elderly received a right to a certain part of the house and an annual payment. This combination of maintenance with a certain independence might have been particularly agreeable to some aging matriarchs. In an 1868 agreement with her children and grandchildren, sixty-eight-year-old Caroline Stribling exchanged her lifetime estate for the "exclusive right to two rooms which she may select" in the plantation house and an annual payment of $120. Even as she passed the reins of property to a new generation, she also affirmed her right to her choice of lodging place and to a monetary payment that would fend off dependence.[16]

All in all, widows from old elite families generally received more responsibility than property in their own right from their deceased husbands in the late nineteenth century. In part this sprang from the couple's conception of their parental role as fostering children, even when that fostering took the form of setting up their children in life. For example, when William S. Dulany's estate was divided among his mother and sisters, his mother Ann Dulany expressed her willingness to accept two tracts of land worth only about half the value of the other shares because those tracts adjoined her other lands and, perhaps more important, this division was "advantageous to the other parties," that is, to her daughters.[17]

Although some historians have viewed the relatively small number of fee-simple bequests in the postwar period as indicating decreased female property holding and autonomy, this was not the case. Implicit in such a view is that notion that women's ownership of property depended on legacies from their husbands. Yet women among the old elite had other sources of wealth, and some who received only life estates from their husbands owned other property outright, most often property inherited from their own relatives. Caroline Stribling received a life estate in her husband's property, but her will reveals that she also possessed in her own right a one-third interest in another farm. Wills drawn up by other married women from the old elite in Fauquier County show that many

15. Will of William Eaton (probated 1873), Warren County Wills, and Testimony in Estate of William Eaton, Warren County Estates, both in NCDAH.

16. Will of Caroline M. Stribling (probated 1887), Fauquier County Wills, vol. 39, pp. 150–51; Caroline M. Stribling to Mildred C. Stribling et al., Aug. 18, 1868, in Fauquier County Deeds, vol. 61, pp. 91–93, both in FCCC.

17. Commissioners to Ann Dulany et al., Nov. 1, 1866, Fauquier County Deeds, vol. 60, pp. 124–27, FCCC.

of them owned property derived in large part from gifts or legacies from parents or other relatives.[18]

Particularly evident in Virginia was the continued importance of the separate estate, set up by either trust deed, marriage settlement, or special bequest. The wealthy in Virginia traditionally had intended such trusts, often drawn up by concerned fathers, to protect property from creditors rather than to create autonomy for women. These wealthy men wanted to ensure that their wealth would pass to their descendants. Virginia seems to have had a somewhat distinctive history in this respect. The existence of chancery courts made the separate estate easier to set up and to enforce there than in North Carolina, where it apparently never gained a similar frequency of use among the old elite. The popularity of the separate estate—as well the elitism of upper-class Virginians—may also help to explain why the Old Dominion was the slowest among southern states to enact a married woman's property act. Because well-to-do Virginians had their own ways of protecting women's property, they remained uninterested in measures that might have aided poorer state residents.[19]

After the Civil War, even as Virginia legislators dragged their heels about expanding married women's legal control of property, members of the old elite continued to resort to the separate estate for their wives and daughters. The testimony of wills, deeds, and marriage contracts, as well as letters and diaries, makes it evident that privileged men—and women—had come to consider such trust arrangements as normal. In her account of recent activities among her extended family in 1883, Sallie Bruce matter-of-factly referred to two such transactions, one of which involved her daughter-in-law, Mary Anderson Bruce: "General Anderson had transferred to Mary $10,000 of Tredegar Stock, on hearing of the birth of her last baby—making $40,000 (with the house) in 12

---

18. Lebsock, *Free Women of Petersburg,* 247–48. Will of Robert M. Stribling (probated 1865), Fauquier County Wills, vol. 29, pp. 420–23; Will of Caroline M. Stribling (probated 1887), Fauquier County Wills, vol. 39, pp. 150–51; Caroline M. Stribling to Mildred C. Stribling et al., Aug. 18, 1868, in Fauquier County Deeds, vol. 61, pp. 91–93, all in FCCC.

19. Some male contemporaries denigrated the importance of the separate estate and its successor, the married women's property act. Fauquier native P. A. L. Smith noted with relish that law professor John B. Minor claimed the "married woman's act was almost a failure, because men generally kicked or kissed their wives out of their property." Presley A. L. Smith, *Boyhood Memories of Fauquier* (Richmond, Va., 1926), 14–15; Lebsock, *Free Women of Petersburg,* 54–111.

Suzanne Lebsock, "Radical Reconstruction and the Property Rights of Southern Women," *JSH* 43 (May 1977): 195–216. See also Carole Shammas, "Re-assessing the Married Women's Property Acts," *Journal of Women's History* 6 (1994): 9–30, which argues for the importance of the statutes; Peter Bardaglio, *Reconstructing the Household: Families, Sex, and the Law in the Nineteenth-Century South* (Chapel Hill, N.C., 1995), 134–36.

months." Sallie Bruce also approvingly noted that Wyndham Robertson had created a separate estate when he married her niece, Ann Seddon: "Wyndham had Ann's property settled on her of his own accord & made Willy Seddon [Ann's brother], her Trustee." In this latter case, Robertson was attempting to convince Ann and her family that he was not a fortune hunter.[20]

In the postwar era, Virginians of both sexes had come to believe that women had an interest in property, whether they had acquired it before marriage or whether it came to them through marriage. A discussion over how best to preserve the Hubard family holdings clearly shows the conviction that Edmund Hubard's wife, Sarah Epes Hubard, deserved to have her property secured to her. Edmund W. Hubard had served during the 1840s as a congressman, and politics seems always to have engrossed him more than the operation of his extensive Buckingham County plantations in central Virginia. The large amounts of money that he borrowed from his brother, Robert T. Hubard, created a rift between the two men that by the 1870s had estranged their families as well. In 1870, R. T. Hubard Jr. (Robert's son and Edmund's nephew) suggested that his uncle secure these debts by drawing up a deed of trust on all his real estate except the home plantation, Saratoga, and an additional 1,200 to 1,500 acres. In return for Sarah Epes Hubard's consent to this deed, Robert Jr. counseled that Edmund settle upon her their personal property and the house and lands at Saratoga. Such an arrangement would, according to the younger Hubard, "save your family from ruin and my father from care." A year later Robert T. Hubard's attempt to buy land from his brother ended in wounded feelings on both sides, as Edmund pronounced the offer to be below the market price. Later that year, when Edmund's debt stood at twenty thousand dollars, R. T. Hubard Jr. again admonished his uncle to set up a separate estate for Sarah Hubard: "You can and ought to settle upon your wife not less than $10,000 worth of personal & real property in consideration of her land & of her dower interest in the other part." Clearly Robert Jr. believed that his aunt Sarah deserved to have her share of the property protected. Apparently Edmund Hubard resisted this line of action, instead selling his plantation in 1874.[21]

In other instances, a wife who relinquished dower rights in some of her husband's land could expect to receive a separate estate as compensation. In 1871, for example, Philip B. Cabell set up a separate estate for his wife, Julia C. Bolling

20. Sallie Bruce to Morelle Bruce, Jan. 13, 1883, Bruce Family Papers, VHS.
21. Robert T. Hubard Jr. to Edmund W. Hubard, July 5, 1870, and Dec. 16, 1871, Robert T. Hubard to Edmund W. Hubard, Feb. 9 and 15, 1871, all in Hubard Family Papers, SHC. On the Hubard plantations, see Percival Moses Thomas, "Plantations in Transition: A Study of Four Virginia Plantations, 1860–1870" (Ph.D. diss., University of Virginia, 1979).

Cabell, in return for her relinquishing her right of dower in Alabama real estate that Philip had conveyed to his cousins. The deed explicitly stated that "Philip B. Cabell & wife" agreed that "she should be compensated in real estate for said relinquishment," and that this compensation should be secured to her sole and separate use. In this case, Julia received the plantation house, Edgewood, in Nelson County, Virginia, and twenty-eight acres surrounding it.[22]

To be sure, the independence granted women by a separate estate varied enormously, according to the stipulations of the deed. In Julia Cabell's case, she received "full power" over the property "as if she were a feme sole" so that she might "sell, exchange, or encumber the same according to the forms of law, may give it away by deed or devise it by will." And because the trustee was her relative, he presumably would have her best interests at heart. Yet if the woman's husband were the trustee, as sometimes was the case, his control over the separate estate might be little diminished from what it would have been under common law. In North Carolina, a neighbor described Mary Pettigrew's separate estate: "She having had her maiden property settled on herself—she treats it however as entirely her husbands and he intends to send an agent here in the fall to commence operations." If a trust allowed a woman little or no control over the property or the trustee, the estate would function almost solely as a device to retain property within the lineage and to defeat creditors. The marriage settlement of April 25, 1861, between Mary Bernard of Caroline County, Virginia, her future husband George Guest of Spotsylvania County, and her trustee, Wyndham Robertson of Richmond, shows how limiting some of these arrangements could be. The trust set up in this settlement covered Mary's inheritance, which included parts of Alabama and Virginia plantations and their slaves as well as bonds and other personal property. While Mary retained the right to sell the property or bequeath it in a will and to choose her trustee, that trustee was instructed to permit her husband "to have possession, control & management without accountability to the trustee or Mary Guest." Such lack of oversight severely undermined Mary's potential autonomy; not surprisingly, Robertson soon relinquished his trusteeship, and Mary designated her husband as her trustee. In this case the property was protected only from George's debts. Although Mary could change her trustee, she had little recourse against any use—or misuse—her husband wished to make of the property.[23]

<hr />

22. Deed of Philip B. Cabell to Julia C. Cabell and Richard M. Bolling, trustee, March 27, 1871, Cabell Family Papers, UVA.

23. Marriage settlement, Mary Bernard to Wyndham Robertson, trustee, April 25, 1861, Guest Family Papers, VHS; Mary Collins to Anne Cameron Collins, June 27, 1871, Anne Cameron Collins Papers, SHC. Lebsock notes the wide variance in the independence that was granted to Petersburg women by deeds of trust. See *Free Women of Petersburg,* 54–67, 79–86.

The last two cases show women simply as the title holders of the property, but some men and women expected a greater respect for women's property rights. Wood Bouldin's response to his niece shows how the notion had taken hold among many of the old elite that the individual rights of women property holders were important. Not only did Bouldin recommend that Mary Cabell secure her property against her husband's debts and that she ensure that the school property be made to pay for itself, he advised her in the "closing statement" of his letter to protect her rights: "William should be ready to accept and act upon the indisputable fact, that in honesty[,] in morality[,] and in law[,] *your* separate property is in no sense and to no extent *his* property and that it is neither safe nor just to you nor proper in itself for him to look to it to any extent as a means of paying *his* debts, nor to so shape his conduct as to impose on you in some sort, the necessity of so applying your separate funds." Bouldin's lengthy disquisition shows that by 1875 women's separate property had gained widespread acceptance as being morally as well as legally correct. Yet his concern about the possible difficulty in convincing William Cabell of such principles suggests that at least some men continued to view the separate estate more as a way to avoid losing property to creditors than as a restraint to their own rights.[24]

Although some trusts barely touched the husband's rights over property, other arrangements veered much closer to the opposite pole of female independence by giving the woman a third-party trustee who served at her pleasure and could be instructed by her. Lucy P. Wickham and her sister held property they inherited from their father, Henry Taylor, under such terms. Taylor had drawn up his will so that each of his two daughters, whether married or single, received at age twenty-one her legacy, to be held by two trustees who paid her its annual income. As in most trust arrangements, the women retained the right to bequeath this property in a will, but their powers in fact went considerably further. While the original trustees were chosen by the executors (Taylor's wife and brother), each daughter had the right to have the trustees "changed at her pleasure." Taylor did not spell out the right to instruct the trustees about the property's management, but their accountability, which could be enforced through the women's right to replace them, meant that Lucy Wickham and her sister retained a voice in the management of their property.[25]

Among Fauquier planter families, the separate estate for women remained common well into the postwar period. Virtually every family among the old elite in Fauquier County could count some married women who held property in

24. Wood Bouldin to Mary E. V. Cabell, July 20, 1875, Cabell-Ellet Papers, UVA.
25. Will of Henry Taylor (probated 1845), Wickham Family Papers, VHS.

their own right as a separate estate. In 1869, elderly Ann Dulany set up a separate estate for her granddaughter, Alberna Jennings, with Alberna's brother, Henry Payne, as trustee. This deed in part showed the reduced circumstances of the formerly well-to-do (Ann Dulany transferred a bond for $650, a colt, a milk cow, two heifers, and a gold watch to Alberna) even as it illustrated a determination that this property supporting the basic needs of life be secured to her granddaughter. Moreover, this trust was to be "free from the debts and control" of Alberna's husband or any other future husband she might have.[26]

Only a handful of Virginians and North Carolinians protected all property given to women by placing it in trust; instead, varying arrangements prevailed according to individual circumstances. When widowed Harriet Ward gave property in trust in 1864 to her daughter, Mary Smith, the trust obviously had been set up to shelter land and slaves from the creditors of Mary's husband, Edwin, as he was designated the trustee with full powers to manage this property. Harriet reserved only minimal autonomy for her daughter: Mary could bequeath her legacy and her assent was necessary if Edwin wished to sell it. Harriet's postwar provisions for her other daughters, however, struck a different note. In the will she wrote in 1865, she placed the property she allotted her unmarried daughter Susan in trust "to her sole and exclusive use and benefit free from all debts, liabilities or control of her husband should she marry." Yet at the same time Harriet made no such provisions for the share of her other unmarried daughter, Annie. Harriet Ward's intentions here cannot be divined. Possibly she was unimpressed by the beau whom Susan would wed a little over a year later; she might have foreseen that Annie would never marry. Most significant here is the element of contingency—the idea that the level of protection for a young woman's property needed to vary according to the individual.[27]

Yet another aspect of inheritance broadened some women's autonomy. One of the most striking aspects of the postwar period was the increased economic power of never-married women among the elite—an economic power derived from an increased equality among offspring in inheritance. Earlier in the century, spinster daughters in rural families could count on little more of a legacy than the right to a home with an inheriting sibling. Since planters linked the

26. See the Will of Inman Horner (probated 1860), Fauquier County Wills, vol. 29, pp. 33–37, FCCC, for an example of a farm given in trust to his daughter, Janet Weaver, during the antebellum period. Ann Dulany to Henry Payne, Oct. 4, 1869, Fauquier County Deeds, vol. 62, pp. 17–18, FCCC.

27. Deed of Harriet Ward to Edwin Smith, June 16, 1864, Fauquier County Deeds, vol. 59, pp. 469–71; Will of Harriet Ward (probated 1871), Fauquier County Wills, vol. 33, pp. 129, both in FCCC.

transfer of property to daughters to the setting up of new households, women not likely to marry did not receive the advancements that their married sisters enjoyed. For example, when William Cain of Orange County, North Carolina, drew up his will in 1828 and wished to make a "competent provision" for his unmarried daughter Peggy, he charged his eldest son William with her support. And the elder William did not make even this maintenance a legally binding, enforceable request. The support of Peggy Cain, who might also have been mentally or physically disabled, depended on the good will and conscientiousness of her brother.[28]

Even by the 1850s, this situation had begun to change. The typical child in old elite Upper South families could expect a share of the patrimony relatively similar to that of a sibling, especially a sibling of the same sex. In his will drawn up in 1851, Duncan Cameron of North Carolina resorted to this newer kind of provision for all his children. While his son Paul, who was married with a family, gained the largest legacy, taking the Fairntosh plantation in Orange County, North Carolina, and land and slaves in Greene County, Alabama, Duncan divided the rest of his slaves among all four children: Paul, his unmarried daughters Margaret and Mildred, and Thomas, who was mentally handicapped and received his share in trust. Mildred, whose health was delicate, and Margaret jointly inherited Duncan's house near Raleigh and its hundreds of acres of land, and Mildred also received the Brick House plantation in her own right. An important aspect of this will was the way it dealt with unmarried daughters in quite different positions: one who was highly likely to marry and another who was equally unlikely to do so. Thirtyish Margaret Cameron had been courted for several years by George Mordecai, a successful banker of Jewish ancestry. Duncan Cameron delayed the marriage, giving as his reason his unwillingness to give up Margaret's oversight of his household and her sister's care. Yet Duncan likely foresaw that after his death, Margaret would marry Mordecai. In bequeathing the Raleigh house and lands, Duncan provided that the property given to Margaret and Mildred could be divided between them upon the marriage of either. Thus, he opened the way for a marriage to take place after his death, but even more significant, he did not penalize his daughters in any way should they not marry.[29]

28. Will of William Cain (probated 1834), Orange County Wills, NCDAH.

29. Jane Turner Censer, *North Carolina Planters and Their Children* (Baton Rouge, La., 1984), 104–18. For an article emphasizing antebellum planters' favoritism and high-handedness, see Joan E. Cashin, "According to His Wish and Desire: Female Kin and Female Slaves in Planter Wills," in *Women of the American South: A Multicultural Reader,* ed. Christie Anne Farnham (New York, 1997), 90–199. Will of Duncan Cameron (probated 1853), Wake County Wills, NCDAH.

In the postwar South unmarried daughters of the old elite could continue to expect a guaranteed home, but they were increasingly likely to receive property of their own. In some cases the law governing division of estates, which treated all children equally, divided property, as when elderly John G. Beale of Fauquier County left no will. Even though his youngest daughter was in her late twenties, only two of Beale's five children (three daughters and two sons) had married. Still, all of them shared equally in his real and personal property.[30]

Others who made wills also adopted equal division and gave unmarried daughters a relatively equal part of the property. For example, Mildred P. Marshall, daughter of Jacquelin and Eliza L. S. Marshall, inherited land in 1868 like her siblings, even though at her mother's death, Mildred was forty-four and unlikely ever to marry. Similarly, her cousins, Maria Willis Marshall and Eliza Jacquelin Marshall, never married but nonetheless shared in their parents' wealth. In 1882, when Claudia Marshall made her will, she gave special monetary legacies, $1,000 to each of her surviving children, but $2,000 to her unmarried daughter, Eliza Jacquelin Marshall.[31]

In Spotsylvania County, Virginia, five of the six Holladay daughters—Huldah, Eliza, Mary, Frances, and Virginia—were unmarried in 1860, when their father died. He attempted a relatively equal treatment, at least according to sex, of his sons and daughters, with the women each receiving $4,000 while their five surviving brothers received land. Grandchildren of deceased offspring, whether sons or daughters, also received monetary legacies. The value of the real estate reserved for the Holladay sons cannot be determined, but it appears to have been relatively similar to the monetary bequests given the daughters and the survivors of the deceased sons. The unmarried Holladay sisters received the more traditional provision as well: "To my single daughters I give the right to reside in my dwelling house with their brother James M. Holladay if they wish it, so long as he may be the owner of it. In the event of the marriage of any one of them, the right, to such one, shall cease."[32]

In at least one North Carolina family, the death of a son in the Civil War led to larger legacies for his unmarried sisters. Before the war, Isaac T. Avery had drawn up a will that gave his lands in Burke and Montgomery counties to his five sons and divided real estate in outlying areas among all his nine children, including two married daughters and two unmarried daughters, Laura and Ade-

30. See Division of Lands of John G. Beale Sr., April 9, 1867, Fauquier County Deeds, vol. 60, pp. 253–56, and vol. 63, pp. 22–24, FCCC.

31. Will of Eliza L. S. Marshall (probated 1868), Fauquier County Wills, vol. 31, pp. 266–76; Will of Claudia B. Marshall (probated 1884), Fauquier County Wills, vol. 38, pp. 81–82, FCCC.

32. Will of Waller Holladay (probated 1860), Holladay Family Papers, VHS.

laide Avery. After unmarried Isaac E. Avery was killed in the battle of Gettysburg, the elder Isaac divided that son's share of the Burke and Montgomery lands between Adelaide and Laura. Moreover, Avery provided that his home plantation lands not be divided "so long, as it shall be the pleasure of my sons Alphonso C. Avery, and Francis W. Avery, and my daughters Adelaide L. Avery and Laura M. Avery to reside together in the family mansion at Swan Ponds." To compensate the children of two other deceased sons, Avery stipulated that these grandchildren receive payments "as will be their respective shares of reasonable compensation for the rents of such portions of said lands." He also provided that the ownership of the family mansion would devolve on Alphonso C. Avery, who was then his oldest living son. Here Isaac T. Avery showed both the expansiveness and the limits of giving property to unmarried daughters. Even in the original will, when nine children were living, Avery bequeathed real estate and an equal number of slaves to his unmarried daughters, providing them with some independent income. But during the war, as his children became fewer in number, Avery admitted the two unmarried women, but not their married sisters, into shares of the core family lands. To be sure, Laura and Adelaide together owned only the one-fifth part equivalent to their deceased brother's legacy. Yet their inheritances, even though not equal to those of their brothers, could support female independence.[33]

Avery's concern that his unmarried daughters have a place to live was echoed by other elite parents well into the twentieth century. As Lucy Wickham tried various strategies for bequeathing her property, she hit upon the device of giving her plantation in trust for a number of years to her son and widowed daughter. Lucy made clear that this complicated arrangement was meant to ensure that Anne Carter Wickham Renshaw, "my beloved daughter may have a roof over her head & I think her Father would wish me to do it. I think he would, as far as I can believe & know." Other testators, especially women, continued this special treatment for unmarried daughters. In the will that she wrote in 1899, Anna Maria Marshall Braxton gave each of her three unmarried daughters $1,000 in land or money and then divided the residue of her estate equally among all seven of her children. Fifteen years later Anna Maria rewrote this will to empower her executors to allow her three unmarried daughters and son Weston to buy her house in Fredericksburg upon their payment of approximately $2,000 (which she estimated to be three-sevenths of its value) to their three

33. Will of Isaac T. Avery (probated 1865), Burke County Estates, NCDAH.

brothers. Over time, the privilege of remaining in a sibling's house had been transformed into ownership of a house of one's own.[34]

A share of family property for all offspring, even for those who might not pass that inheritance on to a new generation, had come to triumph over the earlier view that had linked women's inheritance to their marriage and a new household. Parents no longer made a daughter's legacy contingent on her marital status. The new conception of children and legacies seems to have resulted from parents' broadening their sense of obligation. They had come to believe that all offspring deserved an equivalent start or maintenance in life, regardless of whether they married. Among the planters of the American South, it had never been necessary for sons to marry to inherit property, although marriage had sometimes led fathers to set up their sons with land. But attitudes toward their daughters had changed over the course of the century. In general, this paralleled a national trend that provided greater equality among children in inheritance. Among the southern elite, parental legacies also signal an increasing acceptance of women remaining unmarried. In their willingness to provide property as well as a home in their bequests, these parents guaranteed a modicum of independence to those who had traditionally been most dependent, the daughters who never married.[35]

Still, in the years immediately after the war, when many southern men felt financially strapped, some did not appreciate the financial independence of their unmarried aunts and sisters. An exasperated E. Thornton Tayloe revealed some of the frustration of men who had seen their fortunes decimated and who believed themselves saddled with debts not of their own making. In 1868, Thornton crossly replied to his unmarried aunt Virginia Tayloe's request about her annuity: "My father paid Aunt Anne her annuity regularly during the War & Uncle William yours & you must look to him, he being the surviving executor, I having nothing to do with the business. If you are not satisfied, I wish you would apply to the Court to have another Trustee appointed." Calling her bequest a "troublesome trust," he reminded her that he and other relatives faced hard times: "I myself have not the Thousand Dollars to give away you request nor have I the means to buy real estate in Baltimore. I have now a good deal of Southern land only to try & make a living off, which with the failures of crops,

34. Will of Lucy Wickham (Oct. 28, 1904), Wickham Family Papers, VHS; Will of Anna Maria Braxton (probated 1914), Fauquier County Wills, vol. 47, pp. 106–09, FCCC.

35. The parallel can be followed elsewhere in Shammas et al., *Inheritance in America*, 108–112, who use Bucks County, Pennsylvania, as a test case and argue that some inequality among children's inheritances continued to prevail among the most affluent.

leaves me with very little if any income. We have Relatives more pressed for means to live on these days than you are, with your Annuity, & existence is a struggle. Crops failing, but Annuity is regularly paid." As he recounted his own straitened finances, Thornton could not hide his jealousy of his aunt's security.[36]

Women, married and unmarried, actively used and even disposed of the property they owned according to their own wishes. As a conservative woman who held no brief for women's rights, Sallie Bruce once observed that divorce in a marriage with children was the worst thing that could happen to a woman, but she also believed that a woman had a right to spend the property she brought to her marriage. When one of her sons visited Europe, Sallie suggested that he should buy in Italy copies of "celebrated paintings" for her to hang at in their home, Staunton Hill. After discussing the possible cost, she observed, "Your father has such heavy expenses that he has nothing to spare & I only expect to use what will be my own from the sale of some land belonging to my Father's estate." Other women showed a similar awareness of their contribution to the family's wealth. Even though Leila Dabney's husband was a lawyer and judge, she characterized her family in 1877 to be like that of another relative, just living on the proceeds of "my father's estate."[37]

After inheriting or being given property in their own names, women often carefully guarded their rights to its disposal. Many propertied women among the old elite, especially in Virginia, continued to believe it necessary to arrange their affairs in wills. To be sure, in some cases their menfolk may have suggested that a will would best deal with their business affairs. In an 1908 letter, Henry T. Wickham reminded his elderly mother that her lawyer nephew advised that she be sure to make a will as "very serious complications will arise in the event you do not." Although Lucy Wickham followed this advice and wrote a new will, this was hardly an activity that had to be urged upon her. Over the previous twenty years, she had drawn up at least seven different testaments. Her many wills stemmed not from any whims or passing fancies but from the changing circumstances of her family (although her failure to declare void earlier wills might have complicated the probate). Her intent, as expressed in the first surviving will of 1888, was to divide her estate evenly among her three surviving chil-

36. E. Thornton Tayloe to Virginia Tayloe, Oct. 1, 1868, and Memo, Sept. 1, 1868, Tayloe Family Papers, UVA. Thornton's splenetic outburst stemmed at least in part from Virginia's successful attempts to receive an additional four thousand dollars from her father's estate because she had been paid in Confederate money during the war while a sister living abroad received northern bonds equivalent to gold.

37. Sallie Bruce to Morelle Bruce, June 14, 1873, Bruce Family Papers, VHS; Leila Dabney to Phebe Bailey, Nov. 7, 1877, Bailey Family Papers, VHS.

dren. Over time the changing fortunes of her children dictated different arrangements. The following year, the growing indebtedness of her son, William F. Wickham, led her to bequeath the property in trust for her three children "with the capital & income to be free from any debt of my children." In 1893, she drew up a new will that placed the family plantation in trust, first for her children and then for her grandson, Williams Carter Wickham Renshaw, until he reached age thirty-five. Bequeathing gifts of $15,000 and $20,000 respectively in trust to her son William and daughter Anne Renshaw, Lucy concluded, "I think this is a fair will & the best that I can do for my dear children."[38]

In a letter that she wrote her son Henry Taylor Wickham in 1893 and left with her most recent will, Lucy explained why she had favored his brother William and sister Anne over him. Signing herself, "Your devoted Mama," Lucy declared that her concern for the well-being of all her children dictated the will's provisions: "Your life is so uncertain, Willie's life is so uncertain, Annie's life is so uncertain & precarious & mine even more so—that I think it right & best to make this disposal of my property. I knowing the inside circumstance of my family. . . . Lisa & your children are amply provided for & you & they do not need the little that I give Annie & Willie to keep them from want. I think Mr Wickham would wish me to take care of them—for they don't know how to take care of themselves."[39]

After her son William died in 1900, Lucy Wickham returned to her principle of equal shares. Noting that she had advanced "large sums" to William and to his estate, she declared, "Under these circumstances I cannot at my death give his heirs any share in my Estate having given to him the third of his Fathers & Mothers property." She further justified her actions: "I do this not for want of love to my beloved son, but in justice to my two children & I write this without the least knowledge of either of them." After 1890, probably because of the indebtedness of family members, she was unwilling to give the lands in fee simple. Some of her wills relied on the device of the trust to protect her property and pass it on to the eventual heir; others used the life estate. Her final will chose two grandsons, Williams C. W. Renshaw and Williams C. Wickham, the sons of daughter Anne and son Henry respectively, to receive the plantation after Anne and Henry held it in trust fifteen years.[40]

38. Henry T. Wickham to Lucy P. Wickham, July 10, 1908; Wills of Lucy P. Wickham, Nov. 7, 1888, Aug. 9, 1889, and May 27, 1893, all in Wickham Family Papers, VHS.

39. Lucy P. Wickham to Henry Taylor Wickham, May 27, 1893, Wickham Family Papers, VHS.

40. Wills of Lucy P. Wickham, May 24, 1900, March 20, 1903, Oct. 28, 1904, and July 27 1908, all in Wickham Family Papers, VHS.

Although scholars have disagreed about whether many late-nineteenth-century women were drawing up wills, most women from the old elite in Fauquier County, Virginia, continued to make formal bequests of their property. For example, four daughters of James K. and Claudia Marshall left wills. Their female cousins, the six children of Jacquelin A. Marshall and his wife, Eliza L. S. Clarkson Marshall, similarly relied on legal documents. In this family, three daughters, one daughter-in-law, and two of the sons' daughters drew up instructions about the disposal of their property. The care shown toward the dispersal of their goods indicates how privileged white women, married and single, came to envision themselves as owners of property and sometimes the rebuilders of the family's prosperity.[41]

Privileged women paid attention to their property, but the experience of the Beale women indicates several different approaches to its disposition. In 1865, the heirs of elderly John Beale Sr. were his two unmarried daughters, forty-six-year-old Eliza and thirty-two-year-old Hannah, his married daughter, Mary Gordon, his unmarried son William, and the three children of his deceased son, John G. Beale Jr. Forty-year-old Hannah married in 1873, after drawing up a marriage settlement with her husband-to-be, William Gaskins, that allowed him to hold her property in trust, reserving to her the right to sell or bequeath it. In January 1876, shortly before her death, Hannah G. B. Gaskins wrote a will that left all her property to any child who survived her; otherwise it would go to her husband.[42]

41. For the wills of the daughters of James K. Marshall, see: Will of Maria W. Marshall (probated 1908), Fauquier County Wills, vol. 44, pp. 301–2; Will of Claudia H. Jones (probated 1919), Fauquier County Wills, vol. 48, p. 360; Will of Alice L. Carroll (probated 1919), Fauquier County Wills, vol. 47, pp. 362–63; Will of Eliza Jacquelin Marshall (probated 1918), Fauquier County Wills, vol. 47, pp. 276–77. For the wills of the daughters, a daughter-in-law, and granddaughters of Eliza L. S. Marshall, see: Will of Ellen H. Barton (probated 1920), Fauquier County Wills, vol. 47, p. 414; Will of Mildred P. Marshall (probated 1882), Fauquier County Wills, vol. 37, p. 331; Will of Anna Maria Braxton (probated 1914), Fauquier County Wills, vol. 47, pp. 106–9; Will of Elizabeth W. Marshall (probated 1891), Fauquier County Wills, vol. 40, p. 175; Will of Catherine Travis Marshall (probated 1902), vol. 44, p. 77; and Will of Eleanor Lewis Douthat (probated 1912), vol. 47, pp. 4–5, all in FCCC.

Although Lebsock, *Free Women of Petersburg,* 247, suggests that fewer Petersburg women were writing wills after the Civil War, Shammas et al., *Inheritance in America,* 119–20, indicate that at the end of the nineteenth century, larger numbers of women were drawing up wills. Boswell, *Her Act and Deed,* 97–98, finds only fourteen wills by women for the entire period of 1837–1873 and only one will by a married woman, written in 1862.

42. Power of Attorney of Mary, Hannah, and Eliza Beale to William Beale, Aug. 30, 1865, Fauquier County Deeds, vol. 59, p. 500; Marriage settlement between Hannah G. Beale and William E. Gaskins, Nov. 29, 1872, Fauquier County Deeds, vol. 65, p. 312; Will of Hannah Beale

Hannah's older sister Eliza Beale never married. Along with Hannah, Eliza sold her interest in the farm to the railroad for $17,000 in 1873. With this money Eliza remained an active businesswoman, buying and selling parcels of land. In some cases she took her claims to court, winning judgments against those owing her money. In 1883, when she was in her sixties and "admonished by disease that my stay on this earth is very limited," she wrote a will to distribute her property, giving her brother William and her brother-in-law Charles Gordon the amount of the debt that each owed her plus an additional $500. Her main bequest looked to the future, as she divided her Licking Run farm among her niece and two nephews, the children of her deceased younger brother. Eliza then gave the remainder of her real estate and personal property to her younger sister, Mary Gordon, who was married but childless. Eliza Beale's thinking about female independence might be evident in the provisions of this will that differentiated between bequests to her sister Mary and to Mary's husband, Charles Gordon. To Eliza's way of thinking, marriage had not made them one, with unitary interests. Mary Gordon, in the will she later wrote, left her property to her husband.[43]

The Beale sisters, Eliza, Mary, and Hannah, illustrate some differing ways that women bequeathed property in the nineteenth century. On the one hand, marriage did not mean cutting all one's ties with one's family of origin. In 1870, Mary and Charles Gordon still lived with her unmarried sisters and brother. Yet companionate marriage increasingly meant that the marital relationship between spouses, in the absence of children, tended to override other considerations of kinship. Thus, both Mary and Hannah chose their husbands as their heirs over other kin, much like childless husbands Colin Clark and William Chambers had done in North Carolina.

For unmarried women, kinship remained especially strong, and their inheritance of property often enabled them to aid their own relatives, male and female. Eliza Beale, for example, loaned money both to her brother and her brother-in-law. This practice continued into the next generation. Seventeen years old at the outbreak of the Civil War, Mary Aurelton Beale, like her Aunt Eliza, never married; also like her Aunt Eliza, she helped her brothers in times of need. In November 1897, she loaned her brother John G. Beale $600, secured by a mortgage

Gaskins (probated 1876), Fauquier County Wills, vol. 35, pp. 283–84, all in FCCC. I found no evidence that any child survived Hannah Beale Gaskins.

43. For examples of Eliza's business activities, see Deed of William and Rebecca Russell to Eliza Beale, Aug. 27, 1879, Fauquier County Deeds, vol. 70, p. 26. Will of Eliza Beale (probated 1883), Fauquier County Wills, vol. 38, pp. 52–53; Will of Mary Catlett Gordon (probated 1892), Fauquier County Wills, vol. 40, pp. 370–71, all in FCCC.

on his interest in 180 acres of land. Seventeen years passed before the mortgage was noted as being fully paid and satisfied.[44]

Mildred P. Marshall, who never married, presents a similar case. Her will, drawn up in 1880 when she was in her mid-fifties, divided her property among her seven brothers and sisters, with nieces and nephews standing in for their deceased parents. She gave her brother Jacquelin the land that she had purchased from him, with the proviso that he hold it in trust for his wife and children. If this land, valued at $6,500, exceeded his one-seventh share, he was to reimburse her estate for the excess. Likewise, she noted that any money that her other brother, William C. Marshall, might owe her at her death should be set against his share of the legacy. After Mildred's death, William drew up a mortgage on his farm to protect the portion of the estate that she bequeathed to his wife and children. Unmarried sisters were able and willing to aid their brothers, but sometimes they carefully balanced this aid with their desire to assist other relatives. Thus they placed property for married women in trust rather than allowing it to be swallowed up by the husband's creditors.[45]

By the late nineteenth century, women as property owners had become a bulwark of the propertied class, helping to bolster husbands or siblings against financial hard times. Individualism and the importance placed on the marital bond meant that some married but childless women bequeathed their property to their husbands rather than their families of origin. Never-married women, however, mainly aided their siblings and nieces and nephews.

After the Civil War, women from the old elite also participated in the female economy. A network to sell or trade household merchandise and handmade items had existed for some time, but seldom had involved women of their class. The transition came more easily to the younger generations than the grande dames, who disliked such transactions. When Sarah F. Carraway sold her carriage for $250 to her brother Samuel S. Biddle, she declared, "'Tis the last article I have to sell and shall feel entirely out [of this business] when that is gone." In contrast, her daughter, Mary Norcott Bryan, who had married just before the war began, regularly created and traded items to aid the family economy. "I made a good deal of money myself of which I was very proud," she noted. In 1865, proceeds from her garden paid her husband's fare to New Bern to look after their real estate interests there—property that for the most part came from

44. Deed of John G. and Susan Beale to Mary A. Beale, Fauquier County Deeds, vol. 89, pp. 27–28, FCCC.

45. Will of Mildred P. Marshall (probated 1882), Fauquier County Wills, vol. 37, p. 331, FCCC.

Mary's inheritance and remained in her name. In 1865, M. E. Hill reported that her mother made a little money selling grapes and wine. While such businesses were common immediately after the war, many continued later in the postwar period. Sarah Bruce reported that a daughter-in-law, the daughter of a wealthy iron manufacturer, "is a great manager[,] buys the family groceries with the proceeds of her dairy & hen house."[46]

Other elite women took in boarders, another traditional female occupation that nevertheless had been rare among their social group. Here, too, second- and third-generation women led the way. Obviously operating a boardinghouse, which involved managerial as well as menial labor, tended to be most successful in a city or town, especially a college town. In 1884, when Louisa Carrington Venable considered moving to Hampden Sydney and taking in boarders, her mother Emma Carrington cautioned her to consider thoroughly the amount of work involved:

> In a pecuniary view, it may be better for you, but when I think of the laborious life you led, when there before, it made me dread it for you. The dear girls will do all in their power to relieve you of all trouble, but you as the head of the establishment have all the responsibility, and care of managing. It almost 'put an end' to you, when you made the experiment, and you were glad to return to the quiet of your own home, you recollect. . . . I hope you may not overrate your strength, and that you may be guided to do what is right. . . . It will be a more pleasant home for your dear daughters, and better for the sons, to be at a good school.

Mary Jones, although in poor health, took in ten boarders to support her family. Her sister Sallie Jones Collins, coping with a husband descending into alcoholism and debility, also opened a boardinghouse in Hillsborough, North Carolina.[47]

Business negotiations, especially those with men of a different social class, seem to have been a greater chore than those economic activities traditionally associated with women. The challenges of business dealings intimidated and perplexed some women. The actions of Jane Iredell Meares, the widow of a rice planter and executor of his estate, illustrate how tentatively women of the second

46. Sarah F. Carraway to Samuel S. Biddle, Nov. 27, 1865, Samuel S. Biddle Papers, Duke; Mary Biddle Norcott Bryan Scrapbook, pp. 157, 169, 191, SHC; M. E. Hill to Harriet Benbury, Oct. 28, 1865, Benbury-Haywood Family Papers, SHC; Sallie Bruce to Morelle Bruce, May 4, 1886, Bruce Family Papers, VHS.
47. Emma Carrington to Louisa Venable, June 13, 1884, Carrington Family Papers, VHS; Anne Cameron to George and Anne Collins, July 29, 1866, Anne Cameron Collins Papers, SHC.

generation sometimes moved in matters of business. Jane found it difficult to demarcate areas of decision making between her and her oldest son. Even in the selection of the house the family would rent, he greatly influenced her. "I was rather premature," she confided to an absent daughter, "in saying we had rented a house but I certainly understood Tom was only waiting my signature to take Mrs. McRae's house. He rather inclines now to the Cowan house, has made an offer for it and is waiting for an answer." Surviving family letters do not reveal whether she willingly let Tom take charge or whether he exerted a male decisiveness she found impossible to resist. Nevertheless, her position appears more that of figurehead than actual family head.[48]

Other women, such as fifty-year-old Ann E. George, already twice widowed, apparently took business dealings in stride, even when negotiating with workmen: "I have employed Mr Linskey to finish the well. He is very high priced, but he does his work well, and in the end it will be better. I certainly need it." Six months later she complained that because of election excitement, "Many things have been neglected. It is all over now, and I hope home duties will receive more attention." Mr. Linskey had not finished the well, and she was looking for another workman. Still, even if Ann George dealt competently with such affairs, she did not seem to enjoy them. Even as she assured her son that she wished him to stay in his distant school, she also told him much help he could be to her with farm and business affairs at home, since "what I can't look after myself, I have to leave to Cons [a freedman], . . . I try to keep together what belongs to us, and that is more than I can do."[49]

Probably the experiences of many widows and single women fell between that of Ann George and Jane Meares. Even if they were competent, like Ann George, they might well seek the aid of male relatives in carrying out their business. Martha Clark, the childless widow of a wealthy planter, conducted some business on her own—corresponding with and interviewing people indebted to her and discussing the sale of lands with neighboring planters. Yet the detailed account of her business affairs she wrote to a nephew seems scarcely comprehensible unless she expected his advice and perhaps even help.

In that letter, Martha ruminated about what to do about the large sums that Thomas P. Devereux, a planter and neighbor, owed her. Somewhat surprised by

48. Jane Meares to Jeannie Meares, Aug. 31, 1875, John and William A. Williams Papers, SHC.
49. Ann E. George to Samuel Hairston, May 4, 1884, Nov. 5, 1884, and Oct. 29, 1884, George Hairston Papers, SHC. For a discussion of the strategies of antebellum widows, see Kirsten E. Wood, " 'The Strongest Ties That Bind Poor Mortals Together': Slaveholding Widows and Family in the Old Southeast," in *Negotiating Boundaries of Southern Womanhood: Dealing with the Powers That Be*, ed. Janet L. Coryell et al. (Columbia, Mo., 2000), 110–34.

a letter from Devereux expressing his fear that she would institute a lawsuit to secure the funds, she told her nephew, William J. Hawkins, that she would not sue Devereux: "As he is a member of the Holy Catholic Church I certainly will never agree to anything being done in my name which would be inconsistent with my duty to God." Martha's language suggests an ambiguous business relationship with her nephew. "I am willing," she told him, "to trust to your better judgement implicitly in all worldly matters—for I see that you are right and I feel have my interest in view." While she pronounced herself "*entirely satisfied* so far" with William's advice, she also reminded him that she would not follow his opinion on all issues. Declaring that she wished he were a church member so that he would understand her motives, Martha argued, "As it is I fear you will be provoked and think like a great many (and justly in most cases) others that [a] woman [is] not fit to do business and perhaps I am as unfit as any, but there is no one to suffer for my mistakes but myself and I would rather have a clear conscience than all the world's gold." She finally advised him in the Devereux matter that he might act as though it were his own money, provided he acted as a church member would. Martha wanted advice, but she insisted on her right to set moral parameters around her business affairs.[50]

Over time Martha Clark allowed another nephew, Walter Clark, a lawyer who later in life would serve on the state supreme court, to negotiate and collect some important large debts. While Walter counseled her as well as carried out her orders, he commonly deferred to her for the actual decisions. Although only his side of the correspondence remains, it is clear that she did not always follow his advice. Over the period of almost a year beginning in March 1877, he reported being unable to collect any rent from the Smith brothers in Halifax County, North Carolina. By June, Clark was advising his aunt that if the Smiths did not pay, "there should be a sale." Yet even though Walter Clark received no money and continued to send prodding letters to Martha, only in January 1878 did she consent to let the properties be advertised for sale. She showed scruples about foreclosing too quickly on her friends and neighbors despite the advice of her financially astute nephews. In the end, her business affairs show considerable independence on her part, although she obviously called on a network of male kin to provide legwork as well as advice in difficult cases. Other elderly widows, such as Emma Carrington, might have depended on male tenants or neighbors to sell products from her plantation. "I have sold, and been paid for a little corn," she reported to a daughter. "The poor people buy corn, but cannot pay,

50. Martha Clark to W. J. Hawkins, Nov. 27, 1867, Hawkins Family Papers, SHC (emphasis in original).

till tobacco is sold, and this has not been in 'order,' to send to market before now."[51]

Some women exploited male relatives and friends as important assets. When Elizabeth L. Stuart wished to sell some of the land she had received from her uncle's estate, she informed another uncle that "there are some others who wish to buy but do not offer the value of it" and assured him that she knew he would. With his renowned liberality and judgment, how could he fail to offer the price she wished? Other unmarried women and widows understood the financial world quite well. When M. E. Hill sagely counseled her cousin about general economic conditions in 1865, she indicated both her knowledge of and her experience with financial institutions and merchants: "I do not believe dear Cousin that notes taken before the war will be repudiated but it will be a long time before we can collect any thing on them, several of the merchants here owed me, and they are willing for me to get what I wish and credit it on their notes, but they will not pay me one cent of money. It will be many a long year before the rail road pays any dividends and the Bank never again."[52]

Other second- and third-generation women, especially the never married, seem to have dealt fairly readily with the business world. When in 1884 Nannie Tunstall of Lynchburg contemplated a trip to Europe with her cousin Virginia Clay, she had already calculated the cost and was quite complaisant about borrowing to finance the trip. Nannie described her and her mother's financial situation: "Tho' *we* apparently are well off in this world's goods, we have in fact very little ready money ever at command. By the time that taxes & insurance are paid and the wear & tear on houses, the bank acct is 'nil.'" Yet Nannie foresaw little difficulty in borrowing: "While you have good property, you have no difficulty in borrowing money on it, and in the event of doing so, you see your way to repayment sooner or later." Because of her close friendship with the elderly Washington banker W. W. Corcoran, Nannie first discussed a loan with him: "Sometime ago, I wrote to him and asked him if he would lend me 1000.00 at a low rate of interest for a year or more—on good security. He replied instantly that he was delighted at the prospect of my trip & wished he could go along with us—that he would lend me the money on one condition— that I should make the note payable—on Judgment Day!" Nannie, however, was willing to do business only on business terms: "Mr. C is the *last* person I

51. Walter Clark to Martha Clark, March 28, June 14, and Sept. 29, 1877, Jan. 12, 19, and 31, 1878, Hawkins Family Papers, SHC; Emma Carrington to Louisa Venable, June 13, 1884, Carrington Family Papers, VHS.

52. Elizabeth L. Stuart to Marshall [Hairston], Jan. 5, [1870], Hairston-Wilson Papers, SHC; M. E. Hill to Harriet Benbury, Oct. 28, 1865, Benbury-Haywood Family Papers, SHC.

would like to borrow from. I may not tell you why—only I must be humored in this. His very generosity doubles my reluctance—and if I were really to borrow a thousand dollars I would prefer to go to a bank at once."[53]

For the proposed European trip, Nannie estimated their expenses at $800 each for a four-month stay. She told Virginia Clay, "I thought then, that if you could make 300 at home & I also that amount—I could borrow a thousand at 5 or 6 pr cent and divide with you—500.00 at 6 per cent would require only 30.00 a year interest and you might be able to work that off, as I shall have to do." Nannie had created a detailed plan, although in the end she borrowed from Corcoran's bank. She secured a loan of $1,000, $500 for herself and $500 for her cousin, to finance their trip. The banker provided a "letter of credit to J. P. Morgan[,] Mr. C's banker in London, who will be our banker on the other side &c. Mr C. has said he will give me a note of personal introduction to Mr. M. & as he is in frequent communication with him—there'll be no trouble." Nannie reassured her cousin about the loan, "You can make your mind easy about return of the money as I will be responsible for the whole amount. I would not borrow more than 500 for you—for when that goes out, I'll share with you or come home. The 500 however is an *inside* calculation, & if you could take *more* it would be better. We don't want to come home before November—five months." In Paris, Nannie Tunstall handled her business affairs with the same aplomb. When she ran short of money, she was quite willing to consult the Parisian bankers: "I did not get a letter of credit but shall go tomorrow early to the bankers here & see if they will advance me any—if not, I shall have to borrow, until I get to London."[54]

The Civil War did not create a revolution for privileged white women in terms of property relations, although some changes emerged. Husbands increasingly trusted wives to settle estates and divide them among their children. Families of the old elite continued to give property to their daughters and to try to protect it against debt. In Virginia, the device of the separate estate had over time convinced many men that women, especially their daughters, sisters, and nieces, had a right to property in general and their inheritances in particular. Perhaps this use of separate estates explains why elite Virginians were so slow to institute the more democratic married women's property laws, which often protected wages as well as legacies.

The most important alteration in postwar privileged women's position re-

53. Nannie Tunstall to Virginia Clay, March 21, 1884, Clement C. Clay Papers, Duke.

54. Nannie Tunstall to Virginia Clay, March 21, April 21, and Oct. 10, 1884, all in Clay Papers, Duke.

garding property—one already in the making before the Civil War—came in parents' treatment of unmarried daughters. As parents uncoupled inheritance from marriage, these single women increasingly came to own property in their own right. No longer dependent on the generosity of siblings, some of the better-heeled of these women, like Eliza Beale, could operate in the business world.

Not only did women, including married women, from the old elite continue to hold property, but they continued to take their role in its transmission quite seriously. They carefully wrote wills that divided their property among their loved ones. In particular, unmarried women used their property holdings to aid their siblings and nieces and nephews. In contrast, some married women from the old elite began to behave more like men in inheritance, giving the spouse a special place over and beyond the family.

Overall, changes were gradual, as some elite women had been involved in property ownership and business dealings before the war. Entrepreneurship had not been a prominent trait of the old Atlantic elite, so it should not be surprising that women did not immediately take the plunge into commercial activity. Still, bad economic conditions convinced many to undertake petty business ventures, from boardinghouses to marketing handmade items. Some women from the old elite continued to rely on male relatives to help with business dealings. At the same time, the younger generation could boast women like Nannie Tunstall, who were comfortable dealing with financial institutions and their own finances. All these changes left male property rights reduced but still predominant. Yet women attempted to protect, build, and pass on their possessions to a new generation.

4

WOMEN AND THE OLD PLANTATION

Chief among the causes of that conservatism which gave tone and color to the life we are considering was the fact that ancient estates were carefully kept in ancient families, generation after generation. If a Virginian lived in a particular mansion, it was strong presumptive proof that his father, his grandfather, and his great-grandfather had lived there before him. . . . To the first-born son went the estate usually, by the will of the father and with the hearty concurrence of the younger sons when there happened to be any such.[1]

In this reminiscence about the antebellum Virginia of his forebears, where he only visited rather than lived, George Cary Eggleston sketched a timeless countryside, one where the landed families remained on ancestral plantations and passed them to succeeding generations. In his vision, possession of the plantations was a male affair; women might be housekeepers, but Eggleston never even considered the possibility that they played a role in plantation ownership or management.

Although Eggleston's idealized vision of the plantation little resembled even antebellum reality, the Civil War and the advent of emancipation greatly affected rural life and families. This chapter explores one particular form of women's property—the plantation and its lands—and determines how they fit into the patterns of planter persistence that emerged after the Civil War. As the last chapter illustrated, Virginia and North Carolina women continued to own, buy, sell, and bequeath land. Although they figured little in Eggleston's reminiscence, women in fact helped to shape the plantation landscape of the rural nineteenth-century South. This chapter examines female views of the postwar plantation, the positions that women held on the plantation, and their relationship to its

1. George Cary Eggleston, *A Rebel's Recollections* (1905; reprint, New York, 1969), 29. See also Page Smith, *Daughters of the Promised Land: Women in American History* (Boston, 1970), ch. 15, which assumed that southern plantations were entailed to oldest sons.

management. A close look at these topics reveals the ambivalent role that women of the old elite played after the Civil War. While they would justifiably become known as conservators of tradition—a role in which some later reveled—a significant minority of women helped to spearhead the flight away from the countryside. White women added new fears about social disorder, centering on the freedmen, to their longstanding dislike of the isolation of plantations. These attitudes diminished white women's willingness to live alone, especially in rural areas, and thus discouraged them from operating plantations.

Such realities notwithstanding, numerous images of southern women's responses to the war abounded in popular literary works and, like Eggleston's, soon hardened into stereotypes. The most persistent one has been that of the penniless, helpless southern belle who looked to marriage and a husband as her only salvation, whether he would regenerate the desolate plantation or simply rescue her from it. Even the twentieth-century novel *Gone with the Wind* is a variant of this hoary conceit, albeit one with a particularly enterprising heroine. Northern army officer John W. De Forest was an early chronicler of this sort of romance. The heroine of his postwar novel *The Bloody Chasm* was Virginia Beaufort, a Carolina beauty who, after all the men in her family die in the war, comes to depend totally on the family's former slaves for food and shelter. De Forest's fellow northern novelist Constance Fenimore Woolson created a similar scenario in her story "Old Gardiston," whose heroine possesses neither the training nor the abilities that would fit her for any business or moneymaking activity. In both these tales, marriage to a northern man rescues a vulnerable heroine who is seemingly incapable of self-support. Likewise, in "Meh Lady," one of Thomas Nelson Page's stories of romantic reunion, marriage to a Union soldier saves a young Virginia woman from a chaotic plantation that had been wrecked by the death of its white men and the end of slavery. All three stories predicated patriarchal support as necessary to southern women. In De Forest's and Woolson's accounts, the northern army officer removes the young woman from the broken-down plantation into his care, while Page suggests that his northern hero (who is half-Virginian) will assume control of the old plantation, thus replacing the southern patriarch with a national one.[2]

When southern female authors created literary images of women on the postwar plantation, their scenarios of decay and renewal were quite different. In

2. John William De Forest, *The Bloody Chasm: A Novel* (New York, 1881); Constance F. Woolson, "Old Gardiston," in *Rodman the Keeper: Southern Sketches* (1880; reprint, New York, 1969), 105–38; Thomas Nelson Page, "Meh Lady: A Story of the War," *In Ole Virginia or Marse Chan and Other Stories* (New York, 1887), 83–142.

M. G. McClelland's novels, such as *Princess,* published in 1886, the plantation continues to limp along, impervious to the efforts of men or women to reconstruct it. Her novella "A Self Made Man," featuring the widowed Mary Randolph, depicts the heroine as being forced to sell part of her Virginia plantation in order to support her two sons. The obligatory marriage, in Mary Randolph's case to an impecunious architect, promises little in the way of redemption for the fading glories of the old homestead. Reviving the plantation seems to lie outside the grasp of any upper-class Virginians; only the industrious lower-class white male protagonist can make it pay. Molly Elliot Seawell also pictured a Virginia Tidewater that lay in tatters of its former glory. In Seawell's novel *Throckmorton,* males such as the feckless General Temple live in ramshackle estates in the countryside, but many women are far more astute economically as well as socially. In her depiction of widow Kitty Sherrard, Seawell created a different model of the privileged Virginia woman:

> According to the usual system in Virginia, during the lifetime of the late Mr. Sherrard there was much frolicking, dancing, and hilarity at Turkey Thicket, the Sherrard place, and a corresponding narrowness of income and general behindhandedness. But since Mr. Sherrard's death Mrs. Sherrard, along with the unvarying and sublime confidence in her husband, dead or alive, that characterizes Virginia women, had yet entirely abandoned Mr. Sherrard's methods. The mortgage on Turkey Thicket had been paid off, the whole place farmed on commonsense principles, and the debts declared inevitable by Mr. Sherrard carefully avoided. As a matter of fact, the only people in the county who paid their taxes promptly were the widows, who nevertheless continually lamented that they were deprived of the great industry, foresight, and business capacity of their defunct lords and masters.

Thus Seawell deftly reversed the stereotype, presenting a situation in which women (usually widows), while praising rather than challenging men, are the quiet powers on the plantations and the economic movers and shakers, responsible for whatever renewal the old plantation areas could muster.[3]

In fact, the old elite, in spite of its loss of wealth, still controlled considerable real estate, and women shared in this property. Even though Eggleston depicted the antebellum plantation as a patriarchal perquisite handed down over the generations from oldest son to oldest son, women too had owned plantations and

3. M. G. McClelland, *Princess* (New York, 1886); idem, "A Self Made Man," *Lippincott's Monthly* 39 (Feb. 1887): 195–284; Molly Elliot Seawell, *Throckmorton: A Novel* (New York, 1890), 41–42.

had overseen their operations, and they continued to do so. Most often, these female owners were widows who had inherited plantations. Some of them might have exhibited the business acumen of a Kitty Sherrard and even a few of them the absolute incompetence of the maidens of northern romancers. Overall, not unexpectedly, their record at successful plantation management was mixed. As indicated in the previous chapter, some wealthy men left their entire property, including plantations, to their wives. Lucy P. Wickham of Hanover County, Virginia, was such a widow, inheriting from her husband the plantation Hickory Hill as well as other properties. In other cases, single women and their married siblings inherited real estate, so that some spinsters came to own plantations. The Cabell sisters of Nelson County, Virginia, for example, were the major heirs of their childless aunt, Sallie Cocke Brent. Dying in 1879, Sallie Brent bequeathed her plantation, Recess, to her unmarried niece and namesake, Sallie Cabell, and the remainder of her real estate to Sallie's married sister, Fannie Cabell Campbell.[4]

Yet ownership and management of plantations did not necessarily overlap completely for women either before or after the Civil War. Some widows and wives of politicians had previously managed the growing and selling of crops, buying of provisions, and the like during the antebellum period, even though they probably had depended on an overseer to supervise the farm labor. Other women, though never actually superintending farm affairs, were at least somewhat acquainted with them. Doubtless the Civil War increased many women's involvement in plantation management, since their sons and husbands were off at war. Carey Pettigrew, of a wealthy Washington County, North Carolina, family, supervised many slaves after she removed them in 1862 to a plantation she and her husband owned in South Carolina.[5]

---

4. Henry Taylor to Lucy Wickham, Sept. 17, 1888, Wickham Family Papers, VHS; Sallie Cabell to Philip B. Cabell, Oct. 15, 1879, and N. Francis Cabell to Philip B. Cabell, Sept. 9, 1879, both in Cabell Family Papers, UVA. For an article that surveys women's land ownership from the colonial period to the present in the United States, see Anne B. W. Effland, Denise M. Rogers, and Valerie Grim, "Women as Agricultural Landowners: What Do We Know about Them?" *Agricultural History* 67 (1993): 235–61.

5. Anne Firor Scott, *The Southern Lady: From Pedestal to Politics, 1830–1930* (Chicago, 1970), 34–35, 81–82, 106–10; Catherine Clinton, *The Plantation Mistress: Woman's World in the Old South* (New York, 1982), 188–96; Orville Vernon Burton, *In My Father's House Are Many Mansions: Family and Community in Edgefield, South Carolina* (Chapel Hill, N.C., 1985), 128–31, 134–46. This role can be related to the much earlier one that Laurel Thatcher Ulrich calls the "deputy husband" in *Good Wives: Image and Reality in the Lives of Women in Northern New England, 1650–1750* (New York, 1987), 36–50. For Pettigrew's experiences, consult Wayne K. Durrill, *War of Another Kind: A Southern Community in the Great Rebellion* (New York, 1990), 83–85,

After the war, some elite women controlled plantations and determined their management. As Orville Vernon Burton has suggested, women heading plantation households tended to be older, often with teenaged or young adult sons. North Carolina elite women who shouldered such responsibility were all at least thirty years old. But how far the management of such women reached and how long it lasted is difficult to ascertain. Sisters Susan Skinner and Mary Mosby in northeastern North Carolina clearly hired and fired farm workers. In November 1865, their brother described them as experiencing some "difficulties" with "darkies." The following spring they had "to discharge a good many and get new ones to work their farms." Yet it remains unclear how far their responsibilities and activities extended and how long they lasted.[6]

Some women might have been reluctant to supervise freedmen. M. E. Hill, a wealthy North Carolina widow, described how her mother, faced with obdurate workers in the fall of 1865, resorted to a Freedmen's Bureau agent to back up her authority. Hill added her own acerbic assessment of African American workers: "They will not work, and will soon eat us out of house and home. Mother intends [to] try to get some white man to hire here and work with the negroes for such a part of the crop, but she has not succeeded in getting one yet, she has been worried no little with the lazy field hands, and once they got so she could not stand them and she wrote to Halifax for the Yankee Officer there who came down and gave them a talk and drove off one, which had a good effect for a while." Here we see a woman of the older generation depending on male intervention to deal with her laborers, although one must remember that southern males similarly complained and called upon the Freedmen's Bureau to deal with field workers. Even though this might recall the avoidance of slave management that historian Drew Gilpin Faust found in one Texas woman's experiences during the Civil War, by this time essential parts of plantation management had changed. Even though managing free labor still meant directing the work of men who might become disgruntled, it no longer involved the threats and impositions of whippings that had been so essential to plantation slavery.[7]

The case of Susan Bullock vividly illustrates the difficulty of discovering the

148–49, 153–56, 162–64; Jane H. Pease and William H. Pease, *A Family of Women: The Carolina Petigrus in Peace and War* (Chapel Hill, N.C., 1999), 154–58.

6. Burton, *In My Father's House,* 134–46; George Little to Sally Hamilton, Nov. 17, 1865, William Tarry Papers, Duke; George Little to Sally Hamilton, May 11, 1866, Bullock-Hamilton Papers, SHC (emphasis in original).

7. M. E. Hill to Harriet Benbury, Oct. 28, 1865, Benbury-Haywood Family Papers, SHC; Drew Gilpin Faust, "'Trying to Do a Man's Business': Slavery, Violence and Gender in the American Civil War" *Gender and History* 4 (summer 1992); Clinton, *Plantation Mistress,* 187–95.

full extent of women's roles in plantation management. At her husband's death in 1866, Susan Bullock had four adult sons (ranging in age from twenty to thirty-nine) who lived either with or near her. She depended on them, especially twenty-four-year-old Austin and twenty-year-old Walter, to oversee many plantation duties, whether dividing the crop, picking up guano at the nearby town, or going to the sawmill. Yet Susan clearly perceived herself as responsible for hiring plantation laborers as well as domestic workers. On February 5, 1867, her diary entry recorded that freedmen Mordecai and John were burning a plant bed in preparation for tobacco planting, and she noted, "They are the only field hands I have hired yet[.] To M. I give 120 dollars to John 80 dollars." In February 1868, she indicated that she had hired Woodson for ten months for sixty dollars. These entries contrast with one written six months later that her son "Walter hired two boys this morning." Susan Bullock also chronicled the work on plantation chores and crops that occurred while her sons were absent. After participating in the decision to buy a new reaper, she mentioned two days later that the hands "commenced cutting wheat this morning with the reaper Austin, Walter & myself bought of Mr C. Handy." While she sometimes clearly differentiated between her crops and her children's, writing of "my tobacco" or "my corn" as distinct from what belonged to one of her sons, she most often mentioned "the" wheat or tobacco, whose ownership was indefinite.[8]

Despite her active role in some areas of plantation management, Susan Bullock seems to have considered the plantation and its productions as merely one part of her life, and not the most significant one. She still grieved over the death of her husband and the loss of his companionship, rather than focusing on her authority in regard to plantation work. Although she never seemed to reject plantation affairs as lying outside her sphere, neither did she seem particularly to savor them. The one change in status that most agitated her was giving up management of her household in 1869 (apparently because of poor health). "The morning corresponds with my feelings, gloomy and sad," she wrote. "After keeping house 44 years last Nov. I give it up this morning and take a side seat at Walter's table." On one level this was largely a symbolic change, for her son Walter and his wife Judith had moved in with her over a year earlier. Although her husband's death and the consequently heavier demands of plantation management might have deeply affected Susan Bullock's daily routine, it was relin-

8. Susan Bullock diary, Jan. 5, April 11, Sept. 8 and 9, and Feb. 5, 1867, Feb. 29 and Aug. 5, 1868, July 15 and 23, 1867, and June 17 and 19, 1868, Bullock-Hamilton Papers, SHC. Compare Bullock's lack of surnames for the freedmen in her diary to the usage of another Carolina planter in Edward A. Crudup diary, Duke.

quishing her role as mistress of the household—symbolized by the seating arrangement at the table—that meant the most to her.[9]

Even in the 1880s, as tenantry was on the rise, some women continued to deal directly with African American labor. In November 1884, widowed Ann George reported, "Only one negro here voted radical and that was Bill Ratcliff[.] John Henry, Cons and John Easter voted democratic and the others all stayed home at work. How they have voted on the other places I don't know. I have hired Cons again." Whether Cons's political allegiances had played a part in his hiring (or an earlier firing) is unclear, but the decisions nonetheless belonged to Ann George.[10]

Single and married women also participated in many plantation decisions. Some managerial wives frequently expressed their opinions on numerous aspects of plantation life. Marietta Minnigerode left a detailed description of one such woman, her aunt, Ida Dulany of Oakley in Fauquier County. At Oakley, a plantation where "everyone rose in the morning according to his own sweet will," Ida was the exception: "She was early about her business, supervising a large farm and establishment." In her case, being "ladylike" does not seem to have undercut her authority. While pointing out that Ida Dulany never raised her voice, Marietta Minnigerode emphasized that she "spoke in determined and authoritative tones which left no room for argument." Ida's skills and knowledge were similarly wide-ranging; she "knew all about raising corn and planting wheat and breeding stock and poultry; she knew all about the care of forests, and the proper conservation of timber; she knew all about fertilizers and manure and guano, she knew all about building stone walls and rail fences; she knew all about cooking and preserving and sewing and gardening; and she knew all about God." Ida Dulany, concluded her awed niece, was a "remarkable woman."[11]

In Ida Dulany's case, having a "drinking" husband might have encouraged her to exercise her managerial propensities, but other Virginia wives similarly

9. Ibid., Jan. 1, 1869, and Dec. 6, 1869.

10. Ann E. George to Samuel Hairston, Nov. 5, 1884, George Hairston Papers, SHC. On the rise of sharecropping and black and white tenancy, see Gavin Wright, *Old South, New South: Revolutions in the Southern Economy since the Civil War* (New York, 1986), 81–115; Roger Ransom and Richard Sutch, *One Kind of Freedom: The Economic Consequences of Emancipation* (Cambridge, Eng., 1977), 88–105; Jeffrey R. Kerr-Ritchie, *Freedpeople in the Tobacco South: Virginia, 1860–1900* (Chapel Hill, N.C., 1999), 31–69, 157–80; Lynda Morgan, *Emancipation in Virginia's Tobacco Belt, 1850–1870* (Athens, Ga., 1992).

11. Marietta Minnigerode Andrews, *Memoirs of a Poor Relation: Being the Story of a Post-war Southern Girl and Her Battle with Destiny* (New York, 1927), 63–64. For Hal Dulany's problems with alcohol, consult Margaret Ann Vogtsberger, *The Dulanys of Welbourne: A Family in Mosby's Confederacy* (Berryville, Va., 1995), 181.

assumed an interest and a voice in plantation affairs. When elderly Ann Hairston's husband Marshall was away in Mississippi, Ann advised him on a multitude of issues and gave him a good dose of plantation news. In 1869, she asked her daughter to "tell your father to hurry through his matters there and hasten home; his little mill here will afford him as much pleasant recreation here as his cotten patches there." Because it was "utterly impossible to obtain reliable Overseers," Ann Hairston complained that it would be a "loosing [sic] business to settle the bottom Farm yet." She declared with some asperity, "I cannot think of a man of my acquaintance that would make labourers work. I think we have reasons to believe in a few more years that class of people as well as the labouring class, will learn they have to work or starve. Your Father so far as I am capable of judging from what I hear[,] is doing better renting his lands here than anyone I know in this county working their own lands." Plantation matters were nothing new for Ann Hairston; she had been responsible for updating the plantation register of slaves for three decades.[12]

While some elite women controlled hiring and set wages for freedmen, others remained aloof from direct supervision of plantation labor. Lucy P. Wickham, a second-generation widow, expected her sons to manage the family's plantation enterprises. Soon after her husband's death in 1886, she declared herself a novice at business: "I have never been in the habit of any kind of management. I don't know any thing about money or trying to live comfortably." Yet even with this attitude, she also freely expressed her ideas about business affairs, beginning with a critique of the plantation: "In the first place the farm is an elephant. As far as I know & believe it has never paid the expense of cultivating it." She admitted that she opposed opening a dairy there "because of the difficulty of getting skilled labor and the risk," but she relented when her son William "set his heart on it." Lucy's trepidations apparently were justified, for after several unsuccessful years her son, William F. Wickham, arranged for the plantation to be leased by his brother, Henry T. Wickham, who would pay all expenses and taxes and divide the profits with his mother. However, after a year of this arrangement, Henry declined another year's lease unless his mother agreed to make capital improvements.[13]

Some younger widows as well as older ones leaned on the help of male rela-

12. Ann H. Hairston to Bettie Hairston, Dec. 8, 1869, Hairston-Wilson Papers, SHC. On Ann Hairston and her husband Marshall, consult Henry Wiencek, *The Hairstons: An American Family in Black and White* (New York, 1999), 54–70.

13. Lucy P. Taylor Wickham, "Memorandum of Dec. 10, 1889," Henry Taylor to Lucy P. Taylor Wickham, Sept. 1, 1892, and Henry T. Wickham to Lucy Wickham, July 6, 1893, all in Wickham Family Papers, VHS.

tives or hired managers to supervise workers directly. M. E. Hill planned to rent out her plantation in Mississippi for 1866 and hoped to sell it. She told her widowed cousin, Harriet Benbury, "I am not astonished to hear you say you intend renting out your plantation, I would not be bothered with negroes now, any more than was absolutely necessary." In 1866, Jane Hawkins, a thirty-six-year-old unmarried woman in Franklin County, put both contracting and management in male hands. An agreement for that year with fifteen male freedmen obligated them to work "on the plantation of Miss J. A. Hawkins and in the charge" of Brownfield Clarke. This contract specified monthly wages but did not indicate who would pay them.[14]

After 1870, as most plantations moved from wage labor toward sharecropping and renting, women's attitudes toward management might have become more favorable. The problems of labor would, at the least, be greatly reduced under these systems. Although white men also enjoyed the lack of supervision involved in the rise of various forms of tenantry, these new forms of management allowed women of the old elite to run plantations without overseeing labor in the field. By 1885, widowed Ann Downey Davis of Granville County, North Carolina, was having her tobacco grown by a renter, and she might have been a fairly typical case. The old landed elite often resorted to securing tenants, even in areas like Fauquier County where otherwise tenantry was not widespread.[15]

In Charlotte County, Virginia, widowed Emma Carrington operated her plantations for some years using tenants, but she still retained numerous responsibilities. First of all, she had to secure and dismiss the tenants. In October 1882, she was preparing for a new tenant: "I am to have a new tenant on the upper plantation, and have some arrangements to make for him. He is now here putting in wheat." But Emma Carrington was quite ready, when dissatisfied, to summarily dismiss her tenant. In December 1884, she told a daughter that she was "about to get rid of my present tenant, who has proved a most unsatisfactory one. I hope the one engaged may do better. He is highly recommended by Mr Rice and others."[16] Moreover, Carrington's offhand comments about what her tenants had told her about the crops and other neighborhood news suggest frequent consultations with them. Certainly she was well aware of the rhythms and demands of farm work. One October she determined that neither she nor her unmarried daughter would make any visits because "there is a great deal to do

14. M. E. Hill to [Harriet Benbury], Oct. 28, 1865, Benbury-Haywood Family Papers, SHC; "Agreement with Brownfield Clark," Hawkins Family Papers, SHC.

15. John Downey to Ann Downey Davis, Feb. 9, 1885, Samuel S. Downey Papers, Duke.

16. Emma Carrington to Louisa Venable, Oct. 27, 1882, and Dec. 1, 1884, Carrington Family Papers, VHS.

here and my horses and driver will be fully occupied in hauling up corn &c from the low grounds, before the roads become bad." With the advice of her friends and neighbors elderly Emma Carrington continued to make decisions about cultivation.[17]

Some third-generation women took part in plantation business affairs. Fanny Cooke, granddaughter of John Young Mason, made the arrangements for a sale of timber on a tract called Avents in 1893 at fifteen cents a cord. She enlisted her uncle Lewis Mason's aid in getting an estimate of the kind and amount of the timber and ascertaining the family's title to the property. Early in 1894 she described her activities: "I am hammering away at my trade & will do my utmost to make a sale."[18]

Although some women were involved in all spheres, most plantation women of the old elite understood their activities as typically overseeing dairy, poultry, and gardening departments, while men made decisions about livestock, crops, and general maintenance. While these divisions had existed before the Civil War, women from the old elite showed a greater interest during the postwar period in the moneymaking potential of their part of the plantation. Many of these plantation-based enterprises seem to have been large-scale versions of the kinds of activities that women in white yeoman families had long undertaken. For example, according to Thomas Watson in 1883, his wife and daughter successfully raised poultry on Bracketts, their Louisa County, Virginia, farm. In addition to their ducks and geese, they oversaw one hundred young turkeys and three to four hundred chickens. His daughter Sally was the driving force behind the trade in fowls. "Sally sells a great many eggs too, and she is pretty keen at a bargain, I think," Thomas proudly recounted. "I wanted two chickens to send to an old negro who used to belong to us, now bedridden, and I had to pay her 25 cts apiece for them." He noted that she "carried on a brisk trade & did a good business this last spring in Hens that were ready to begin incubation."[19]

Sarah Hubard of Buckingham County, Virginia, depended on her production of vinegar to buy various household necessities as well as to refurbish the wardrobe of her marriageable daughter. Similarly, after her marriage in 1874, Jeanette Ryland Gwathmey of King William County, Virginia, sold butter and chickens to acquaintances in Richmond. One of her customers declared the last

17. Emma Carrington to Louisa Venable, July 21 and Oct. 27, 1882, Carrington Family Papers, VHS.

18. Fanny Cooke [Jr.] to Lewis E. Mason, Dec. 15 and 19, 1893, Jan. 15, 1894, Mason Family Papers, VHS.

19. Thomas Watson to Sally Johnston and Julia Holladay, June 15, 1883, Latané Family Papers, UVA.

shipment of butter "simply perfect" and added, "My two neighbors and myself would gladly divide another dozen chickens if you have them."[20]

Although some women from the old elite worked hard to maintain family holdings, a considerable number of the old families left the plantation districts of North Carolina and Virginia after the Civil War. A small but significant part of the gentry had seen their plantation mansions destroyed during the war. The number of houses razed was larger in Virginia, where so many battles raged, than in North Carolina, which remained largely untouched by war. Ironically, Virginians, who had been among the most reluctant secessionists, were among the most likely southerners to have had ravaged plantations. Destruction was heaviest in and near the James River peninsula, Fredericksburg, Richmond, Petersburg, and parts of the Shenandoah Valley. Robert E. Lee and his family stood among the largest losers; the national government confiscated Mary Custis Lee's childhood home, Arlington House, and turned it into an enormous cemetery for the Union dead. Union soldiers also burned White House, a Lee family property located on the Pamunkey River, during the Seven Days battles of 1862. Other elite Virginians experienced similar losses. Jennie Friend later recalled the shock of her first trip back to her family plantation, White Hill, near Petersburg: "Now all was desolation. . . . Quarters, barns, overseer's house, out houses, and fencing were all gone. Farm roads obliterated and army roads made instead. All appearance of a domestic habitation gone." She was struck particularly hard by the fate of their once beautifully tended home: "The gaping, eyeless frame of a big house, porchless, doorless, windowless stood before us. Within could be seen battered walls, falling partitions, and within and without, the thickly strewn debris of army life, such as pieces of garments, canteens, shot and shell."[21]

In other cases, Virginians and Carolinians lost their plantations and other lands only after the war. Once slave property was gone and real estate prices became depressed, debts that had been accumulated in the antebellum period became overwhelming. Before the war, the extended Smith family of Scotland Neck had been one of Halifax County, North Carolina's richest clans, but these

20. Josephine to Jeannette Gwathmey, June 18, n.d., Gwathmey Family Papers, VHS. In this case the customer was paying a total of $7.80 for a dozen chickens ($4.80) and ten pounds of butter.

21. Paul C. Nagel, *The Lees of Virginia: Seven Generations of an American Family* (New York, 1990), 269–70, 286, 292–93; Emory M. Thomas, *Robert E. Lee: A Biography* (New York, 1995), 230, 239; Jennie F. Stephenson, "My Father and His Household, before, during and after the War" (unpub. ms., April 1897), 40–41, Blanton Family Papers, VHS. See also David F. Allmendinger, *Ruffin: Family and Reform in the Old South* (New York, 1990), 162–64, about the Ruffin family's losses at Beechwood and Marlborough in Prince George County, Virginia.

families tottered on the verge of bankruptcy in the immediate postwar period. In that same county, wealthy lawyer Thomas P. Devereux, who had inherited several plantations from a wealthy unmarried uncle, was forced to declare bankruptcy and lost Conneconara plantation.[22]

Although the wealthiest southerners appeared rooted compared to the wanderings of the young and landless, the nineteenth century had long seen much geographical mobility among elite families. Even among the prosperous, western investments beckoned, and sons and daughters moved away. Careers, marriages, and living preferences all sometimes led to a certain amount of flow into and out of home counties. Before the Civil War, Thomas Devereux's son, John Devereux, and his Raleigh-born wife divided their time between Runiroi plantation in Bertie County and a large house in the capital city.[23]

The Civil War made such a lifestyle, divided between rural plantation and town residence, impossible. As straitened circumstances came to rule, some families were marooned on the rural family property; others gravitated toward the cities. Women of the old elite often did not regret these urban relocations. While twentieth-century popular fiction tends to dwell on the affection of aristocrats for their ancestral acres, the attitudes of nineteenth-century privileged women toward plantations were far more ambivalent.[24]

Studies of southern locales as diverse as east Texas, central Virginia, and blackbelt Alabama have argued that the persistence of the gentry was much the same after the war as before it, but this observation misses important differences between the antebellum and postwar periods.[25] Geographical mobility had been

22. Claiborne Thweatt Smith Jr., *Smith of Scotland Neck: Planters on the Roanoke* (Baltimore, 1976), 99–119; Walter Clark to Martha Clark, March 28, June 14, and Sept. 29, 1877, Jan. 12, 19, and 31, 1878, Hawkins Family Papers, SHC. Beth G. Crabtree and James W. Patton, eds., *"Journal of a Secesh Lady": The Diary of Catherine Ann Devereux Edmondston, 1860–1866* (Raleigh, 1979), xxiii–xxvii.

23. Crabtree and Patton, eds., *"Journal of a Secesh Lady"*, xxi-xxvii.

24. See Steven M. Stowe, "City, Country, and the Feminine Voice," in *Intellectual Life in Antebellum Charleston*, ed. Michael O'Brien and David Moltke-Hansen (Knoxville, Tenn., 1986), 295–334, for a discussion of how such elite women as Susan Petigru King and Mary Boykin Chesnut were pessimistic about the countryside.

25. For examples of studies of the persistence of landed elites before and after the Civil War, see Randolph Campbell, "Population Persistence and Social Change in Nineteenth-Century Texas: Harrison County, 1850–1860," *JSH* 48 (May 1982): 185–204; A. Jane Townes, "The Effect of Emancipation on Large Landholdings, Nelson and Goochland Counties, Virginia," *JSH* 45 (Aug. 1979): 403–12; Jonathan Wiener, "Planter Persistence and Social Change: Alabama, 1850–1870," *Journal of Interdisciplinary History* 7 (autumn 1976): 235–60. A study with a longer timespan is Roger Shugg, "The Survival of the Plantation System in Louisiana," *JSH* 3 (Aug. 1937): 311–25. In general the studies of geographical persistence of city dwellers and the landless have stressed the

high before the war, but among the elite it had focused on agriculture, as ante-bellum planters had left the Southeast to seize new, untapped farm lands. The agricultural economy of much of the antebellum South had been robust; with the exception of a roughly five-year period in the late 1830s and early 1840s, cotton prices had been excellent. Large profits on the southwestern frontier beckoned to the owners of many slaves. Cotton growing, even in eastern North Carolina and the Charlotte area, had exploded during the 1850s. While tobacco, corn, and wheat prices never reached the boom levels of cotton, planters could generally count on good returns during the middle decades of the nineteenth century. In contrast, agriculture in the postwar South lurched from crisis to crisis, as commodity prices dipped ever lower and land values stagnated. Postwar migration by the old elite largely stemmed from a desire to escape the plantation rather than the antebellum plan to move it to newer, richer lands.[26]

Moreover, scholars comparing prewar and postwar elite persistence have generally focused on the period immediately following the war. This most likely overstates postwar elite persistence, for it appears that many planters gave agricultural life a brief try only to abandon it in a few years. In 1872, Judith Page Rives commented about Albemarle County, Virginia: "Our neighbors seem to be selling out, at least many of the places around us are offered. Dr Meriwether, Dickinson's[,] Mr Minor, Dr Hancock and others. You have probably heard that Carlton is to be sold in May—the proprietor thereof smashed completely." The flight from these plantations seems to have continued into the agriculturally depressed eighties and nineties. In 1889, Sallie Bruce, surveying Charlotte County, Virginia, from her mansion Staunton Hill, lamented the retreat of the gentry from the countryside: "All the ladies and gentlemen are disappearing from this country and in 20 years there will be none left in this section I am sure—it makes me sad to realize this melancholy fact."[27]

In this depressed era, women would be in the vanguard of hostility to plantation living and agricultural pursuits. Sue Hubard, despite the family's holdings

---

mobility of these groups. See Peter Knights, *The Plain People of Boston: A Study in City Growth* (New York, 1971).

26. Joan E. Cashin, *A Family Venture: Men and Women on the Southern Frontier* (New York, 1991), 59–60, 91–98; Jane Turner Censer, "Southwestern Migration among North Carolina Planter Families: 'The Disposition to Migrate,'" *JSH* 57 (Aug. 1991): 407–26; Christopher Morris, *Becoming Southern: The Evolution of a Way of Life, Warren County and Vicksburg, Mississippi, 1770–1860* (New York, 1995), 40–41, 156–68.

27. That the federal census of 1870 was the last to give the value of land belonging to those individuals enumerated may be one reason that many studies of economic and geographic persistence use that date as an endpoint. Judith Rives to [W. C. Rives Jr.], March 31, 1872, William C. Rives Papers, LC; Sallie Bruce to Morelle Bruce, April 8, 1887, Bruce Family Papers, VHS.

in Buckingham County, Virginia, was openly contemptuous of rural life. During a visit to Baltimore, she attended a concert during Lent, but she justified her behavior by pointing to the monotony of rural life: "As it is Lent of course a great many people will not go to places of amusement but I tell them we have Lent in Buckingham all the year round & I can't think it a great harm to see a little pleasure when I am in town." A decade later, after her father's death, Sue Hubard suggested that her mother live in Washington or Baltimore and take in boarders. She ridiculed her brothers' reservations about the plan: "I think the boys' idea about boarders is the most utter nonsense. The very best people here are glad enough to get them. I have no sympathy with any such pride. I think it is not only foolish but sinful." Denouncing life in the countryside, Sue declared that she would "never consent to go back to such a life of poverty & humiliation." Even though she was unsure of her own future, she was certain that she wanted her mother to join her in the city.[28]

For those who sought a rich cultural life and intellectual work, the towns and cities became enormously appealing. In 1888, Virginia Hankins, who had grown up at Bacon's Castle in Surrey County, Virginia, explained to her brother why living in Baltimore made her so happy: "I prefer living in a city[,] have church privileges and can watch the world go round. I enjoy going to the opera and theatre and have a plenty of books to read." While Virginia Hankins stressed the advantages of the city, other women focused on the disadvantages of the countryside, which sometimes seemed a boring, barren wasteland. Although Frances Christine Fisher used the proceeds from her writings to maintain the family plantation home, which she dubbed "Castle Rackrent," she believed that living in North Carolina hindered her literary work. In 1872, she wrote that she yearned "for the liberty that a great city brings in its manners and customs. In truth, I pine for a city as exiles are said to pine for their native air. As a pure matter of taste, I cannot bear the provinces, and as a matter of business it is a serious bar to my success, being here. If I had only had myself to consider, I should have shaken my native dust forever off of my feet long ago—but it has been a question of duty which has kept and still keeps me here." Frances Christine Fisher made careful calculations whether she could afford either New York or London. Two years later, she told her friend Paul Hayne, "Since my visit to New York I am more than ever anxious—if that be possible—to leave this place. There is nothing, absolutely nothing, to keep me here. The climate is horrible, and we have not one single advantage of any kind. If I had only myself to con-

---

28. Sue Hubard to Sarah Hubard, March 5, 1869, and April 20, [c. 1879?], Hubard Family Papers, SHC.

sider I should go to New York at once, but my aunt—unfortunately for herself as well as for me—will not consent to that, so I scarcely know where else to turn." She dismissed the idea of Baltimore or other southern cities: "You know what the Southern cities are—mere large towns, pleasant enough socially, but without any save social culture, and unhealthy besides." Yet she worried that London would be overly expensive and she would have to begin anew to create a literary reputation. Frances Christine Fisher never left for London, but a late marriage (in her forties) to a mining engineer led to her extended residence in the Southwest and Mexico before she returned, as an elderly widow, to her native Salisbury.[29]

Even women without the cultural and literary aspirations of a Sue Hubard, Virginia Hankins, or Frances Christine Fisher preferred town or city life to the plantation. Some, like Rosa Biddle, who had grown up on a Craven County, North Carolina, cotton plantation, complained of a dependence on agricultural cycles. In 1879 she told her fiancé, a bank officer, "I have no faith in cotton, have all my life been dependent upon it & when I thought of going to Charlotte, it was a relief to me that I would not immediately be connected with it." For others, the location of plantations and their lack of social life made the country-side unappealing. Mary Biddle's adult offspring thought that her experiences while a refugee from their plantation during the Civil War had left her less tolerant of life in rural North Carolina: "Ma does not fancy Fort Barnwell very much after living near Louisburg. I guess she finds it rather lonely." Carey Pettigrew's sons worked hard to rescue the family plantations at Lake Scuppernong, North Carolina, from debt, but her five daughters, she wrote, wanted to get away: "Naturally enough the girls get tired of living down here, the neighborhood is very narrow, the associations common! common!" Sarah Hubard, faced with her daughter's frequent visits to Richmond and Baltimore, admitted that she wished their Buckingham County plantation "was in a more pleasant location or near a city—the country is quite attractive with 'its garb of green': but we have no society & but for our home circle it would be devoid of interest."[30]

Women of varying ages applauded the movement away from the old planta-

29. Virginia Hankins to Louis Hankins, April 19, 1888, Hankins Family Papers, VHS; Frances Christine Fisher to Paul Hamilton Hayne, June 19, 1872, and June 6, 1874, Paul Hamilton Hayne Papers, Duke; Edwin Anderson Alderman et al., eds., *Library of Southern Literature,* 15 vols. (New Orleans, 1907–10).

30. Rosa Biddle to S. P. Smith, June 22, 1879, and Mary Bryan to Rosa Biddle, Jan. 28, 1866, Samuel S. Biddle Papers, Duke; Carey Pettigrew to William S. Pettigrew, June 6, 1880, Pettigrew Family Papers, SHC; Sarah A. Hubard to Sue Hubard, May 10, 1870, Hubard Family Papers, SHC.

tions and sometimes attempted to engineer it. Even during the Civil War, Mary Ann Mosby, then in her fifties, confided to a niece that she wished that her husband had sold their plantation in eastern North Carolina: "I have seen so much trouble at this place and so little society that I am really anxious that Mr M should sell it and pay his debts with the money." In 1872, Sarah Hubard rejoiced that her husband seemed likely to sell their lands to an English buyer: "It would be for the best as I could never be happy on a farm unable to contribute to the advancement of my children and they scattered over the country." Sarah Bruce Seddon gossiped to her sister-in-law about a Richmond family, "Mr Stanard is bent on selling his place & settling in Gloucester, & his wife is equally opposed." Similarly, when Mary T. Meares reported in 1875 that her husband was "very anxious" to sell his upcountry Carolina plantation, she added, "We all find plantation life *very dull*—Sundays to me are particularly long and dreary."[31]

While widows such as Josephine Loftin in New Hanover County, North Carolina, tried to sell her "fine body of land," younger married women also tried to avoid the old plantations. Anne Cameron Collins helped to convince her husband not to repurchase any of the lands at Lake Scuppernong where the Collins family plantation, Somerset Place, was located. George Collins reluctantly agreed about the financial riskiness of such a commitment and assured her that he "would be extremely unwilling to do anything in which I would not have your hearty approval & cooperation which I would not have." The compromise the Collinses found—George managed her father's Mississippi plantations while Anne stayed in North Carolina—created long separations, but it did not strand Anne on a remote plantation. No doubt Anne Cameron Collins agreed with the neighboring Pettigrew family about the lack of agreeable social life. Many women found the confinement of the postwar plantation worsened by the lack of money to finance visits to town or city.[32]

To be sure, women still tolerated and sometimes even chose rural life for various reasons, many of which were economic. Susan Polk Rayner, descended from the wealthy North Carolina Polk family, acquiesced when her lawyer-politician husband, Kenneth Rayner, decided after the Civil War to migrate to Memphis, Tennessee, near the Mississippi cotton plantations he had purchased. The venture went belly up, and Kenneth Rayner, ill and depressed, declared bankruptcy

31. Mary A. Mosby to Sally Hamilton, March 17, 1864, William Tarry Papers, Duke; Sarah A. Hubard to Sue Hubard, March 11, 1872, Hubard Family Papers, SHC; Sally B. Seddon to Sallie Bruce, Oct. 26, [c. 1868], Bruce Family Papers, VHS; Mary T. Meares to Fred Meares, March 20, 1875, William B. Meares Papers, SHC.

32. Josephine E. Loftin to Charles W. Dabney, Oct. 23, 1883, Hawkins Family Papers, SHC; George P. Collins to Anne Cameron Collins, Feb. 8, 1874, Anne Collins Papers, SHC.

in 1868. Although for almost thirty years Susan Rayner had been refusing to spend summers on the North Carolina plantation they had owned, she boldly checked out various pieces of land. In 1869, without consulting her husband, she used the remainder of her own legacies to buy a farm south of Memphis in Desoto County, Mississippi, where she moved her family. Still, to Susan Rayner, the plantation merely was a way station, not a permanent home. After the Rayners recouped their finances, Kenneth received a government appointment to the Alabama Claims Commission in 1874, and they then moved to Washington, D.C.[33]

By the 1880s and 1890s new problems in the countryside compounded for many the isolation and poor social life of the plantation. In 1887, when middle-aged Adeline Carrington faced a decision about the family plantation, Ridgeway, she turned to her neighbor and kinsman, Charles Bruce. With the decline in commodity prices, the plantation was not raising enough to pay its expenses and interest on its debts, even as the death of Adeline's brother meant that his estate would begin to demand interest on the mortgage he had held on Ridgeway. While Adeline called it a "very great trial to us, even to *think* of parting with a place so endeared to us by the tender associations of a life-time," she argued that her mother's "growing infirmities and increasing difficulties of the times, with the loss of her eldest son (the only person to whom she could look in emergency, for substantial aid), all of these things, combine, to render this more and more an undesirable home for us." Adeline's avowed attachment to the house appears rather formulaic and unconvincing compared with the disadvantages she listed. Decrying their "lonely and unprotected condition" and "isolation from all privileges," Adeline deemed her home "scarcely more than a comfortable prison!" Declaring that there were "very few,—scarcely more than two or three ties left to us in our old neighborhood," Adeline asked Charles Bruce to help her find a buyer:

> If we could only exchange this home—where we are harassed by a thousand cares—for a few plain *rooms* in Rich[mon]d, with an income even of the *smallest*, compatible with comfortable subsistence, we would esteem it a most blessed consummation; for then my precious old Mother could enjoy the society of her brothers, & sister, and her little grandchildren, and go to church, sometimes, and spend the evening of her days, in tranquillity and peace! Oh my dear Cousin, if you will help me to effect this, I will bless you for the rest of my life!

33. Gregg Cantrell, *Kenneth and John B. Rayner and the Limits of Southern Dissent* (Urbana, Ill., 1993), 49–58, 152–60, 313, explores the Rayners' marriage and the wealth Susan Polk brought to it.

In Adeline's opinion, this state of affairs had been looming for many years. The low price of real estate, however, had kept them in a holding pattern, deferring sale: "We thought that while real estate in this section, was so low, we would have to sacrifice *more* in selling, than the accumulation of interest would amount to!"[34]

This dislike of the impoverished social life of plantations converged with another postwar social phenomenon—a growing fear of African Americans, especially African American men. Black men were leaving elite white households, and over time whites grew suspicious of the African American presence in the countryside. Increasingly, whites deemed blacks to be threatening. During Reconstruction and later, white conservative newspapers magnified any incidents of crime or violence as part of a growing lawlessness among blacks. In the decades after the war, white women became increasingly uneasy about living alone or without white males in the household. This had not always been the case; during the antebellum period, some white widows showed little fear about remaining alone on isolated plantations. Wealthy Ruth Hairston of Pittsylvania County, Virginia, provides an example. Her grandson Peter W. Hairston described an antebellum visit with her: "I rode up to Berry Hill to see Grand Mama. I found her entirely alone with a large black cat sitting at her feet. She told me that she remained ten days at a time without seeing a single white person when the weather was very bad." Peter dined with her and returned home; another visit three days later again found her alone. Other widows similarly lived in isolation with only their slaves to keep them company.[35]

The Civil War marked a transition period for such a discourse of fear, as disorder appeared to white plantation families to be more the rule. Certainly some women of the old elite grew more timid as both rumors and newspaper reports created the perception that law and order were breaking down. Yet even in the early postwar period, many white women continued to live alone on the plantation. Late in 1865, Ann Rutherfoord described her life on the plantation with her nine-year-old daughter and six-year-old son: "My life at this season is especially lonely for I shall be here until sometime in January without a white person on the place but myself and little children. We have lately been sur-

34. Adeline M. Carrington to Charles Bruce, [c. 1886–87], Bruce Family Papers, VHS (emphasis in original).

35. Peter W. Hairston diary, Dec. 24 and 27, [1851], SHC. For an example of another rather isolated widow, see John Hammond Moore, ed., *A Plantation Mistress on the Eve of the Civil War: The Diary of Keziah Goodwyn Hopkins, 1860–1861* (Columbia, S.C., 1993).

rounded by snow and ice but when I can arrange everything here for the coming year I shall go to Richmond to see Ma."[36]

For some women from the old elite, overt racism and a dislike of living among blacks seem to have fueled their distaste for the plantation. For Charlotte Carrington, in Charlotte County, Virginia, in 1870, visits to town were respites from her plantation, which she characterized as "this 'New Africa,' this vale of tears, this Poverty Hollow." Reports that reached women both personally and through the newspapers bred a growing paranoia that helped to push them away from the countryside.[37]

Not surprisingly, 1868—a year of political changes and the enfranchisement of the freedmen—made rural whites uneasy about the state of the social order and prone to fears of possible uprisings or black disorder. In a letter written that year, L. J. Crenshaw opined, "Robbing is quite fashionable these days of Republicanism." She reported that not only had a local doctor in their section of eastern North Carolina been terrorized by a group of thieves, but also that "Cousin Sally Hicks was treated in the same manner, some have been arrested in her case but no decision yet." That same year in rural Granville County, North Carolina, Susan Bullock worried about the behavior and activities among African American workers, including her own employees. When a cousin's house burned, many believed that his servants had started the conflagration. Susan anticipated other incidents as well. Watching her corn being gathered, she gave vent to her frustrations: "[I] find a great deal stolen from the fields by the negroes, they steal from us so much *God* only knows how we are to live among them." Only a month later she declared, "Nelly and Jane had their trial for barn-burning and were cleared[.] came home last night." That these cases lacked a clear-cut culprit and resolution seems to have added to Bullock's distrust of African Americans.[38]

Over time, even self-possessed dowagers such as Judith Page Rives became more conscious of being isolated on the plantation. In 1865, Rives pooh-poohed rumors of a possible insurrection among the former slaves in Albemarle County,

36. Ann S. Rutherfoord to [William C. Rives?], Dec. 22, [1865], Rives Papers, LC.

37. Charlotte Carrington to Maria Louisa Carrington, March 16, 1870, Saunders Family Papers, VHS.

38. L. J. Crenshaw to Mary Biddle, Oct. 1, 1868, Samuel S. Biddle Papers, Duke; Susan Bullock diary, Aug. 8, Nov. 12, and Dec. 11, 1868, John Bullock-Charles E. Hamilton Papers, SHC. See Gail Williams O'Brien, *The Legal Fraternity and the Making of a New South Community, 1848–1882* (Athens, Ga., 1986), 124–25, on one North Carolina newspaper's "steady stream" of articles on black crime in 1868.

Virginia: "I cannot see what these creatures could gain but 'harm and loss' from such an attempt, and ignorant as they are, I think they have more sense than to make it." Ten years later she reported that she and her unmarried daughter Ella were the "only people in the neighborhood who have not a man in the house."[39]

The younger generations of women from the old elite became more easily intimidated, both in town and on the plantation. White men encouraged their fears. In 1872 in Wilmington, Kate Meares told her son that because she had no servant, "Grandpa didn't like me [to] stay on the lot by myself." Over a decade later, she justified a niece staying with her: "I don't know what I'd do without her as my present maid doesn't sleep on the lot." Similarly, in Washington, Georgia, Fanny Andrews, who lived a mile away from the female seminary where she taught, confided to her diary in 1871 that "though I have a pretty path through the woods that shortens the distance nearly one half, I never dare to walk it alone, for fear of stray niggers." Fanny made it clear that rumors had fueled this fear in her: "One hears so many dreadful things of them now, that I would sooner meet a lion in a lonely place, than a 'nigger fellow.'"[40]

To be sure, some white men themselves had become increasingly uneasy with African American workers. William Clark, who had grown up on large plantations in Beaufort County, North Carolina, expressed such feelings in a depressed letter that he wrote his sister-in-law. Unfortunately Clark omitted the year from his heading, but the letter was written between 1869 and 1886, probably either in 1875 or 1880. Describing his field workers as "drawn from every part of the country," he characterized them as "uncontrollable . . perfectly wild." Declaring that the weather had been so bad that he merely wished to cover his expenses, Clark continued, "I never felt in all my life so desolate as I do now. Before the war I felt safe at home with the old family negroes around me; and many of whom would have periled their lives for me, but they have changed with the times." Now, Clark concluded, neither did he have confidence in his workers nor did he feel safe.[41]

By the late 1880s, the language of "protection" had begun to permeate writ-

39. Judith P. Rives to Sadie Rives, Dec. 7, 1865, and Judith P. Rives to [William C. Rives Jr.], March 20, 1875, both in Rives Papers, LC.

40. Kate Meares to Louis H. Meares, Aug. 5, 1872, and Kate Meares to Richard A. Meares, July 30, 1884, both in Meares-DeRosset Family Papers, SHC; Eliza Frances Andrews, *Journal of a Georgia Woman, 1870–1872,* ed. S. Kittrell Rushing (Knoxville, Tenn., 2002), 45. See Joel Williamson, *The Crucible of Race: Black-White Relations in the American South since Emancipation* (New York, 1984), 57–60.

41. William Clark to Alabama Clark, July 11, n.d. [1869–1886], Henry Selby Clark Papers, Duke.

ings by and about women. In Virginia this might have been related to two decades of white newspaper editorializing about black men as menacing to white
women, especially young unprotected ones. The black menace was a favorite
scare tactic used to build a white backlash against the interracial political coali-
tions found among the Readjusters, those Virginia politicians who wanted to
repudiate a part of the state's antebellum debt. In 1887, when Lewis Harvie's
daughter planned, after a visit to Richmond, to journey to Dykelands, the family
plantation in Amelia County, to spend the summer, he left explicit directions
with his unmarried sister: "I will tell her to write from R[ichmon]d saying what
train she will go on. Please ask one of the boys to be certain to meet her. I don't
want her to go from the Depot alone, and please see that she never goes anywhere unprotected. I have a great horror of my Daughters going about the country without some protector."[42]

Perhaps the woman of the second generation who put the matter most
bluntly was Mary Mason Anderson, a Richmond resident. Like her brothers and
sisters, Mary often obsessively revisited the decline of the family plantation,
Fortsville, in Southampton County, Virginia. She and her siblings individually
and collectively bemoaned a state of affairs in which, as they saw it, only the
freedmen profited from and enjoyed the plantation. In 1884, Mary lectured her
brother Lewis Mason, who had moved out of Fortsville after a quarrel with his
unmarried sister: "I write now to beg and insist upon your going back to Fortsville to live. It is your proper home and you are the proper protector of your
sisters. Archer and I have never felt satisfied that you were not there and in these
troubled times, it is not proper for females to live alone." In the years after Susan
and Saidie Mason secured paid employment and moved to the city, Mary Anderson made even clearer her objections to women residing alone on the plantation. In 1891, while making plans to visit the plantation where her brother then
lived, Mary demurred about staying there even one week during his absence.
Since her oldest son would be unable to accompany her, she considered cancel-
ing the trip: "We will be without a protection, so we do not know about going
and I think the children will cry for a month if they cannot go out to Fortsville
but I am afraid to stay there without a white man." The following year Mary
Anderson mused that her family probably would not visit Fortsville that summer: "We have no horse and no man to stay there at night and I am a *COW-
ARD*." In the decades after the Civil War, genteel matrons increasingly perceived

42. Edwin J. Harvie to Josephine Harvie, June 25, 1887, Harvie Family Papers, VHS. See Jane
Dailey, *Before Jim Crow: The Politics of Race in Postemancipation Virginia* (Chapel Hill, N.C.,
2000), 68–102.

the countryside as a place where ladies needed not just escorts, but "protectors."[43]

Over time, white paranoia had increased, and it was greatest in rural areas. In the 1870s and 1880s, Kate Meares in Wilmington felt safe with either a black maid or a white female companion, but by the 1890s Mary Anderson believed that only a white male provided sufficient protection on the plantation. Such language of danger and menace proved intimidating to those women who tried to function on their own without "protection." A discourse that sprang from southern elites who argued that white supremacy and the suppression of African American civil rights were necessary to protect white women, it also played back into those hands. Whites who assaulted and lynched black Virginians and North Carolinians could fall back on the rationale of the so-called necessity to protect women. Although white Virginians committed a smaller number of lynchings than their compatriots in Georgia and the Deep South, they justified a large proportion of the lynchings in Piedmont and Tidewater Virginia during the nineteenth century by claiming to be avenging and discouraging sexual assaults.[44]

Thus, both because of the long-felt social drawbacks of the plantation and the new terrors of the countryside, many women of the old elite wished to move to town and city life. Their views might have carried added weight with husbands and brothers because economic factors simultaneously made the late-nineteenth-century plantation a poor investment. As Thomas Watson of Louisa County, Virginia, complained in 1883, "Agriculture is at such a low ebb, in the Green Springs, that no hope is held out to us—and I find it impossible to support my family by the revenue from this farm." He declared it was only a "question of time" before the plantation would be sold "and my children scratch for a living as they can." Social and economic factors came together with racial fears to alienate the old elite from the plantation.[45]

43. Mary Mason Anderson to Lewis Mason, Nov. 10, 1884, April 22, [1891], and March 27, 1892, all in Mason Family Papers, VHS. See also Mary Bryan to Rosa Biddle, June 15, 1875, Samuel S. Biddle Papers, Duke.

44. The information on lynching in Virginia comes from the excellent work of W. Fitzhugh Brundage, *Lynching in the New South: Georgia and Virginia, 1880–1930* (Urbana, Ill., 1993), 64–72, 141–43, 153–60. See also Williamson, *Crucible of Race,* 111–39.

45. Thomas Watson to Julia Holladay, Feb. 2, 1883, Latané Family Papers, UVA; Edward L. Ayers, *The Promise of the New South: Life After Reconstruction* (New York, 1992), 56, 63, documents this flight from rural districts but ascribes it only to single women's desires. James Roark argues that elite men who wished to shed plantations were motivated largely by financial considerations. See *Masters without Slaves: Southern Planters in the Civil War and Reconstruction* (New York, 1977), 176–81.

Given women's demonstrated concern for retaining property and these attitudes toward the countryside, the role that elite women played in the perpetuation of family plantations is especially instructive. In 1900 in Fauquier County, some members of the old elite still owned plantation houses, but they had been slowly growing apart from their lands. In some cases, they slipped away from the lands; in others the land slipped away from them, as the old gentry slowly melted away from the countryside. The wills that the women in the extended Marshall clan drew up in the late nineteenth century show an insistence on giving property to kin, but at times an indifference about whether the land itself was retained. In her will of 1880, Mildred P. Marshall, who never married, gave in trust land she had purchased from her brother Jacquelin to his wife. Yet Mildred directed her executors to sell her other real estate and divide the proceeds among her nieces and nephews. Mildred's unmarried cousin, Maria W. Marshall, similarly provided in her will of 1899 that her land would be sold and the proceeds divided among her various nieces (Maria omitted her nephews). To be sure, by the twentieth century, some Marshall women wished to hold on to their ancestral lands. Ellen Marshall Barton not only retained her own legacy of Prospect Hill plantation, but also purchased Wheatly and the Mountain Farm from her brother, Jacquelin Marshall Jr. In the will that she drew up in 1911, Ellen Barton further decreed that none of her real estate should be sold during her daughter Mary Smith's lifetime, "but at her death all such property both real and personal to be divided equally between my four grandchildren or their heirs."[46]

Women in other wealthy Fauquier families shared a willingness to part with family lands. In 1873, Hannah and Eliza Beale sold over fourteen hundred acres to the railroad. That this was not simply a sale caused by financial distress is revealed in the fact that Eliza Beale continued to buy and sell parcels of land through the 1870s.[47]

As they chose heirs for their lands, one finds among the Marshall women, as among other members of the Virginia and North Carolina elite, three main

46. Will of Mildred P. Marshall (probated 1882), Fauquier County Wills, vol. 37, p. 331. In 1892, Mildred's nieces and nephews reported that they found such a sale "impracticable" and requested the court to divide the lands among them. Deed of Harrison Robertson Jr. et al. to Eleanor Douthat, Oct. 13, 1892, Fauquier County Deeds, vol. 84, pp. 322–24; Will of Maria W. Marshall (probated 1908), Fauquier County Wills, vol. 44, pp. 301–302; Will of Ellen Barton (probated 1920), Fauquier County Wills, vol. 47, p. 414, all in FCCC.

47. Deed of Eliza L. and Hannah G. Beale to Washington City, Virginia Midland, and Great Southern Railroad Company, May 13, 1873, Fauquier County Deeds, vol. 65, pp. 199–202. For examples of Eliza Beale's real estate, see William and Rebecca Russell to Eliza Beale, Aug. 27, 1879, Fauquier County Deeds, vol. 70, p. 265, and Charles Gordon, trustee, to Eliza Beale, Oct. 10, 1879, Fauquier County Deeds, vol. 70, p. 309, both in FCCC.

approaches. The least common of these strategies, chosen by only a few, was to designate only one major heir. Eliza Jacquelin Marshall, a never-married daughter of James K. Marshall, chose this course when she gave the bulk of her property, including her parents' home, Leeds plantation, to her niece, Claudia B. Stribling. Some, like Marion Carter Oliver, chose to pass on a plantation to a male heir. She and her sister Alice inherited Shirley plantation, but both were childless. By the time that Marion Carter Oliver looked to the future in the 1930s, she relied on patriarchal principles for inheritance, bequeathing it to a male cousin who was a lineal descendant of her grandfather.[48]

More common among women, whether married or not, was partitioning one's lands among numerous heirs. Eliza Jacquelin Marshall's sister, Claudia Marshall Jones, divided her plantation Shelburne, "given me by my husband," among four of her children and bequeathed the "property I inherited from my father James K. Marshall deceased, and the property joining it that I bought from the heirs of Miss Maria W. Marshall deceased" to all five of her children. Such shares might not be exactly equal in these cases, yet all offspring received a part. Claudia and Eliza's sister-in-law, widowed Isabella Reaney Marshall, took a similar tack, dividing her Glenora lands among six of her children after a seventh had received a legacy of money. This liquidation of family land holdings paralleled inheritance practices elsewhere in late-nineteenth-century America.[49]

Yet a third approach among the Marshalls and other elite women was to choose a smaller group of heirs among one's relatives. This, like the choice of one heir, was a strategy confined mainly to unmarried or childless women. Thus Alice Marshall Carroll divided her property among numerous nieces, giving small legacies to most of them, but dividing her plantation Ashleigh among three of them, Alice G. Marshall, Claudia Stribling, and Lucy Jones.[50]

Even though the Marshall women usually divided their lands among several heirs, this did not always break up plantations. As some of these wills and deeds testify, lands sometimes circulated among family members. Claudia Jones purchased a tract from the heirs of her deceased sister, much like her cousin Ellen

48. Will of Eliza Jacquelin Marshall (probated 1918), Fauquier County Wills, vol. 47, pp. 276–77, FCCC; Marion Carter Oliver memorandum, n.d., Shirley Plantation Papers, CWF.
49. Will of Claudia H. Jones (probated 1917), Fauquier County Wills, vol. 47, p. 360, and Will of Isabelle Reaney Marshall (probated 1923), Fauquier County Wills, vol. 50, p. 121, both in FCCC. For liquidations of farms and businesses, see Carole Shammas, Marylynn Salmon, and Michel Dahlin, *Inheritance in America: From Colonial Times to the Present* (New Brunswick, N.J., 1987), 103–22.
50. Will of Alice L. Carroll (probated 1919), Fauquier County Wills, vol. 47, pp. 362–63, FCCC.

Barton had done from the latter's brother. Other large landholders, either from the ranks of the old gentry or from the ascending middle class, also sought these plantations. In Fauquier County, Robert Beverley from the old elite rapidly expanded his holdings in the postwar period, as did the Glascocks, who before the war had been substantial farmers rather than large planters.

Up until the twentieth century, women showed more ambivalence than enthusiasm for family lands. The case of Shirley plantation shows how such attitudes sometimes changed over time. After the Civil War, elderly Hill Carter requested his son, Robert Randolph Carter, then forty years old, to return to and manage Shirley plantation, on the James River. Robert's wife, Louise Humphreys Carter, found her father-in-law difficult and disliked the plantation. On her thirty-eighth birthday, she poured out to her diary her feelings of unhappiness at Shirley. While she rued the return to Shirley, she realized that her children had a different view. Her daughters Marion and Alice felt far more attached to the plantation. They loved canoeing with their father on the river and spending time on the grounds. Thus it was that Marion, after successfully managing Shirley for several decades, self-consciously passed it on as a family holding. By 1908, Lucy P. Wickham was expressing the wish to her two surviving children, Henry T. Wickham and Anne C. W. Renshaw, that the family plantation, Hickory Hill in Hanover County, Virginia, not be sold—a desire that she had never explicitly voiced in any of the wills she had been drawing up for two decades.[51]

By the turn of the century, white women of the old elite came to a new relation with the old plantation. In part they shared in an increased affection for plantation lands as the past and their ancestral lands came to seem increasingly desirable and even idyllic. Despite their ambivalence in the decades after the war, women had played a role in preserving the old plantations. But as mythmakers like George Cary Eggleston constructed visions of prewar plantations, women appeared at most as ornaments and minor characters rather than owners and managers.

Over the course of the late nineteenth century, elite women reacted in varying ways to plantation life. Many had long preferred a town existence that seemed both more civilized and convivial than rural life. Moreover, the town and city offered more paid employment that would promote the nondependence that many women idealized. Some also sought activity and nondependence on

51. Louise Humphreys Carter diary, Oct. 29, 1870, and Alice Carter diary, Nov. 28, 1874, and April 21, 1875, both in Shirley Plantation Papers, CWF; Lucy P. Wickham will (July 27, 1908), Wickham Family Papers, VHS.

the old plantation. There, most found limited success, since managing the late-nineteenth-century plantation was generally a losing proposition for both men and women of the old elite. For every Shirley that endured, there were many Conneconaras, Shelburnes, and White Hills that either were lost to debts, divided up, or simply sold away from their antebellum owners. But even as white gentry families were giving up on the plantation as it was, the plantation as it might have been, in that hazy time before the Civil War, increasingly became a seductive image. As women grappled with hard realities of economic life, they were also exploring new identities and possibilities both in rural and urban areas.

5

WOMEN IN PUBLIC: SCHOOLTEACHERS
AND BENEVOLENT WOMEN

Despite the altered composition of the southern household and the organization of work within it, the most striking changes for women of the old elite in the postwar South came in their access to and activities outside their homes. While genteel white women had never been as thoroughly sequestered in practice as in theory, they greatly increased their paid and volunteer labors after the war. This chapter surveys both forms of activity. While detailing some of the various forms of benevolent activity, my focus is on schoolteaching, the paid employment that not only involved the largest number of women but also seemed to give them the greatest satisfaction.

The Civil War did not create female southern schoolteachers, but it certainly made them far more common and far more visible. More important, the rise of both public and private schools in the postwar South encouraged the creation of an alternative culture for women, one that valued intellectual activities and power that differed from some of the normal prescribed behaviors for women. To be sure, schoolteaching emphasized many values that women already held dear, encompassing idealism and love of literature. At its best, it was a high-minded outlet for bookish girls who wanted something more than the Victorian domesticity that was then becoming so firmly rooted in the South. Most schoolteachers firmly believed in propriety, temperance, and the maintenance of a social and intellectual hierarchy. Such attitudes often landed them in a no-holds combat with the "good old boy" culture that historian Ted Ownby has delineated. The world of the school promised power and respect to teachers and gave them the ability to aid their relatives financially. Although life in the classroom included its share of drudgery, and the priggish aspects of schoolteacher culture provoked ridicule from men and women alike, teaching provided a meaningful place in society for unmarried women and an alternative to domestic life.[1]

---

1. Ted Ownby, *Subduing Satan: Religion, Recreation, and Manhood in the Rural South, 1865–1920* (Chapel Hill, N.C., 1990).

As they looked out over the changed economic landscape after 1865, women from privileged white families in Virginia and North Carolina explored various kinds of paid employment. Although women who had been forty or older at the war's beginning rarely engaged in paid work, those in the second generation (born between 1820 and 1849) more frequently did so. While some married women taught school, most salaried women and even most teachers were either widows or had never been married. Financial need, either to educate their children or relatives or simply to support themselves, impelled women toward paid positions. In 1874, Ann Biddle Pope probably called on her connections as the daughter of a deceased wealthy Baptist minister to become the housekeeper of the Baptist school in Raleigh. Not only did she take up salaried employment, but she uprooted herself from her former eastern Carolina residence. Similarly, Isabella Rives Coleman moved with her young daughter Pinny from central Virginia to Missouri in the mid-1870s to serve as the matron of an Episcopalian orphanage near St. Louis. Her sister-in-law worried that Bella was not "pleasantly situated," explaining, "She has a great deal to do and the pay is only some three hundred or three hundred and sixty dollars for the years work, and the officials in the institution she has not much confidence in, and add to her laborious duties." Yet Isabella apparently preferred to remain in her job, telling her relatives that she needed "to work for a living, and is doing as well as she could elsewhere and has the comfort of having Pinny with her, board free." Saidie Mason less happily found employment in the 1880s and 1890s, first as a companion to wealthy women in Washington, D.C., and later as a judge's housekeeper in St. Louis.[2]

Such positions as institutional matron or housekeeper generally were given only to older women. As a result, both second- and third-generation women (born between 1850 and 1869) looked to clerical positions, which, in the wake of the Civil War, were slowly becoming available to females. In both North and South, the exigencies of the Civil War had opened governmental work to women; in a few cases, young unmarried women had been recruited to fill a handful of clerical posts. After the war, state governments also hired some women; by 1879, Mamie Cain, a young woman from Orange County, North Carolina, was in Raleigh "writing for the legislature."[3]

After the Civil War, unmarried women of various ages sought out positions,

2. Mary E. Biddle to Rosa Biddle, Aug. 4, 1874, Samuel S. Biddle Papers, Duke; Martha Elizabeth Ambler to Phebe Bailey, March 22, 1875, and March 17, 1876, Bailey Family Papers, VHS; Saidie Mason to Lewis Mason, Aug. 15, 1892, and Susan Mason to Lewis Mason, Feb. 27, 1895, both in Mason Family Papers, VHS.

3. Anne Collins to Anne Cameron, Jan. 12, 1879, Anne Cameron Collins Papers, SHC.

most often as clerks, with the federal government. Lineage no doubt helped Susan Mason, who landed in the library of the office of Naval Records in the War Department; her deceased father had been a prominent senator from Virginia. Other Virginia women, such as Virginia Preston Carrington, then in her forties, also searched for work in the federal bureaucracy. In this period, youth sometimes offered more roadblocks than it removed. When twenty-four-year-old Caroline Pettigrew explored the possibilities for a clerical position in 1884, she at first received no encouragement from her state's congressmen. According to her mother, "Several of the delegation entirely opposed her applying for a place on the score of the wickedness and bad reputation of the positions." At that point, Senator Matthew Ransom promised to help her, and Caroline Pettigrew discovered that her female friends in Baltimore, many of whom were Carolina expatriates, disputed the men's low opinion of female workers, saying, "Doubtless there were many bad people in the departments, but many ladies against whom there wasn't a whisper." Although Caroline failed to land a governmental job, others of her generation did.[4]

By the late 1880s, a few young women from old elite backgrounds were undertaking even more unconventional work. In 1890, a female relative of the Faison family in Duplin County, North Carolina, was clerking in a store. By the end of the century, some women had begun to attend schools that promised more highly specialized training. Some women—including women from old elite families—attended art schools in hopes of a commercial career. Positions in medicine began to open to females; some attended nursing schools, while a few pioneering young women even sought to become doctors. After medical school in Philadelphia, Annie Lowrie Alexander taught at a medical college in Baltimore. She returned to her native Mecklenburg County, North Carolina, in 1887 to practice medicine. In the 1890s, Kate Waller Barrett decided that, even though she had a minister husband and a growing family of children, a medical degree would fit her for the sort of reform work she wished to undertake. All these possibilities were supplemented by writing and editing, topics which will be explored in the following chapter.[5]

Still, when circumstances pushed genteel women to find a way to earn

4. Susan Mason to Lewis Mason, Aug. 26, 1890, Mason Family Papers, VHS; Joseph Henry to Virginia Carrington, July 11, 1877, Preston Family Papers, VHS; Carey Pettigrew to William S. Pettigrew, Feb. 28, 1884, Pettigrew Family Papers, SHC.

5. William S. Powell, ed., *Dictionary of North Carolina Biography,* 8 vols. (Chapel Hill, N.C., 1979–), 1: 13; Edward L. Ayers, *The Promise of the New South: Life After Reconstruction* (New York, 1992), 88; Katherine G. Aiken, *Harnessing the Power of Motherhood: The National Florence Crittenton Mission, 1883–1925* (Knoxville, Tenn., 1998), 36.

money, teaching seems to have come first to mind. Although Alethea Collins Warren seems never to have worked as an educator, she contemplated it at several different times. In 1879, she told her niece, "I have thought after I can get my children to school and have paid my visit to my sister that it would be right I should try and look up something for me to do in the way of support and not be a burden on my relations." Three years later Warren wrote, "I have been reading and studying all Winter with a view of teaching." Even though she believed that her sister would disapprove, she asserted, "It does seem to me that I might go to work and help about my children." Similarly, when Sue Hubard, just out of school, first considered working for pay, she looked for a position as a governess or as a young lady's companion.[6]

The vast majority of women in the old elite who pursued paid positions were teachers, and in the last forty years of the nineteenth century, they began to change the face of education in the South. Earlier in the century, Virginians and North Carolinians, like other southerners, had become accustomed to a few women, mainly northerners, who had taught in schools or private families. Some antebellum southern women were instructors in schools that were family businesses, although such establishments had been mainly managed by males. In a Warrenton, North Carolina, school owned by the Mordecai family, the Mordecai daughters were a vital part of the staff, and later Daniel Turner and his wife operated a female academy there. By the time of the Civil War, the aristocratic Misses Nash and Kollock had been running their boarding school for girls in Hillsboro, North Carolina, for over a decade. By the 1850s, Richmond had become a center of female education with schools headed by women, some of whom hailed from the local elite.[7]

During the Civil War, female schoolteachers in North Carolina increased from under 10 percent to around 40 percent of all teachers. This percentage dropped sharply when men returned to peacetime pursuits. For example, in

6. Alethea Warren to Sallie Collins, April 21, 1879, and May 23, 1882, Anne Cameron Collins Papers, SHC; Mary L. Roberts to Sue Hubard, Aug. 1868, and Alma E. Mitchell to Sue Hubard, c. fall 1874, both in Hubard Family Papers, SHC.

7. Stanley L. Falk, "The Warrenton Female Academy of Jacob Mordecai, 1809–1818," *NCHR* 35 (July 1958): 281–98; Edgar Wallace Knight, *Public School Education in North Carolina* (1916; reprint, New York, 1969), 201; Margaret Meagher, *History of Education in Richmond* (Richmond, Va., 1939). For the best survey of antebellum southern women's education, see Christie Ann Farnham, *The Education of the Southern Belle: Higher Education and Student Socialization in the Antebellum South* (New York, 1994). For the social characteristics of teachers nationally in 1850 and 1900, see John L. Rury, "Who Became Teachers? The Social Characteristics of Teachers in American History," in *American Teachers: Histories of a Profession at Work,* ed. Donald Warren (New York, 1989), 9–33.

1870 women in North Carolina formed only slightly over 25 percent of all public school teachers. This decline occurred in part because women faced male
competition for positions in education. Young males, whether just home from
the war or just emerging from school, also were searching for work; schoolteaching had been and continued to be a traditional entry job for an educated young
man. That salaries for southern schoolteachers did not exhibit as large a differen-
tial between the sexes as elsewhere in America probably did not aid the southern
woman seeking a teaching position, although it might well have helped the
woman who actually secured one. In both Virginia and North Carolina, women
came to form around one-half of the public school teachers during the last decades of the nineteenth century; by the early twentieth century, they constituted
a majority. These proportions most likely underestimate women's participation
in education, since such statistics did not include governesses and many teachers
in private schools.[8]

Even as young men from old elite families continued to try their hand at
education, either as teacher or principal, some of them denigrated teaching as
an occupation for their female relatives. Twenty-one-year-old Edmund W. Hubard Jr., serving in 1873 as principal of the Covington Male and Female Academy, counseled his twenty-two-year-old sister Sue not even to consider a
position in education. "I don't agree with you about teaching, what can you
make at it?" he challenged her. Contrasting teaching with marriage to the
wealthy widower to whom Sue was then engaged, Edmund argued that if she
took a teaching position, she would sacrifice her "happiness for a lifetime, lose a
fortune & a most acceptible companion (for life) for the small sum of $400,
$500 or even a $1000." As "one who feels the greatest interest in you," he im-
plored her to "abandon the idea of teaching." In his estimation, "To a man it is
one of the most unsatisfactory ways of making a living and to a woman it would
be a second hell." The future in teaching that Edmund sketched for Sue promised few rewards, financial or otherwise: "Your beauty would fade, your health
become impaired and laying all considerations of [your fiancé] Steinberger out
of the question, you couldn't make more than would keep you going, besides
while hard licks & practical experience is necessary for a man, it is equally unnecessary and uncalled for & objectionable in a woman." His final advice was,
"Give up the idea." Edmund's admonitions might have affected his sister's cal-

8. Cornelia Camp, *Some Pioneer Women Teachers of North Carolina* (n.p., 1955); Joel Perlmann
and Robert A. Margo, *Women's Work? American Schoolteachers, 1650–1920* (Chicago, 2001), 34–
103. As Perlmann and Margo searched for causes for antebellum southern women's smaller numbers in the teaching field, they found female education and age at marriage to be similar enough
between North and South that these factors could not account for the difference.

culations. Although she briefly taught the children of the freedmen on the family plantation after the war, she only desultorily searched for teaching positions. She seems to have expected to make her way in the world via writing and an advantageous marriage—and obviously her brother favored the latter course. Yet other women would expect and receive more from teaching.[9]

Several reasons led white women from the old elite to teaching as a way to earn money. In part, no other occupation then open to them seemed to utilize their education and yet provide flexibility in hours and a steady income. Teaching required only a general education rather than specialized training, and work experience was often unnecessary. Moreover, teaching was a socially acceptable occupation that squared with expanded rather than radically altered gender roles. Although some men thought that women should not teach males, especially those beyond the primary grades, even the most rigid traditionalists believed that instructing young children was appropriate for females, at least within the home.

Teaching school was no standardized position, but encompassed several different kinds of occupations grouped under the same rubric. Well into the 1890s, a teacher could still be the live-in governess so often described in English and American novels. In truth, this generally was an entry-level occupation. Some people considered the work of a governess especially appropriate for a young woman just beginning to teach because it always included board with the family. For example, when Maria Louisa Carrington considered possible positions for a female relative, she thought governessing the only viable option because the young woman was "too young to board any where, but in the family where she teaches."[10]

Obtaining a position as a governess could be relatively easy and painless for young women from privileged families. Although some positions were advertised, many people hiring governesses asked family and friends among the old elite to recommend promising young ladies. When Sue Hubard considered working as a governess, she drafted a letter that described her case and sought to capitalize on such informal networks: "Carefully educated by the best teachers, she anxiously looks out for a situation as Governess. But here in Va no schools

9. Edmund W. Hubard Jr. to Sue Hubard, July 10, 1873, Hubard Family Papers, SHC. Lyon Gardiner Tyler was another case of an elite young male in education. From Memphis, Tennessee, the son of the former president assured his mother in 1882, "My school & prospects for making enough money to publish my book are fine just now." Lyon Gardiner Tyler to Julia Tyler, Jan. 16, 1882, Julia Tyler Papers, VHS. See also the Bondurant-Morrison Family Papers, UVA, and Saunders Family Papers, VHS.

10. Maria Carrington to Betty Saunders, Sept. 22, 1876, Saunders Family Papers, VHS.

not even private ones are open during the summer & to advertize in a Northern paper at such a distance would be useless. The object of my letter is to ask, if in yr circle of friends, you know of any one who wishes a governess. If so, all that I wish is that you will write me the name & address."[11]

Sometimes neighbors provided initial employment opportunities. Bessie Carrington's first position came in the family of Wood Bouldin, a wealthy lawyer and neighboring planter who knew Bessie well and socialized with her widowed mother and other relatives. In other cases, an elaborate network of friends and relatives among the elite tried to steer jobs toward "deserving" young friends and relatives. John Taylor wrote Maria Louisa Carrington about a possible position in Kentucky that "might suit" his niece, Lucy Taylor. He had heard "from good authority" that Colonel Johnston, brother of the Confederate general Albert Sydney Johnston, was seeking a teacher. As proof that this distant position would be a suitable one for his niece, Taylor offered the testimony of Johnston's former governess, who had since married: "Mrs Pendleton speaks in terms of gratitude for the uniform kindness offered her & is sure the same will be offered her successor." Taylor seems to have written Maria Louisa Carrington because as a teacher herself as well as a relative of Lucy Taylor, she could offer a recommendation. In the 1870s, Maria Louisa Carrington served as something of a clearinghouse for both those seeking teachers and those seeking teaching positions. In 1876, she checked whether her daughter and another relative had received the addresses she had forwarded of people who needed teachers.[12]

To be sure, some young women scoured their networks of friends and acquaintances to little avail. Maria Hatcher told Kitty Dabney, who was looking for a job, that her visit to the Tidewater county of Westmoreland had convinced her that the people there had no money to hire governesses. Neither had a stay in Baltimore turned up any promising situations. Caroline Pettigrew also failed in her first attempts to find work.[13]

John Taylor's analysis of the position offered his niece focused on the status of the family and the conditions of work rather than the work itself or the salary. Others echoed this emphasis. Describing Lucy Taylor's position to another relative, Maria Louisa Carrington drew an idyllic picture of "how kindly, and deferentially Lucy is treated, she is the *queen* of the house and they all seem to wish to make her happy. I doubt if she could find, anywhere, so pleasant a situation."

11. Sue Hubard, draft of letter, n.d., Hubard Family Papers, SHC.

12. Maria Carrington to Betty Saunders, Aug. 3, 1868, and Sept. 22, 1876, and John Taylor to Maria Louisa Carrington, Feb. 10, 1871, all in Saunders Family Papers, VHS.

13. Maria Hatcher to Kitty Dabney, Oct. 16, 1868, Saunders Family Papers, VHS; Carey Pettigrew to William S. Pettigrew, Aug. 1, 1878, and June 6, 1880, Pettigrew Family Papers, SHC.

The emphasis on the genteel family setting and the governess's treatment as a social equal might have made governessing more acceptable to many parents and even some young women, but it also made it difficult for these women to see themselves as professionals. This was especially the case when the governess was a relative, since she might seem only one step removed from being on a family visit. Two young matrons who discussed the teaching prospects of their mutual relative expected her, if jobless, to spend the winter as company for their recently married sister.[14]

In perhaps the most egregious example of such a possible disjunction in expectations, Fannie Dabney found herself in the embarrassing position of asking her cousins to clarify whether they believed that they had employed her for wages or that she was merely visiting them. Fanny seems to have arrived at Bleak Hill, the Piedmont Virginia home of Peter and Betty Saunders, early in January 1867. According to Betty, "We find her a very sweet pleasant person. She helps me a good deal besides teaching Edward, and has a quiet way of accomplishing a great deal. I find her already a great comfort & the children are devoted to her." It is not clear how long Fanny stayed at Bleak Hill, but in the summer of 1867 she took advantage of a visit to her own home to write Betty Saunders, asking for a clarification of her status:

> Let me ask you my dear cousin what I have wanted to know for a long while. In what light am I to consider my living at Bleak Hill? Am I engaged as a teacher or not? Cousin Cornelia made the arrangement between us, and as she does some odd things occasionally I don't know that I understood her, or that you did either. You know after the war you invited one of us to live with you, and while we thanked you for your great kindness and highly appreciated it we could not conscientiously accept your offer. After that I learned through cousin C. that you wished to employ a teacher.

After living with her cousins and receiving no salary or explanation about her lack of pay, Fanny tentatively broached the subject with them. She depended on the eccentricities of cousin Cornelia to explain any misunderstandings. Fanny Dabney brought up the subject only after many months had elapsed, and she insisted both on her affection for her family and her need for a paid position to support herself. In making her claim to be a teacher rather than a dependent poor relation, Fanny put her case as a question of self-respect and self-support.

14. Maria Louisa Carrington to Eliza Dabney, Nov. 23, 1867, and Maria Louisa Carrington to Betty Saunders, Sept. 22, 1876, both in Saunders Family Papers, VHS.

Her cousins' response has not been discovered, but even if they acknowledged her hopes, she apparently did not continue to teach at Bleak Hill.[15]

Most governesses were paid, but salaries generally were extremely low. The emphasis on living conditions seems to have helped keep salaries depressed. Willie Carrington referred to a position that was touted as good despite its extremely low salary: "Mother got a letter from Mrs Gordon yesterday telling of a situation near Baltimore which she thought a very desirable one although the salary is only a hundred & fifty." Much the way many other governesses must have done, Willie argued that such a position would be better than idleness: "Still how much better this would be than holding your hands in grinding poverty."[16]

In addition to the emphasis on gaining experience in a pleasant family situation, other factors militated against a governess trying to gain a more substantial salary. The governess was more likely to receive small gifts than a large payment. Kitty Dabney noted in June 1870 that her scholars had presented her with a "beautiful fan and neck ribbon," while their mother had given her a "beautiful white & black striped ribbon sash." Such trinkets tended to suggest that the governess was a household guest rather than a professional teacher. Even when the question arose of Kitty's remaining to teach the Holcombe children, the conversation barely touched upon money. Apparently Kitty had come to the Holcombes in part to help copy a manuscript for Mr. Holcombe, but she had instructed the children during the illness of another teacher. She deemed her discussion with Mr. Holcombe a "very sweet & gratifying conversation." Not only did Holcombe assure her that "no one could have been more agreeable to them in every respect"; he also asserted that "if he could afford it . . . I should be a fixture at Bellevue but of course it would be expensive to him to keep two female teachers." For her part, Kitty skirted the question of wages: "I told Mr Holcombe that I was very willing to leave the business part of the arrangement in his hands, that I knew he was straightened & that I had rather for this remnant of time stay for less at Bellevue than to go anywhere else." The outcome of this conversation was that Mr. Holcombe "said that I might rest assured that he would *do the best he could* for me" but, should Kitty receive a better offer of a situation, she would be at liberty to accept it. Instead of bargaining for a higher salary, Kitty Dabney affirmed her ties to the Holcombe family. Still, this situa-

15. Betty Saunders to Eliza Dabney, Jan. 29, 1867 [misdated 1866], and Frances Dabney to Betty Saunders, Aug. 26, 1867, both in Saunders Family Papers, VHS.

16. Williamine Cabell Carrington to Betty Saunders, Nov. 23, [c. 1868–70], Saunders Family Papers, VHS.

tion covered only the "remnant of time" remaining in her engagement, and Kitty had secured her freedom to accept other positions.[17]

Lula Bondurant's experiences with a family near Lexington, Kentucky, gives us yet another view on the life of a governess. Cheerful in her letters back home to Buckingham County, Virginia, Lula described the children as easy to teach and the family as wealthy and religious. On Sundays she made the drive of seven miles to the church in Versailles, where her employer was, in her view, the wealthiest man in the church. Such a position, in which a young lady simply moved to the supervision of a new family, sometimes better pleased the parents than the young teacher. Although Lula Bondurant complained little about her situation, one drawback apparently was the lack of other young people nearby. When a Virginia expatriate from her area invited her to visit his Kentucky home, she regretted that bad weather had prevented it: "I would love dearly to go to Dr. G's. There are so many young people and I know I would have a lovely time." In part because Lula herself was quite religious and straitlaced and also because she worked only a few years until her marriage, she seemed little affected by the strictures of governessing. Other young women tested the limits of family governance over the governess. In Virginia, Powhatan County matron Leila Bankhead reported that she was on the lookout for a new governess, even though her present one was willing to continue teaching: "My last teacher wishes to return, but she acted imprudently with the young men in our neighborhood." For that reason, William Pope Bankhead, Leila's husband, opposed rehiring the governess, and Leila seems to have acquiesced, musing, "I may get my niece Carrie Willis."[18]

Governessing promised a home environment to shelter young women, but that very environment could also expose them to sexual advances. In 1883, elderly Emily Dupuy questioned her daughter about a scandal that had erupted over the alleged seduction of a governess by the father of the family for whom the young lady worked: "Minnie in her letter didn't speak of the scandal about J. J. Price & his governess, which is going the rounds in the papers, it is certainly a most unfortunate affair for the young lady, if in her youth & inexperience she has been led astray by Price. What is thought about it in the neighborhood?" For her own part, Emily Dupuy, who herself had taught school, tended to blame the governess's parents, writing, "There must have been want of discretion in

17. Kitty Dabney to Eliza Dabney, June 2, 1870, and Feb. 10, 1871, Saunders Family Papers, VHS.

18. Lula Bondurant to Alexander J. Bondurant, Nov. 8 and Dec. 20, 1891, Bondurant-Morrison Family Papers, UVA; Leila Dabney to Phebe Bailey, Sept. 20, 1878, Bailey Family Papers, VHS.

her parents, to allow their daughter to go into such a family to get her first experience in teaching, without any salary. I hope it may prove a warning to other girls. If she has innocently been imprudent, her character has received a taint, which will be hard to remove."[19]

In the postwar period, the position of governess was becoming somewhat archaic and less common among women from privileged families. To be sure, teachers in one-room rural schools continued to board with their students' families, either staying with one family or "boarding around." By the end of the nineteenth century, however, such positions in rural areas were usually filled by farmers' daughters, seldom by the offspring of the old elite.[20]

Operating a school, like governessing, was a traditional way of obtaining work that often relied on family ties and local allegiances more than on academic credentials. The kinds of schools available varied widely, and the teaching duties in them varied according to whether they were ungraded or had more formalized curricula. In some cases, governesses supplemented their pay by teaching additional day students from the neighborhood. While teaching in a day school in one's own home might have differed little in curriculum from governessing, it was usually mature women or married couples, rather than young single women, who opened schools in their homes or elsewhere in towns and cities.

Several reasons can be found why women who founded schools were of mature age. Operating a school entailed a variety of tasks that young women with no business experience might find difficult, such as charging pupils' parents and handling the monies received. The oversight of a school sometimes also required finding an appropriate space, although only the larger residential schools needed much of a physical plant. In other cases, women taught out of their own homes or rented spaces that included living quarters. When Bettie Quince began a day school in July 1865 with twenty scholars, her relatives praised her "peculiar fitness" for it. By 1868, Lucy Williams was teaching a small day school near her home area of Littleton, in Warren County; she apparently continued it for some years.[21]

When young women organized schools, they usually relied on parental or family support. In 1869, at the urging of their mother, Lavalette Dupuy and her sister Nannie decided to run a school at their plantation rather than be governesses elsewhere. They justified this decision to a cousin on grounds of their health:

19. Emily Dupuy to Mary Watkins, Feb. 1, 1883, Emily Dupuy Papers, VHS.
20. William A. Link, *A Hard Country and a Lonely Place: Schooling, Society, and Reform in Rural Virginia, 1870–1920* (Chapel Hill, N.C., 1986), 45–70.
21. Rebecca S. Davis to Kate Kennedy, July 29, 1865, DeRosset Family Papers, SHC.

Nannie & I have concluded, at Mamma's suggestion, to open a little school at home and will be very glad to have your two little girls live with us and be among our pupils. I have just recovered from an attack of pneumonia and am perhaps not strong enough to undertake a school entirely by myself, and as Nannie & I are the only ones now left at home, we had rather not be separated, and think too by having a joint school and sharing the duties between us, we will both be better able to stand the confinement of the school-room.

Their mother, Emily Dupuy, a northern-born woman, had been a schoolteacher herself before her marriage to a wealthy Prince Edward County, Virginia, planter in the 1840s; she thus was comfortable with a school being opened on her plantation. Emily also wrote to her nephew, telling him, "I think it probable you would prefer one of the girls to come to your house to teach your school, which they would readily do were it not for the reasons mentioned in L's letter. Indeed her health has been so delicate since Oct. that I have felt great uneasiness about her, & should be afraid to have her engage in a school without Nannies assistance." The contingency of such schools can been seen in Emily Dupuy's parting comment that the school would begin on "the 1st of Feb. if we succeed in making it up." It is unclear whether the Dupuy sisters actually operated this school. Ironically, given the worries about Lavalette's health, it was her sister Nannie who died young. Nannie's death and Lavalette's eventual marriage meant that neither of these young women were longtime schoolteachers.[22]

Other women of the second generation started relatively long-lasting residential schools. As unmarried women aged respectively thirty and thirty-four in 1862, Martha and Mary Mangum looked straightforwardly at the hard facts of reality—their beloved father, a longtime senator from North Carolina, had died a year earlier, broken by the loss of his idolized only son early in the war. Their plantation, Walnut Hill, near Hillsborough, North Carolina, had never been particularly profitable; it would not support them and their elderly mother. They quickly seized their best alternative—a select boarding school for young ladies at their home. With Martha's hardheaded business sense, and advice from their male cousins who were successful lawyers and businessmen, the Mangum sisters operated their school for almost three decades.[23]

22. Lavalette Dupuy to William Purnell Dickinson, Jan. 3, 1869, and Emily Dupuy to [William Purnell Dickinson], Jan. 4, 1869, both in Emily Dupuy Papers, VHS.

23. On the Mangum sisters, consult Sandra Lee Kurtinitis, "Sally Alston Mangum Leach, A Profile of the Family of a Plantation Mistress: An Analytical Study of the Correspondence of the Family of Willie P. Mangum" (Ph.D. diss., George Washington University, 1986), 150–56, 205–207, and the Willie Mangum Family Papers, Library of Congress, Washington, D.C.

Similarly, in Mecklenburg County, Virginia, near Clarksville, the four unmarried Carrington sisters—Agnes, Mildred, Isabella, and Emily—began Sunnyside School in 1872 at their plantation of the same name and continued it for
the next thirty-six years. One student remembered, "My first year there was the
session 1872–73. I was one of eight boarders that year. There were twenty to
twenty-five day pupils from Clarksville, which was then a mile from the school.
. . . Misses Belle and Mildred were teaching elsewhere that year, but later taught
at home, and as the school grew we had teachers of both German and French."
The combination of boarders and day pupils employed all four Carrington sisters. Susie Webb Yarbrough recalled the division of responsibilities: "Miss Agnes
looked after the farm and garden and was called the man of the family. Miss
Emily taught Mathematics, French, and general grade work. Miss Belle taught
Music and Miss Mildred taught Art History and English." Yet another student
remembered Miss Agnes as "our Mother Confessor. If our morals or our manners needed correction, she would call us to her room quietly, one at a time, and
in a gentle but firm way would reprimand us, and tell us how to mend our
ways."[24]

Among family-owned institutions, long-lived schools appear to have been a
significant minority. Those schools that existed a considerable time usually depended on the involvement of more than one member of the family. For example, when Agnes Carrington died in 1887 at age fifty-four, her three remaining
unmarried sisters continued the school. That the Mangums and the Carrington
sisters lived in the rural countryside, near small towns, also aided the survival of
their schools. A city like Richmond, in contrast, saw a great turnover of schools.
In cities, the private institutions that most often survived for decades had been
founded or were supported by a church.[25]

These different kinds of schools, proprietorial as well as public, offered different occupational tracks to teachers. In the late nineteenth century, probably
most female instructors began as governesses and taught only a few sessions before marriage. These were not the teachers that one finds chronicled in the histories of schools or teaching; instead, evidence about them emerges primarily
from family letters or in fiction. In some ways they fit the ideals conveyed in
British and American novels. *Jane Eyre,* with its story of straitlaced Jane wooed
by the irascible and compelling Edward Rochester, was but the most famous

24. J. D. Eggleston, ed., "Misses Carrington's Sunnyside School for Young Ladies, 1872–
1908" (unpub. ms., c. 1930s), pp. 14, 18, 11, VHS.

25. Ibid., 33. See, for example, Peace Institute and St. Mary's School, both in Raleigh, North
Carolina, as examples of long-lived schools which were church-related.

version. Sallie Brock, a young Virginia woman, chronicled in *Kenneth, My King* the long, involved story of Harriet Royal, the governess for a family in the Virginia Piedmont, who, after four hundred pages of courtship and adventure, marries the family's sardonic and handsome scion. Not content merely to describe one form of teaching, Brock sends her heroine to teach in the "Finishing school of the famous Madame de Blande" in New Orleans, where she works "like an automaton." After three terms there, Harriet Royal launches a successful literary career and is then rediscovered by the hero, who marries her and takes her home to Virginia. Harriet might have married more successfully than other governesses, but the variety of her employers suggests the experience of many teachers, who remained longer in teaching and had different sorts of experiences than governessing. The employment patterns of several of these women provides insight into the ways that women incorporated teaching into their lives.[26]

Most long-term teachers from the old elite spent much of their later lives in relatively stable private schools and urban public schools. These generally were not entry jobs, but instead went to older teachers who had demonstrated skills or a classroom reputation. The experiences of three teachers of the second generation—one from North Carolina, two from Virginia—illustrate the careers of mature women who taught in the decades immediately following the war. As these examples suggest, the teachers among the second generation included many women who either were or had been married.

The career of Kate DeRosset Meares, whose husband was killed in the Seven Days' battles, shows how some young widows of the middle generation balanced work and family obligations through teaching. Before the war, Kate married the merchant son of a wealthy planter from the Wilmington, North Carolina, area and lived a conventionally successful and apparently happy life, largely in New York City. Although her letters do not express a yearning for a life of independence, the need to support her three young sons apparently pushed her to provide for them and herself. While her parents wanted her to live with them and she continued to rely on her father for financial advice, Kate preferred to make her own living and her own life. Over the next fifteen years she moved among different teaching positions—some obviously chosen to be near her sons, who were away in school, and others to be with her parents in Wilmington.[27] After briefly teaching in Granville County in 1868 and later heading the music department in a school run by a relative in Wilmington, Kate Meares organized a free school there in 1871 at the elite Episcopal church of St. James. In 1875 she

---

26. Sallie A. Brock Putnam, *Kenneth, My King* (New York, 1873), 373, 384–404.
27. Eliza J. DeRosset to Louis H. DeRosset, Feb. 4, 1868, DeRosset Family Papers, SHC.

moved to Germantown, Pennsylvania, where she taught elocution, French, and music at a girls' school. She returned to North Carolina when Aldert Smedes asked her to become the "lady principal" of St. Mary's Academy in Raleigh—a position she held for several years.[28]

The experiences of Maria Louisa Carrington of Charlotte County, Virginia, provide another perspective on how widows of the second generation came to teaching. At the outbreak of the war Maria Louisa's husband had already been dead a decade, and she lived with his family. The death of her mother-in-law and marriage of her sisters-in-law led Maria Louisa to assume responsibility for the household and the care of her elderly father-in-law, Henry Carrington. In 1866, she discussed her "duties" and how she, rather than an unmarried sister-in-law, should perform them: "I greatly prefer keeping house to Emma's doing it, I feel much more independent to do something for Father, when he is constantly, doing so much for me, and mine[.] directing every thing myself, I get on with less trouble than you would suppose." That autumn, when she began to teach her niece Louise Carrington, Maria Louisa remarked that "this brings me a little money every month—and I would be glad to get some other little girls, and thus make something these hard times."[29]

The experience of teaching her niece was something of a turning point in Maria Louisa's life and marked the beginning of her professionalization. In December 1866, she admitted to her sister that receiving payment for Louise's instruction had changed her orientation: "I find her a very pleasant scholar, and the only objection I have to teaching her is, that it confines me very much. When I taught my own children only, I could stop whenever I pleased, but now that I receive money for teaching Louise, I feel that I must be perfectly regular, I think a little of taking some more scholars, but have not entirely decided on it." Several months later Maria Louisa decided that her unwillingness to interrupt lessons for a long period meant she could visit her sister for only a month.[30]

Even as she kept regular hours in the schoolroom, Maria Louisa Carrington,

28. James Sprunt, *Chronicles of the Cape Fear River, 1660–1906*, 2nd ed. (Raleigh, N.C., 1916), 612–13. Kate Meares to Louis H. Meares, Oct. 24, 1871 and Oct. 10, 1872, Kate Meares to Armand and Richard A. Meares, Feb. 4, 1875, Kate Meares to Richard A. Meares, Sept. 25, 1875, Alice Daves to Kate Meares, Aug. 27, 1877, all in Meares-DeRosset Papers, SHC; William Lord DeRosset, *One Hundredth Anniversary Commemorating the Building of St. James Church, Wilmington, North Carolina, April 30th and May 1st, 1939: The Two Hundred and Tenth Year of the Parish* (Wilmington, N.C., 1939), 11.

29. Maria Louisa Carrington to John and Eliza Dabney, April 7, 1866, and Maria Louisa Carrington to John Dabney, Nov. 9, 1866, both in Saunders Family Papers, VHS.

30. Maria Louisa Carrington to Betty Saunders, Dec. 11, 1866, and March 31, 1867, both in Saunders Family Papers, VHS.

in concert with her father-in-law, had decided by the summer of 1867 that a residential school could earn money for both of them. She told her sister that the opening of the school was planned for the first of November: "For both his benefit, and mine—We both need pecuniary help sadly, so we have determined to try to do this." This plan was derailed when Maria Louisa's father-in-law suffered a massive stroke that October and died two months later.[31]

After Henry Carrington's death, Maria Louisa again faced choices. Her parents offered to let her and her daughters live with them, but she thought otherwise. Instead she proceeded with the plan for a school at the old family plantation, this time with her brother-in-law. He would pay her $250 plus the tuition charges of the scholars and would receive the payments for board for her daughters and the other resident scholars. Maria Louisa was firm that only a business arrangement would be fair to both of them: "This arrangement makes us perfectly independant, and if I don't like it, I will change it, after our session." In fact, this division of responsibility boded well for her: "If we succeed in our school, I shall have a good income, and be very comfortable."[32]

Perhaps not surprisingly, given its secluded location, a residential school for girls in Charlotte County, Virginia, did not immediately catch hold. By the spring of 1868, Maria Louisa was again weighing her options. In May 1868 she was considering an offer to teach in an established Richmond school, and she confided to her mother that if the school's proprietor "acceeds to my terms, I think [I] shall go there. It will be most painful to me to break off from my friends here, but I must go where I can make a living, and must lay my feelings aside." By that summer, Maria Louisa had decided to teach in Richmond at the Southern Female Institute that had been founded by the Powell family. Sad as she was to leave friends and relatives, the school offered an advantage that her older daughter Bessie had pressed her to take: free tuition for her younger daughter, Willie. According to Maria Louisa, "This determination I have come to, is at Bessies earnest solicitation. She is so anxious for Willie to have the advantages of Mr. Powells school, and by her supporting herself, we look to be able to meet our expenses. My services will pay all of Willies school bills—and amounts to near a thousand dollars."[33]

Once in Richmond, Maria Louisa Carrington quickly became an advocate of

31. Maria Louisa Carrington to Betty Saunders, Aug. 2 and Oct. 3, 1867, both in Saunders Family Papers, VHS.

32. Maria Louisa Carrington to John and Eliza Dabney, Dec. 8, 1867, Saunders Family Papers, VHS.

33. Maria Louisa Carrington to Eliza Dabney, May 30, 1868, and Maria Louisa Carrington to Betty Saunders, Aug. 3, 1868, both in Saunders Family Papers, VHS.

the Southern Female Institute. Her responsibilities kept her so busy that she felt "in a perfect whirl ever since I came down, and my duties are all so new to me, that it will take a little time for me to become accustomed to them." Declaring that she had never been in a "better ordered house, or one where the comfort of the inmates was better attended to," Maria Louisa pronounced it the "best school in its arrangements I know anything about, and if the girls don't learn, it is their own fault."[34]

Given her high opinion of the Southern Female Institute, it is not surprising that Maria Louisa was willing to run it in 1871. Seven years later, with both her daughters married and rearing families, she decided to relinquish control of the school. At first she intended merely "to get rid of all the care and responsibility" of administration and concentrate on teaching. A relative commented about her decision, "I am so glad to hear of dear Sister's arrangement with regard to her school, as she says to teach six hours a day and have all the rest of her time to herself will seem as nothing to her."[35]

Virginia Hankins provides yet another variation on these themes and a third example of how the second generation entered teaching. In 1870, when her father died, the family's Tidewater Virginia plantation was lost. Virginia, as one of the older children, was particularly concerned that her youngest brother and sister be educated. In the eighteen years that elapsed between 1870 and her death, Virginia taught in schools in her native state (Surrey County, Newport News, and Norfolk, Virginia), Montgomery, Alabama, and Baltimore, Maryland. Although she left little information about her early positions, by 1881 she was a skilled teacher who at times served as a division superintendent or a matron.[36]

All three of these women came to teaching only after the war, in response to family reverses or needs. Without the war's toll in lives and property, none of them might ever have considered teaching for wages. Although they were a well-educated group, their training had not been meant to prepare them for public classrooms; this older group of southern-born teachers had simply received a good education by the lights of their day. The most compelling history of antebellum southern women's schooling has asserted that this education

34. Maria Louisa Carrington to Betty Saunders, Oct. 11, 1868, Saunders Family Papers, VHS.

35. Betty Saunders to Chiswell Dabney, May 19, 1878, Saunders Family Papers, VHS.

36. Yet another example can be found in widowed Nora Cannon, who also taught at St. Mary's in Raleigh at least from 1871 until 1875; she moved to Fayette County, Tennessee, where in 1881 at the age of fifty-two she was elected superintendent of public schools. Beth G. Crabtree and James W. Patton, eds., *"Journal of a Secesh Lady": The Diary of Catherine Ann Devereux Edmondston, 1860–1866* (Raleigh, N.C., 1979), 738–39.

could be rigorous and demanding precisely because parents and teachers neither expected young women to pursue gainful employment nor to compete with men.[37]

Young women of the third generation received quite different educations, especially in terms of preparation for teaching. Girls educated during the war had to cope with interrupted schools, while after the war numerous other privations sometimes affected their instruction. Some attended private schools or had governesses, but others were educated in public schools or even charitable institutions. This was a change that the old elite only haltingly and hesitantly embraced. Marietta Minnigerode Andrews declared that even though public schools were clearly superior to private tutoring, it made no difference to her mother, who sent "our boys and girls to Cousin This or Cousin That." Emily Morrison Bondurant also expressed doubts about the propriety of public schooling, saying, "I do not like a free school, I do not like the people or society thrown around girls in Lynchburg." Yet she let her daughter Lula attend the public high school there before Lula began governessing.[38]

Perhaps more important than where this third generation was schooled was the direction its education took. After the war, both young women and their parents saw education as preparation for teaching. Leila Dabney thus justified a request for financial help to her aunt on the grounds that learning music would fit them for teaching. Elizabeth Worthington set out her thoughts on the subject very clearly when she discussed her daughter Lizzie's education and prospects in life:

> I am undecided what Lizzie will do this Fall, she is very anxious to begin her life as a teacher, and I am more than anxious she should continue at school for [a] couple more years. Leache-Wood is one of the best schools I know of, is thorough & their standard of excellence is very high. I want Lizzie to be prepared as a *No 1 teacher* when she begins, & with full recommendations from Miss Leache— also as pupil, during her last term, to be given charge of some of the minor branches to teach to fit herself better. I have had a struggle to educate my children, & for Lizzie I wish her to have every opportunity to be thoroughly competent to support herself in the future.

Elizabeth Worthington, while seeking a thorough education for her daughter, also wanted her to leave school with the necessary recommendations and teaching experience to be, in her reckoning, a first-class teacher.[39]

37. Farnham, *Education of the Southern Belle,* 28–32, 68–93.

38. Emily Bondurant to Alexander L. Bondurant, Feb. 7, 1887, Bondurant-Morrison Family Papers, UVA.

39. Leila Dabney to Phebe Bailey, Sept. 4, 1877, Bailey Family Papers, VHS; E. D. F. Worthington to Emily Benbury Haywood, Aug. 6, 1888, Benbury-Haywood Papers, SHC.

Other second-generation women were determined that the younger generation be given more choices through education. While not necessarily advocating a "career" or lifetime work, such mothers implicitly wanted their daughters not to feel pressured into marriage—and especially not into an "unequal" marriage. Elizabeth Worthington's peers were women such as Maria Louisa Carrington and Carey Pettigrew. The latter, despite the wreckage of her family's fortunes, secured educations for her many children. With the help of her bachelor brother-in-law, William S. Pettigrew, who dedicated his small salary as an Episcopal priest to pay for the schooling of his nieces and nephews, she embarked upon a decades-long education program. And this ethic was absorbed by her children, such as her daughter Caroline, who wanted a teaching position because she "was very anxious to do something for herself, to assist in paying off Mr Smedes [bills for education] and to help with her younger sisters." In Georgia, Fanny Andrews noted that she was taking pains with her young niece. "I shall do my best to give her a good education," Fanny vowed, "for it is all I shall ever be able to give her, I expect, and it will make her independent."[40]

By the 1880s and 1890s, a few southern women sought educations at the best women's colleges, founded during the last few decades in the North. In 1881, after being schooled by her sisters in Prince Edward County, Virginia, Martha Burton Watkins entered Wellesley College at age twenty-three. By 1885, she was teaching at Stuart Hall in Staunton, Virginia; she held later posts at Agnes Scott and Flora Macdonald Colleges in Georgia and North Carolina. Elizabeth Avery Colton, after studying at Statesville Female College, spent two years at Mount Holyoke and later attended Teachers' College at Columbia University.[41]

The educations of third-generation women differed from that of their mothers and grandmothers mainly in the emphasis on preparation for teaching. Some young women, especially North Carolinians, looked to special training in the normal schools that were founded after the 1870s. For example, Lena Smith first attended St. Mary's, a Raleigh school long popular with elite Carolinians, and then studied at the new state normal summer sessions. A newspaper account of Vine Hill School, where Lena taught as part of the "Female School," declared in 1879: "Miss Smith is now at the State Normal where she is keeping up with the most approved and recent methods of teaching, and increasing her present knowledge of kindergarten." Caroline Pettigrew received a scholarship to the newly created Peabody Institute for teachers in Nashville, Tennessee. According

40. Carey Pettigrew to William S. Pettigrew, July 1, 1879, and Aug. 1, 1878, Pettigrew Family Papers, SHC.

41. Camp, *Some Pioneer Women Teachers,* 53–57, 192–93; Eliza Frances Andrews, *Journal of a Georgia Woman, 1870–1872,* ed. J. Kittrell Rushing (Knoxville, Tenn., 2002), 40.

to her mother, Caroline "would be prepared for any position as a teacher after this course." Similarly, Viola Boddie of Nash County, North Carolina, won a two-year scholarship to the Peabody Institute after scoring well in the competitive examination.[42]

To be sure, many third-generation young women who began schoolteaching in the 1870s and 1880s gained their first experience much like teachers of the older generations. Viola Boddie's experience before attending Peabody had been as a "governess, teacher in a co-educational academy, work in a one-room rural school, teaching seventy-two primary children in a graded school, and a brief period in each of two denominational colleges for girls." Similarly, Mary Alves Long's older sisters, who came to maturity in the 1870s, were both governesses at some point. Some young women, like Roberta Lord, continued to gain their first teaching experiences with their younger siblings or the children of relatives. In 1876, Roberta instructed ten scholars, charging each $1.50 per month. When Lena Smith returned to Scotland Neck, North Carolina, after graduating from St. Mary's School, she began instructing first her younger sisters and then neighborhood children. In 1871, Thomas Watson pronounced his daughter Ellen a "good girl!" because "she stays at home, and teaches the three youngest."[43]

Yet aside from these entry-level jobs, crucial differences between generations show up vividly in the work experiences of third-generation teachers. They were far more likely than their elders to work in public schools in the North and the South. Second-generation teachers frequently worked in proprietary and other private schools and academies, but younger women more often saw and took advantage of the expanding possibilities in public education in the South. Alone among the southern states, North Carolina had instituted a public school system before the Civil War. This school system, revived and expanded after 1870, offered remunerative employment. In Virginia, public schools formed a flash point of the Funder-Readjuster political quarrels between those "Funders" who believed Virginia should pay its prewar debts and their "Readjustor" opponents who wanted to repudiate or scale down those payments. Funding the debt would absorb monies that otherwise could be applied to public education and other public services. Because of this controversy, women from the old elite in

42. "Typescript," July 7, 1879, Peter Evans Smith Papers; Carey Pettigrew to William S. Pettigrew, June 6, 1880, Pettigrew Family Papers; Camp, *Some Pioneer Women Teachers*, 36–37.

43. Camp, *Some Pioneer Women Teachers*, 36–37, 172–73; Mary Alves Long, *High Time to Tell It: "Ah, Distinctly I Remember"* (Durham, N.C., 1950), 151–60; Kate Meares to Richard A. Meares, Oct. 15, 1875, and Eliza DeRosset to Kate Meares, Jan. 16, 1876, both in Meares-DeRosset Papers, SHC; Thomas S. Watson to Julia A. Holladay, Dec. 4, 1871, Latané Family Papers, ser. 1, UVA.

Virginia more slowly entered the ranks of public school teaching. Nonetheless, public school teaching, in part because of its better pay and more secure jobs, increasingly attracted the younger generation of schoolteachers. Particularly in North Carolina, some teachers moved back and forth between positions in public and private schools. For example, Catherine Cameron Shipp taught in the public schools of Raleigh and Charlotte before opening a private school for girls in Lincolnton, North Carolina. Sometimes women parlayed experience gained in northern school systems into positions in women's seminaries and other institutions of higher learning. Jane Long, after a stint substitute teaching in the public schools of New York City, gained a post teaching English at Peace Institute, a female college in Raleigh.[44]

Among all the female teachers in the late-nineteenth-century South, probably the majority of women taught only as a bridge from girlhood to marriage or at times when family needs were pressing. No doubt the level of commitment to and satisfaction in teaching varied a great deal. Many governesses and teachers might well have had little commitment to their work; after all, the possibilities for paid work were extremely narrow, especially for young white women. Some young teachers worked only because their families needed their wages or to bring a different experience to their humdrum lives. Jeannie Meares, for example, was a short-term teacher who seemed content to relinquish it for marriage. She offered no rejoinder or argument when her suitor told her, "I feel so sorry for you in that hot schoolhouse today, my darling." Even more committed teachers found some positions more appealing than others and had their ups and downs in dealing with numerous children. Lena Smith's school was flourishing, but her grandmother noted that the students were "mostly young beginners that it is not much pleasure to teach."[45]

Yet both second and third generations contained a considerable number of women who taught students for a decade or longer and made teaching a long-term, if not necessarily a lifelong, occupation. For some widows, such as Kate Meares and Maria Louisa Carrington, teaching supported them financially and filled up their time. Later in life they retired to other activities. Maria Louisa

44. Knight, *Public School Education in North Carolina*, 201; Camp, *Some Pioneer Women Teachers*, 168–70; Long, *High Time to Tell It*, 151–60. On the Funders' suspension of Virginia public schools, see Jane Dailey, *Before Jim Crow: The Politics of Race in Postemancipation Virginia* (Chapel Hill, N.C., 2000), 48–102; Raymond H. Pulley, *Old Virginia Restored: An Interpretation of the Progressive Impulse, 1870–1930* (Charlottesville, Va., 1968), 24–57.

45. W. A. Williams to Jeannie Meares, June 18, 1881, John and William A. Williams Papers, SHC; Grandma to Rebe Smith, Aug. 20, 1882, Peter Evans Smith Papers, SHC. See also Thomas Pettigrew to Caroline Pettigrew, April 30, 1883, Pettigrew Family Papers, SHC.

Carrington, for example, lived briefly in New York with one of her daughters and then shuttled between her two daughters' homes in Richmond. Other second generation teachers were more dedicated. Virginia Hankins seems to have contemplated retirement only when her health, weakened by tuberculosis, began to fail her; up until that point she had looked forward to the time when she might open her own school. In Georgia, Fanny Andrews complained about teaching when she first began in 1870, but by her second term she was finding it "less odious." Soon she began to express a dedication to her scholars, and she taught for much of the next thirty years.[46]

Even more elite women of the third generation spent many years teaching and helped to make it increasingly a "woman's occupation" by the end of the nineteenth century. Mary Lord began teaching in 1868 when she was twenty-three years old. Many of her positions were in Brooklyn and the environs of New York City. In 1878, a cousin reported, "Mary Lord is so happy at her school." Her teaching continued for over another decade, until her marriage. More impressively, Adelaide Meares taught over four thousand students during forty-two consecutive years at the same school. Meares and other lifetime teachers have left relatively little testimony about their commitment to schoolteaching, yet their love of learning and education was apparent even early in life. In 1875, teenaged Adelaide Meares had pronounced herself "perfectly delighted" with her school, Tileston Institute in Wilmington. Two years later, while averring her intention "to study several years longer," she declared, "Father thinks it is a great mistake for girls to stop school and go out into society so soon, and I do also, so I am not anxious to be a young lady."[47]

Some of the most erudite and enterprising of the third-generation teachers moved into higher education. Although the intellectual level and rigor of southern female colleges and seminaries varied wildly, these institutions depended on long-term teachers to inspire and stimulate their students. Some teachers, like Elizabeth Avery Colton at Meredith College in Raleigh (then known as Baptist Women's College), dedicated themselves to raising standards of female education. In the 1890s, the growing number of normal schools created to educate teachers also employed female teachers and principals. While normal schools continued to hire many male faculty, women who looked at teaching as a long-

46. Maria Louisa Carrington to Eliza Dabney, March 22, 1880, and Dec. 24, 1882, Saunders Family Papers, VHS; Virginia Hankins to Louis Hankins, [c. 1887], and April 19, 1888, Hankins Family Papers, VHS; Andrews, *Journal of a Georgia Woman,* 40.

47. Kate Meares to Richard A. Meares, Jan. 11 and March 10, 1878, Meares-DeRosset Papers, SHC; Adelaide Meares to "Dear Miss Mary," c. Oct. 11, 1875, and Adelaide Meares to "My Dear May," Feb. 14, 1877, both in Adelaide Savage Meares Papers, Duke.

term occupation increasingly found berths at these schools. Viola Boddie began to teach Latin and French at North Carolina State Normal and Industrial School in 1892 and remained there until her retirement in 1935. Sue May Kirkland became the first "lady principal" of North Carolina State Normal in 1892, a position that she held until her death in 1914.[48]

The testimony left by teachers of the second and third generation suggests that many enjoyed teaching, less because of the actual activity involved than the influence and lifestyle it allowed them. Relatively few testified to the joys of working with young people; when they described teaching in terms of students, they emphasized the impact that the teachers could make on the next generation. The teachers exhibited, all in all, more a love of influence than of children. Perhaps women who enjoyed young children preferred marriage and traditional domesticity.[49]

Some teachers, especially those in the younger generation, seemed to have liked their occupation precisely because it formed a practical alternative to the domestic life. In 1877, Esther Meares only half-jokingly told her cousin, "I was so sorry your Mother could not get me a [teaching] situation. It would be so much better than cooking, don't you think?" Within three years Esther had her teaching position—a school with thirty-eight scholars. Not only did she prefer teaching to housework for her family, but her sarcastic comments about her suitors as "country beaux" who were "tiresome" suggest that she chose teaching over the marriages available to her. She laughingly fended off her admirers' hints about marriage. Whether she cared little about marriage or simply the men who offered it to her, Esther lived a long life unmarried.[50]

Like Esther Meares, many schoolteachers never married; others married relatively late. As Chapter One indicated, schoolteachers were not the only females who never married; other women from elite families remained single. Still, schoolteachers, as a group, seemed most sanguine about their unmarried state. For some, the friendships they formed with other teachers were a fulfilling alternative to or substitute for marriage. Some of these relationships provided both love and intellectual stimulation. At Leache-Wood, a school in Norfolk, Vir-

48. Camp, *Some Pioneer Women Teachers*, 36–37, 53–57,114–15; Amy Thompson McCandless, *The Past in the Present: Women's Higher Education in the Twentieth-Century American South* (Tuscaloosa, Ala., 1999), 36–38; Jean Bradley Anderson, *The Kirklands of Ayr Mount* (Chapel Hill, N.C., 1991).

49. See, for example, Long, *High Time to Tell It*, passim.

50. Essie Meares to Louis H. Meares, Nov. 7, 1877, March 25 and April 15, 1877, Meares-DeRosset Papers, SHC; Mary T. Meares to Fred Meares, Nov. 20, 1880, William B. Meares Papers, SHC.

ginia, Irene Leache and her devoted friend and fellow teacher, Anna Cogswell Wood, spent thirty years together, punctuating their summers not only with uplifting study but with numerous foreign trips to places as exotic as Italy, Russia, and Egypt. In *The Story of a Friendship*, a memoir written by Anna Wood after Irene's death, Anna chronicled not only their teaching and travels but the strength of their relationship, which she called an "opulent friendship." Although she always referred to Irene Leache as "Miss Leache," she spent many pages detailing her friend's magnetism and charisma. "The matchless charm of her countenance was its smile," Anna wrote, "only to be described, however, by its effect on others." She quoted her journal, in which she had described Irene's eyes as "lucid with thought, lucent with love," calling them "lamps that have lighted my footsteps through the dreary labyrinths of this nether world."[51]

In this case, two fellow teachers happily constructed their own world, a place where they pursued love, truth, and beauty. After a childhood in Fauquier County, Irene Leache had governessed and taught in West Virginia to support her younger siblings. In 1868, twenty-nine-year-old Irene first encountered eighteen-year-old Anna Wood at the Valley Female Seminary called Angerona near Winchester; they never parted. While we can not determine the sexual orientation of these women, Wood's narrative makes it clear that theirs was indeed a loving partnership. Her description of the garden at Angerona that first spring suggests that a marriage, at least of their minds, had occurred there. "What a delight we found in wandering through this garden," she reminisced, "giving to fancy all she craved of freedom." According to Wood, "The pageant of spring before us took on the aspect of a wedding for which each plant in turn hurried to make ready." In this case, "The centre of all this loveliness was the bride, a laurel that leaned half of her snowy blossoms against a cedar, which, in his suit of perennial green did us service for the groom."[52]

Together Leache and Wood opened Leache-Wood in Norfolk in 1871 and educated girls of all ages. The school not only included higher learning for young women; in 1880 they began a kindergarten for children between ages three and eight. According to Wood, they deliberately kept the school at a size

51. Anna Cogswell Wood, *The Story of a Friendship: A Memoir* (New York, 1901), 9. Idem, *Idyls and Impressions of Travel* (New York, 1904) also described their worldwide adventures.

52. Wood, *Story of a Friendship*, 19–21; Eleanor Ramsay Williamson, "Exceptional Attainments and Constructive Force: Women, Education, and the Arts in Norfolk, 1871–1933," *VC* 47 (spring 1998): 64–75. Jo Ann Mervis Hofheimer, *Annie Wood, a Portrait: The Life and Times of the Founder of the Irene Leache Memorial* (Norfolk, Va., 1996), 40–45, describes Wood and Leache as "thoroughly Victorian women who . . . had neither the concept of, nor the terms for, a lesbian relationship."

and scope they could control: "Through the gradual increase of pupils and teachers, besides the addition of kindergarten, music, and arts departments, Leachwood bid fair to reach more than mere local fame; but here we called halt to ambition; for effort to compass material gain together with size, structure and success would soon have used up Miss Leache's strength and subverted the real interests of the school. We determined therefore, early in the action not to become the slaves of our work." Although Leache-Wood became well known for its rigorous curriculum, it also included numerous activities for the student body. Productions and musicals helped to make the school a special place to teachers as well as students. Wood thought dramatic recitations a "prompt and effective medium for conveying knowledge and for enabling the mind to grasp subjects as a whole instead of in parts." Considering the theater and opera house to be "serious schools of art," Leache and Wood set about to foster a cultural community that reached beyond their students to others in Norfolk. On Saturday evenings the Fireside Club, composed of local adults, met in the teachers' apartment. According to Anna Wood,

> Twenty or thirty callers often dropped in of an evening; there was a mingling of ages and sexes, of gray hair with the vivid heads of youth, there were men and women of the world. . . . Some came to see what was going on, whether this was to be a "Ballad Evening" or whether a minuet was to give the finishing touch to a French comedy. Others came for no purpose but to talk with Miss Leache, and it was amusing to note the skill with which these last avoided social entanglements and stuck to the parlor doorway, measuring the length and breadth of the rooms until they had singled out the well known figure clothed in dress of uncut brown velvet.

The summers that Leache and Wood spent exploring faraway places further extended their world of truth and beauty. The residential schools promised and sometimes delivered a community for women that was most removed from everyday domesticity. In contrast, other long-term teachers lived with their families. Yet even in the case of those who continued to be involved with their families, most were at least somewhat removed from household cares.[53]

Teaching was paid work, and most teachers seem to have needed the income, at least when they began. To be sure, teaching generally did not promise a financial bonanza. Many historians have pointed out that salaries for men were miserable and those for women even lower, although southern female teachers

---

53. Wood, *Story of a Friendship*, 87, 109, 104; Williamson, "Exceptional Attainments and Constructive Force," 68–69.

seem to have fared better than their northern peers, who often received only one-half or one-third the salary of men. High turnover helped to keep wages low. Even if they operated their own schools, teachers faced the problem of extracting money from the impoverished parents of their pupils, and profits often were small. Still, historian George Rable's argument that "poverty drove women into the classroom, but the classroom could not lift them out of poverty" seems overstated. In contrast to his assertion that "most teachers barely supported themselves, let alone their families" stand both the goals and the actual achievements of schoolteachers.[54]

Teachers seem to have envisioned two interrelated ideals, both of which depended on earning money: they wished to aid their families and to provide a measure of achievement and autonomy for themselves. While governesses might have found it difficult to ask for raises, long-term teachers seem to have become adept in negotiating for better pay. For example, when Virginia Hankins taught at Mrs. Chilton's female seminary in Montgomery, Alabama, she found that she constantly had to demand her salary. After at least two years, in 1880 she threatened to resign if she were not paid monthly. Her employer then sent her an advance and promised to do better, claiming she would be "heartbroken" if Virginia left. Yet leave Virginia did, for a position as "Principal of the Intermediate & Primary Departments" and teacher of rhetoric, composition, and reading at the Norfolk College for Young Ladies. There she received $500 yearly plus room and board, and her salary was paid in a timely manner, as she remarked in November 1881.[55]

Virginia experienced a problem that may have been widespread—adjusting her expectations for her salary with her preferences as to working conditions and location. When she decided that being a matron was too wearing on her health and that she would revert solely to teaching, she confided to her brother that "I like it here right well—but I don't like Norfolk much." She left for a position in Newport News that she preferred even though it paid only $300 yearly. Later she relinquished it for a school in Baltimore, noting, "They are all so nice to me here and my room is so pretty, I certainly am sorry to leave it for Baltimore & an uncertainty. But if I only can keep well—it will be better to make $600 than $300." Despite her reluctance to move to Baltimore, Virginia quickly came to enjoy the city and its cultural and gastronomic opportunities: "I enjoy going to

54. George C. Rable, *Civil Wars: Women and the Crisis of Southern Nationalism* (Urbana, Ill., 1989), 278; Perlmann and Margo, *Women's Work?* 86–89.

55. Virginia Hankins to Louis Hankins, June 27 and Sept. 8, 1880, and Nov. 18, 1881, Virginia Hankins to R. M. Saunders, June 13, 1881, all in Hankins Family Papers, VHS.

the opera & theater (and have a plenty of books to read)—then what is an important thing to me, I have good food, well-cooked." While better paying, the position in Baltimore did demand greater exertions. Virginia knowingly remarked, "They are all very nice with me, but of course I shall have trouble in managing so many undisciplined & indulged young people."[56]

Family correspondence of female teachers reveals them doing their part in propping up families, supporting parents, and educating siblings, sometimes even nieces and nephews. Even as Virginia Hankins fretted over receiving her salary promptly, she paid for the education of her younger sister and brother. For some teachers, this was a labor of love; for others it was a labor of duty. Armand DeRosset expressed such expectations when he wrote about his niece, "I think she would be wrong in losing any good opportunity of aiding in the support and education of her sisters and relieving her grandmother of the burden which she cannot well bear, and which seems likely to rest upon her alone." Whatever the demands, some families deeply appreciated such aid. Lena Smith taught for many years at Vine Hill Academy in eastern North Carolina, where she supervised the school for girls. When she was but twenty-five years old, her father, prodded by his failing eyesight, wrote a grateful tribute to her and her "sense and energy."[57]

An even greater admiration imbued the letters that Virginia Hankins received from her siblings. As early as 1880, one of her brothers thanked her for the "thousands of things" she had done for him and voiced the hope that a possible raise in his salary would enable him to begin repaying her. Far more touching was the letter that her favorite brother wrote Virginia shortly before her death, attributing his own and his brothers' successes in life to her: "My Darling sister you do not know how much we all love and honor you, and how much we all feel that it has been through your loving kindness and untiring zeal and love and prayer for us that have made us all what we are. We feel, dear sister, that we owe it all to you. What would Willie, Charlie or myself be today, if we had not received the helping hand and support from you. It has been through your work at St. Louis, Montgomery and at Norfolk and in Surry, that we have been able to prepair [sic] ourselves for the positions in lifes work that we now hold."[58]

The entrance of southern elite women into paid employment marks the

56. Virginia Hankins to Louis Hankins, April 16, 1883, May 15, 1887, April 19, 1888, and n.d. [1887].

57. A. J. DeRosset to Kate Meares, April 22, [1868], DeRosset Family Papers, SHC; Peter E. Smith to Lena Smith, July 13, 1880, Peter Evans Smith Papers, SHC.

58. Charlie Hankins to Louis Hankins, March 31, [c. 1880], and Louis Hankins to Virginia Hankins, Dec. 19, 1888, both in Hankins Family Papers, VHS.

emergence of a new ethic in the South—one that praised economic self-support and independence among women. For many, schoolteaching was not only a means to self-support but also was a form of independence. In her decision to retire from teaching because of her health, fifty-three-year-old Virginia Hankins lingered over the advantages of urban life and culture that she had enjoyed as a teacher. Yet her greatest regret, she wrote her brother, was the impending loss of independence: "I shall never be able to do as well again—because you know, dear Louie I enjoy spending my own money because I work for it. I love to control my own actions and to feel as if I can go or stay when I choose." Against this satisfaction she set the "fatigue and heavy weariness of an overtaxed body"—a body that would succumb to tuberculosis in less than a year.[59]

Other women pointed to the many achievements of the teacher. Emily Dupuy drew an explicit comparison between fashion and good works when she contrasted the superficial luxury of a young female acquaintance with the hard work of her granddaughter: "Kate Lee Holland left yesterday for New Orleans to visit relatives there, & to be present at the Mardi Gras when it comes off. Her wardrobe is a very splendid one, many of her dresses bought in Paris. With it all, I expect she is no happier than you are; usefully employed in teaching, imparting knowledge to others, at the same time gaining it yourself, besides making you feel independant, that you can support yourself. I feel quite proud of my grand-daughter, think I have reason to be."[60]

While securing their independence and helping their families could ofttimes be pursued in tandem, these goals sometimes conflicted with more traditional emotional relationships with kin. Mary Lord was tormented by the conflict between her desires for both attachment and self-sufficiency. From her teaching job in Brooklyn, New York, she anxiously wrote her cousin, "I am so distracted all of the time to go home, and so frantic for fear that I might have to do so." For Mary, the separation from her motherless younger siblings weighed most heavily: "I get perfectly wretched when I think of the children losing their dependence on me, and it is so hard to be separated from them; still I wouldn't go home for anything, and at the same time look forward to it with the greatest eagerness as the end & sum of my desires."[61]

Even though the school community might have lessened the pain of familial separation for some women, even those who did not overtly yearn for home and kin thought that a position combining both work and family would be ideal.

59. Virginia Hankins to Louis Hankins, April 19, 1888, Hankins Family Papers, VHS.
60. Emily Dupuy to Emmie Watkins, Jan. 18, 1883, Emily Dupuy Papers, VHS.
61. Mary Lord to Kate Meares, May 9, 1876, Meares-DeRosset Family Papers, SHC.

Less than two years before her death, Virginia Hankins hoped to open her own school with the assistance of her younger sister: "I think the year here [in Baltimore] will be a splendid preparation for me in case I can ever have a school of my own. I still want to have my own school & Mary to live with me and help me." She included visits from her younger brother, an itinerant engineer, in this vision: "And then you can come and be at my house sometimes."[62]

To be sure, not all employed women viewed their positions positively. Saidie Mason, then in her mid-fifties, worked first as a companion and later as a housekeeper in Washington, D.C., and St. Louis. She knew her employment was necessary to support herself and her impoverished brother, but she greatly resented it. While emphasizing the luxuriousness of her surroundings and the thoughtfulness of her employers, she also chafed at what she saw as a lack of independence. Constructing her own chronology of her employment, Saidie averred that she and her sisters had left home because there "it was impossible to eke out a decent support." In her letters, Saidie returned often to the tropes of her fettered existence and her separation from the family estate in Southampton County, Virginia. She feared a future dependence on her wealthy brother-in-law, Archer Anderson: "Should ill health overtake me[,] to have to give up my present comforts & to struggle or what is worse to fall back upon dear Archer, who is the only one who could help me, is distressing & humiliating to say the least." Only two years later, she again complained to her brother, "I have every comfort but I am not my own mistress." Mary Mason Anderson, Saidie's sister, believed that the problem was that Saidie's employers "do not show her the respect due to her." Mary asserted, "I should rather have less grandeur and more equality if I were Saidy."[63]

In contrast, women in clerkships and librarianships often seemed far more contented with their work. In addition to their own achievements, they seemed to value their independence and the admiration of others. Susan Mason, unlike her sister Saidie, happily recounted events during her days as a library clerk at the naval library in Washington. When she received a promotion, she proudly wrote her brother that the "money-increase is very *inconsiderable* but it is the appreciation of my own chief & my secretaries that pleases me." Even querulous Saidie admitted, "I don't mean to say that Sudy is not happier working to support herself."[64]

---

62. Virginia Hankins to Louis Hankins, n.d. [1887], Hankins Family Papers, VHS.

63. Saidie Mason to Lewis Mason, Sept. 16, 1890, and Aug. 15, 1892, Mary Anderson to Lewis Mason, Aug. 18, 1893, all in Mason Family Papers, VHS.

64. Susan Mason to Lewis Mason, Aug. 8, 1891, and Sarah Mason to Lewis Mason, Sept. 16, 1890, both in Mason Family Papers, VHS.

Long-term schoolteachers have left few testimonials about their life's work, but it seems likely their views echoed the best-selling fiction of Augusta Jane Evans: they valued teaching for what it could do for others and for themselves. In *Beulah,* Evans's enormously popular 1859 novel, the eponymous heroine, although taken under the guardianship of a wealthy doctor, remains determined to earn her livelihood as a teacher. A heated argument erupts after Beulah's graduation from the public school that she had insisted on attending when she announces her intention to teach school, even though her guardian wishes legally to adopt her. Over the course of the remaining three hundred pages of the large novel, Beulah works as a teacher. Almost never does Evans venture into the schoolroom with Beulah; instead, the novel chronicles her many relationships and her intellectual odyssey as she becomes a writer of philosophy. Evans skips over Beulah's actual teaching with the phrase that she "attended to her school duties"; perhaps the longest description of Beulah as teacher indicates that she "came home from school more than usually fatigued; one of the assistant teachers was indisposed, and she had done double work to relieve her."[65]

At one point Cornelia Graham, a wealthy invalid friend, questions Beulah, "Does not life look dreary and tedious when you anticipate years of labor and care? Teaching is not child's sport; are you not already weary in spirit?" Beulah's reply is resolute: "No I am not weary; neither does life seem joyless. I know that I shall have to labor for a support, but necessity always supplies strength. I have many, very many sources of happiness, and look forward, hopefully, to a life of usefulness." Cornelia presses her point. What will Beulah's future be; should she look to marriage to free her from this kind of labor? "Beulah made a gesture of impatience. 'That is a mode of exemption so extremely remote that I never consider it. I do not find teaching so disagreeable as you imagine, and dare say, at fifty (if I live that long), I shall be in a schoolroom.'"[66]

Most likely a majority of women teaching school at any one time in the late nineteenth century would have shuddered at the thought of many more years of such employment. Yet a significant number of women saw teaching not only as a temporary expedient but as a long-term solution to the question of how they would support themselves and what they wished to do with their lives. When the University of North Carolina created a summer normal school in 1876–77, almost half of the two hundred students who enrolled were female teachers, even though males formed the great majority of teachers. Moreover, the early teachers

65. Augusta Jane Evans, *Beulah,* ed. Elizabeth Fox-Genovese (1859; Baton Rouge, La., 1992), 143–47, 393.
66. Ibid., 310.

described here presented a model of what an educated woman could be in southern society. They pioneered an ethic of women's self-support, capability, and intellectual achievement that would be amplified in the normal schools that proliferated after 1890.[67]

Even as some women from the old elite ventured outside the household to work and teach for wages, others also moved in public spaces. Over the last few decades of the antebellum period, women had gained access to more public areas. Historian Lisa Tolbert has mapped the geography of mid-southern towns in the antebellum period, showing how over time the town square and retail area became more welcoming to female shoppers. As the railroad came to southern towns, industrial zones of warehouses and the like clustered around it, while the center of town became a more refined retail space suitable for ladies. Women gathered in churches and cemeteries or shopped in specialty stores that sold dry goods or furniture; groceries and local courthouses remained more ambiguous spaces, often given over largely to males. Maria Louisa Carrington attested to this phenomenon, telling her sister that Dr. Bagby was slated to deliver a speech on barons and queens at the courthouse, and that "we want to go to hear him, if any ladies go." In this case, Maria Louisa, despite her position as a thirtyish widow of a good family, was checking to make sure that the crowd at the courthouse would include other women of her social position. Often elite women, rather than make the trip to the county courthouse with its political talk and male swagger, attested to deeds before local justices of peace or depended on men to carry out their legal business.[68]

67. Pamela Evelyn Dean, "Covert Curriculum: Class, Gender, and Student Culture at a New South Woman's College, 1892–1910" (Ph.D. diss., University of North Carolina at Chapel Hill, 1995), 21, 36–41; Pamela Dean, "Learning to Be New Women: Campus Culture at the North Carolina Normal and Industrial College," *NCHR* (July 1991): 286–306. Although Dean emphasizes how much this first generation of normal school graduates differed from their mothers and grandmothers, I would argue that the normal school graduates resembled the most dedicated of the second- and third-generation women teachers and continued their commitment to independence and a life of the mind.

68. Lisa C. Tolbert, *Constructing Townscapes: Space and Society in Antebellum Tennessee* (Chapel Hill, N.C., 1999), 95–101, 123–29, 140–52. Maria Louisa Carrington to Betty Saunders, May 7, 1866, Saunders Family Papers, VHS. For examples of women who attested to deeds before justices of the peace who were neighbors or relatives, see Mortgage of William and Catherine Marshall to R. Taylor, Oct. 1, 1886, Fauquier Deeds, vol. 77, pp. 458–59; Mortgage of Gray and Alice Carroll et al. to Alexander Payne, April 10, 1866, Fauquier Deeds, vol. 59, pp. 807–808. Examples of women performing such business at the courthouse can be seen in Deed of Janet C. Weaver, Janet H. Weaver, and Meta W. Lee to Julian P. Lee, Nov. 12, 1872, and Deed of Mary H. Smith to George W. Grafflin, Aug. 24, 1874, Fauquier Deeds, vol. 66, pp. 96–97, both in FCCC.

Women from the old elite continued another activity that had emerged in the antebellum period, assuming leadership roles in voluntary charitable efforts for community institutions and organizations. While some of these activities were commemorative and memorial, women also moved toward involvement in more overtly political affairs. Women's benevolent efforts, especially in support of churches, were of long standing; the ladies of southern towns and cities had been undertaking religious and charitable work for much of the nineteenth century. Newspaper accounts and personal letters alike suggest that these activities continued at as busy a pace as the general economic conditions would admit. This work included women's participation in church services and other programs, as well as the ongoing maintenance of churches' physical plants. In addition, women were involved in conceiving and carrying out fundraising and other events in support of special, often relatively large, undertakings.[69]

In both the North and the South, women came during the nineteenth century to form the backbone of churches. In most congregations they comprised the majority of the membership and were the most frequent participants in church activities. As historian Elizabeth Hayes Turner has pointed out for Galveston, Texas, worship services in many different Protestant denominations showed the impress of female activity. Maria Gordon Rice, in her reminiscence about life in late-nineteenth-century Charlotte County, Virginia, drew a detailed picture of Roanoke Presbyterian Church, which much of the local gentry attended. Before church services began, the men stood outside, discussing "politics and crops," while the women inside the church "conversed in stage whispers, often passing from pew to pew to chat with their friends." This was their space, even if they talked quietly when gossiping about secular topics. During services the sexes were separated, each with its own set of benches. Maria Rice suggested that social rather than religious reasons governed this separation. Only upon the second hymn did the men come "noisily trooping to their seats." She continued, "This custom, joined to the less defensible habit of tobacco-chewing, was, probably the reason for the separation of the sexes in church."[70]

At Roanoke Church, the organ and organist took center stage. According to Maria Rice, "In the middle of the church was a singular structure with green baize curtains. . . . Its purpose was made clear when Miss Adeline Carrington appeared, went within the curtains and drew them closely around her, whisper-

69. For the best introduction to the voluminous literature on women's benevolence, see Anne Firor Scott, *Natural Allies: Women's Associations in American History* (Urbana, Ill., 1993), especially chs. 4 and 5 on the late nineteenth century.
70. "Reminiscences of Maria Gordon Pryor Rice," unpublished typescript, c. 1920, LVA.

ing a few directions to the singers outside. Soon, from the modest seclusion, the little organ began a hymn known as the 'voluntary.'" Ironically, as Rice herself noticed, Adeline Carrington's insistence on veiling her participation only highlighted it. Elsewhere, women needed less window dressing for their part in their church's musical offerings. Second-generation matron Rebecca Norfleet Hill Smith long served as the organist at Trinity Church, an Episcopal church in Halifax County, North Carolina.[71]

Elite women of different generations also were active in teaching the Sunday schools that increasingly were a part of the postwar church. Teenaged Alice Lee Saunders continued this activity among third-generation women, sending back special greetings to her "Sunday School scholars" when she visited Richmond. Teaching Sunday school tended to run among the pious descendants of the Dabneys; Willie and Bessie Carrington and their cousin Alice Saunders all were Sunday school teachers as young adults. As historian Anastatia Sims has noted, the major Protestant denominations in North Carolina were welcoming women's societies and auxiliaries in aid of missionary work by the 1870s and 1880s. By this time, some young southern women of the third generation were willing to go as missionaries to foreign countries, as when Lizzie Dabney undertook what her relatives considered a "great, and noble work."[72]

Finding support for building, renovating, or expanding the physical plant of churches often depended on female efforts. As the Presbyterians in Danville, Virginia, finished a new church in 1882, the women of the church were particularly active. Maria Dupuy Anderson, according to her mother, "with the other ladies has been busy the past week in fixing the grounds around the presbyterian church, the gentleman are so busy they do not have time to attend to it, there was cleaning up, grading & sowing in grass seed, which the ladies have superintended." When a large fire in New Bern, North Carolina, razed Christ Church in 1871, Maggie Haughton delayed distributing other fundraising circulars because she knew that rebuilding the church would engross everyone's energies. And in fact the women held a series of fairs and feasts to pay the contractor. Judith Page Rives proudly spearheaded the group repairing the chapel of her local Episcopal church. In 1875, she told a son that most of the $225 on hand

71. Ibid., 21–22; Claiborne Thweatt Smith Jr., *Smith of Scotland Neck: Planters on the Roanoke* (Baltimore, 1976), 118.

72. Anastatia Sims, *The Power of Femininity in the New South: Women's Organizations and Politics in North Carolina, 1880–1930* (Columbia, S.C., 1997), 15–18; Scott, *Natural Allies*, 86–93. Alice Lee Saunders to Addie Saunders, Nov. 1, 1886, and Maria Louisa Carrington to Eliza Dabney, May 14, 1871, and April 12, 1880, all in Saunders Family Papers, VHS. See Suzanne Lebsock, *"A Share of Honour": Virginia Women, 1600–1945* (Richmond, Va., 1984), 110–11.

had been raised "by the sale of fancy work done by Ella and me, and a few donations." In Halifax County, North Carolina, Peter Evans Smith jokingly remarked in 1886 that in his daughters' absence, "it will be very lonesome for your mother . . . she will have to amuse herself in looking after the Rectory work." In this case, Rebecca Hill Smith had already busied herself in church affairs, serving as first president of Trinity Church's Ladies Sewing Circle in 1878 to raise money to build a church rectory. As in Galveston, Texas, where women's efforts resulted in church buildings that conformed to their aesthetic ideas and also celebrated their contributions to the church and Christianity, women of the old elite were putting their own stamp on the places in which they worshipped. Declaring that the rectory was a memorial to Rebecca Smith "and other devoted and consecrated women," Trinity Parish's historian found it "especially appropriate that this should be a home."[73]

Although Judith Rives and her never-married daughter single-handedly crafted items and raised money for their church, more commonly fund-raising was an endeavor undertaken by a community of women. In December 1887, ladies in Warrenton, North Carolina, staged an oyster supper to benefit the Methodist Sunday school there. In numerous towns and localities, female church members staged bazaars and entertainments that depended on exhibiting their own and their female relatives' talents. Churches had begun to model some of their activities on more profane entertainment; they would continue to do so because the cause, in public opinion, justified women's and even young unmarried girls' appearance on stage. For example, Kate Dabney borrowed sheet music from a relative for an upcoming musicale because "I am invited up to the Seven Mile Ford to meet some company from Abingdon & three of us ladies are desired to play at a concert for the benefit of the church."[74]

Outside the arena of church affairs, southern aristocratic women continued to undertake and even expanded their benevolent activities related to family, religion, and education. In Wilmington, North Carolina, Kate Meares turned her work in education and her Episcopal piety toward new ventures. She was

73. Emily H. Dupuy to Minnie Watkins, Oct. 9, 1882, Emily Dupuy Papers, VHS; Maggie Haughton to Jane Hawkins, April 17, 1871, Hawkins Family Papers, SHC; Gertrude S. Carraway, *Crown of Life: History of Christ Church, New Bern, N.C., 1715–1940* (New Bern, N.C., 1940), 177–79; Judith P. Rives to Will Rives, Aug. 15, 1875, William Cabell Rives Papers, LC; Peter E. Smith to Lena Smith, Sept. 23, 1886, Peter E. Smith Papers, SHC; Elizabeth Hayes Turner, *Women, Culture, and Community: Religion and Reform in Galveston, 1880–1920* (New York, 1997), 40–54; Smith, *Smith of Scotland Neck,* 118–19.
74. George W. Alston to Lucy T. Alston, Dec. 9, 1887, Lucy Tunstall Alston Papers, SHC; Kate Montgomery Dabney to Kitty Dabney, Nov. 17, 1872, Saunders Family Papers, VHS.

instrumental in establishing the St. James Home, which operated as the charitable adjunct of St. James Episcopal Church, one of Wilmington's most elite Episcopal churches. For four years, Kate Meares threw herself wholeheartedly into the work. She helped organize the home's free school (which had sixty students by October 1872) and started an infirmary. The orphanage was well underway, and she was so involved in educating the poor that she was willing to befriend a northern schoolteacher who was instructing the children of freedmen. Kate announced to her son, "We are going to have a boarder—a young lady from Wisconsin who is sent here by the Missionary Society to teach the negro children at St. Barnabas . . . poor thing nobody would take her in, & as she came to do Church work, I thought the church Home was the place for her." Kate also anticipated opening a boarding school for girls. Although some of her friends and relations were aiding her exertions, she wanted and demanded more assistance: "But don't you see how work is gathering up—if God will only send me some more ladies to help do it!" She continued her benevolent work until 1875, when she was took a teaching position near her sons and had to relinquish her responsibilities to others.[75]

Other ladies, especially townswomen, occupied themselves with benevolent institutions such as orphanages. In Richmond, the Female Humane Society had supported an orphanage for girls since the early nineteenth century, but the Civil War both destroyed its endowment and vastly increased the numbers of children needing its services. Anna Greenough Burgwyn, an elderly matron who shuttled between plantations in North Carolina and Richmond, was in 1869 one "of the Managers of St. Paul's Orphan Asylum"; she was involved in a host of other activities as well. Active in the Church of the Savior, an Episcopal church, she rejoiced when her society decided to ask the male members of the church to contribute toward an organist. In 1886, she supported efforts by her Ladies Aid Society, which frequently met as a sewing circle, to raise a contribution of $100 toward building a schoolhouse. On a typical day in North Carolina, sixty-nine-year-old Anna visited her daughter-in-law and played with her grandchildren, then attended her society meeting. She had earlier cut out aprons that the society intended to make, and at the meeting they sewed up four of them.[76]

75. Kate Meares to Louis H. Meares, Dec. 10, 1871, and April 27, 1872, both in Meares-DeRosset Family Papers, SHC. On home missions, see John Patrick McDowell, *The Social Gospel in the South: The Woman's Home Mission Movement in the Methodist Episcopal Church South, 1886–1939* (Baton Rouge, La., 1982).

76. E. Susan Barber, "Anxious Care and Constant Struggle: The Female Humane Association and Richmond's White Civil War Orphans," in *Before the New Deal: Social Welfare in the South, 1830–1930,* ed. Elna C. Green (Athens, Ga., 1999), 120–37; Anna Greenough Burgwyn diary,

Some women saw benevolent work as the way to a contented as well as productive life. When Sallie Bruce mused over what would make her daughter-in-law, Mary Howard Bruce, a more contented wife, she decided that the answer lay in activities in town rather than life on the plantation, since Mary "will never rest until she gets in or near a town & I really believe that she would not only be a happier, but a better woman, if she could have her time taken up with society, church work & other things which occupy the attention of her set in cities."[77]

The sectional crisis and Civil War had stimulated women's interest in politics, and this continued after the war on a range of issues. Given their class position and their racism, most women opposed—and some bitterly—the political reconstruction of the South in the late 1860s and 1870s. The immediate post-war events called forth the greatest comments from them, but in 1866, Maria Louisa Carrington despaired of Virginia's political prospects as growing "more and more dreadful" because the radicals were "filled with every fiendish feeling." In 1871, young Lavalette Dupuy worried about the Republicans carrying her home county of Prince Edward and observed, "How mortifying it is! though I rejoice to see that the Old State is redeeming itself and has given a large Conservative majority." Election day the following year called forth mixed feelings in Sallie Bruce, who reported to her son, "The South is so oppressed that it is impossible for our States to be prosperous & Grant's re-election assures another 4 years of misrule. I never saw your Father so despairing as far as political matters are concerned—he seems to realize that no change for the better will take place in his day."[78]

In Virginia much of the old elite distrusted and disliked General William Mahone and the Readjusters, the interracial coalition that he put together in the 1870s. The issue of how best to pay off the state's debt loomed large in Virginians' minds, but, as historians such as Jane Dailey have pointed out, it was inescapably entwined with racial politics. Virginia women of the old elite who expressed political views tended to denounce the interracial alliance of Readjusters who wanted to provide public schools rather than retire the debt. In 1879, when Leila Dabney looked to the woes of Orange County, Virginia, she

Sept. 14, 1869, May 25, June 1, and Nov. 23, 1886, Burgwyn Family Papers, SHC; Henry W. Lewis, *Northampton Parishes* (Jackson, N.C., 1951), 115.

77. Sallie Bruce to Morelle Bruce, Dec. 18, 1886, Bruce Family Papers, VHS.

78. Maria Louisa Carrington to Susan Taylor, Feb. 6, 1866, Saunders Family Papers, VHS; Lavalette Dupuy to Mary Watkins, Nov. 14, 1871, Emily Dupuy Papers, VHS; Sallie Bruce to Morelle Bruce, Nov. 8, 1872, Bruce Family Papers, VHS. See also Martha Elizabeth Coleman Ambler to Phebe Bailey, March 22, 1875, Bailey Family Papers, VHS.

blamed the freedmen: "I am sorry to see so many persons coming to poverty and I believe it is all due to negro schools." Sharing the conservative distaste for General Mahone's interracial alliance, Sarah Bruce Seddon gloated when John S. Wise—one of Mahone's allies with ties to the old elite—was blackballed by an exclusive Richmond club. "The line cannot be drawn too distinctly between the sheep & the goats," she exulted, "and honest, true men should not be mixed up in any way with Gen Mahone and his foul disgusting followers." When in 1883 Governor Mahone appointed three African Americans as election judges, Sallie Bruce angrily declared, "How long will these wretches rule I wonder!" A month later she returned to the theme of black election judges and added, "It is awful to think of such savages being used as tools to degrade our state by that wretch Mahone."[79]

To be sure, some aristocratic families—such as the Harvies, Hubards, and Wises—supported Readjuster politics, especially in its early stages. The women in these families, however, were less vocal about political affairs and left no evidence that they approved of the Readjusters. Whether elite white women supported or deplored the Readjuster movement, it was not something that galvanized them into direct participation in politics. They were unwilling, or at least hesitant, to form political organizations, despite urgings from some male Funders. In Warrenton, Virginia, such pro-Funder efforts came to naught. The local newspaper reported in March 1878 a meeting of what it called a "goodly number of matrons and young ladies" to "initiate a movement which should inculcate an honest and healthy sentiment touching the public debt, and to concert measures to contribute something of themselves towards its payment." Although the article claimed that "two ladies" had persuaded former governor William Smith to address the gathering, it also acknowledged that the newspaper had issued the call for the meeting. Despite the newspaper's claim that "resolutions were proposed looking to permanent organization and future procedure," no further news appeared about such a female organization.[80]

While the Funder-Readjuster controversy dominated Virginia politics in the 1870s and 1880s, North Carolina during that period dealt with a host of other issues. At the end of Reconstruction, temperance legislation came to the fore in North Carolina state and local politics. In 1881, upon the prodding of prominent church groups, the state legislature passed a prohibition measure and put it

79. Leila Dabney to Phebe Bailey, Aug. 13, 1879, Bailey Family Papers, VHS; Sarah Bruce Seddon to Sallie Bruce, n. d. [1878], Sallie Bruce to Morelle Bruce, April 13 and May 19, 1883, all in Bruce Family Papers, VHS; Dailey, *Before Jim Crow*, 132–57.

80. James Tice Moore, *Two Paths to the New South: The Virginia Debt Controversy, 1870–1883* (Lexington, Ky., 1974), 54–82; *Warrenton (Va.) True Index,* March 28, 1878.

to a plebiscite for voter approval, a measure that spurred both white and African American women to action. In Charlotte, North Carolina, the "better classes" of both races worked in separate organizations for the common cause of temperance, much as they had done for the impoverished and the hospital association. Although prohibition lost badly in the election, women's groups continued to press for it through local option elections. At this time, the Woman's Christian Temperance Union (WCTU), founded in Ohio, was reaching out to a national audience, especially after the accession of Frances Willard to its presidency in 1879. In November 1883 she spoke in Greensboro, North Carolina, to inspire the temperance workers there. For the next decade and a half, black and white women labored both together and separately, as African American women formed their own local. It would take the white supremacist campaigns of the 1890s to drive apart these groups of women.[81]

Yet this cooperation was tentative and did not completely allay white fears about black behavior. Many blamed African Americans when prohibition failed during the 1881 plebiscite. Elite white women took special note of the black vote, even when temperance forces won local elections. Rejoicing that politics was seconding her reform interests, elderly Anna Greenough Burgwyn reported the success of a local option election in Northampton County, North Carolina, where her son George Burgwyn had served as an election judge: "George came over in the eve[nin]g & reported that the town had 'gone dry' 16 to 49. This was a great pleasure to all of us. Many Negroes had voted in favor of it." Although the WCTU organized in Virginia during this period, its beginnings there were tentative. The ladies, while pressing for temperance instruction in the schools and a raised age of consent for sexual activity for young women, gained no legislative victories in the 1880s.[82]

Historians, while long recognizing the importance of female benevolent activ-

81. Sims, *Power of Femininity*, 19–28; Glenda Elizabeth Gilmore, *Gender and Jim Crow: Women and the Politics of White Supremacy in North Carolina, 1896–1920* (Chapel Hill, N.C., 1996), 31–59; Janette Thomas Greenwood, *Bittersweet Legacy: The Black and White "Better Classes" in Charlotte, 1850–1910* (Chapel Hill, N.C., 1994), 64–113. On Frances Willard and her southern campaign, see Ruth Bordin, *Woman and Temperance: The Quest for Power and Liberty, 1873–1900* (New Brunswick, N.J., 1981), 52–88; Scott, *Natural Allies*, 93–103. For the North Carolina state and local campaigns, see Daniel J. Whitener, *Prohibition in North Carolina, 1715–1945* (Chapel Hill, N.C., 1945), 53–105. On other issues in North Carolina postwar politics, consult Paul D. Escott, *Many Excellent People: Power and Privilege in North Carolina, 1850–1900* (Chapel Hill, N.C., 1985), 85–195.

82. Anna Greenough Burgwyn diary, June 7, [1886], Burgwyn Family Papers, SHC; Lebsock, *"A Share of Honour,"* 123–24. For the role of George Burgwyn, Anna's son, in opposing African American participation in the Union League, consult Escott, *Many Excellent People*, 151.

ities, have been perplexed by women's efforts in support of the "Lost Cause," that is, for memorializing the Confederate dead. Some historians have interpreted such work as an expression of women's conservatism and their attachment to reactionary political movements, arguing that female support for Confederate causes was part of an unholy bargain in which women assented to their subordination as a sex in order to protect their class position. Although this explanation may well hold true for Confederate memorial activities of the 1890s, it misses some of the distinctive features of the early movement, an effort that offers a window on the entire range of women's civic activities.[83]

In the years after the Civil War, many southern towns and cities honored their Confederate dead through memorial organizations in which elite women took the lead and remained in the forefront. Many of these southern societies organized during the spring and summer of 1866, and they commonly called themselves Ladies Memorial Associations (LMAs), although they remained local, decentralized groups until late in the century. Historians have pointed to numerous reasons for the founding of these societies, ranging from women's commemorative and mourning activities to their role as political mouthpieces for their disenfranchised menfolk. Some scholars link these societies to women's wartime work of nursing and mourning. Those who focus on the political aspect of these societies tend to emphasize the role that men played in encouraging the formation of these societies and supporting their continued activities.[84]

In the immediate postwar years, women of the old elite, aided by male friends and admirers, undertook the enormous task of building and caring for cemeteries. After a farmer plowing his fields near Winchester, Virginia, uncovered the

83. For the Lost Cause as a futile distraction that pulled women away from working for their own social, legal, and political advancement, see Suzanne Lebsock, *The Free Women of Petersburg: Status and Culture in a Southern Town, 1784–1860* (New York, 1984), 244–49. LeeAnn Whites, *The Civil War as a Crisis in Gender: Augusta, Georgia, 1860–1890* (Athens, Ga., 1995), 160–208, sees the societies as propping up male dominance. She makes the argument more forcefully in "'Stand By Your Man': The Ladies Memorial Association and the Reconstruction of Southern White Manhood," in *Women of the American South: A Multicultural Reader*, ed. Christie Anne Farnham (New York, 1997), 133–49. Drew Gilpin Faust, *Mothers of Invention: Women of the Slaveholding South in the American Civil War* (Chapel Hill, N.C., 1996), 247–57, believes that postwar women were involved in what she calls the "rehabilitation of patriarchy."

84. Whites, *Civil War as a Crisis in Gender*, 181–88; Faust, *Mothers of Invention*, 187–95; Gaines Foster, *Ghosts of the Confederacy: Defeat, the Lost Cause, and the Emergence of the New South* (New York, 1987), 38–42, 127–34; E. Merton Coulter, "The Confederate Monument in Athens, Georgia," *Georgia Historical Review* 40 (Sept. 1956): 230–47; Catherine W. Bishir, "'A Strong Force of Ladies': Women, Politics, and Confederate Memorial Associations in Nineteenth-Century Raleigh," *NCHR* 77 (Oct. 2000): 455–91.

remains of two soldiers, several local men and women discussed how to deal with this problem. Their solution—one that quite a few other groups in the Upper South would imitate—was to form a memorial society and to obtain land for a cemetery. The Winchester group began its labors in the fall of 1865; by that winter its efforts were receiving attention in the local press. In March 1866, a neighboring newspaper reported that the "ladies of Winchester" had received $250 toward "removing and suitably re-interring" the Confederate dead "scattered throughout the Valley." Early that spring, other groups in Virginia and elsewhere took shape and began their attempts to bury and suitably to memorialize southern soldiers.[85]

The problem of soldiers' graves strewn about the southern countryside seems to have driven these early organizations. Many of the earliest societies in the Old Dominion were located in wartorn areas, where residents wished to bring both order and commemoration to the dead so obviously and untidily in their midst. Although North Carolina had seen less military action, Raleigh too had hundreds of Confederate soldiers' graves near what had been the Confederate hospital. The most striking common factor of these organizations, ranging from Spotsylvania through Petersburg and Appomattox to Raleigh, was the desire to gather soldiers' graves into a common cemetery and to see that they were mounded, marked, and neatly kept. It was a form of civic housekeeping, intended to rationalize and tranquilize the towns and countryside where war had so recently wreaked havoc.[86]

The minutes of the Appomattox society indicate that it first met at the courthouse in May 1866, where members elected officers and wrote a constitution. The organization's purpose was "to provide suitable interment for the Confederate Soldiers who came to their end by battle or decease in the latter part of the late war in this part of the country, whose bodies have not been deposited in some regular burying-ground." The Appomattox group claimed as its inspiration a letter that a Richmond lady had written to an Appomattox resident in appreciation of the care given a deceased son. Yet the formation of other societies also influenced the Appomattox group, as it signaled an interest in creating a "Ladies Association similar to the Ladies Memorial Associations in other parts of the South."[87]

The Petersburg Ladies Memorial Society also took shape in May 1866, but

85. For the history of Ladies Memorial Associations written by the local societies themselves, see Confederate Southern Memorial Association, *History of the Confederated Memorial Associations of the South* (New Orleans, 1904); *Warrenton (Va.) True Index,* March 2, 1866.

86. Whites, "'Stand By Your Man,'" 138, also sees part of the problem as "purely practical."

87. Minutes of the Appomattox Ladies Memorial Association, May 18, 1866, VHS.

it announced its purposes in far more grandiloquent language: "Whereas a mysterious Providence has devolved on us a duty which would otherwise have been a nation's pride to perform; we the ladies of Petersburg now assume our share of the melancholy yet grateful task of doing honor to the remains of her noble sons." In their founding statement, the Petersburg ladies imagined a "spectral band" of dead soldiers arising from their "neglected graves" and "demanding a Christian, an honorable sepulture." That September, the Spotsylvania society called for assistance "to identify and remove the remains of the Confederate dead who are buried in this and adjoining Counties, to a cemetery," in order to "make their last resting-place worthy of the precious dust it shall contain, and of Virginia, who will guard with jealous care the dead sons of her bereaved sisters, still suffering from the desolations of a cruel war." Thus, the Winchester group apparently set both the stage and the agenda for the early LMA societies in the Upper South.[88]

Even though the memorial societies became best known for the traditional womanly duty of decorating graves, early in their existence many of them had more serious agendas. The aim of erecting and expanding cemeteries might seem a dubious task for "gentle womanhood," yet it was the primary task of some societies in the 1860s. In particular, the memorial societies of Petersburg and Raleigh carried out long, involved programs of finding, identifying, and moving Confederate soldiers into cemeteries under their supervision. In Raleigh, the LMA moved Confederate soldiers into a new cemetery when their old resting place became a national cemetery for the Union dead. In June 1870, the society voted to transport the bodies of more than one hundred Confederate soldiers buried near Gettysburg, Pennsylvania, back to North Carolina.[89]

Here the women's societies, as historian Gaines Foster has pointed out, sought and usually received the support and assistance of many men. Political bodies—such as town governing councils, and even the North Carolina state legislature—sometimes fell into line in aiding them. In Raleigh, the Ladies Memorial Association of Wake County also had male members and, according to a modern historian, "adhered to a traditional gender division of labor," with men carrying out business arrangements and public speaking. By June 1866 the common council of Warrenton, Virginia, had purchased almost four acres for an addition to the local cemetery and appropriated $300 to the ladies for "making and somewhat adorning" the graves of the Confederate dead there.[90]

88. Minutes of the Ladies Memorial Association of Petersburg, Va., May 6, 1866, p. 1, Records, 1866–1912, accession 24254, organization records collection, LVA; *Warrenton (Va.) True Index*, Sept. 15, 1866.

89. Bishir, "'Strong Force of Ladies,'" 456–62; Sims, *Power of Femininity*, 13–15.

90. Ibid.; *Warrenton (Va.) True Index*, June 16, 1866.

The Petersburg society, which left a thorough record of its labors, was very ambitious; at its inception it envisioned several different projects. First, the women set up committees to oversee the various cemeteries in the environs of Petersburg, ensuring that the graves were well cared for and marked with a wooden headboard. They also sought a burial section for Confederate soldiers in Blandford Cemetery and supervised the moving and marking of the graves of numerous soldiers there. It was a long struggle, even with the assistance that they could command. In October 1866, the ladies showed their appreciation to the two men who had moved more than a thousand graves by designating them honorary members of the association. The Petersburg LMA also asked the southern railroads to provide free transportation of Confederate corpses and further demanded "that this resolution be published in our city papers, to be transferred to all Southern papers, requesting each President to notify his assent to our Corresponding Secretary." Whether the group actually received that much free publicity, it did convince railroad presidents to help their cause.[91]

In her semiannual report in December 1866, Margaret F. Joynes, president of the Petersburg LMA, noted that the organization had been overseeing the "procuring and erection of headboards over the graves of those soldiers, whose names were known." Calling the duty "both troublesome and expensive," she declared that, of the five thousand graves they had located, the LMA had "erected 454 headboards, 130 more are ready to be placed in position, and about 60 are now in the course of preparation." Mrs. Keiley, the treasurer, indicated that $184 had been spent on this project, almost $100 of which had gone directly to moving bodies. In February 1867, the Petersburg group asked for bids for preparing four thousand headboards, appointing three ladies to oversee the proposals and choose the lowest bid.

In June 1867, President Joynes reported that the Common Council had donated a part of the cemetery large enough for five hundred graves. With the help of a committee of men, the land was to be laid off as a "Confederate square . . . , for the graves of such of the Confederate soldiers as cannot be properly attended to elsewhere, and in due time we shall be able to mark with some appropriate monument their resting place." The president congratulated the various committees for securing a "degree of cleanliness and care with respect to the several cemeteries of soldiers under our charge, which has fully equaled our expectations."[92]

91. Minutes of the Petersburg LMA, May 30, 1866, p. 6, July 11, 1866, p. 7, Oct. 23, 1866, pp. 8–11, LVA.
92. Ibid., Dec. 5, 1866, pp. 12–14, 14–46, Feb. 6, 1867, p. 19, June 11, 1867, p. 25–29, LVA.

The grim work continued. A year later, in June 1868, the treasurer reported that the LMA had spent almost $1,000 to move bodies, and the members resolved to proceed until their treasury was exhausted. Although they had disinterred and reinterred over 275 bodies, a report to the society cautioned that there were "good many more bodies that ought to be removed." Three years later, in addition to their annual decoration of soldiers' graves, the ladies returned to the task of moving the remains of soldiers—in this case, from the cemetery near the fairgrounds to Blandford. For this purpose they raised and quickly expended $300.[93]

In Petersburg, the LMA seemed almost obsessed with a chore shared by the Appomattox and Raleigh memorial societies—that of creating a space set aside for dead soldiers and for those who wished to mourn them. The Raleigh society spent much of its earliest years removing remains to the new Confederate cemetery there and seeing that the graves received painted name markers. In the 1870s, the Raleigh society replaced the painted wooden grave markers with granite posts. The memorial societies thus brought the soldiers "home," removing them from battlefields to a space that not only was accessible to women and families but also to some extent was controlled by females. Thus, at their inception, the societies' annual decoration of graves played a relatively small role compared to the women's desire to order and sanitize the presence of death in their midst. Some historians think that women found it easier to deal with the homogeneous "Confederate dead" than the actual soldiers who had ofttimes been far cruder than "heroes" should be.[94] Yet it is clear that the Petersburg and Raleigh women, in their insistence that names of the dead be discovered and preserved on grave markers, were emphasizing the individual and trying to ensure that he was not forgotten. Similarly, the ladies of the Appomattox society appended to their minutes a list of the seventeen Confederate soldiers buried in their cemetery. In the case of those whose names were unknown, the index very carefully noted where each had first been buried. Rather than simply being part of an anonymous mass, each body had its own history and individuality, which was recorded in the hope that it would eventually be identified by name.[95]

Thousands of women removed the Confederate bodies to their own dominion and promptly took control of mourning for them. Through this memorial work, women carved out a civic space where they not only were welcome, but to some extent called the shots. The Appomattox society, for example, arranged

93. Ibid., June 13, 1868, pp. 42–44, LVA.
94. Whites, *Civil War as a Crisis*, 166–68.
95. Minutes of the Appomattox LMA, appendix to constitution.

an order of parade that put themselves thoroughly on display. The "orators of the day" and clergymen led the way, closely followed by the ladies of the association themselves. Bringing up the rank and file were the local Sunday schools and the general populace. In Petersburg, the LMA chose June 9, the anniversary of the 1864 Confederate defense of Petersburg, as the day on which the soldiers' graves would be decorated. In Raleigh, the memorial society celebrated May 10, the anniversary of Stonewall Jackson's death in 1863 and of the founding of the LMA in 1866. In their early commemorations, the Petersburg ladies struck a strongly religious note. Like the Augusta, Georgia, association, the Petersburg LMA's founding statement cast the Confederate dead in Christlike terms: "We come together to devise means to perpetuate our gratitude and admiration for those who died for us," and to have them "sepulchred in Blandford's consecrated ground." Over time the activities of commemoration societies would change in most places. In Petersburg, the LMA shows both the cooperation and the contestation between women's and men's commemorations.[96]

Petersburg began with two parallel organizations, the male Confederate Memorial Association and the Ladies Memorial Association. The LMA offered membership to all women, but consigned men to the status of honorary members. At first, cooperation was the watchword, and the ladies' association worked out an agreement to this effect with its male counterpart. At the second meeting of the LMA, the president, two of her vice presidents, and the corresponding secretary formed a committee to "confer with a committee from the gentlemen's society," which had requested a conference. Apparently the men wanted this to be a standing committee "for mutual aid." In reply, in October 1866 the women passed a resolution that requested the "officers of the Gentlemen's Memorial Association" to confer with the executive committee of the Ladies Memorial Association "for the purpose of procuring a suitable Cemetery for the Confederate dead in this vicinity." In this instance, the male society apparently withered, and by July 1867 the ladies were requesting that "in view of the present demands upon our nearly exhausted treasury, we respectfully suggest that the funds &

96. Whites, *Civil War as a Crisis,* 182–85; Minutes of the Appomattox LMA, April 20, 1870, VHS; Minutes of the Petersburg LMA, May 6, 1866, p. 1, c. Nov. 1866, p. 11, and May 19, 1881, p. 59, LVA. Contrast these celebrations to Antoinette G. Van Zelm, "Virginia Women as Public Citizens: Emancipation Day Celebrations and Lost Cause Commemorations, 1863–1890," in *Negotiating Boundaries of Southern Womanhood: Dealing with the Powers That Be,* ed. Janet L. Coryell et al. (Columbia, Mo., 2000), 71–88. Van Zelm's examples of lost cause commemorations generally come from the later period.

subscription list of the [male] Con. Mem. Society be turned over to our association."[97]

Although some Georgia and Carolina female memorialists turned over their business dealings to men, the Petersburg women were admiring of business techniques and seemingly adept in them. At the second meeting, President Joynes reminded her fellow members that energy "was necessary and money equally so." When the members eulogized one of their vice presidents who died suddenly, they did so by pointing to her businesslike virtues, remembering her as one "whose clear head, sound judgement, and systematic energy, must always be seriously missed by our Association." In the 1860s and 1870s, the Petersburg society oversaw a mixture of male and female activity. Like other early female commemorative societies that depended on men for financial support and other aid, the women of the Petersburg LMA relied on their own husbands, male relatives, and friends, who seem to have carried out the women's initiatives. The ladies delegated the laying out of the graveyard to a deputation of men and chose a minister as their deputy to oversee the retrieval of bodies, even while they superintended their own business affairs.[98]

As early as 1867, the Petersburg LMA began to express exasperation about the level of male support for their efforts. Frustration lurked in the resolution that it passed that September: "In view of the work before us, with means so inadequate to its accomplishment, we call upon the manhood of our city for contributions or to become members by the payment of twenty five cents monthly." By March 1868, the ladies had resorted to blunter speech: "Resolved, That as we have found gentlemen seemingly unwilling to assist the ladies in this Society, we (the ladies) have determined to take the matter in hand; and persevere over every difficulty until its object is accomplished. As patriotism and heroism appear to be entirely dead, we have been forced to this decision." The following year the association even more directly questioned the attachment of local men to the cause. President Joynes reported that, despite economic vicissitudes, the ladies' organization had survived and "almost unaided" was continuing "to discharge the duties for which it was created," the "rescue of the remains of our gallant dead" and their reinterment.[99]

97. Minutes of the Petersburg LMA, May 16, 1866, pp. 3–4, May 30, 1866, p. 5, Oct. 23, 1866, p. 11, and June 12, 1867, p. 29, LVA.

98. See for example, ibid., May 16, 1866, p. 4, and June 12, 1867, p. 29, LVA; Foster, *Ghosts of the Confederacy,* 37–38.

99. Minutes of the Petersburg LMA, Sept. 4, 1867, p. 34, March 7, 1868, p. 38, and Jan. 16, 1869, p. 47, LVA.

Whatever the origins of the Petersburg group, the Virginia women soon set their own course and did not hesitate to criticize their townsmen. Some historians picture the Georgia women's groups almost as "fronts" for male political bids; such female societies could evade northern strictures against male Confederate revivals. Yet the early emphasis of the Petersburg and Raleigh female memorialists on cemetery building was all their own. Stressing the importance of the Confederacy as a bid for southern independence, in 1869 the Petersburg ladies contrasted their own "patriotism" with the unfeeling stance of the city's men: "The cares of business, the absorbing demands of the present and the selfishness which is born of those may account for, if it does not excuse the lukewarmness of southern men in the honored cause, but the reason is only, therefore, stronger and deeper why we, the women of the south, should forever keep green in our hearts the memory of those who vainly died for southern independence." From the inception of their organization, the Petersburg ladies had asserted that both their womanly nature and their patriotism had involved them in the work of commemoration: "Untrue would we be to the instincts of nature, as well as to our birthright of glory, untrue to the land of a Washington and a Lee, did we not give every energy to this work."[100]

In regard to whether these female associations were undertaking "social mothering," some discussion of their social composition seems helpful. Although commemorative activities have sometimes been associated with loss, a pattern of grieving mothers is not apparent among the Petersburg LMA. Married women, some of whose husbands had been officials or officers, formed the bulk of the membership, but some unmarried ladies were included among their number. Young unmarried women in Petersburg, Appomattox, and Raleigh served on committees that were expected to solicit contributions and subscriptions for their LMA. This reliance on young women indicates that young women were being thrust into public, if not into the limelight, by being encouraged to ask local businessmen as well as friends and relatives for contributions to the cause. One might consider this an early usage of the motif of daughterhood that by the 1890s, with the creation of the United Daughters of the Confederacy, would become such an important part of Confederate memorialization. In this earlier version, young women were supplicants rather than decorations. Moreover, at the inception of the ladies' societies, it was not exclusively

---

100. Ibid., Jan. 16, 1869, pp. 47–48, and May 6, 1866, p. 1; Whites, *Civil War as a Crisis*, 181; E. Merton Coulter, "The Confederate Monument in Athens, Georgia," *Georgia Historical Review* 40 (Sept. 1956): 230–47.

young women who raised money. For example, late in 1867 Mrs. William S. Simpson—along with Miss Anna Joynes (the president's daughter) and Miss Mary Simpson—comprised a committee to collect delinquent subscriptions. Such a service seems to have functioned more to make the society a female united front than to advertise the devotion of daughters.[101]

Over time the Confederate memorial organizations would change. The Petersburg organization passed through several different phases. After its early burst of activity in burying as well as mourning the Confederate soldiers, the organization by the early 1870s had moved to annual meetings and then ceased recording its minutes. Other than the annual Memorial Day celebrations, the society appeared almost moribund. One chronicler wrote about the yearly meeting: "No interest is manifested in these meetings except by the Executive Committee and one or two other ladies." By the 1880s, the longtime president, Margaret F. Joynes, was in ill health; she resigned her office in 1883. Despite its lack of activity in the early 1880s, the Petersburg society still showed some pride in its work for the cemetery. While admitting they had "been generously assisted by the public," the LMA argued that its work had civic as well as patriotic utility: "The only trouble is, many feel that we are working for a sentiment, not for a sacred duty, and in these hard times think the money could be put to better uses; however since we have made such decided improvements in our Cemetery, which reflects credit on our city, I hope they will continue their help for which we thank them."[102]

Even as the Petersburg LMA was languishing, it took part in a new venture: the erection of a galvanized iron arch for the cemetery entrance in 1883. For many LMAs, a memorial to the Confederate dead was the second item on a long-term agenda and came after the remains of Confederate soldiers had been transferred to beautified cemeteries. Like other early Confederate monuments, the Petersburg arch was located in the soldiers' section of the local cemetery. In 1868, the ladies of Middleburg, Virginia, had directed the building of a "beautiful shaft of white marble" in the local cemetery as a monument to Confederate soldiers. In general, women commemorating the Confederacy in the 1870s and 1880s looked to monuments that would inspire reverential or spiritual feelings. Art historian Kirk Savage has documented the long struggle in Richmond, Virginia, between the Ladies Lee Monument Committee and the Lee Monument

---

101. Minutes of the Petersburg LMA, May 16, 1866, p. 5, and Nov. 1867, p. 35, LVA; Bishir, "'Strong Force of Ladies,'" 458.

102. Ibid., June 1880, p. 58, [no month] 1882, p. 59, LVA.

Committee, composed of men. The ladies pressed their point that the statue should be an aesthetic accomplishment, an outstanding work of art, whereas the men were more concerned with a properly martial Lee.[103]

By the early 1880s, the Petersburg LMA began to lose control over the memorial day. In 1883, when the celebration was to fall on a Saturday, the LMA, after gentle prompting from the newspapers, acknowledged that it was an "inconvenient one to the business public" and changed it to Friday.[104] Many of the association's founders had died or moved away, and the Petersburg LMA then functioned more as a social club, at one point in 1885 sponsoring an excursion trip to Norfolk and Virginia Beach. Moreover, the ladies of the revitalized society did not exhibit the autonomy in business affairs that had marked the earlier society; they had Mr. Jarratt undertake "entire management" of the excursion. Instead, the ladies' part was to supply the refreshments, or "collations" as they were called, for local worthies, such as when the governor and his staff visited the 1886 commemoration.[105]

In this period, interest in the Confederate cause waned among some women of the old elite. After all, the Petersburg LMA in the mid-1880s spent as much time on a social outing as other affairs. Still, among privileged white families at that time, disparagements of Confederate organizations tended to be muted or expressed only to one's inner circle. Kate Meares, whose husband had died in battle during the war, expressed in 1884 some of this feeling of weariness combined with an unwillingness to criticize, writing about a party thrown by the local memorial society for the benefit of the Confederate home in Raleigh: "Somehow I cant feel much interest in it—for it seems to me that in the 20 years just past the urgent need existed & was not met & by the end of the next 20 the Confederate survivors will all have passed away and then what becomes of the Institution? Nevertheless one must give countenance to such a cause—so our crowd will be in attendance."[106]

In the late 1880s and 1890s, new, more martial forms of Confederate com-

103. Ibid., April 26, 1883, p. 60; *Warrenton (Va.) True Index*, Nov. 25, 1868; Kirk Savage, *Standing Soldiers, Kneeling Slaves; Race, War, and Monument in Nineteenth-Century America* (Princeton, N.J., 1997), 129–61; Van Zelm, "Virginia Women as Public Citizens," 82–86, also documents tensions between men and women over monuments. Catherine W. Bishir, "Landmarks of Power: Building a Southern Past in Raleigh and Wilmington, North Carolina, 1885–1915," in *Where These Memories Grow: History, Memory, and Southern Identity*, ed. W. Fitzhugh Brundage (Chapel Hill, N.C., 2000), 139–68, shows the Raleigh Confederate monument to have been in the later tradition of celebration rather than the earlier one of mourning.

104. Minutes of the Petersburg LMA, April 26, 1883, p. 60, and June 28, 1884, p. 71.

105. Ibid., July 29, 1885, p. 75, and June 1886, p. 76.

106. Kate Meares to Richard A. Meares, July 23, 1884, Meares-DeRosset Family Papers, SHC.

memoration gained ground and increasingly either instructed or simply elbowed
aside the LMAs. When in 1887 the Robert E. Lee Camp of the Confederate
Veterans, a male commemorative society, requested the Petersburg society to
change its memorial day from June 9 to May 30, the LMA fell into line, although indicating its regret at "giving up the day so sacred to us." Similarly, in
an 1889 meeting, the Petersburg LMA president, Mrs. Callender, opposed asking the 4th Virginia Regiment, Governor Lee, and his staff to participate in
ceremonies on Memorial Day. The Petersburg Grays, however, decided to invite
these political and military worthies and successfully overrode her objections. At
the same time they requested the LMA's assistance "in preparing a collation."
The ladies succeeded only in changing the day of commemoration back to June
9. By 1891 the LMA was holding some of its meetings at the A. P. Hill Camp,
a part of the Confederate Veterans Society. The following year the A. P. Hill
Camp asked the society to become auxiliary to it "for the purpose of assisting in
caring for the destitute widows and orphans of Confederate soldiers." The LMA
agreed, retaining its independent name but continuing its work under the aegis
of the male organization.[107]

In Raleigh, North Carolina, in the 1890s the North Carolina Monumental
Association (NCMA), created to erect a Confederate monument for the state,
came to overshadow the local LMA. The NCMA included a female "board of
managers"; its president was Nancy Branch Jones, daughter of Nancy Haywood
Blount Branch, who had served as the first president of the LMA in Raleigh.
Despite the participation of ladies, a recent history of the NCMA has noted that
men exerted more influence in it than in the earlier LMA. Moreover, through
its male supporters the NCMA became heavily embroiled in state politics. The
organization gained a $10,000 appropriation from the state legislature in 1893
and raised $5,000 from private sources but was still $10,000 short of the necessary sum. In 1895, the NCMA used the same race-baiting techniques of the
white supremacy campaign in North Carolina, criticizing the legislature for passing a resolution honoring the deceased African American leader Frederick Doug-
lass while delaying the promised $10,000 loan for the monument. While elite
women participated in the NCMA and supported its positions, they were by no
means its strategists.[108]

During the quarter century that had passed since the inception of the Petersburg LMA, an almost complete turnover had occurred in its membership.

107. Minutes of the Petersburg LMA, May 2, 1887, p. 78, April 5, 1889, p. 81, May 4, 1891,
p. 90, Feb. 8, 1892, p. 93, and March 1892, p. 97.
108. Bishir, "'Strong Force of Ladies,'" 471–80.

Equally large had been the changes in the members' conception of their role and the work of the society. The original Petersburg LMA, much like others in the Upper South, cared about identifying and congregating the graves of the Confederate dead as well as adorning them. Their commemoration involved the proper burial of the dead; in claiming the cemeteries they gave themselves a civic arena and platform for their mournful evocation of a failed crusade for independence. Through the 1870s, the ladies called on their unmarried daughters and the men of their community for fundraising but continued to control the LMA's activities.

As Memorial Day became more martial and more under the control of the business community, the ladies ceded authority to veterans and military groups. By the 1890s, the LMA appeared an auxiliary of the male veterans organization. Although the formation of the United Daughters of the Confederacy in the 1890s did provide a new woman's group, it was one whose name and origins bespoke a distinctly subordinate status. Begun as an auxiliary to the Richmond-based Robert E. Lee Camp of the United Confederate Veterans, the United Daughters were visualized by veterans as adoring dependents. In the early twentieth century, the possible erection of a memorial to the women of the Confederacy exposed the divisions among these women. Some, like Virginia Clopton-Clay, the redoubtable Alabamian who had accompanied her cousin Nannie Tunstall to Europe, wanted an industrial college for women; others wanted a monument. But preparations for a monument ran aground entirely when the representatives of the veterans organizations objected to the "amazonian proportions and warlike attitude" of the first design, and the Daughters objected to the alternate—a woman admiring a wounded soldier—as suggesting frivolity in the former and weakness in the latter.[109]

This chronology suggests that the LMAs functioned as different sorts of organizations at different times. In the war's wake, the women of the Petersburg LMA saw themselves not as bolstering male self-confidence but as patriots undertaking an important duty to the dead and to their communities. Over time, their fervor waned, so that by the 1880s they had allowed men to make many of the decisions about commemoration.

109. Foster, *Ghosts of the Confederacy*, 175–79; see also Angie Parrott, "'Love Makes Memory Eternal': The United Daughters of the Confederacy in Richmond, Virginia, 1897–1920," in *The Edge of the South: Life in Nineteenth-Century Virginia*, ed. Edward Ayers and John C. Willis (Charlottesville, Va., 1991), 219–38; Cita Cook, "Women's Role in the Transformation of Winnie Davis into the Daughter of the Confederacy," in *Searching for Their Places: Women in the South across Four Centuries*, ed. Thomas Appleton and Angela Boswell (Columbia, Mo., forthcoming 2003). See also Susan Hamburger, "We Take Care of Our Womanfolk: The Home for Needy Confederate Women in Richmond, Virginia, 1898–1990," in *Before the New Deal*, ed. Green, 61–77.

By the end of the 1880s and 1890s, elite women who belonged to Confederate memorial societies were taking a different tack from their earlier compatriots
of the 1860s and early 1870s. New societies that were dedicated to a celebration
of the Confederacy, often by the erection of monuments in prominent civic localities, joined and even overshadowed the LMAs. Elite women who became
involved in the commemorative societies of the 1890s found themselves in demand more as figureheads of pure white southern womanhood than as dedicated
workers. Their activities were also used explicitly in support of programs of
white supremacy and African American disfranchisement.

By the 1890s new interests were taking hold, as women's clubs and organizations gained increased popularity in the South. A panoply of organizations
sprang up, available even to the rural women, ranging from the self-help aims
of book clubs to the genealogical interests of the Colonial Dames and Daughters
of the American Revolution and even the agitation of the suffrage and women's
rights organizations. Some women combined interests in a number of such organizations; others focused more narrowly. Although Anna Bodeker had sponsored a short-lived woman's suffrage association in the early 1870s, more than
twenty years passed before Virginia would have a permanent suffrage organization. Historian Marjorie Spruill Wheeler has demonstrated the privileged background of southern woman's rights leaders; she also has shown that after 1890,
the National American Woman Suffrage Association tried to recruit southern
white women. In part, the national organization did this by softening its stance
on racial equality and accommodating itself to southern prejudice. While a few
second-generation women—such as Sarah Russell, wife of North Carolina governor Daniel Russell—campaigned for women's rights, it was primarily the third
generation and their daughters and nieces who were particularly active in the
suffrage movement. Studies of southern suffrage leaders and the most prominent
"anti's," groups formed to oppose women's suffrage, have emphasized their aristocratic origins. Members of prominent old elite families, such as Amélie Rives,
participated in the women's rights campaign, while others, like Molly Elliott
Seawell, became vocal antisuffragists. One difference lay in landed wealth—
those who remained on plantations tended to be less supportive of women's
rights than townswomen.[110]

110. Sims, *Power of Femininity,* 80–188; Sandra Gioia Treadway, *Women of Mark: A History
of the Woman's Club of Richmond, Virginia, 1894–1994* (Richmond, Va., 1995), 3–53. On the rich
history of women's fight for and against woman's suffrage in the South, see especially Sandra Gioia
Treadway, "A Most Brilliant Woman: Anna Whitehead Bodeker and the First Woman Suffrage
Association in Virginia," *VC* 43 (spring 1994): 166–77; Suzanne Lebsock "Woman Suffrage and
White Supremacy: A Virginia Case Study," in *Taking Off the White Gloves: Southern Women and
Women Historians,* ed. Michele Gillespie and Catherine Clinton (Columbia, Mo., 1998), 28–42;

Some women from Virginia and North Carolina old elite families played prominent roles in reform organizations both within and outside their native states. Sarah Cowan Denson, known as Daisy, would in 1903 succeed her father as secretary to North Carolina's Board of Public Charities. Educated at Leache-Wood School, Daisy earlier had assisted her father in teaching in the family school. Historian Sarah Wilkerson-Freeman has painstakingly documented how Daisy Denson pushed for greater social services in the areas of child welfare and more humane treatment of juvenile offenders. For over fifteen years she relied on women's organizations to help her lobby for expanded facilities. At the same time, she included women on the grass-roots level to help inspect public facilities.

Other women from the old elite also became more involved in pushing state and local governments to assume new responsibilities. Elizabeth Evans Johnston, known as "Johnsie," was the daughter of a wealthy North Carolina planter and the wife of a wealthy lawyer, Robert Daniel Johnston. Both she and her husband took a prominent part in the prohibition campaign in Charlotte, North Carolina. After her husband accepted the presidency of the Birmingham National Bank in 1887, Johnsie Johnston, through the tutor of her teenaged son, met some of the young convicts in a prison there. During the next decade she focused on the establishment of a separate institution for young offenders, the Alabama Boys' Industrial School, which opened in 1900 with an all-female board of managers. In addition to this work, Johnsie Johnston was a long-term member of a book club and also served as a state regent for the Ladies Mount Vernon Association. Responsible for locating and obtaining at least fourteen of George Washington's personal effects, she took that organization, like her other memberships, very seriously.[111]

Kate Waller Barrett of Virginia similarly began a lifelong commitment to reform in the 1880s. The granddaughter of one of Fauquier's most prominent planters, Robert Stribling, Kate married Episcopal clergyman Robert South Barrett. She began to aid unwed mothers after an experience that occurred while her husband headed a church in one of Richmond's poorer neighborhoods. One Christmas season a few years after their marriage, Kate and her husband took in an unwed mother and her child who arrived at their door asking for assistance.

Elna C. Green, *Southern Strategies: Southern Women and the Woman Suffrage Question* (Chapel Hill, N.C., 1997), chs. 1–3; Marjorie Spruill Wheeler, *New Women of the New South: The Leaders of the Woman Suffrage Movement in the Southern States* (New York, 1993).

    111. Sarah Wilkerson-Freeman, "Women and the Transformation of American Politics: North Carolina, 1898–1940" (Ph.D. diss., University of North Carolina at Chapel Hill, 1995), 113–55; Mary Johnston Avery, *She Heard with Her Heart* (Birmingham, Ala., 1944), 40–48; Greenwood, *Bittersweet Legacy,* 104–13.

The sight of the two sleeping infants, her own child and the illegitimate one, and the realization that they were likely to have radically different lives, profoundly moved the young wife: "As I thought of the deep gulf the world had fixed between them—my child with every door open to him, hers with all the powers that society could bring to damn him and keep him down—how my heart burned within me at the injustice, the blindness, and the inequalities of the world." Kate Waller Barrett's answer was the establishment of shelters that would help unwed mothers retain and rear their children: "I vowed a vow that night beside the couches of those babies that, by the power of the God that ruled the universe, I would spend my life in trying to wipe out some of the inequalities that were meted out to my sisters who were so helpless to help themselves." In Atlanta, Georgia, and Washington, D.C., she pursued "rescue work," aiding women whose sexual missteps had made them social outcasts. A request for aid from philanthropist Charles Crittenton and the Barrett family's move to Washington D.C. in 1894 led to Kate's work with the National Florence Crittenton Mission. Later she became the organizer and supervisor of the mission's many homes for unwed mothers.[112]

In the postwar period, elite women's work, whether salaried or unpaid benevolent labor, was in transition in various parts of the public sphere. The schoolteacher quickly became the premier symbol of genteel women in the workplace. Despite low salaries, women still appreciated the increased authority and intellectual life that came with teaching or the emerging field of librarianship. By the 1890s a few hardy souls had entered the field of medicine as doctors or nurses.

Some scholars—and even some of the elite women I have depicted—might find peculiar a discussion of these choices in the midst of the economic depression that followed the Civil War. Would not economic necessity provide sufficient explanation of the changed behavior of women and their paid employment outside the home? No doubt in many cases, altered economic circumstances served as a precondition to the new responses of elite women. Given the choice, the great majority of them would perhaps have preferred less work at home or abroad—preferring comfort and ease is after all a fairly widespread human trait. But the generations divided on these issues. Generally, the two younger generations—women born after 1820—sought paid employment not simply to avoid

112. National Florence Crittenton Mission, *Fourteen Years' Work among "Erring Girls"* (Washington, D.C., [1897]), 58–60; Aiken, *Harnessing the Power of Motherhood*, 36. See also Regina Kunzel, *Fallen Women, Problem Girls: Unmarried Mothers and the Professionalization of Social Work, 1890–1945* (New Haven, Conn., 1993), which classes Kate Waller Barrett among middle-class reformers.

starvation, but to educate their children (or their brothers and sisters) and to regain an honored place in the world. Some teachers who had been excellent students probably also sought to live in a world of books, ideas, and gentility. Both schoolteachers and other working women sought their ideal of nondependence, in which they would be a benefit to themselves and others rather than a burden. Such aspirations often led to long-term paid employment. In particular, the third-generation included women who spent most of their adult lives as teachers. Their actions, even more than their words, suggest that work begun out of necessity might have continued out of commitment. For much of this period the youngest generation, born after 1849, was responding to a hard world. For them, the call and needs of family sounded like a clarion, so that a woman like Mary Lord was torn between seeing her younger siblings grow up without her and wanting to continue her teaching career in the high-paying North.

The growing importance and variety of female benevolent work also indicate that women were becomingly increasingly comfortable in the public sphere of the postwar South. Women who did not need to work for wages nevertheless found opportunities to contribute to their society. These contributions and the role that women played in them varied over time and place. The changing face of Confederate memorial societies gives some idea of these changes. At the war's end, elite women turned to memorial societies to create a sanitized space to mourn the dead soldiers and the defunct Confederacy. Over time some ladies' memorial societies, like the LMAs in Petersburg and Raleigh, yielded their forms of commemoration to veterans' and business interests that had brought a new martial emphasis to the memory of the Confederacy. By the 1890s, privileged white women in commemorative societies found themselves embroiled in militant forms of southern nationalism and white supremacy, where their presence was most appreciated for its decorative quality.

As some members of the old families attained economic prosperity or at least stability, the postwar labors of women continued in churches and aid societies. While few women looked to electoral politics, some of them attempted to right what they considered the wrongs of society—whether by outlawing drink, helping unwed mothers, or reforming wayward boys. In the 1870s and 1880s, women worked at their churches and in other benevolent activities. By the 1890s, new forms of southern nationalism that emphasized white supremacy and a renewed patriarchy were resurgent. Some women of the old elite participated in these reactionary movements while others looked to reform; more than a few even attempted to mesh these contradictory movements. Southern female authors from the old elite showed much the same attitude toward the public sphere even while their writings revealed these warring tendencies toward southern nationalism and modernism.

6

BECOMING AN AUTHOR IN THE

POSTWAR SOUTH

Since I can first remember[,] it has been my highest ambition to take an active part in the drama of life[;] not to sit quietly with folded hands witnessing with indifference, the struggles of my fellow men and unmoved to hear the cries of downtrodden genius, but with my soul strengthened and nerved by prayer, to arise, give here a helping hand, there a kindly word, and still more precious gift, a tear to those who need it, teaching them so to live that death shall be robbed of its sting.

In August 1867, sixteen-year-old Sue Hubard, who lived with her family on a plantation in Buckingham County, Virginia, penned these hopes for her future. Her vision might seem a quasi-religious mission that could be fulfilled by benevolent works, but in fact this was only a part—and probably a small one—of what Sue had in mind for herself. She had recently finished the bestselling novel, *St. Elmo,* written by fellow southerner Augusta Jane Evans, and she could not resist the temptation to share her innermost ambition with "Miss Evans." More than anything, Sue had a burning desire to be an author. "I have been writing short sketches & pieces of poetry ever since I could grasp a pen," she confessed, "and altho' I feel how far short they fall to anything which I desire, yet Hope points upward and onward and shows me the goal which I may attain by study and perseverance and oh what hardships are too great to be encountered and overcome with such an end in view!" Despite the lofty superstructure Sue Hubard erected around her dream, her immediate goal was quite practical: she asked Augusta Evans to suggest a course of study that would prepare her to be an author. More poignantly, Sue also asked the famous author to be her friend and correspondent, evidently envisioning a kind of mentorship that could help guide her career.[1]

It is far from clear that Sue Hubard ever worked up courage actually to mail

1. Sue Hubard to Augusta Jane Evans, Aug. 31, 1867, Hubard Family Papers, SHC.

this letter to Augusta Evans. The voluminous Hubard papers yield no trace of any response from the well-known author, even though Evans's biographer indicates that she answered a large correspondence from her admirers. If Evans received this note, she might well have been at somewhat of a loss about how to reply. Certainly Sue Hubard's vision of literature as inspiration would have jibed well with Evans's own high-mindedness and religious goals. And given Evans's sometimes tortured prose, she might not have found Sue Hubard's prolix and breathless style off-putting. Nonetheless, Augusta Evans believed traditional marriage and domesticity to be the proper lot of most females; it seems doubtful that she would have actively encouraged a young woman considering an alternative lifestyle. Moreover, in Evans's own books, the kind of heroine who wrote books possessed a self-reliance that needed few props (such as the friendship of a literary lady). Even though Evans aided at least one female literary aspirant, she probably would not have wanted to encourage a young and impressionable girl. Sue Hubard's ambition would have most likely appeared to her as somewhat unseemly as well as naive. Finally, by this postwar period, Augusta Evans was moving in elite circles in Mobile, Alabama, and her surviving correspondence reveals few Virginians among her friends. Had Sue Hubard discreetly mentioned that her father was a former congressman and that her grandfather's first wife had been Maria Jefferson, daughter of the former president, she might have been more likely to receive at least a polite reply, even if it discouraged her ambitions at authorship.[2]

In many ways this letter, juxtaposing as it does an unknown, young sixteen-year-old with the best-selling southern female author of 1867, suggests the range of privileged white women interested in authorship as well as women's literary goals and activities in the postwar period. Beginning with a backward look at the antebellum world of reading and writing, this chapter explores the evolving southern female experiences with authorship after the Civil War. Examining the lure of print in the late nineteenth century for southern women of the old elite, it also profiles postwar women writers, examining some of the differences in their privileged backgrounds, their varied reasons for seeking authorship, their paths into the literary arena, and the reactions that their activities elicited from the literary establishment and the general reading public.

Most of these elite Carolinian and Virginian authors have received relatively little attention. Antebellum southern female writers have been increasingly re-

---

2. William Perry Fidler, *Augusta Evans Wilson, 1835–1909: A Biography* (University, Ala., 1951), 146–47. For the novelist's assistance to other aspiring writers, see Rebecca Cameron to Paul H. Hayne, March 26, 1872, Paul Hamilton Hayne Papers, Duke.

read and reinterpreted, but most scholarly accounts of literary life in the postwar South discuss only Kate Chopin, Ellen Glasgow, and a handful of others. Histories of the late-nineteenth-century South often suggest that relatively few women wrote for publication. For example, Anne Goodwyn Jones sees postbellum southern women as having had little literary voice; those few who did merely parroted the Confederate memorialism of male writers. Indeed, Jones assumes the patriarchy of the slave regime to have continued into the postwar period, simply in a slightly different guise.[3]

Yet Sue Hubard's letter to Augusta Evans illustrates that in the postwar South, privileged women, especially younger ones, were coming not only to want to write but also to visualize themselves as writers. In their dreams, they built upon the work of earlier generations of women writers. A consideration of prewar female writers across the South thus helps to contextualize the hopes and achievements of postwar women.

By the 1850s, considerable numbers of antebellum southern women had begun to enter the world of literature as producers as well as consumers. As southern girls and matrons helped to elevate the religious domestic novel to bestseller status, women south of the Mason-Dixon line were penning their share of the flood of sentimental literature that poured off the presses. A young Virginian, Mary Virginia Hawes, who wrote under the pen name Marion Harland, produced one of the most popular novels of mid-1850s, *Alone*. After marrying a minister and moving to New Jersey, Mary Virginia Hawes Terhune continued to churn out novels, advice columns, and books on housewifery.[4] And Terhune was far from alone. Augusta Evans was also thrilling audiences with her strong-willed heroine, *Beulah*, published in 1858. A southern Jane Eyre, Beulah Benton is a free-thinking, self-supporting orphan who, after chapters and chapters of individualistic action and philosophical meanderings, finally finds religion. At

3. The standard work on southern women writers is Anne Goodwyn Jones, *Tomorrow Is Another Day: The Woman Writer in the South, 1859–1936* (Baton Rouge, La., 1981), which focuses on seven authors, only two of whom wrote during the nineteenth century. For antebellum southern women writers, consult the contrasting interpretations in Elizabeth R. Varon, *We Mean to Be Counted: White Women and Politics in Antebellum Virginia* (Chapel Hill, N.C., 1998), 102–24; and Elisabeth Moss, *Domestic Novelists in the Old South: Defenders of Southern Culture* (Baton Rouge, La., 1992). General surveys of antebellum female writers include Mary Kelley, *Private Woman, Public Stage: Literary Domesticity in Nineteenth Century America* (New York, 1984); Nina Baym, *Woman's Fiction: A Guide to Novels by and about Women in America, 1820–1870*, 2nd ed. (Urbana, Ill., 1993).

4. Varon, *We Mean to Be Counted*, 114–17; Mary Virginia Terhune [pseud. Marion Harland], *Marion Harland's Autobiography: The Story of a Long Life* (New York, 1910).

the end of the novel she marries her guardian to convert him to an evangelical brand of Christianity.[5]

Terhune and Evans enjoyed national fame, but lesser known Virginian and Carolinian privileged women also participated in the world of letters of the 1850s; they wrote popular novels and penned poetry and other articles and squibs for local publications. In 1853, as a twenty-six-year-old wife and mother, Mary Bayard Devereux Clarke of North Carolina anonymously edited two volumes of poetry. She and Margaret Junkin Preston of Virginia both published poems, singly and in collections. Other elite women worked in various genres of nonfiction, whether sketches of admirable people and histories, religious devotional literature and hymns, or housewifery and etiquette manuals.[6]

The sectional crisis and the Civil War greatly altered southern women's writing. As the political situation became more unstable, women throughout the South increasingly wrote politicized fiction and nonfiction. The publication of Harriet Beecher Stowe's *Uncle Tom's Cabin,* with its critique of slavery, pushed southern novelists like Maria McIntosh and Caroline Hentz and nonfiction writers such as Julia Gardiner Tyler, wife of the former president, into print. According to historian Elizabeth Varon, Virginian women during the 1850s produced fiction that, in the romances depicted between northerners and southerners, preached union and forbearance, urging northerners to be more tolerant of southern institutions such as slavery. Yet writing could also serve as a form of defense and southern nationalism. Although a New Yorker by birth, Julia Gardiner Tyler demonstrated her southern fealty when she wielded her letters to the Duchess of Sutherland as a polemical weapon on behalf of the South.[7]

The Civil War gave new justifications for women's writing. Once again Augusta Evans proved herself in the vanguard of literary effort, penning *Macaria, or Altars of Sacrifice,* the most important Confederate novel of wartime nationalism. The heroine Irene, a fierce patriot, dedicates herself to the cause of southern independence and willingly consecrates her lover to the war. There he dies a

5. See the reprint of Augusta Jane Evans, *Beulah,* ed. Elizabeth Fox-Genovese (1859; reprint, Baton Rouge, La., 1992).

6. William S. Powell, ed., *Dictionary of North Carolina Biography,* 8 vols. (Chapel Hill, N.C., 1979–), 1: 380–82; Edward T. James et al., *Notable American Women, 1607–1950: A Biographical Dictionary,* 3 vols. (Cambridge, Mass., 1971), 342–44; Beth G. Crabtree and James W. Patton, eds., *"Journal of a Secesh Lady": The Diary of Catherine Ann Devereux Edmondston, 1860–1866* (Raleigh, N.C., 1979), 729, 737–38; Mary Price Coulling, *Margaret Junkin Preston: A Biography* (Winston-Salem, N.C., 1993), 61–63, 80–82.

7. Varon, *We Mean to Be Counted,* 112–14; Evelyn L. Pugh, "Women and Slavery: Julia Gardiner Tyler and the Duchess of Sutherland," *VMHB* 88 (April 1980): 186–202.

heroic death. With *Macaria,* Evans turned the romance into a tool of the state. She would be the first muse of the Confederacy but certainly not its last.[8]

The Civil War also called forth fictional works, especially poetry, from elite Upper South women such as Mary Bayard Clarke, Margaret Junkin Preston, and Cornelia Jordan, who during the war published many pro-Confederate poems. Similarly privileged Virginian and Carolinian women gained a new, more powerful voice in nonfiction. Some of their writing started as personal jottings: a chronicle of the war in diary form or in letters to be shared with family or friends. The importance of the Civil War seemed to demand that such writings become public—extending them beyond the family. Thus, by war's end, young white Virginians such as Constance Cary and Sallie Brock were writing up their wartime experiences and observations and putting them into print.[9]

These elite Upper South women joined a chorus of southern women who during the war had written not only about their daily life, but also about the needs and demands of their new nation. The experience of war allowed women to assert their opinions and share their plans; for female Confederate patriots, it even seemed to mandate such assertive actions. It is not surprising that such a self-assured literary light as Augusta Evans advised J. L. M. Curry what speeches might best maintain Confederate homefront morale, but women with far less experience in the public eye were also ready to make their opinions known. Maria Louisa Fleet, a plantation mistress and doctor's wife in King and Queen County, Virginia, straightforwardly put forward her suggestions in November 1863 regarding the tithe, a tax in kind. Complaining about the five pounds of wool lying uncollected in her attic, she asked the help of the newspaper's editor in securing permission to shortcut procedures and return the tithe to the government in the form of socks for the soldiers. Fleet saw this as an alternative that should be adopted by the entire country: "Of course I should expect help from my neighbors; but I have never seen the lady who is not willing to help the soldiers, and what I propose could be done by some influential, trustworthy lady in every neighborhood throughout our entire Confederacy." When Fleet had received no response after two months, she pushed ahead with her project, telling the *Richmond Enquirer:*

8. See the reprint edition, Augusta Evans, *Macaria; or, Altars of Sacrifice,* ed. Drew Gilpin Faust (1864; Baton Rouge, La., 1992).
9. Cornelia Jane Matthews Jordan, *Flowers of Hope and Memory* (Richmond, Va., 1861); idem, *Corinth and Other Poems of the War* (Lynchburg, Va., 1865); Powell, ed., *Dictionary of North Carolina Biography,* 1: 380–82; Coulling, *Margaret Junkin Preston,* 139–46; Sallie Brock Putnam, *Richmond during the War: Four Years of Personal Observation,* ed. Virginia Scharff (1867; reprint, Lincoln, Neb., 1996); Drew Gilpin Faust, *Mothers of Invention: Women of the Slaveholding South in the American Civil War* (Chapel Hill, N.C., 1996), 167.

I have concluded 'silence gives consent,' and intend to take the responsibility and have it done as soon as possible. My only object in troubling you again is to urge that others may do likewise. By just one lady in every neighborhood knitting up her tithes, with the assistance of her friends and neighbors, we can produce socks enough for our army, and I venture to say, we will not consume as much wool and cotton as would be otherwise wasted; and the soldiers would be sure of them. For, when the ladies undertake anything, you know they generally succeed.

To further her plan for better supplying the army with socks, Maria Louisa Fleet resorted to speaking in the newspaper under her own name, and she did so with authority. Her call to action not only trumpeted female competence; it seemed to place women war workers virtually on a par with the soldiers in terms of patriotism. As she argued, "Let us work for them with our needles as long as they defend us with their bayonets, and then when our glorious cause triumphs, let us share with them the victory."[10]

After the war, women from the old elite in Carolina and Virginia continued to seek access to magazines and newspapers. The sectional crisis, as Elizabeth Varon has noted, had politicized the whole business of authorship. For many, their first nonfictional works were intensely personal ones, such as the diary, travel journal, or reminiscence. Encouraged by their sense of "history in the making" to write of their own experiences, new authors found that first person accounts were a relatively easy way to break into print in newspapers. Over time, large numbers of women turned to other forms of nonfictional writings— histories (especially texts for children), housekeeping manuals and cookbooks, and religious writings.

Prewar southern female authors of fiction, such as Augusta Evans and Mary Virginia Terhune, concentrated almost exclusively on what we would now consider romances but were then called domestic stories. This sentimental fiction focused on the trials and tribulations of a young woman and usually rewarded her virtue with the happy ending of marriage. Such tales of love and marriage continued to be a staple of women's writing, but the postwar female authors examined here experimented with other genres, such as local color (including dialect tales), and would by the 1880s bring sexuality into their stories. At times these female writers of fiction, like their nonfiction-writing counterparts, would deal with topics of political and social importance to their region and themselves.

Any attempt to limn the typical female writer of the late-nineteenth-century South must make a distinction between women who merely wanted to write

10. Betsy Fleet, ed., *Green Mount After the War: The Correspondence of Maria Louisa Wacker Fleet and Her Family, 1865–1900* (Charlottesville, Va., 1978), 8–9.

and those who were successful at it—at least by their own and their society's terms. Although Amélie Rives's bestseller probably sold over three hundred thousand copies, neither she nor any other of these privileged female writers found their way into the literary canon, the ranking of "important" writers, then being formed. Some of these female authors were then relatively well-known and published in leading periodicals and with prominent publishers. They garnered reviews in the *Atlantic, Harper's Monthly,* the *Nation,* and other important journals, even if such reviews were sometimes hostile or condescending. Only in the twentieth century have these women been almost totally overlooked. Their literary careers form a contrast with the lesser-known writers who published exclusively in regional or even local publications.[11]

Major now-forgotten writers would include Frances Christine Fisher, who wrote under the name Christian Reid, and who was certifiably one of the most prolific female authors of the 1870s and 1880s. Other prominent female authors include Henrietta Hardy Hammond, Mary Greenway McClelland, Mary Tucker Magill, Julia Magruder, Margaret Junkin Preston, Amélie Rives, and Mollie Elliott Seawell. Preston, a poet, barely fits with this group, most of whom were far younger. Fisher, Preston, and Magill were all publishing by 1870. Hammond seems to have broken into print in the mid-1870s but died in 1883. Although Rives, McClelland, and Magruder all began publishing in the mid-1880s, Seawell's first book appeared in 1890. By 1910, only Fisher, Seawell, and Rives were alive and writing for publication.[12]

11. This chapter draws upon the biographies of roughly thirty-three Virginia and North Carolina women who published fiction, nonfiction, or poetry between 1865 and 1895. In this discussion, I consciously omitted writers such as Mary Virginia Terhune, Constance Cary Harrison, and Lillie Devereux Blake, who, despite Upper South birthplaces, made their primary residence in the North during the post–Civil War period.

12. Biographical information on all these writers tends to be scattered and in several cases quite scanty. On Amélie Rives, see Welford Dunaway Taylor, *Amélie Rives (Princess Troubetzkoy)* (New York, 1973), and the bibliography of critical reactions to her work in George C. Longest, *Three Virginia Writers: Mary Johnston, Thomas Nelson Page and Amélie Rives Troubetzkoy* (Boston, 1978). See also Emily Clark, *Innocence Abroad* (New York, 1931), 74–84; Wayne Mixon, "'A Great, Pure Fire': Sexual Passion in the Virginia Fiction of Amélie Rives," in *Looking South: Chapters in the Story of an American Region,* ed. Winfred B. Moore Jr. and Joseph F. Tripp (Westport, Conn., 1989), 207–16. James, *Notable American Women,* vols. 2 and 3, contains biographies of both Rives and Julia Magruder.

Biographical sketches of Julia Magruder and Mary Greenway McClelland can be found in the *National Cyclopedia of Biography* and in Edwin Anderson Alderman et al., eds., *Library of Southern Literature,* 15 vols. (New Orleans, 1907–10), 8: 3321–24, 3477–82. A contemporary illustrated article that includes Magruder, McClelland, and Rives is Charles Coleman, "The Recent Movement in Southern Literature," *Harper's New Monthly* 74 (May 1887): 837–55. See also Harriet R.

More than twenty other women published enough to put them on the edges of professionalism. This second group included Jane Stabler, Nannie Tunstall, Fanny Murdaugh Downing, and perhaps even the grown-up Sue Hubard, who pursued her dream of writing for most of her short life. While the first rank of authors generally wrote at least three novels or other books for major publishers, women in this second grouping published at least one book and sometimes some short stories and poems as well. In their own opinions they lived, at least for a short time, in the world of letters and literary achievement.[13]

Next to these women, all of whom left some mark on the literary world, stood a host of other female would-be writers who managed to publish only an article, a poem, or a novel with a local printer. Some, like Maria Louisa Fleet or Kitty Dabney, found their public voice with just a local newspaper story or two to their credit. The pages of Mary Tardy's 1870 biographical directory of southern female authors brim with women from Virginia and North Carolina, most of whom were from well-to-do families, who are not included in the above categories. Despite Tardy's and their own self-designation as "authors," these women published either so little or in such obscure journals that the modern researcher can find almost none of their printed efforts. Yet their inclusion in a biographical volume shows their aspirations. Despite differing publication levels, all of those women wanted to write for publication and make their views and stories known. While their limited participation might have satisfied some of these authors, others clearly hoped for a larger audience.[14]

Holman, "Mary Greenway McClelland, 1853–1895," *Virginia Magazine of History and Biography* 56 (July 1948): 294–98. For Mary Tucker Magill, consult Mary T. Tardy, *The Living Female Writers of the South* (Philadelphia, 1870), 438–39; Alderman et al., eds., *Library of Southern Literature,* 8: 3305–3308. For information on Henrietta Hardy Hammond, see Alderman et al., eds., *Library of Southern Literature,* 15: 179.

13. I have included twenty-five women in this group: Myrta Lockett Avary, Emma Lyon Bryan, Letitia MacCreary Burwell, Helen Hamilton Chenoweth Day, Mary Jane Haw, Sue W. Hubard, Cornelia Jane Matthews Jordan, Mary Lewis, Louise Manly, Emily Virginia Mason, Mary Minta Pleasants, Sallie Brock Putnam, Judith Page Rives, Martha Harrison Robinson, Jane Lathrop Stabler, Mary Jane Stith Upshur Sturges, Nannie W. Tunstall, Susan Archer Talley Weiss, Anna Cogswell Wood, Margaret Breckinridge Wren from Virginia; and Maria Taylor Beale, Rebecca Cameron, Mary Bayard Devereux Clarke, Fanny Murdaugh Downing, and Rosalie Bankhead Winston from North Carolina. Among the most helpful sources in identifying these women and their productions were Mildred Lewis Rutherford, *The South in History and Literature: A Hand-book of Southern Authors from the Settlement of Jamestown 1607 to Living Writers* (Atlanta, 1906); Richard Walsh, *Literary North Carolina: A Brief Historical Survey* (Raleigh, N.C., 1970); Welford D. Taylor, *Virginia Authors Past and Present* (n.p., 1972); and the fifteen-volume *Library of Southern Literature,* edited by Edwin Alderman, whose volume 15 is composed of short entries on numerous writers.

14. Tardy, *Living Female Writers.*

Privileged female authors came from families that had owned slaves before the war, but their backgrounds were not uniform. Some of these families had suffered reverses, especially during the war. Mollie Elliot Seawell, a granddaughter of President John Tyler, had primarily inherited a distinguished name. The death of Charles Fisher, Frances Christine Fisher's wealthy and successful father, at Bull Run left his daughter to support her siblings and aunt after the war. Mary Greenway McClelland, despite a host of wealthy planting relatives in Piedmont Virginia, described her own parents as poor. Another social group that gave rise to many writers was the professional grouping of ministers, teachers, and professors. In Virginia and North Carolina, many such professionals shared ties of kinship with the planter and mercantile classes. Margaret Junkin Preston stands as an excellent example of this: the daughter of a clergyman, she became the second wife of a wealthy planter.[15]

The educational backgrounds of many privileged women writers remain elusive, in part because mid-nineteenth-century education was so sporadic and unsystematized. What is known suggests certain similarities. Most of them attended a boarding school or seminary at some point in their career; governesses and other teachers played a part in their training. In almost all cases, whether their formal education had been extensive or sketchy, these women had ready access to books and reading materials. Two interacting factors make their educational backgrounds appear particularly shadowy. The Civil War and its aftermath disrupted schools and schooling and also cut into the wealth of elite southerners. This tended to intensify a resort to governesses or other education at home, which was less expensive than schools. Second, literary conventions of the time, especially those concerning "genius" in creative writers, led some novelists—male as well as female—to mute their educational attainments and instead focus on how they had been writing since childhood, if not since infancy. For example, it is unclear whether Amélie Rives actually attended the boarding school in Mobile operated by Elizabeth Whitfield Bellamy, a writer of dialect stories for national magazines, or simply was tutored by Bellamy. Yet contemporaneous biographical accounts tended to emphasize her lack of time in any schoolroom.[16]

Privileged women writers shared similar geographical backgrounds in that they tended to hail from the Piedmont rather than the Tidewater. Jane Lathrop Stabler and Nannie Tunstall from Lynchburg, Mary Tucker Magill from Win-

15. Ibid., 436–39; Alderman et al., eds., *Library of Southern Literature,* 11: 4729–31, 12: 5369–70; Holman, "Mary Greenway McClelland," 298; Tardy, *Living Female Writers,* 379–80; Coulling, *Margaret Junkin Preston,* 88–151.

16. See, for example, "Some Days with Amélie Rives," *Lippincott's Monthly* 42 (April 1888): 531–33; Kate Orgain, *Southern Authors in Poetry and Prose* (New York, 1908), 141.

chester, Frances Christine Fisher from Salisbury, North Carolina, and Amélie Rives from Charlottesville all called the prosperous towns and plantations of the Piedmont home. To be sure, poet and editor Mary Bayard Clarke lived in Tidewater New Bern, but even she had spent much of her life in Raleigh. In part these numbers may reflect the population shift to the Piedmont that had occurred in both Virginia and North Carolina.

Another common characteristic was that many of these women writers could boast relatives who had written for publication. Frances Christine Fisher's father had been a newspaper editor as well as a lawyer; Julia Magruder's lawyer father authored historical biographies as well as writing on religious questions. Mary Tucker Magill could harken back to her grandfather, St. George Tucker, as well as her uncle, Beverley Tucker, as men who had published a great deal. Similarly, Amélie Rives's family brimmed with literary relatives. Her grandfather, the well-known Virginia politician and statesman William Cabell Rives, spent the last years of his life writing biographies of Madison and Jefferson, his mentors in politics. The Rives women—including both Amélie's grandmother and the aunt for whom she had been named—also wrote. Amélie's grandmother, the redoubtable Judith Page Rives, had published her first book after her husband had served as minister to France in the 1840s. In her case, the Civil War provided the impetus for her memoirs reminding her grandchildren, North and South, of the valor of their ancestors and the beauty of their ancestral home. While Judith Page Rives wrote nonfiction, primarily travel accounts, her daughter Amélie Louise Rives Sigourney penned but never published numerous poems and short stories before her untimely death in the sinking of the steamer *Ville de Havre*.[17]

While most female writers from the old elite shared these similarities, several characteristics distinguished the major writers from the lesser-known. For one thing, major writers differed in marital status and responsibilities. Like the postwar female local colorists that literary historian Ann Douglas has surveyed, the majority of the most successful in this group never married. Julia Magruder, Mary Magill, and Mary Greenway McClelland all remained single. Amélie Rives married but did not have children; Frances Christine Fisher, who began to publish at age twenty-four, did not marry until her forties and remained childless. In part, this seems to have been a generational characteristic of privileged southern women born after 1850; their rates of marriage were lower than for their older relatives. The small number of mothers among the married successful authors contrasts with the prewar female writers, few of whom remained childless;

---

17. Alderman et al., eds., *Library of Southern Literature*, 8: 3305, 3321–22, 12: 5369–70; Taylor, *Amélie Rives*, 20–23; James, *Notable American Women*, 3: 169–70.

it also distinguishes them from their less successful peers. Of course, one should not assume that an unmarried status completely exempted these women from domestic responsibilities. Mary G. McClelland, for example, wrote of fitting her compositions into the hurly-burly of the domestic scene. But for others, like Frances Christine Fisher, who for many years lived with her unmarried sister and aunt, domestic responsibilities seemed to weigh lightly.[18]

Another trait distinguishing these major writers from the great mass of the others was the amount of writing that they packed into their careers. Once they began writing, they remained active, retiring from publishing only for short intervals. Only death could still their pens, though several had relatively abbreviated careers. Both Henrietta Hardy Hammond and Mary Greenway McClelland were dead by age forty. In contrast, long-lived Amélie Rives and Frances Christine Fisher loosed streams of books and other publications.

The most successful women writers among the old elite generally were born after 1845, often after 1850, and began their writing careers in the 1870s or 1880s. In contrast, older privileged women, those born before 1835, tended to be less successful unless they had already published pieces before the war. Margaret Junkin Preston and Mary Bayard Devereux Clarke, both of whom had been active before and during the war, were the prototypical successful second-generation women. After the war, Mary Clarke, born in 1827, served first as assistant editor for *Southern Field and Fireside* and then in 1868 became the editor of *Literary Pastime.* She continued to compose poetry, but she also produced remunerative hymns, book reviews, short stories, travel sketches, and reminiscences. In 1879 she assisted her husband, William J. Clarke, in editing a Republican newspaper called the *Signal.* Mary Tucker Magill and a few schoolteachers like her form the major exception to this grouping. After writing two novels in the early 1870s, Mary Magill followed them up with a state history of Virginia intended for classroom use, which was republished many times in numerous editions. Similarly, Anna Cogswell Wood, after many years teaching school, not only published two novels but also a memoir and a travel account.[19]

More often, older privileged women who turned to writing simply wished to translate their love of reading into an aptitude for writing. Some of these women

18. Alderman et al., eds., *Library of Southern Literature,* 8: 3305, 3321–22, 3477–79, 12: 5369–70; Ann Douglas Wood, "The Literature of Impoverishment: The Women Local Colorists in America, 1865–1914," *Women's Studies* 1 (1972): 3–45; Frances Christine Fisher to Paul H. Hayne, Jan. 31, 1873, and Sept. 12, 1878, Hayne Papers, Duke.

19. Crabtree and Patton, eds., *"Journal of a Secesh Lady,"* 729, 737–38; Coulling, *Margaret Junkin Preston,* 61–62, 139–40, 152–61; Jo Ann Mervis Hofheimer, *Annie Wood, a Portrait: The Life and Times of the Founder of the Irene Leache Memorial* (Norfolk, Va., 1996), 147–56.

had actively kept a diary for years and expected to proceed from journal writing to more formal pieces. South Carolinian Mary Boykin Chesnut presents the most famous case of this; she attempted to rewrite her wartime diary for publication. In the course of working out how best to present her diary, she attempted several novels that remained unfinished and unsubmitted. Unsuccessful in her own day, she nevertheless produced a manuscript that upon its publication in the twentieth century surprised readers by its novelistic elements.[20]

Others shared Mary Chesnut's interest in making the transition from private journal keeping to writing for a public audience. Gertrude Clanton Thomas of Georgia, who had been keeping a diary for over twenty years, decided by 1869 to try to write for periodicals: "I have hoped to write and publish something of what I write." When she sent her story, "How One Woman Loved," to the *New Eclectic,* published by Daniel H. Hill, he rejected it, telling her that the magazine then published only extracts from other periodicals. Thomas was disappointed that Hill did not include his opinion of her story: "As an editor he could judge if it was worthy of publication. . . . I do not think I am cowardly. If the surgeon's knife is necessary I could nerve myself for it and I would be glad of an unbiased opinion from a good judge." In fact, Thomas did not expect rejection to obliterate her interest in writing: "I expect then I would write because I could not help it, but then I would forego the wish to publish." She remained so interested in writing for publication that a few months later, when she and family members consulted a psychic in New York, her last question was, "Can Gertrude write well enough to make it profitable and for what paper?" With the hour's consultation up, Gertrude Thomas received only the teasing statement, "She can." But even if she could, she never really did. She produced only a few pieces for local papers and other specialized publications. Instead she turned to benevolent work, especially the Woman's Christian Temperance Union, Confederate memorial societies, and women's rights, to express herself.[21]

A number of factors might have played a part in limiting mature women's success as writers. Some of them might have had fewer educational opportunities. More likely, many of the second generation, though far from all of them, had led a more sheltered existence than their younger relatives. This might have played itself out in several ways. Those in more straitened circumstances might have had less time to devote to imaginative flights of fancy. Women such as

20. Elisabeth Muhlenfeld, *Mary Boykin Chesnut: A Biography* (Baton Rouge, La., 1981), 136–223, gives the most sensitive account of Chesnut's endeavors. For the rewritten journals, see C. Vann Woodward, ed., *Mary Chesnut's Civil War* (New Haven, Conn., 1981).

21. Virginia Ingraham Burr, ed., *The Secret Eye: The Journal of Ella Gertrude Clanton Thomas, 1848–1889* (Chapel Hill, N.C., 1990), 324–25, 338, 14–20, 447–54.

Mary Chesnut and Gertrude Thomas might have been less prepared to deal with the rejection notices that so often formed an important—if discouraging—part of publishing. Despite the novels, stories, and nonfictional accounts that she wrote, Mary Chesnut seems to have submitted little for publication. Only a single story, a reminiscence of the war in the Charleston newspaper, was published during her lifetime. Gertrude Thomas does not seem to have tried other publishers when her story was rejected. Middle-aged and older women might have lacked the heart or self-confidence—or simply the energy—to persist in a quest for publication.

Moreover, the winds of change were at work in the publishing world. New literary genres were emerging, which might have accounted for some of the relative lack of success for older women. Women of the 1870s could not expect prompt publication and a widespread readership with the same sort of fiction that had been most popular during the previous two decades. The domestic novel centering around pious, nearly perfect heroines had never enjoyed high literary repute, and in the postwar period it seems to have been sinking in popularity with readers. Even younger women writers who wrote romances tended to recast them and introduce new elements of local color or realism. The sorts of themes appealing to this third generation will be explored more fully in the following chapter. Here, it is important to note that the flexibility of these younger postwar writers and their willingness to write local color fiction or adapt the romance to this new form gave them a greater measure of publishability.[22]

While beginning to write during or even past middle age would not seem to point toward success in publishing, it was the way that a considerable number of privileged white southern women maneuvered their views into print. A number of older women published their memoirs late in the century, especially after 1890, when it became practically a fad; more surprisingly, they also published fiction and other writings. Why did this spate of writing occur in their later years? The relative leisure of middle age might have finally allowed them to break into print. But still, while they gained some local following and fame, they made little impress on the larger literary world.

For all their common circumstances, privileged women writers in action dif-

22. Local color was immensely popular in the 1870s and 1880s. A nuanced discussion of the several varieties of it can be found in Helen Taylor, *Gender, Race, and Region in the Writings of Grace King, Ruth McEnery Stuart, and Kate Chopin* (Baton Rouge, La., 1989), 15–20. For a New England version, see Susan Allen Toth, "'The Rarest and Most Peculiar Grape': Versions of the New England Woman in Nineteenth-Century Local Color Literature," in *Regionalism and the Female Imagination: A Collection of Essays,* ed. Emily Toth (New York, 1985), 15–28. An unsympathetic interpretation can be found in Wood, "Literature of Impoverishment," 3–45.

fered in tone and style. Frances Christine Fisher and Amélie Rives, to choose only two, would probably have found themselves quickly at odds over the proper behavior of heroines. Fisher's high-minded heroines could never have shown the sensuality of Rives's. And it is difficult to imagine that Julia Magruder would have conversed long with Mary Tucker Magill about the Confederacy or ladies' memorial organizations without coming to argument. If their backgrounds and milieu look relatively similar on the surface, how did they differ among themselves? This may be best answered first by exploring the different reasons that compelled them to write, as well as considering the different sorts of novels and stories they composed.

Why did women write? The motivations of authors and artists have long received attention in terms of psychology. Some analysts point to books as a kind of intellectual offspring, while others look to psychological pain as a spur to creativity. Bertram Wyatt-Brown's recent examination of the aristocratic Percy family of Alabama and Mississippi has pointed to battles with depression as inspiring much of that talented family's literary output. In particular, his study of the women of the Percy family targets the experience of parental loss and deep melancholia as motivating these women's creativity. Although psychological factors might have played a role in sparking artistic creations of various sorts, none of the evidence about Carolina or Virginia authors suggests that writing was a way to deal with emotional problems or depression. Thus this chapter of necessity focuses on the social factors that allowed and even encouraged women's writings.[23]

The reasons that women gave for writing are almost as many and varied as the individuals involved and seem to have changed over time. Many antebellum female authors, whether northern or southern, justified their publishing primarily as a way to earn money, most often because of the precarious economic positions of their families. Historian Mary Kelley has carefully delineated some of these prewar writers, such as E. D. E. N. Southworth and Maria McIntosh. Such antebellum women did not easily enter the public arena and were particularly uncomfortable with putting forth a notion of themselves as authors. Convinced by the prevalent societal notions that publication was unladylike, they found it difficult to valorize their work or to deal with it as a business.[24]

The justification of writing as a way to earn a living was, over time, joined

23. Bertram Wyatt-Brown, *The Literary Percys: Family History, Gender, and Southern Imagination* (Athens, Ga., 1994). Wyatt-Brown also sees depression as playing a major role among the male Percys in inspiring their writings; see his *The House of Percy* (New York, 1994).
24. Mary Kelley, *Private Woman, Public Stage: Literary Domesticity in Nineteenth-Century America* (New York, 1984), 164–78.

by other economic considerations. Some young women of the old elite used their writings as a kind of part-time work—a way to make money in a time of need. Their writing was a way to buy things for themselves, similar to the way that young women in New England made palm hats and spent their earnings at the general store on items of apparel or for their trousseau. Kitty Dabney, according to her older sister, bought barege, a kind of sheer silk-blend dress material, with the five dollars she gained from a "literary effort," and the purpose of her planned writings had a distinctly materialist cast: "She has hopes a future effort may get her ten dollars."[25]

Female authors sometimes claimed to write mainly for money. Frances Christine Fisher, later Frances Christine Fisher Tiernan, was perhaps the most emphatic in calling her writing a business proposition: "All I wished, all I desired was to make a little money by working at the drudgework of the literary profession." Yet over the course of her eight-year-long correspondence with South Carolina poet Paul Hamilton Hayne, she tended to give differing emphases to her motives for writing fiction. At one point she claimed it was the possibility of writing about the Confederacy that inspired her. She called it a "duty [that] was all the more incumbent because the struggle had failed." But to undertake such a demanding subject meant that she had to work to improve her skill in writing. She described her efforts: "I commenced a novel on the War. But the greatness of the theme soon made me pause. I was unwilling to try my prentice hand on such a subject. I put aside my ms..and partly as a course of literary education, but principally as a pecuniary necessity, began to write on ordinary subjects, with the mental reservation that if I ever obtained sufficient skill and reputation as a writer, to justify me in touching with reverent pen our greatest page of history and manners, I would resume my first effort." In another letter, she pointed to the impoverishment of her family as the only reason that she had taken up writing: "It was only this poverty—the very sternest form of real necessity—which forced me into the career I seem to have chosen. Nothing else would ever have induced me to come before the public even under the friendly shade of a *nom de plume*. But I *was* forced. . . . I never even dreamed that anything I could write would attract even the most passing notice—else even necessity would have urged in vain."[26]

Even though she emphasized stern necessity as her taskmaster, Fisher also

25. Thomas Dublin, *Transforming Women's Work: New England Lives in the Industrial Revolution* (Ithaca, N.Y., 1994), 29–75; Maria Louisa Carrington to Eliza Dabney, May 16, 1869, Saunders Family Papers, VHS.

26. Frances Christine Fisher to Paul H. Hayne, March 4 and Jan. 25, 1871, Hayne Papers, Duke.

cast herself as a working woman. In one long passage, she fulminated over the distractions caused by her wealthy friends and relations: "Idle people can't understand the necessities which compel the labour of working people, and unfortunately (I don't mean that word the least bit ungratefully) I have a large number of friends and relatives who belong entirely to the former class and who beset me with kind temptations into which I fall." For Fisher, writing was an occupation, as she made clear:

> Try as I will I cannot make my world of butterflies understand that I am not a butterfly like themselves (in confidence I will tell you that I should amazingly like to be,) but a sober, industrious, hard working bee! They won't understand that I write for money (not for fame, or for pleasure,) and that if I did not do this for a support, I should have to do something else. They refuse to recognize any such degrading necessity and, with all their kindness they often drive me to wish that I lived in some spot and among some people who knew what labour was.

Her emphasis on the importance of her work made her chafe at social obligations that interfered with it. Fisher would have bridled at anyone questioning her credentials as a lady, but nonetheless she disliked it when entertaining guests detained her from writing. Complaining that "Southern people—of town or country—have, as a general rule, not the faintest idea of the value of time," she continued her excoriation of them: "I think I should bear the infliction with tolerable patience if it were only a question of being bored, but since it is a question of being forced to neglect my work which is very important, I often long for the liberty that a great city brings in its manners and customs." Yet when too many deadlines had exhausted her, she sounded as though she wished never to write again: "Of all drudge-work I do think that literary drudge work— when the interest in your labour is *nil,* when imagination is absolutely dormant, and when it is simply the matter of so much per hour—is the hardest."[27]

Although most of Frances Christine Fisher's books in the 1870s and 1880s were published by Appleton's, she often looked around for better deals. After contributing to a journal entitled *Today,* she confessed to Hayne, "The publishers are respectable but not first class, yet, strange to say, they make liberal offers and fulfill them promptly. This fact will account for my contributing to their journal, which is not at all of a kind that I fancy."[28]

Despite all her emphasis on "drudgework," Frances Christine Fisher acted as

27. Frances Christine Fisher to Paul H. Hayne, Jan. 19, April 10, and June 19, 1872, all in Hayne Papers, Duke.
28. Frances Christine Fisher to Paul H. Hayne, March 8, 1873, Hayne Papers, Duke.

BECOMING AN AUTHOR IN THE POSTWAR SOUTH   223

a businesswoman and professional and cared both about her recompense and the quality of her work. Sometimes, when she was unhappy with her writing, she ascribed its deficiencies to the necessity of meeting her deadlines. In the spring of 1873 she explained a long silence to Hayne as the result of an excellent deal on a serialized novel that then had to be completed: "Hence on the first Monday in January, I sat down to begin a serial of twenty chapters which was to be delivered—the whole Ms—on the first of February. You can imagine, therefore, whether or not I had need to work by night as well as by day, and you can also judge how much 'inspiration' was connected with this severe strain of physical and mental labour." Recalling how Hayne had mentioned the "imperious voice of genius," she satirically contrasted it to her situation: "The imperious voice which urged me on was essentially that of outward necessity, and the work would have been much easier if, from the first word to the last, it had not been so entirely forced from a sluggish brain and a dormant imagination. I do not complain, however, for it is over now, and has been remunerated."[29]

Frances Christine Fisher was indeed able and willing to assess shrewdly where opportunity best lay in securing adequate recompense for her literary efforts. Discussing the efforts of a fellow female Carolinian, she argued that magazine articles rather than novels paid best for the "facile" writer:

> If she were my own sister I would advise her to leave novel writing alone, and to use her talent for facile composition on magazine articles. This kind of literature is certainly well-paid, for the shortest sketch to a first-class periodical brings fifty dollars, and there are numbers of excellent writers who devote their lives to it. But—as you well know—everybody in the South who writes at all must needs write a book. It does not seem to enter their conception that there are other means of living by the pen, and that some forms of talent are peculiarly fitted to this mode of composition. As a novelist, I can see only failure before Miss Cameron, but as a magazine writer it strikes me that she might support herself. . . . If she is of my way of thinking she rates material success considerably above notoriety, and would accept the former in preference to a little local fame.

Of course, this was easy for Fisher to say, because as Christian Reid she was achieving both fame and material success.[30]

29. Ibid.

30. Frances Christine Fisher to Paul H. Hayne, April 2, 1872, Hayne Papers, Duke. For a work that argues that the relationship between magazine editors and their contributors was not adversarial, see Carol Klimick Cyganowski, *Magazine Editors and Professional Authors in Nineteenth-Century America: The Genteel Tradition and the American Dream* (New York, 1998).

Although Fisher stressed the moneymaking aspect of her work and often negotiated for a better deal, writing for her possessed a professional aspect that went beyond moneymaking. This was the author's obligation to the craft. In Frances Christine Fisher, professionalism and moneymaking remained somewhat at odds. Her complaints had a common subtext: deadlines were the reason why she could not scale the literary heights to which she aspired. She frequently criticized her own work on the grounds it had been completed too quickly. She characterized one of her novellas as having "in it the *material* for a good thing, but it is utterly spoiled by bad and hasty execution. I wrote it in a month, and went to the press without any revision whatever—a fact very apparent in its style. It was thrown off carelessly just for money, and I am sorry now that I wasted in such a manner really good and valuable conceptions."[31]

Despite her strong front as a businesswoman, Frances Christine Fisher lacked self-assurance. "I often envy people who are very self-confident," she confided to Paul Hayne. "I often wish I had a larger amount of self-esteem, behind which to entrench my self. But I did not need for a phrenologist who once examined my head to tell me that self distrust is a morbid sentiment with me." Even as she bewailed her lack of self-confidence, she justified her writing as a moneymaking proposition: "My pen makes my bread, and so I must continue to breast as well as I can, the tide of adverse criticism." Her letters leave no doubt that the world of literature deeply engrossed her; she loved reading and critiquing the latest novels, and she wanted her own work to match or excel them. Her earnings provided the shield of professionalism that allowed her to continue writing.[32]

Other writers from the old elite also linked payment with professionalism. Julia Magruder complained that the amount she had received from the *North American Review* for a short article was "less than I had a right to expect." She expressed an unwillingness to surrender her copyright to the article unless better compensated: "I notice that you call on me to resign also copyright of the article. This is something I've not been asked to do for a magazine article before—but I should not object to doing it, provided I got a satisfactory price for the magazine publication."[33]

The moneymaking aspects of writing attracted other privileged women.

31. Frances Christine Fisher to Paul H. Hayne, Oct. 2, 1874, Hayne Papers, Duke.

32. Frances Christine Fisher to Paul H. Hayne, March 21, 1872, Hayne Papers, Duke.

33. Julia Magruder to Editor, *North American Review,* March 30, 1905, Julia Magruder Papers, Duke. See Susan Coultrap-McQuin, *Doing Literary Business: American Women Writers in the Nineteenth Century* (Chapel Hill, N.C., 1990) for an examination of five different women writers' relationships with their publishers.

Amélie Rives, because of the landed wealth of her family and the postwar earnings of her engineer father, generally enjoyed a comfortable life. In 1886, however, her father lost his position with the railroad and also ran into speculative
reverses. Even though he still owned the family estate, Castle Hill, near Charlottesville, Virginia, he despaired about what would become of his family. For
her part, Amélie wished to turn her writing to the family's advantage. In July
1886, she asked her well-to-do uncle William Cabell Rives Jr. to lend money to
her father and emphasized her own ability to repay it:

> It will be my fondest, happiest task to work for *him*—I mean to work until I can
> repay you the debt which I will incur for him. You know dear Uncle this is not
> idle and the high flown sentiment of a school girl. I find—thanks to a good God
> that I can make money—that such brain as He has given me, means downright,
> sterling coin. For my last accepted story I received $175. My latest (unaccepted)
> they tell me is worth six hundred. I have eight or nine more—I have several hun-
> dred verses—Several dramas. It will be a matter of time I know. Some years.
> Maybe a good part of my life, but it will make me happy, *happy* to feel this debt
> on my shoulders.

When William C. Rives Jr. responded by preaching economy and avoiding the
"delusive bog of debt," Amélie angrily retorted that she recently had made many
of her own clothes and closed her letter by again alluding to her forthcoming
writings: "I thank the dear God that by His help, I have lately been placed in a
position which will enable me unassisted to assist those who are most dear to
me."[34]

While some women from the old elite began writing mainly to earn a living
or supplement other income, other impulses also pushed them into the publishing world. That Augusta Evans could inspire Sue Hubard with a view of authorship as public service and achievement shows one model available to young
women in the 1860s and 1870s. The appearance of larger numbers of Sue Hubards in the South—relatively well-educated young women who ambitiously
wished activity in the public sphere in general and a life of letters in particular—
marked a change in female aspirations and threatened to alter the southern literary scene. Some privileged young women, the third generation in this study,
were dreaming new dreams about what they could be and do. The literary world
seemed an arena where they could achieve their goals and suffer relatively few of
the disabilities customarily faced by women in public.

34. Amélie Rives to William C. Rives Jr., July 18 and Aug. 17, 1886, and William C. Rives
Jr. to Amélie Rives, July 26, 1886, William C. Rives Papers, LC.

Young women's interest in a professional identity can be seen in the kinds of names under which these Carolinians and Virginians faced the world. Although some prewar authors, like Augusta Evans, had published under their own names, male pseudonyms were often the rule. Increasingly, however, young women writing in the 1880s followed Evans's example. To be sure, some of the younger authors had to work up to a full disclosure. Amélie Rives's first short story appeared anonymously in 1886, but by March of that year, when she was still a mere twenty-two years old, she was authorizing her publisher "to use my real name in signing the articles written by me, which you propose publishing in 'The Century.'" Similarly, Julia Magruder's first book, *Across the Chasm,* appeared anonymously in 1885, but later books appeared under her name.[35]

Even those elite female authors who resorted to pseudonyms in the postwar period seem to have been thinking more about practical and literary success than personal modesty. While earlier prewar female writers such as Judith Page Rives, who published as "A Lady of Virginia," or Mary Jane Stith Upshur, who wrote as Fannie Fielding, merely hid their names, the younger generations tended to mask their sex by resorting to either male or sexually ambiguous names. Henrietta Hardy Hammond wrote at least some of her novels as Henri Daugé, while Anna Cogswell Wood published books as Algernon Ridgeway, her father's given names. Some were more deliberate in their choices. A contemporary biographer and neighbor of Frances Christine Fisher noted: "In choosing Christian Reid for a pen name, she was actuated by the desire to find a name which would be simple, and applicable to either man or woman." Mary Greenway McClelland used only her initials, becoming M. G. McClelland, while Rebecca Cameron wrote as H. M. LaGrange. This latter practice was not limited to the Upper South. Katharine Bonner McDowell of Mississippi published her short stories and novel, as well as her newspaper columns, under an appellation derived from her middle and family birth names, Sherwood Bonner. These choices suggest that privileged women writers were building identities as authors whose sex was not immediately evident in order to avoid identification as "scribbling females," rather than shielding their names because of feminine modesty.[36]

Although writing as achievement for its own sake interested women, many of them, especially those in the two older generations, wrote with ideological purposes in mind. Most often their goals were at least partly moral in nature. Living in the midst of Victorian earnestness and Christian piety, these women wished

35. Amélie Rives to Richard W. Gilder, March 22, 1886, Amélie Rives Papers, Duke.
36. Alderman et al., eds., *Library of Southern Literature,* 12: 5371.

to advance both ideals. Like Augusta Jane Evans, they took upright moral positions. Evans's strong-minded and rigidly pious heroines undertook philosophical studies but ultimately preached the necessity of true religion and resignation to God's will. Although postwar writers often softened this religious message, some of them clearly believed that their works could play a part in the moral regeneration of America. Sue Hubard revealed this sentiment in her letter to Augusta Evans, exclaiming, "Oh, that the task might be mine of assisting in the great & noble work of improving and aiding mankind." Business-minded Frances Christine Fisher also emphasized the virtuous nature of her work when, late in life, she summed up her career: "I have never for a moment lost the sense of the responsibility of the written word, which has persisted in me from the outset of my career as a novelist. My purpose has always been to inculcate high standards of living, to influence none to do wrongly. I have tried never to write 'one line that dying I would wish to blot.'"[37]

Some female authors of the third generation tended to frame their writing as an irrepressible force of their nature, against which they could not resist. When Thomas Nelson Page asked Mary G. McClelland to describe her method of writing, she effusively replied, "For my methods—Cousin, how *can* you reduce me to shame & confusion of face—My method is *no* method. I write because I cant help it, and should keep on writing if the world should never see a line. I don't remember when I didn't make stories! I do a lot of housework (we are poor) and sewing and housekeeping, and the stories work about the mass somehow." This was not the only metaphor of involuntary action that McClelland used to describe her writing. She recalled her early life: "I began to pick among books pretty soon, collecting twigs and grass, bits of string and colored rags to form that queer little nest which is called my 'education' and in which stories were to be hatched out after awhile." When stories simply hatch themselves out of one's "education," the writer really has little control. Yet McClelland's description of her writing process suggests that she enjoyed the creative exercise. Other privileged southern women also indicated that their compositions enthralled them. Fanny Andrews of Georgia, who published three novels, described her fiction writing as a sinful indulgence, almost an addiction, that tempted her to neglect her household chores. "This little steel tipped staff of pine is my fairy wand, that charms all cares away," she rhapsodized about her

37. Sue Hubard to Augusta Jane Evans, Aug. 31, 1867, Hubard Family Papers, SHC; Alderman et al., eds., *Library of Southern Literature*, 12: 5374. Morality was not the only ideology, as women writers also had political positions which will be explored in Chapter Seven.

pen in 1871. "As soon might an opium eater relinquish his drug—as soon might the flowers bid adieu to sunshine, as I give up the one friend that has never failed me."[38]

Undoubtedly, some women authors among the old elite of the Upper South primarily sought renown and fame, if not outright notoriety. Writing promised a reputation for intellectuality and creativity that otherwise proved elusive to many women in this period; it allowed influence, intelligence, and fame to become intertwined. When Carolinian author Maria Beale thanked a reader for his kind letter about her book, she noted, "One of the most unexpected pleasures which the story has brought me, is in the knowledge which occasionally comes home to me through such letters as yours, that at moments when I have been overwhelmed with personal cares and distresses[,] some distant and strange human being has been thinking kind thoughts of me though I did not know it."[39]

The Civil War changed the climate of opinion about white women's participation in at least some public arenas, including that of publication. As former Confederates remembered their past nation and enumerated their heroic feats in its defense, they included female activity and bravery. Whether spying for the Confederacy, defying Yankees, nursing and saving soldiers, or preserving the family homestead from invaders, some southern white women became renowned for accomplishments that lay outside the home and deviated far from domestic activities. All this subtly affected the ways in which young women imagined themselves being celebrated and admired.

These changes in aspirations are instructive about the history of the South. In some ways these dreams showed that privileged young southern white women shared much with their counterparts elsewhere in America. Louisa May Alcott captured adolescent female dreams of authorship in her character of Jo in *Little Women*, first published in 1868. A year earlier Sue Hubard had articulated the same goals in her letter to Augusta Evans. In other cases the evidence is less direct. An 1870 notice of Sallie Brock's work noted that in the author's youth, "Her fondness for books grew upon her; in the course of time, she devoted herself to studying oil-painting, and she indulged the dream of *authorship*." The outbreak of war changed that self-styled lady's course: "Dreams of distinction were hushed before the stern demands of duty." Yet in Brock's case, the "demands of duty" pulled her away from writing for only a short time. By the end

38. Holman, "Mary Greenway McClelland," 298, 297; Eliza Frances Andrews, *Journal of a Georgia Woman, 1870–1872,* ed. S. Kittrell Rushing (Knoxville, Tenn., 2002), 46.

39. Maria Beale to Richard B. Shepard, June 7, 1895, Maria Taylor Beale Papers, SHC.

of the war, she was describing in print her experiences in a besieged city, and she immediately went on to edit a book of poetry and write articles and a novel.[40]

In the end, many women's motivation for writing mixed goodly doses of a desire for earnings, achievement, and moral uplift with the newer and still somewhat unseemly hankering after celebrity and fortune. Female authors themselves tended to conflate their motives in a hopeless muddle. Sue Hubard's letter to Augusta Evans mixed images of ambition and religion in describing how reading Evans's novel *St. Elmo* had left her determined to be an author: "It seemed the scales had fallen from my eyes & I could see the glorious career which Hope & Ambition said might be mine." Fanny Murdaugh Downing supposedly announced the beginning of her literary career to a friend: "I shall write first to see if I can write; then for money, and then for fame!" Downing's first book, *Nameless,* a melodramatic novel replete with English lords and ladies, was allegedly written in ten days "as proof whether or not she could write prose" as well as poetry. Writing offered the possibility of many things: the construction of alternative worlds, entrance into the world of literature, the acquisition of renown and moral authority. Assessing the relative influence of these various motives is difficult, since it varied from author to author.[41]

Whatever their motives, elite women's training in authorship, like their educational and geographical backgrounds, adhered to a broad similar course with numerous individual deviations. One might describe publication as a journey; would-be writers traveled down the same and parallel byways, even though some went much further than others, and a few discovered shortcuts to that high road to fame. In most cases working alone, they tried to find entrances into literary America, which then centered around Boston and New York. Yet many of them attempted to do this without leaving home either physically or emotionally. With more hope than knowledge, privileged young southern white women knocked at the gates of authorship. Few guideposts existed to help them; in terms of organizational support, the best situation for women was probably a reading society composed of a few like-minded people.

In the 1860s and 1870s, elite Carolinian and Virginian women who aspired to be authors found several overlapping literary arenas were available to them. First, and most readily available, were local newspapers. Needing copy to fill their pages (as well as subscribers), they often published local writers. In Granville County, North Carolina, for example, the pages of the *Oxford Torchlight,*

40. Tardy, *Living Female Writers,* 405–06. See the biographical entry, "Sarah Ann Brock," in *Dictionary of Virginia Biography,* ed. John T. Kneebone et al. (Richmond, Va., 1998), 2: 247–49.

41. Sue Hubard to Augusta Jane Evans, Aug. 31, 1867, Hubard Family Papers, SHC.

Granville Free Lance, and *Oxford Leader* offered a forum for poems, essays, and short stories, as well as numerous nonfictional pieces. Historian Laura Edwards has noted that "Granville County's local elites wrote for and commented on much of the material themselves." Some women participated in this forum: "Elite white women eschewed certain public arenas, such as the courtroom, where poor white and black women appeared. But their names were highly visible and their voices were distinctly audible in the pages of the local newspapers." Similar to local papers were the religious weeklies and monthlies that also offered a venue for fledgling writers.[42]

The next step up the publishing ladder was the market of newspapers of southern cities and regional magazines. During the Civil War, the *Magnolia,* published in Richmond, was a favorite of beginning female writers because it was written by them for themselves and other young women. After the war, a southern white woman attempting to publish an article might first try the *Southern Magazine,* edited by William Hand Browne, or Daniel Harvey Hill's *The Land We Love.* In approaching a southern magazine, the would-be writer could escape the prejudice that many feared would greet them in northern editorial offices. Moreover, publication in southern journals, especially in the period immediately after the war and in the 1870s, was seen as a patriotic gesture. Some agricultural magazines also included writings by and for women.[43]

Beyond the local and regional outlets lay the "big time," national publishing, which was centered in Boston, Philadelphia, and especially New York. Major firms, such as Harper Brothers, J. B. Lippincott, and D. Appleton, not only published books, but also magazines that serialized novels and included poems and short stories. Other influential journals, such as *Scribner's* and *Atlantic Monthly* (under the editorship of William Dean Howells), published the best of American literature. The *Nation* and *North American Review* tended more toward nonfiction and the political. In addition, there were a host of other magazines, such as the *Galaxy, Home and School,* and *To-Day,* even though many of them folded soon after their founding. Frances Christine Fisher, who wrote for some of these (if they paid enough), characterized them as respectable but not first-rate.[44]

Thus the postwar literary world was a melange of the national, regional, and

42. Laura F. Edwards, *Gendered Strife and Confusion: The Political Culture of Reconstruction* (Urbana, Ill., 1997), 108–09.

43. Tardy, *Living Female Writers,* 410, 415.

44. Kathleen Diffley, *Where My Heart Is Turning Ever: Civil War Stories and Constitutional Reform, 1861–1876* (Athens, Ga., 1992), xi–xlvii; Frances Christine Fisher to Paul H. Hayne, March 8, 1873, Hayne Papers, Duke.

local; moving in one of these literary circles did not necessarily preclude participating in another. Even with all these competing forums, the easiest way to become a published author was to be "discovered" and acquire a literary godparent
who opened the necessary doors. Mentorship in the late nineteenth century was,
as a literary historian has argued, essential for success, especially for women. Female authors who prospered in the postwar period usually had an important
backer. Despite her youth and inexperience, Sue Hubard grasped the very important principle that an influential mentor could be extremely helpful.[45]

Yet mentorship remained unstructured and available to only a few. Women
without ties to the urban northern elite found it difficult to garner the notice of
the nabobs of the intelligentsia. Amélie Rives was among the most fortunate
Upper South female writers in terms of her connections. She was "discovered"
while yet in her teens when a family friend from Boston read one of her stories
and showed it to *Atlantic* editor Thomas Bailey Aldrich. Rives later told an admirer, "Do you know it seems strange, but I never published a story in my life
until 'A Brother to Dragons,' and it is the first short story I ever wrote of the
kind." Although her story appeared anonymously, she immediately received
much notice for it and many requests for future stories. This mentorship did
not last long, however; Aldrich seems to have been disappointed by her other
writings. By 1886, the relationship between the two had become so strained that
Rives told *Century* editor Richard W. Gilder, "I thank you with all my heart for
your kind word to Aldrich on my behalf, and hope that someday he will be my
friend again. I owe him so much."[46]

Amélie Rives's experience was shared only by a lucky few among elite Virginians and Carolinians. Augusta Evans was very sympathetic to Rebecca Cameron
from North Carolina. Cameron pronounced Evans a *"noble* woman," and detailed her assistance: "She has spared no pains to advance my success, even when
she was overwhelmed by family misfortune, and illness. I was *nobody*—unknown
to her even by name—when she so generously interested herself in my cause,
and tried to get the Appletons to publish for me. . . . I only hope some day it
may be in my power to show as much kindness to some poor struggling soul, as
has been shown to me."[47]

Elsewhere in the South, a few elite women made fortunate acquaintances. A
meeting with Julia Ward Howe when that renowned lady came to New Orleans

45. Taylor, *Gender, Race and Region,* 29–40; Shirley Marchalonis, ed., *Patrons and Protégées:
Gender, Friendship, and Writing in Nineteenth-Century America* (New Brunswick, N.J., 1988).

46. Amélie Rives to Mrs. Holloway, July 6, 1888, and Amélie Rives to Richard W. Gilder,
July 20, 1886, both in Amélie Rives Papers, Duke; Taylor, *Amélie Rives,* 25–26.

47. Rebecca Cameron to Paul H. Hayne, March 26, 1872, Hayne Papers, Duke.

launched Grace King's career. Sherwood Bonner, a Mississippian who moved to Boston to learn to write, so impressed Henry Wadsworth Longfellow with her charm and ability that he gave her a position and lent her money. It was his praise for her first novel that convinced Harper Brothers to publish her novel.

Some would-be authors sought help from famous writers in their own region. Margaret Junkin Preston, who had published many poems, felt almost overwhelmed by numerous requests for her mentoring; she vented her anger in a long letter to her literary friend and fellow poet, Paul Hamilton Hayne. "Dear Mr. Hayne," she queried,

> does every literary fledgling who writes a poem or a book, send you the MSS. and ask you to put them in shape for the press? Does everybody who wants to get a story published in Scribner or Harper write and request you to arrange the terms for them? Does every poetling who writes a jingle insist that you shall prepare such book notices as will make it sell forthwith? Do the people who translate send you their MS to revise? Does everybody ask you for special poems for this, that and the other public (or private) affair? Well, they do me!

Declaring, "I am tormented by this sort of thing to such a degree that I have to set all manner of work aside, to answer these letters or do these jobs!" Preston further detailed the sorts of demands that she had recently received: a man whom "I have never seen and never expect to see" wanted her to edit and revise his translation, and a woman from Kentucky suggested that Preston might arrange to sell her book of poems ("the merest doggerel") and the photographs taken to illustrate them. Preston finished her list: "Here lies a book from a woman in Old Virginia begging me to procure her such patronage for it through writing it up, that it will sell in Maryland!"[48]

Margaret Junkin Preston's discussion of her mail is suggestive on several different fronts. First of all, it indicates the range of activities involved in literary patronage, from advising writers and editing manuscripts to opening negotiations with publishers. In 1895 Julia Magruder, who by that time had published at least ten books, requested that editor Robert U. Johnson give her friend an opinion of the novel the latter had written. After a story or novel was published, a literary mentor could "puff" the piece by praising it in the book notes or review sections of various journals. Preston's tirade wondering whether Hayne too received such demands suggests that she might have wondered whether such requests came only to women. Would strangers dare to ask a literary man for such favors?[49]

48. Margaret J. Preston to Paul H. Hayne, Dec. 1, 1881, Hayne Papers, Duke.
49. Julia Magruder to R. U. Johnson, April 23, 1895, Magruder Papers, Duke.

In fact, Hayne, as a southern poet with a national reputation, also received many requests for him to assist fellow authors. After he wrote a laudatory review of one of Frances Christine Fisher's works, she opened a correspondence with him that lasted almost a decade. While theirs was a literary friendship that often focused on reading the same authors, Fisher deferred to Hayne, praising his poems and occasionally asking his advice about a plot for a story or novel that she was writing. On his side, he praised her work for its high-mindedness. Other would-be literary women of Hayne's acquaintance asked far more than Fisher. When Carrie Aiken Harris of Wilmington, North Carolina, planned to publish a southern literary magazine called *The South Atlantic,* she solicited Hayne for an original poem for the inaugural issue, while expressing her regret that her limited funding would not allow her to pay him for such a piece. "I am sure you desire the successful establishment of such an enterprise sufficiently to induce you to give me a few pages of ms in order to insure that success," she somewhat disingenuously argued.[50]

For women lacking a mentor, another way to vault into print or win increased attention was to win a prize. Increasingly, privileged white women attempted to garner such notice. Julia Magruder began her writing career at seventeen when one of her short stories won a prize competition at the *Baltimore Sun.* Although Mollie Elliot Seawell had produced children's stories and a couple of novels, winning the *New York Herald*'s $3,000 prize for a novelette in 1895 enabled her to begin publishing with Scribner's.[51]

A certain chronology can be traced for women authors in the Upper South and elsewhere. They were much more likely to gain entry into national magazines after 1880. Even women like Amélie Rives, Grace King, and Sherwood Bonner, who were sponsored by nationally known mentors, mainly published after 1876 and the end of Reconstruction. Northern publishers then became more open to local color and distinctively southern stories. Perhaps another part of the story is that southern women had to learn to write for a larger audience. These later stories generally seem fresher and more exciting to a modern-day audience; at the time they were also more in tune with the new currents of literature, such as local color.[52]

50. Carrie Aiken Harris to Paul H. Hayne, Aug. 3, 1877, Hayne Papers, Duke. For Hayne's review of Fisher's *A Daughter of Bohemia,* see "Literature at the South," *Southern Magazine* 14 (June 1874): 651–55.

51. Alderman et al., eds., *Library of Southern Literature,* 8: 3322, 11: 4729–30.

52. For the change in genres, see the various articles in Louis Rubin, ed., *The History of Southern Literature* (Baton Rouge, La., 1985), 178–278; Louis Rubin, *The Writer in the South: Studies in a Literary Community* (Athens, Ga., 1972); Wayne Mixon, *Southern Writers and the New South*

Yet even the careers of the unsuccessful or barely published among the Virginian and Carolinian women can yield important information. Many of these writers aspired to literary fame, only to gain little. The outlines of Sue Hubard's progress as a fledgling writer emerge from the voluminous Hubard family papers as a case in point. Even with no mentor to lead the way, Sue Hubard followed a course common to other would-be female authors in the South. Her first published writings were both local and anonymous. In March 1869, less than two years after her letter to Augusta Evans, Hubard debated a young "Sir Galahad" in the Richmond newspapers over the morality of waltzing. Mr. Moseley, editor of the *Richmond Whig,* seems to have encouraged her writing. At one point an out-of-town trip by Moseley meant that he received Hubard's description of commencement activities, probably at the University of Virginia attended by her brother, too late for it to be timely. To be sure, writing did not consume all of Hubard's time. A winter visit to New York City and a spring in Baltimore gave her new material and fresh interests in life. While she pursued her dream of becoming an author, she looked to other possibilities, such as teaching or marriage to an older man of wealth and power. She explored these avenues through visits to friends in Washington, Baltimore, Petersburg, and Raleigh. In the spring of 1873, she began a love affair with an affluent northerner, A. B. Steinberger.[53]

Even during this intense courtship, Sue Hubard continued to write. In August 1873, the *Southern Magazine,* produced in Baltimore, published her poem, "Fragment" (which she signed "S. W. H.") and accepted her short story, "Beck." When the story appeared two months later, the local newspaper complimented her on its publication. That autumn Hubard was working on several different sorts of writing projects. Although the *Galaxy,* a national publication, accepted her poem, "If," for publication, it was returned to her because the journal's "supply of poetry" was so large that hers would not soon appear. At this point, Hubard was hard at work on a novella, "His Reward," meant for serialization. After William Hand Browne of the *Southern Magazine* rejected "His Reward," writing, "It is contrary to our custom to publish continued stories," he passed it on to *Appleton's Journal.* That December Edmund Hubard reported his daughter to be "busy writing."[54]

Movement, 1865–1913 (Chapel Hill, N.C., 1980); Merrill Maguire Skaggs, *The Folk of Southern Fiction* (Athens, Ga., 1972).

53. Sue Hubard to [unknown], April 3, 1869, A. Mosely to Sue Hubard, April 25 and July 29, 1869, Sue Hubard to E. W. Hubard Jr., March 15, [1873], and Sue Hubard to George, Oct. 13, 1869, all in Hubard Family Papers, SHC.

54. Sarah A. Hubard to E. W. Hubard Jr., Oct. 7, 1873, John Lillie to Sue Hubard, Oct. 6, 1873, William Hand Browne to Sue Hubard, Jan. 14, 1874, and E. W. Hubard to E. W. Hubard Jr., Dec. 14, 1873, all in Hubard Family Papers, SHC.

Sue Hubard's experience indicates the range of authorial projects available to aspiring writers. Even as she was experiencing both acceptances and rejections of her stories and poems, she tried her hand at other possibilities. In the summer of 1874, when she visited White Sulphur Springs, she asked Charles Dana of the *New York Sun* whether he needed a correspondent at the spa. He declined to employ her but offered to consider publishing any letters she might write, cautioning her that he would pay "liberally" for those "important enough in their matter or containing genius enough in their manner to make it necessary to print them," but that he would pay nothing for those "less impressive in their quality."[55] In addition to newspaper articles, Hubard attempted playwriting. After she forwarded one of her plays to the manager of New York City's Fifth Avenue Theater, he advised how best to rework it. Along with her small triumphs, she was learning by experience, as when she discovered that she had not retained the copyright to a story that she had sold to *Frank Leslie's* which had been reprinted. She also gained employment, spending part of the summer of 1876 in New York as a correspondent for the *Baltimore Gazette*. Her greatest success seems to have been winning second place in a short story competition sponsored by the *Baltimore Sun*.[56]

Throughout the 1870s, Hubard was trying to realize her destiny and create a better life for herself. Although she considered teaching or becoming a young lady's companion, writing for publication remained her major ambition. A long obituary of her father, written by a family friend in 1878, included the line: "His children are all worthy of honor and his brilliant daughter bids fair to take her stand among the first writers of the country." Sue Hubard's many projects continued to bubble along. She never realized her ambition to be a famous author, but she did publish a book in 1880, when J. B. Lippincott's brought out—with her paying the costs—her novel, *As Thyself.* In 1881 she wed an elderly editor of the *Baltimore Sun,* who died several months later. It is impossible to know whether she would have continued to write, as she survived her husband by less than a year and died in 1882 at age thirty-one.[57]

Young women like Sue Hubard dreamed of writing and becoming writers. Letters, diaries, and other writings document such aspirations. The pages of newspapers and journals, not to mention the wares of bookstalls, indicate that a

55. Charles A. Dana to Sue Hubard, July 24, 1874, Hubard Family Papers, SHC.

56. Augustine Daly to Sue Hubard, Jan. 21, 1875, J. R. Trehon to Sue Hubard, April 7, 1876, Sue Hubard to Sarah A. Hubard, July 29, 1876, and fragment, n.d., all in Hubard Family Papers, SHC.

57. Alma E. Mitchell to Sue Hubard, c. fall 1874, W. Stoddard, ms. obituary of E. W. Hubard, n.d. [c. 1878], and Authors Publishing Company to Sue Hubard, June 7, 1880, all in Hubard Family Papers, SHC.

goodly number of women were realizing their desire to see their work in print, though few were able to attain the fame of the best-selling "Marion Harland" or even an Amélie Rives. Yet general literary histories have remained quite reticent about postwar southern women writers. Anthologies of either women's or southern writing tend to include few other than Ellen Glasgow and Kate Chopin. And some of those literary historians most interested in discovering a tradition of southern women's writing have looked primarily to those who wrote nonfiction or who never published anything. Meanwhile, those female authors who did publish have been thoroughly forgotten.[58]

Why has this been the case? In part, these novelists dropped from view because of the contemporary southern opinion of women's writings; for various reasons, they were often dismissed as unimportant. In the twentieth century, the best-known Virginian female author, Ellen Glasgow, posthumously would, in her own literary autobiography, add to the legend that southern women had no public voice by suggesting that she was a pioneer. It might be argued that the female writers of the 1870s and 1880s used hackneyed plots and had slender talents, but the same arguments can be made about males of similar talents who were read well into the twentieth century. Yet John Esten Cooke and Thomas Nelson Page continued to be anthologized, while Amélie Rives and Julia Magruder were not.

In the nineteenth century, contemporaries—especially southern males—were reluctant to take women's writings or even women authors themselves very seriously. This was true of a wide swath of the southern intelligentsia, from ministers to writers and critics. Soon after Lynchburg native Nannie Tunstall published a North-South romance entitled *"No. 40": A Romance of Fortress Monroe and the Hygeia,* a friend, the Presbyterian minister Dr. Hoge, wrote her a critical letter. Nannie described the note to her cousin:

> Dr. Hoge wrote, scolding me for publishing *such* Junk (!) as "No. 40"! &c, &c, &c. "But a wilful woman, will have her way, & so I will have mine until I get a

---

58. See, for example, Fred Lewis Pattee, *A History of American Literature since 1870* (1915; reprint, New York, 1968); Mixon, *Southern Writers and the New South Movement;* Robert Bain and Joseph M. Flora, eds., *Fifty Southern Writers before 1900* (Westport, Conn., 1987). Those searching for a southern woman's voice in literature include Carol S. Manning, who uses books by Belle Kearney and Anna Julia Cooper (both of whom wrote only nonfiction) to show an "emerging renaissance of Southern women." See Manning, "The Real Beginnings of the Southern Renaissance," in *The Female Tradition in Southern Literature,* ed. Carol S. Manning (Urbana, Ill., 1993), 37–56. Similarly, Lucinda H. MacKethan, *Daughters of Time: Creating Women's Voice in Southern Story* (Athens, Ga., 1990) focuses on unpublished writers such as Catherine Hammond as well as better known authors. See also Carolyn Perry and Mary Louise Weeks, eds., *The History of Southern Women's Literature* (Baton Rouge, La., 2002), 123–230.

husband to manage me which is a blessing I should pray for (!!)" I felt like replying that it is said the *prayers* of a *righteous man* avail, & perhaps it would be advisable for *him* to invoke the needful blessing for me! Instead, however, I have not written at all. So the other day he sent a paper containing an eulogium on his late address before the Medical students of the College of Penn in Phila. The vanity of men! the vanity of men![59]

While some would-be authors like Nannie Tunstall could shrug off the negative reception of their work, such reactions did little to encourage a high opinion of women's participation in the literary world. Dr. Hoge's reaction was private, but other cultural critics were more open in their disdain of female writing. When newspaper editor Henry Grady of the *Atlanta Constitution* urged a new, revitalized southern literature, or poet Paul Hayne discussed what was wrong with southern literature, both claimed that amateurism and the lack of forceful criticism were what ailed southern letters. Yet they spoke in gendered terms, and by their definition the amateur was a woman. In a call for the South to contribute to the nation's literature, Henry Grady couched his criticism of contemporary southern writings in this way: "Does a publisher fill a paper full of trash from the composition books of romantic schoolgirls?" Grady's example of the prototypical bad southern writer was the fictional "Miss Sweetie Wildwood," who in his estimation got "together a lot of sickening doggerel." When Grady constructed his ideal author, male descriptors suddenly replaced Miss Sweetie: "You may be very sure that the man who does it will not care whether he is developing and building up southern or northern literature."[60]

Paul Hamilton Hayne, then the foremost southern man of letters, was similarly unhappy with what he called the "fungous school" in southern literature. To him, this was a group of "factitious growth," that, like mushrooms, would perish "of their own inherent feebleness." Still, he thought this "class of writers" to be dangerous because "through the influence of their peculiar productions, [they] have been involuntarily, but not the less surely, the worst enemies of the intellectual advancement and repute of their section." Hayne carefully cataloged the prime failings of these authors: "Writing at the command of impulse, not inspiration, with little mental training or artistic experience, with but slight knowledge of life beneath its conventional surfaces, and no marked originality or natural genius to counterbalance such disadvantages, they boldly challenge the public admiration by works as ambitious often in scope and design as they

59. Nannie Tunstall to Virginia Clay, March 21, 1884, Clement C. Clay Papers, Duke (emphasis in original).

60. [Joel Chandler Harris], "Literature in the South," *Atlanta Constitution,* Nov. 30, 1879.

are feeble, inefficient, and worthless in execution." When Hayne turned to hypothetical examples of this ill-educated and ill-conceived art, he found only female works: "Mrs. Duck-a-love's 'pathetic and passionate romance, that marvellous revelation of a woman's famishing heart,' or Mrs. General Aristotle Brown's 'profound philosophic novel.'" Moreover, he asserted that the femininity of these authors was a bar to necessary criticism: "For it be observed, that to deny the genius or undervalue the achievements of a literary *lionne* is not only to insult the *lionne* herself, but all her adherents male and female, . . . who defend the author's intellect, art and productions as lustily as if they were defending her fair fame."[61]

Hayne seemed to decry localism and want a broader literature, but he nonetheless expected southern authors to respect the racial and political shibboleths of their region. His review of Sherwood Bonner's novel *Like unto Like,* which centered around a romance between a southern woman and a northern man who had been an abolitionist, clearly reveals his views. Although conceding the novel was "very clever, sometimes brilliant," Hayne quite frankly was shocked. "How a Southern woman . . . could have patiently conceived such a personage [as Roger Ellis, the racially egalitarian hero] or at least lingered with such apparent pride, satisfaction and delight over the many traits of his ultra Radical nature, and many expressions of his ultra Radical belief," Hayne railed, "seems to be utterly unaccountable." He then accused Bonner of "selling out" to the Yankees or, as he put it, "yearning towards the tents of the Aliens." Her work was unacceptable not because of its amateurism, but because of its ideology.[62]

Thus, as the South was attempting to build its own literature, women writers

61. Paul H. Hayne, "Literature at the South," *Southern Magazine* 14 (June 1874): 651–55. Hayne's blast might well seem like that of a realist sickened by the genteel tradition and sentimental literature, especially that produced by women. Yet, in fact, he was more complex on the counts of both gender and genre. Hayne was unfailingly kind and even helpful to many female authors, even those such as Rebecca Cameron, whose productions the modern reader might well deem labored and showing little talent. Moreover, Hayne was a believer in the genteel tradition; he was appalled by Walt Whitman's *Leaves of Grass* and believed that highly emotional fiction by females was not sufficiently pure and high-minded. See Rayburn S. Moore, ed., *A Man of Letters in the Nineteenth-Century South: Selected Letters of Paul Hamilton Hayne* (Baton Rouge, La., 1982); idem, "Paul Hamilton Hayne and Northern Magazines, 1866–1886," in *Essays Mostly on Periodical Publishing in America: A Collection in Honor of Clarence Gohdes,* ed. James Woodress (Durham, N.C., 1973), 134–47.

62. William L. Frank, *Sherwood Bonner (Catherine McDowell)* (New York, 1971), 140, 139, 137. The best biography of Sherwood Bonner is Hubert Horton McAlexander, *The Prodigal Daughter: A Biography of Sherwood Bonner,* 2nd ed. (Knoxville, Tenn., 1999). See also the introduction of the reprint edition of her novel, *Like unto Like,* ed. Jane Turner Censer (Columbia, S.C., 1998), xi–xxix.

were singled out not as gifted amateurs but as badly educated exhibitionists who, in Hayne's words, were the "worst enemies of the intellectual advancement and repute" of their region. Perhaps even more galling than these incompetents were traitors like Bonner, who sought northern attention and acclaim. Only when a female author could be commended for her work's high moral purpose —such as Frances Christine Fisher's creation of a heroine who was a "fascinating embodiment of womanly pride and purity"—did a contemporary critic like Hayne find much to praise. With such lavish criticism on the one hand and such guarded praise on the other, women writers generally were considered as merely popular; their work was not seen as possessing any staying power.[63]

In addition to hostile commentators, few institutional supports in the South were available to authors and none to women. In particular, nineteenth-century southern women writers had neither formal nor informal organizations to pass on their knowledge of the literary world and its workings. Most would-be authors, including Ellen Glasgow, began on their own. In her posthumously published autobiography, Glasgow, who tended to dramatize her life, discussed the disastrous episodes she remembered as marking her early incursions into authorship. With a group of other young ladies from Richmond, at age eighteen she visited New York City, where she consulted a "'distinguished' literary critic," who for a fee of fifty dollars advised young authors about the best publisher for their novels. Glasgow quickly cut this meeting short when the "critic," after telling her she was "too pretty to be a novelist," queried, "Is your figure as lovely in the altogether as it is in your clothes?" and tried to kiss her. Four years later, when she had produced another manuscript, Glasgow found Price Collier, the reader for Macmillan, more circumspect and courtly, but no more encouraging. "'The best advice I can give you,' he said with charming candor, 'is to stop writing, and go back to the South and have some babies.'" Macmillan then declined the book, which was published by another company as *The Descendant*.[64]

Both of Glasgow's anecdotes portray a woman intruding into uncharted terri-

63. Hayne, "Literature at the South," 651, 654. Gayle Tuchman, *Edging Women Out: Victorian Novelists, Publishers, and Social Change* (New Haven, Conn., 1989) argues that in the late nineteenth century in Britain, authorship of novels was rising in prestige. As this occurred, men entered the field in greater numbers and criticized the work of women writers.

64. For a northern group of men and women who shared literary experiences, see Nicole Tonkovich, "Writing in Circles: Harriet Beecher Stowe, the Semi-Colon Club, and the Construction of Women's Authorship," in *Nineteenth-Century Women Learn to Write,* ed. Catherine Hobbs (Charlottesville, Va., 1995), 145–75. Ellen Glasgow, *The Woman Within* (New York, 1954), 96, 95–97, 108. See also E. Stanly Godbold Jr., *Ellen Glasgow and the Woman Within* (Baton Rouge, La., 1972); J. R. Raper, *Without Shelter: The Early Career of Ellen Glasgow* (Baton Rouge, La., 1971).

tory—she was going, in her own mind, where no southern woman, or at least no Virginian woman, had gone. She pronounced publishers an unknown race to her, and southern writers as nonexistent: "Southerners did not publish, did not write, did not read. Their appetite for information was Gargantuan but personal; it was either satisfied by oratory, or it was sated by gossip." Even as she caricatured southerners as determinedly nonintellectual, she provided her own sketch of the inner circle of northeastern writers: "The autocrats of American literature composed a self-centered group of benevolent old gentlemen in the Authors' Club. . . . Yet, even though I couldn't read their pale, consumptive novels, I longed . . . to know these old gentlemen, who, however, uninteresting in print, were at least 'literary.' And to be 'literary' appeared to my deluded innocence as an unending romance. If only I could meet a few 'people who wrote,' and listen, humbly, while they discoursed, I might learn something I ought to know, something that would make the practice of writing less difficult."[65]

Interestingly, Glasgow suggested that no women novelists had preceded her. Yet at the time Glasgow describes, Virginians Julia Magruder, M. G. McClelland, and Amélie Rives were publishing with national houses. Why, given that background, did Glasgow make her experience seem so pathbreaking? One possible reason is that none of these female authors lived in Glasgow's native Richmond. Rives and Magruder had national and international ties, but insofar as they stayed in Virginia, Charlottesville, rather than Richmond, tended to be their base. Even though they were very much identified and even self-identified as Virginians, they figure not at all in Glasgow's narrative.

The key to this omission lies in what one scholar has called Glasgow's self-construction as an artist. In her chronicle of her quest to become an artist, Glasgow remembered her past as one solely of obstacles with little encouragement: "A vast discouragement overwhelmed me, and, while it endured, I tried to forget that I was born a writer, that, as far back as I could remember, I had wanted to be a novelist." She felt that she had to triumph over the hurdles both of gender and region. In the telling of her tale of hardships overcome, other southern authors—and especially female ones—became obscured.[66]

At one point, Glasgow herself had been much more accurate and generous about the existence of other female writers and their influence upon her. In an article published in *Harper's Magazine* in 1928, she alluded to Amélie Rives's

65. Glasgow, *Woman Within*, 105, 109.
66. Ibid., 94, 95; Nancy Walker, "The Romance of Self-Representation: Glasgow and *The Woman Within*," in *Ellen Glasgow: New Perspectives,* ed. Dorothy Scura (Knoxville, Tenn., 1995), 33–41.

influence on the coming of the Southern Renaissance. Even if Glasgow as a beginning writer had not known how to find help and solace among fellow writers of her region, she soon was able to find an informal community of support. Literary scholars have documented Glasgow's close friendships with other female authors, such as Amélie Rives and the northern writer Louise Chandler Moulton. In 1905, Glasgow indicated that she felt a great kinship of spirit with Rives, who was ten years her senior. She told Moulton, "It is the liberation and the reconciliation of the spirit that I would make the joy that we hold and feel together, Amélie and you and I." Earlier in that letter, Glasgow had exclaimed, "You brought the spirit very close to me and because of this I know—I feel, oh, my friend, with a sense that is above and beyond knowledge that we have come together—as Amélie and I have come—for some wonderful and lovely end."[67]

Perhaps because toward the end of her life Glasgow felt unfairly excluded from the literary canon, she depicted herself as struggling and triumphing alone. Literary historian Nancy Walker has argued that Glasgow cast herself both as "victim and heroine." Because female literary companionship was slow in coming and because she saw herself as the lonely, misunderstood artist, Glasgow overlooked her literary forebears in her account of her pilgrimage as a writer. Of course, her position is more interesting than it was injurious: it was the male critics and cultural pundits, such as Grady and Hayne, who had already belittled the importance of these earlier female writers. Glasgow's account of becoming a writer conveys, nonetheless, the lack of formal institutions among women authors. Although by the 1890s Virginian women had been publishing popular books for over fifty years, it was only in the early twentieth century that circles of literary friends and acquaintances began to appear.[68]

Nothing better shows the interest that postwar white women from the old elite held in participating in the public sphere than the growing lure of authorship. As historian Drew Faust has compellingly shown in her book on southern women during the Civil War, privileged, literate women were voracious readers

67. Ellen Glasgow, "The Novel in the South," in *Ellen Glasgow's Reasonable Doubts: A Collection of Her Writings,* ed. Julius Rowan Raper (Baton Rouge, La., 1988), 68–74; Ellen Glasgow to Louise Chandler Moulton, Oct. 5, 1905, in Pamela R. Matthews, "Between Ellen and Louise: Female Friendship, Glasgow's Letters to Louise Chandler Moulton, and *The Wheel of Life,*" in *Ellen Glasgow: New Perspectives,* ed. Scura, 108.

68. Walker, "The Romance of Self-Representation," 33–41. For two accounts that explore in different ways Glasgow's conflict with women's traditions, see Linda W. Wagner, "Ellen Glasgow: Daughter as Justified," in *The Lost Tradition: Mothers and Daughters in Literature,* ed. Cathy N. Davidson and E. M. Broner (New York, 1980), 139–46; Pamela R. Matthews, *Ellen Glasgow and a Woman's Traditions* (Charlottesville, Va., 1994).

and consumers of fiction and nonfiction. These literary worlds cast their spell over a generation of readers, some of whom then wanted to create fiction themselves and to be known for it.[69]

Among these southern women, the unmarried and those with few domestic responsibilities were most successful at breaking into the national world of publishing. Women with ties to the North and those who could secure mentorship usually fared best. Although being a paid writer appealed to many women, their other motives ranged from the altruistic to the self-aggrandizing. Yet their desires to make money and to voice their views on life reflect the nondependence that characterized other parts of their lives and careers. While these aspiring women writers shared similar backgrounds, the range of success they experienced varied wildly. A fortunate few went on to become nationally recognized authors, but small earnings, local fame, and the pleasure of having participated in the world of literature and culture were the rewards that most could garner from their fictional and nonfictional writings.

69. Faust, *Mothers of Invention*, 153–78.

7

WOMEN WRITING ABOUT THE

NORTH AND SOUTH

E ven as twentieth-century scholars have reread and reinterpreted American literature, late-nineteenth-century Southern fiction, especially fiction written by women, has engrossed them little. For years only Mark Twain and George Washington Cable were deemed worthy of interest among the southerners who wrote before 1890, and relatively few novelists of this period have found a place in the literary canon. In the face of this general lack of interest, few southern women novelists have emerged from the shadows. Even recent and inclusive compendia of southern and women's literature allocate little space to those preceding Kate Chopin, Ellen Glasgow and the new generation of writers in the 1890s. As the previous chapter has shown, Glasgow and Chopin stand as pioneers of critical writing about women's position in the South. Although these authors represented a deviation from the sentimental tradition, inclining toward more realistic depictions of the South, other southern female authors had already been experimenting with such treatments. This chapter explores the imaginative writings of elite women of the Upper South, scrutinizing their themes and their shifting interests over time. In this account the late-nineteenth-century South no longer appears as a static monolith, completely outside larger cultural and intellectual trends. Yet deep divisions remained between North and South, and female authors sought to address some of these rifts.[1]

Insofar as modern literary historians and critics have mentioned the writings of postwar southern women, they have usually dismissed these works as formulaic, predictable, and sickly saccharine, or as mindlessly upholding the Lost

1. Louis Rubin, *The Writer in the South: Studies in a Literary Community* (Athens, Ga., 1972), xi-xii, 36–45. See, for example, Edward L. Ayers and Bradley C. Mittendorf, eds., *The Oxford Book of the American South: Testimony, Memory, Fiction* (New York, 1997); Cathy N. Davidson et al., eds., *The Oxford Companion to Women's Writing in the United States* (New York, 1995); Sandra Gilbert and Susan Gubar, *The Norton Anthology of Literature by Women: The Traditions in English,* 2nd ed. (New York, 1996).

Cause. To some extent, male nineteenth-century critics and authors created these interpretations. Northern novelist John De Forest made one of his southern heroines inordinately fond of Confederate poetry (though he did not depict her as writing it herself), while southern critic Paul Hamilton Hayne asserted that southern women produced sentimental twaddle.[2]

Postwar women confronted a changing world of fiction, and a fledgling writer looking to make a name for herself could not simply rely on continuing the old domestic novels and frothy romances. Although some women participated in the Confederate and Lost Cause writing that began during the Civil War, they did not lead the way in that genre. Nor was it the only subject they addressed. The postwar period saw a recasting of genres, as literary elites and popular readership alike appeared to find adventure, naturalism, and regionalism (best known as local color stories) more interesting than the rather shopworn romance. Elite southern women experimented with all these kinds of stories.

The topics and themes that these women used tells us much about a range of dreams and realities in the postwar South. While creating a certain amount of escapist literature, often set in Europe or peopled with aristocrats from the Continent, southern female writers also pursued themes of sectional reunion in the romance. While their stories often dealt with gender relations, they sometimes examined the interactions among different classes. Although far from free from class biases themselves, some female writers began to explore the lives of lower-class whites in a newer, more empathetic manner. In their treatment of race relations, many women took an understated approach. In doing so, they adopted and used the stereotypes of the day, though more slowly and sometimes more kindly than southern men. In the late nineteenth century, some southern women produced fiction that was quite critical of their own region, though often in muted or humorous ways. But by the very end of the century, a more defiantly self-congratulatory fiction arose in the South, one that included female writers in its ranks. By that point, women's use of racial stereotyping had definitely increased and had become less distinctive from southern male writing.

In their fiction, female authors sought inclusion in a national print culture and an international society of writers. Such popular Victorian writers as Alfred Lord Tennyson, William Thackeray, George Eliot, and the Brownings greatly influenced them. Whether Julia Magruder choosing an aphorism from Tenny-

2. Paul H. Hayne, "Literature at the South," *Southern Magazine* 14 (June 1874): 651–55. An exception to this would be Anne Firor Scott's depiction of what she calls the "fiction of dissent" written by women novelists in the New South. See Scott, "Women in the South: History as Fiction, Fiction as History," in *Rewriting the South: History and Fiction,* ed. Lothar Hönnighausen and Valeria Gennaro Lerda (Tübingen, 1993), 22–34.

son to begin one of her books or Frances Christine Fisher praising Thackeray in her private letters, they looked to the Anglo-American publishing world for their models and inspiration.[3]

Southern women also wrote fiction that fulfilled fantasies, although their fantasies were not always those of love and marriage. In addition to producing stories in which intelligent young women were rewarded, female authors met other cravings of their readers, primarily women readers. Among the most important was a fascination with the exotic and the beautiful. Novels with a quasi-travelogue of a plot, or foreign characters (especially titled ones), satisfied some of this desire for the unusual. These novels constitute a great proportion of the worst-written and most poorly plotted books by female authors. *Helen Erskine*, written by Martha Robinson in 1872, is a prime example. Set largely in Scotland and England, it is replete with British and Italian characters and high-flung language. For example, the heroine, Helen, worries about the health of her younger sister in these terms: "Whither could she translate this fading flower for reinvigoration ere it perish?" For writers who were more nationalistic and less knowledgeable about Europe, New Orleans provided an ornate locale for stories, since it combined the peculiarities of the Deep South and Europe and seemed to offer a luxuriant landscape where out-of-the-ordinary events were possible.[4]

Other, more skilled, writers also created works with these elements of fanciful characters and intriguing locales. After she produced several popular romances, Frances Christine Fisher adopted foreign characters and settings in several of her works. The principal protagonists of *A Daughter of Bohemia*, while American in origin, had lived extensively in Europe. Fisher's novels of the late 1870s and early 1880s still used the genre of romance, but her descriptions became longer and more florid. In *The Land of the Sky*, published in 1876, she set the romantic encounters during a summer trip among the mountains of North Carolina. Not only the Asheville area, but also the valley of the French Broad River, Swannanoa, Caesar's Head, and other prominent western Carolinian scenery received a lush, detailed description. In contrast, the six or seven major characters, including an almost omniscient narrator, were barely developed. Similarly, *Heart of Steel*, published in 1883, provided numerous word pictures of ancient sites and cathedrals, primarily in Rome, as well as descriptions of natural beauty. Here the author turned her talents toward giving substance to the beautiful and the

---

3. Consult, for example, the epigram from Tennyson in Julia Magruder, *Dead Selves* (Philadelphia, 1898); Frances Christine Fisher's reference to Thackeray's genius in Frances Christine Fisher to Paul Hamilton Hayne, Nov. 7, 1871, Paul Hamilton Hayne Papers, Duke.

4. Martha M. Harrison Robinson, *Helen Erskine* (Philadelphia, 1870), 184.

sublime, relying heavily on adjectives, metaphors, and other poetic devices meant to display the beauties of nature or historic places. This emphasis on descriptive prowess, while in keeping with writing's "artistic" component, holds far less appeal to today's society, awash with far more direct forms of visual imagery. In the nineteenth century, these long descriptions helped to give the stories an additional appeal beyond the plot line, especially when one person read them aloud either to the rest of the family or to a group of women engaged in sewing or other handiwork.[5]

An important theme of the literature produced by southern women from the 1870s into the 1890s was its intense fascination with the North and northerners. That so much of the South in this period remained an impoverished, rural or semirural society meant that women from the old elite found northern cities, like European locales and aristocrats, exciting. Yet in the 1870s and 1880s this appeal went beyond a mere desire for the outlandish; instead, depictions of the North allowed women authors to address the problems and possibilities of their own society. While some of these writers simply described northern locales and characters, others consciously juxtaposed the North and the South and the inhabitants of each region as a way to explore individual and regional values and character.

The varying ways in which different authors refashioned and reshaped sectional images in the wake of a long and bloody war reveal interesting aspects of late-nineteenth-century cultural history. Historian Nina Silber has explored the different visions of the South that northerners were disseminating as they projected their own anxieties about gender, race, and industrialization. Other scholars have plumbed the South's renewal and refashioning of its own image in this time—whether its revival and resuscitation of the plantation myth or its creation of the "New South" in the 1880s. Curiously, little attention has focused on southern depictions of the North and northerners in the postwar period. Perhaps this stems from the assumption that southern defensiveness and touchiness in regard to the North remained constant over time and did not vary after the Civil War. In such a view, the South appears too busy with its own internal storytelling and mythmaking to consider the North.[6]

To be sure, postwar southern women novelists could easily have found and adapted to their purposes existing hackneyed depictions of the North. One sur-

5. Frances Christine Fisher [pseud. Christian Reid], *"The Land of the Sky"; or, Adventures in Mountain By-Ways* (New York, 1875); idem, *Heart of Steel, A Novel* (New York, 1883).

6. Nina Silber, *The Romance of Reunion: Northerners and the South, 1865–1900* (Chapel Hill, N.C., 1993), 63–64, 111.

vey of antebellum southern domestic novelists has argued that these authors, while trying to conciliate relations between North and South, revealed their distaste for the North by depicting northerners as villains. Virtually every evilly disposed character, according to this analysis, could be equated with a northern vice. Such stories, even when they included southern villains, fought the propaganda war between the sections by focusing on northern shortcomings.[7]

Some of the immediate postwar fiction extended this tradition of northerners as villains, as some female writers in the late 1860s and 1870s picked up the Lost Cause as a literary theme. In large part, it was the mature women of the first and second generations, whether novelists or poets, who admiringly chronicled the Confederacy and focused on the wickedness of its northern enemies. Mary Magill, born in 1830 and in her forties when she published her first novel, exemplifies the Confederate memorialists. Two of her novels, *The Holcombes* and *Women* (both published in 1871), glorified Virginia's past. *Women*, set in the midst of the Civil War, presents a large cast of Virginian characters, most of whom figure among the noblest people ever to walk the earth. The Yankee villains are particularly cruel and heartless in their reprehensible deeds; they represent little more than brutality, evil, and pollution. Even though Magill wrote at war's end, her book fired volley after volley in verbal defense of the defunct Confederacy.

Magill's rather convoluted story of the war's effects on two Virginia families drew on her own experiences in Winchester, Virginia, and reflected her own pain and anger at that town's occupation by the Union army. Although in good Victorian style, she carefully pointed out that the Yankees left white southern womanhood unmolested sexually, she nonetheless described the bluecoats with images of violence and outraged sexuality. In her story, when Union forces occupying Winchester search the room of young, unmarried Ellen Randolph to ensure that no Confederate soldiers are hidden there, Ellen treats the incident as a violation, "feeling her household is outraged by this invasion of her home." After ordering the Union soldier not to touch her clothes, Ellen vents her indignation to her mother: "Mamma, please have everything changed in my bed to-night. The idea of that man's touching it! I never will get over it, never! I never will feel the same in that room again." And when the occupying Union general seizes furnishings for his family, Ellen Randolph gives up her own bedroom furniture, since her mother wants to retain the bed where four of her children had died. Magill's labeling of this intrusion an outrage, then a synonym for sexual assault,

7. Elisabeth Moss, *Domestic Novelists in the Old South: Defenders of Southern Culture* (Baton Rouge, La., 1992).

and her emphasis on beds—whether Ellen's virginal one or her mother's bed of childbirth—have clear sexual overtones. Magill treats the Yankee occupation as a violent intrusion upon and appropriation of southern domestic space as a metaphor for the symbolic rape of young, patriotic Confederate women.[8]

The villains of Magill's story are capriciously cruel or simply unfeeling Yankees. Chief among them is a doctor who had courted one of the heroines before her marriage; he exults in burning her house and forcing her into exile. Magill resorts to demonic imagery to describe such wickedness: "He turned toward her, and if his Satanic Majesty looked forth from human eye, she saw him then." The southern villains are a less devilish breed; they simply lack sufficient gumption to resist the Yankees. One such malefactor is a Confederate from Maryland who joins the Confederate army yet cannot stay the course, while another is a poor white Virginian who, in his ignorance, supports the Union. Slaves who are duped by the promises of the Yankees form yet a third class of southern offenders. A conversation between Mrs. Holcombe and her married daughter, Margaret Murray, sets out Magill's notions about enslaved men and women during the waning days of slavery in Confederate Virginia:

> "I shall be relieved when they are all gone now. They are a dead expense and no profit," said Mrs. Holcombe.
> "Ungrateful creatures!" said Margaret indignantly.
> "I think there are a great many excuses to be made for them. Of course they love the thought of freedom, and they believe that this Northern army has come down here solely on their account, and that the South is fighting to retain them in bondage; necessarily it has its effect."
> "But they know we never did deceive them," said Margaret.
> "That don't make any difference. Their minds are warped now. They don't think of the past, except its hardships, for which they make their masters responsible."

In the remainder of the dialogue, the women declare Mammy to be disgusted with her fellow blacks because "Mammy is above most of the others, she has been so much with white people."[9]

While Mary Magill resorted to stock villains in her depiction of northerners as vindictive devils, such characterizations changed by the end of Reconstruction. The 1880s were a time of positive representation of the North by southern pens, and considerable numbers of female authors in Virginia and elsewhere in

8. Mary Tucker Magill, *Women, or Chronicles of the Late War* (Baltimore, 1871), 125.
9. Ibid., 198, 186–87.

the South wrote stories that set the North in an extremely favorable light. Briefly, the North became the standard against which these women judged the South and found it wanting. These authors constructed a variant of the common romance that focused on male roles and suggested that southern men had much to learn from their northern counterparts. Although some historians have argued that southern women were trying to bolster the egos of men disheartened by defeat and poverty, these stories suggest that some female authors had a different sort of reconstruction in mind—one that more reformed than consoled their menfolk.[10]

A small group of elite women developed a romance of reunion that deviated from the hackneyed war story that John W. De Forest and a host of less talented authors had been writing. The standard North-South romance celebrated the Union war triumph by showing fictional northern soldiers conquering Confederate beauties with billets doux, not bullets.[11] Southern men scarcely figured in such accounts, largely by northerners, which lauded northern martial splendor, but female authors changed the focus. In 1878, Sherwood Bonner of Mississippi published what is apparently the first romance of reunion that featured women's concerns, but Virginians Mary Greenway McClelland, Julia Magruder, Amélie Rives, and Nannie Whitmell Tunstall all followed her lead with novels or stories of intersectional romance that differed from the northern model. These women authors created in the 1880s a new version of the national romance, one taking place after, not during, the war. Like so many stories written by southern

10. Drew Gilpin Faust, *Mothers of Invention: Women of the Slaveholding South in the American Civil War* (Chapel Hill, N.C., 1996); LeeAnn Whites, *The Civil War as a Crisis in Gender: Augusta, Georgia, 1860–1890* (Athens, Ga., 1995).

11. Paul H. Buck, *The Road to Reunion, 1865–1900* (Boston, 1937), 196–235, surveys both northern and southern fictional writings in two paired chapters. See also Joyce Appleby, "Reconciliation and the Northern Novelist, 1865–1880," *Civil War History* 10 (June 1964): 117–29; Silber, *Romance of Reunion*, 63–64, 111; Anne Rowe, *The Enchanted Country: Northern Writers in the South, 1865–1910* (Baton Rouge, La., 1978); Richard Weaver, *The Southern Tradition at Bay: A History of Postbellum Thought* (New Rochelle, N.Y., 1968), 295–98. Constance Cary Harrison, who lived in Virginia during the Civil War and had privileged connections, and British-born Frances Burnet Hodgson also wrote romances of reunion similar to those detailed here.

For northern versions of the romance of reunion, see John William De Forest, *The Bloody Chasm: A Novel* (New York, 1881); idem, "Parole d'honneur"(1868), reprinted in Kathleen Diffley, *Where My Heart Is Turning Ever: Civil War Stories and Constitutional Reform, 1861–1876* (Athens, Ga., 1992), 80–115; *Miss Ravenel's Conversion from Secession to Loyalty*, ed. Gordon S. Haight (1867; reprint, New York, 1955); Constance F. Woolson, "Old Gardiston," in *Rodman the Keeper: Southern Sketches* (1880; reprint, New York, 1969). Thomas Nelson Page, "Meh Lady: A Story of the War," *In Ole Virginia or Marse Chan and Other Stories* (New York, 1887), 83–142, is a version by a southern male similar to the northern ones.

women, these romances feature intelligent, determined southern heroines who deserve the best of futures. But it is in their depiction of males, northern and southern, that these authors drive home their critical points.[12]

In the romances of reunion written by men, Union soldiers were the northern heroes, but only Tunstall created a hero with that occupation. Southern women novelists carefully described their heroes, often using the North and northern men as foils to show what southern men should become. Both M. G. McClelland and Julia Magruder resorted to the popular romantic convention used by Jane Austen—a romance in which the heroine picks the "right" suitor over the "wrong" one.[13] Since the suitors represent the North and South, choice here carries both sectional and political implications—some of which were followed up by the authors, and others at which they only hinted. McClelland and Magruder generally went beyond the typical conventions of good looks and brooding personality to create protagonists who were wealthy, intelligent, personable, kind, and self-controlled. In addition, the northern heroes in their stories emit an intensity that gives them a sexual appeal completely absent from northern reunion stories. In Magruder's *Across the Chasm,* the northern hero, architect Louis Gaston, is wealthy, but his hard work and devotion to his career form part of his attractiveness. "He has quite a nice little fortune," reports his sister-in-law, "and there's no earthly reason why he should work so hard, except that he likes it; . . . Louis undoubtedly finds his chief pleasure in application to his profession." When Gaston stays up all night finishing a set of plans, the heroine Margaret Trevennon realizes that she has never seen such male diligence in her native Virginia.[14]

Like many other novelists, Magruder utilized doubling—that is, using two or more characters of the same gender and similar age to illustrate significant differences in character—in this case, as a way to show Gaston's superiority over his three southern rivals. Each of the three represents a flaw rife among southern men. The industriousness of Gaston points up the indolence common to southern male culture, which was exemplified by the character of Charley Somers. In an early scene in *Across the Chasm,* the heroine discovers Charley, her childhood sweetheart and an impoverished Virginia aristocrat, lounging at the town drugstore: "After one swift glance, she had received a distinct impression of Mr. Som-

---

12. See Jane Turner Censer, "Reimagining the North-South Reunion: Southern Women Novelists and the Intersectional Romance, 1876–1900," *Southern Cultures* (summer 1999): 64–91, for an exploration of the rise and fall of this genre.

13. For the common use of doubling in romantic rivalries, see Jean Kennard, *Victims of Convention* (Hamden, Conn., 1978).

14. Julia Magruder, *Across the Chasm* (New York, 1885), 28, 77–79.

ers' whole manner and attitude, as he sat with his chair tipped back against the wall, his heels caught on its topmost round, his straw hat pushed back from his delicate, indolent face, and a pipe between his lips. In this way he would sit for hours, ringing the changes on the somewhat restricted theme of county politics with the loungers who frequented 'Martin's.'" Obviously, an architect who works all night can far outpace the somnolent Charley Somers. Infuriated by Somers's behavior, Margaret "could not grow accustomed to it, in spite of long habituation." Here, indolence and a lack of application to self-improvement stand as southern male attributes that call for reform. Margaret's reaction shows that concerned southern women did not share such failings.[15]

Magruder drove home her comparison in other areas. The northerner and southerner, Gaston and Somers, share a talent—superb singing voices. But whereas Somers possesses a great deal of natural aptitude and little application, Gaston credits his ability almost exclusively to study and practice. Even while studying architecture in Germany, he practiced singing for three or four hours daily. In addition, Gaston's polished appearance, which was scrupulously neat "in every detail, the very cut of his short dark hair, parted straight in the middle, and brushed smoothly down on top of his noticeably fine head," highlights Somers's typically southern male untidiness.

Magruder presents hard work as one side of northern superiority; sexual appeal, combined with morality and restraint, stands as another. Louis Gaston avoids the wiles of a "married belle," while a second southern suitor, Alan De-Courcy, though seemingly a model of gentlemanly deportment, carries on just such an affair. DeCourcy joins selfishness and indolence to his lack of integrity and sexual self-indulgence. Although thirty-three years old, he has not yet opened his law office and begun to practice. Beautiful manners, handsome appearance, and a considerable fortune cannot compensate for his lack of discipline and self-control.[16]

A third southern suitor, the former Confederate soldier Major King, highlights the northern hero's courtesy and search for a companionate marriage. Magruder never mentions whether Gaston served in the Union army, but her southern veteran serves almost as an antihero. Major King dresses badly in an old, ill-fitting suit, but his unattractiveness is less physical than moral, a failing apparent in his uncouth demeanor and arrogant manners. The heroine finds herself contrasting the "gaunt Southerner, whose features were, in reality, the handsomer of the two, and the Northern man, in his quiet evening dress." In

15. Ibid., 4–5.
16. Ibid., 65, 50–51, 121.

this comparison the northerner "looked so greatly the superior. Mr. Gaston's attitude despite its stiffness, was dignified and impressive, and Major King's notwithstanding its ease, was slouching and ungainly." In an interminably long visit, King "sat and talked and laughed and told jokes with a ghastly hilarity." Not only "arrogant and ill-bred," he also is poorly educated and "loud, familiar and irritating." Indeed, King, whose very name signals his pretensions to patriarchal rule, is no monarch, only a pretender—an intriguing twist for Magruder, whose great uncle, Confederate general John Bankhead Magruder, had been commonly known as "Prince John."[17]

Magruder depicts Major King's self-absorption as abusive and destructive. During his visit, he sits in a "delicate little gilt chair," which he then tips backward, so that "his heavy weight caused the slight wood-work to creak ominously." Upon leaving he glances at a beautiful book and tosses it down so carelessly that "its delicate leaves [were] crushed open beneath its heavy cover"—an action suggesting that King would reign over his household with a similarly callow insensitivity and careless destructiveness. Despite King's belief that he is better than the best Yankee that ever lived, he is deeply inferior to a northerner such as Gaston. In Magruder's formulation, northern men, with their self-control and sensitivity, offer the best of all worlds: companionate marriage with sexual fidelity and a well-ordered household.[18]

Other women authors, such as M. G. McClelland and Nannie Tunstall, created similarly admirable northern suitors during the 1880s. Nannie Tunstall's romantic lead is a middle-aged Union officer, General Carson, who is wealthy, kind, and modest; his northern competitor, Hugh Gardner, is a handsome Harvard graduate and author. As in Magruder's account, it is through domestic virtues rather than military derring-do that the northern man triumphs. Quite often the triumph is in part intellectual. In *Princess,* published in 1885, M. G. McClelland sets up a romance between her heroine, Pocahontas Mason, and Nesbit Thorne, a New York suitor who is a brilliant Harvard graduate; his aristocratic southern rival, Jim Byrd, having inherited Shirley plantation and a crushing load of debt, works diligently, though unsuccessfully, to rebuild the family's fortunes. Pocahontas Mason's mother, explaining her daughter's lack of romantic interest in Jim Byrd, comments: "Noble fellow as he is, he has not the intellectual power which commands admiration."[19]

Even more striking than the intelligence and sensitivity of these northern

17. Ibid., 96, 98, 99.
18. Ibid., 100–01.
19. M. G. McClelland, *Princess* (New York, 1886), 42.

males is their magnetic sexuality. Magruder's northern hero is an ardent lover who addresses Margaret Trevennon with "fervent, tender eyes" and a "caressing voice." Magruder heightens the reader's sense of Gaston's sexuality by juxtaposing it to his enormous self-control: his eyes were "wild with longing," his lips "stern with repression," as he "held his breath in passionate expectation that, as she turned at the bend of the stairs, she might give him one last look." After the passionate kiss that seals their love, he speaks in a "stern, sweet voice which thrilled and conquered her." Although Magruder gives her northern hero sexual mastery to win the heroine's love, she always situates sex appeal within the rubric of companionate love. Even as the lovers say goodnight, they part "with the blessed consciousness that they would meet to-morrow in the same sweet companionship—with the thought in the mind of each that the future was to be always together never apart."[20]

McClelland makes sexual attraction even more powerful in her romance, *Princess.* Along with his intellect and Harvard degree, Nesbit Thorne possesses great magnetism that indicates his sexual potency. He is one of those men who "are lodestones which attract events; whirlpools which draw to themselves excitement, emotion, and vast store of sympathy." This hero is well aware of his own attractiveness: "Thorne was no fatuous fool, blinded by his own vanity, but his power over women had been often tried, fully proven, and he had confidence in himself." A scene in which Pocahontas innocently misfires a gun and promptly faints serves to increase the sexual tension. This incident makes Thorne realize his "fierce desire to change her passivity of regard into wild activity of passion." Intoxicated by Pocahontas's beauty at the local Christmas ball and jealous of the jessamine flowers she wears from Jim Byrd, Thorne tries— quite successfully—to make her love him.[21]

In these depictions of sexually attractive men, McClelland and Magruder found their virile imagery in men who were darkly handsome. Thorne is a "slender dark man, with magnificent dark eyes" and Gaston possesses a "straight and well-carried figure and a dark-skinned, intelligent face." The black imagery resembles that given Rhett Butler by Margaret Mitchell, but unlike Butler, these northern men remain virtuous, even while sexually appealing.[22]

To be sure, the women novelists present some southern men who have been "reconstructed" through reform. Charley Somers, while rejected by the heroine,

20. Magruder, *Across the Chasm,* 281, 300, 308, 309.

21. McClelland, *Princess,* 16, 120, 128.

22. Ibid., 15; Magruder, *Across the Chasm,* 50. See Joel Williamson, "How Black Was Rhett Butler?" in *The Evolution of Southern Culture,* ed. Numan Bartley (Athens, Ga., 1988), 87–107, for a discussion of black imagery in *Gone With the Wind.*

decides that "he would win her approval though he could never win her love." Rather than return to the South "and the old stagnating life, which had already made its sad impress upon his mind and character," he joins a group of his friends going to South America to seek their fortune. Jim Byrd does not win the heroine, but sells his plantation and takes an engineering job in Mexico to recover his fortune. "Strong . . . yet very gentle," he places Pocahontas Mason's happiness above his own and encourages to follow her heart and marry Nesbit Thorne.[23]

George Throckmorton, the eponymous hero of Molly Elliot Seawell's first novel, published in 1890, provides yet another variant of the upstanding northerner and the reconstructed southerner combined into one character. Throckmorton is a southerner who at the same time is a northerner, at least in his political inclinations. As a Virginian and an officer in the regular army, he remained loyal to the Union and served in the Union army throughout the Civil War. He returns to his inherited plantation in Tidewater Virginia after the war, only to encounter a populace that is slow to forgive and forget. Despite an ill-fated love affair with a young woman, Throckmorton eventually woos and wins the widow of a Confederate soldier. Although Seawell does not thoroughly explore his motivations and political inclinations, he is clearly the best man in her novel, far better suited to and more worthy of the heroine than her late husband.[24]

In these novels, the northern men and reconstructed southern men exhibited the virtues that southern women most admired: hard work and its concomitant economic success, attachment to home, sexual fidelity, and modesty. Southern men who lack these virtues cannot even make a contest of it. Yet it is the force of sexuality that allows northern men to triumph over otherwise admirable southerners. Compared to these virile exemplars of virtue, the southern male aristocrats appear somewhat insipid, both sexually and intellectually.

Perhaps most surprising is the relative dearth of swashbuckling Confederate heroes produced by southern female novelists before the 1890s. Confederate soldiers dot the pages of Mary Magill's *Women,* but even her roseate account of virtuous Confederate warriors does not produce the sort of heroes who later became commonplace. Magill's heroic Confederates are most upstanding because of their devotion to duty and their willingness to face death or crippling injury for their country. Mary Holcombe, her primary heroine, weds a veteran who, because he has lost an arm in the war, offers to break their engagement. When

23. McClelland, *Princess,* 273; Magruder, *Across the Chasm,* 258.
24. Molly Elliot Seawell, *Throckmorton: A Novel* (New York, 1890).

Mary assures him that she will be "arm and all" to him, he, "all the manliness shaken out of his voice by illness and agitation," questions whether she can give herself to a "cripple." Her answer, of course, is that he must not give her up. She vows that his injury means "you need me ten thousand times more now than you ever did" and reasons that "I may be able to repay you in some small degree for your long faithfulness and love." Here the author highlights the post-war heroism and strength of the heroine, rather than the hero.[25]

In the 1880s, Mary Greenway McClelland dealt most ambiguously with the Confederate past. Pocahontas Mason, the heroine of her reunion novel *Princess,* can barely remember her father and brother, both named Temple Mason, who died in the Civil War—the father at Malvern Hill and the brother of disease in a Union prison camp. In a sentimental scene, Pocahontas discovers that her Yankee neighbor, General Smith, had tried to aid her deceased brother. This discovery makes her revisit the past, trying to remember her brother: "With tender imagination, she exaggerated his youth, his courage, his hardships, and glorified him into a hero. Everything connected with him appeared pitiful and sacred; his saber hung above the mantle, crossed with his father's, and she took it down one morning and half-drew the dulled blade from the scabbard. The brass of the hilt and the trimmings of the belt and scabbard were tarnished and even corroded in places." Pocahontas polishes the swords of both father and brother, apparently a direct renewal of filiopietism and a bow to patriarchal domination. Yet McClelland simultaneously undercuts this patriarchy by suggesting the "pitiful, corroded" nature of these martial relics. Moreover, the novelist implies there is little factual basis for Pocahontas's proud memories. Young Temple Mason appears only a casualty rather than a warrior. Still, McClelland's criticism is muted; she simply presents forlorn victims in a long ago, faraway war. Pocahontas's remaining brother, Berkeley Mason, is a Confederate veteran who lost an arm in the war. Although a stoic, admirable character, he never appears as a family patriarch who could control Pocahontas's actions or marriage.[26]

In other books, the Confederate soldier fares even more poorly. While Julia Magruder's Colonel King provides one of the few outright vicious Confederate veterans, most others are more gregarious than martial. Magruder's General Reardon is a career U.S. Army officer who "went with the South" in 1861. Good natured but rather dull-witted, General Reardon projects neither heroism nor

25. Magill, *Women,* 366–67. The Confederate veterans depicted by women contrast greatly with those of southern male writers of the day, who compared them to gallant knights. See Ritchie Devon Watson Jr., *Yeoman versus Cavalier: The Old Southwest's Fictional Road to Rebellion* (Baton Rouge, La., 1993), 142–65.

26. McClelland, *Princess,* 30–32, 49, 52–55, 96–99.

brilliance; his conversation about his business activities simply repeats the wise sayings and actions of his younger wife.[27]

In the 1890s, as heroic Confederate knights became more frequent in other fiction, a paler tradition of criticism also continued, with later Confederate veterans figuring as broadly humorous characters. Molly Elliot Seawell's Confederate veteran, General Temple, is a totally impractical man of exquisite courtesy, whose heroism in war had been matched only by his lack of martial abilities. Seawell invidiously contrasts this courtly but inept general with Major Throckmorton, who had fought for the Union: "General Temple knew that Throckmorton had been mentioned half a dozen times in general orders, and had got several brevets, while General Temple had narrowly missed half a dozen courts-martial for being where he didn't belong at a critical time. The fact that he was in imminent personal danger on all these occasions, General Temple considered not only ample excuse, but quite a feather in his cap." Seawell also implies that the heroine's deceased husband, killed while grappling with a Union soldier, had actually been shot by one of his own men. Such heroism, when not bumblingly humorous, appeared at best useless, if not positively dangerous.[28]

In 1899, Julia Magruder created her own humorous Confederate veteran, Colonel Augustine Chiltern of Flowery Dell. Chiltern, the heroine's uncle, is an ineffectual and pompous figure, who was "supposed never to have rallied from the effects of the failure of the Confederacy." A bombastic little old man whose exploits in the war loom larger with each retelling, Chiltern is above all a laughable figure. Yet his effect on his womenfolk is more somber. His five unmarried sisters minister to his every need and constantly attend him; when he goes out, they follow him in a small procession carrying his pipe and medicine. In the fifteen years that had elapsed since *Across the Chasm,* Magruder had found a new target: women who devoted their lives to the Lost Cause. While condemning the adoration of Colonel Chiltern by his sisters as their "religion," Magruder's heroine becomes increasingly tolerant of these elderly aunts, as she comes to believe that "it was their all too mistaken hero-worship of him which gave the romance, intensity, poetry, enthusiasm, to their starved and colorless lives."[29]

In the 1880s, the reunion novels presented heavily idealized pictures of the North; but by the end of the decade, a stronger chord of criticism was creeping into depictions of the North. "Inja," a short story by Amélie Rives, shows yet another side of the North-South romance. This tale begins with a wealthy north-

27. Magruder, *Across the Chasm,* 225–30.
28. Seawell, *Throckmorton,* 141–42.
29. Julia Magruder, *A Sunny Southerner* (1899; reprint, Boston, 1906), 73–78.

erner, Ruthven Lely, courting India "Inja" Sterling, a poor farmer's daughter. Yet the focus is not on Lely, who merely represents plutocratic wealth. Reuben Sterling, a farmer, is quietly contemptuous of his daughter's suitor as a man who smells sweet rather than of leather and cannot properly whistle for his dogs. The story centers on how the opulence and excitement of a distant society pulls a young woman away from her father, who adores but does not understand her, into a world that values only money and position. Reuben, with his distinctive yeoman Virginian accent, symbolizes integrity and selfless love, but when he pays an unannounced visit to his daughter in the city, he is mistaken for the overseer of the family plantation that has become part of her reconstructed past. Inja's flame-red dress and the rubies in her hair tell of the sale of self and family that mark her marriage for money. Rives juxtaposes the apple-green dress that India's father had wished to give her with the scarlet of sin and display, and the wealth of the Lelys with the poverty of the little newsboy whom Sterling meets in the city. All in all, the North appears to be the home of dismaying disparities of wealth as well as of shallowness, materialism, and social climbing.[30]

Although "Inja" invidiously contrasts northern urban life with southern rural mores, the North in novels and stories of the 1880s more often appears as a superior intellectual center. Southern female novelists frequently focused on upper-class life in the North, and writers such as Henrietta Hardy Hammond penned romances featuring upstanding, intelligent northern characters. As Amélie Rives's story of Inja makes clear, southern women were experimenting with the duality of country and city as well as that of North and South. New York remained the exemplar of the city, with its polish, its excitement, and above all its high society of glitter and glamour. At the same time, New York, and to a lesser extent, Washington, symbolized impersonality and heartless social climbing, places where wealth and social pretension were valued over the true richness of strong character. Such was the common exposé of nineteenth-century New York.

Even as southern women writers in the 1880s criticized the pretensions and hypocrisy of New York, they also suggested that the rural South was far from ideal. Mary G. McClelland probably was least critical of life in the South, populating her James River community of Wintergreen largely with gentry families, who at their worst are merely provincial and overly inbred. In contrast, Seawell's picture of a Tidewater Virginia community, while not sketched in any depth, suggests a narrowness and at times a cruel provinciality. Not only does social opinion snub the local son who had stayed in the Union army, but it freezes out

30. Amélie Rives, "Inja," *Harper's New Monthly* 76 (Nov. 1887): 31–50.

a young lady considered "fast." Community condemnation not only is swift but deeply punitive. While Henrietta Hammond in *The Georgians* depicted southern religion quite sympathetically, her opening scene of a Georgia plantation is far from idealized. On reaching her inheritance, the European-born heroine finds "all the disorder of the average Southern country-place—the weedy grass, the broken hedges, and neglected shrubbery, straggling spiraea-bushes, rose vines swaying from rotten trellis work, and the wrecked stalks of tall ornamental grasses."[31]

Julia Magruder, while suggesting that southerners were comparatively less class-conscious than northerners, still described Virginia as awash in sloth, with men like Major King depending on a delusional superiority of character. Because she blamed slavery and the war for the lazy and degraded intellectual condition of the South, Magruder did not see the past as a key to its regeneration. For her, worship of the Confederate past positively hindered women who were forced to cope with either Major King or Colonel Chiltern; such filiopietism impeded change and improvement. In her stories, women and northerners share the primary virtues of hard work, dedication, and religious feeling; they, rather than Confederate veterans, can be the agents of change, much as Margaret Trevennon inspires southern aristocrat Charlie Somers to seek his fortune through work.

Although the writings of the 1880s showed an increasing ambiguity regarding the North, this picture considerably darkened in the 1890s. Southern women still wrote tales with northern protagonists, but northern virtues had become less evident. Perhaps the economic downturns of the 1890s and the excesses of the Gilded Age, as well as southern men's emphasis on patriarchal pride and a martial Confederate past, played a part in this change. What had been northern hard work and perseverance now appeared as mere obsessiveness and greed. In this decade, both McClelland and Magruder wrote very different tales of North-South romance from their earlier novels, ones that showed less admirable northern men.

McClelland's *Broadoaks,* published in 1893, presents a radically altered view of the North and its denizens. Again McClelland sets her scene in Virginia, this time in the Piedmont, narrating a tale of romantic rivalry in which Rebie Kennedy, a young woman, chooses between two suitors—Geoffrey Bruce, a Confederate veteran and former neighbor just returned from seeking his fortune in Texas, and Stuart Redwood, a northern mining engineer. Her courtship, however, turns out to involve little contest. Embodying "courage and physical

31. Henrietta Hardy Hammond, *The Georgians* (Boston, 1881), 33.

strength," Bruce immediately captivates Rebie because she "had all a primitive woman's reverence and admiration for [such qualities]." In contrast, Redwood varies between a satanic deceiver and an animal. His only chance lies in deceit and bribery. At one point he literally tries to entrance Rebie by hypnotically invoking the "delights of wealth" in the North. His evil purpose—mastery through material goods—is illustrated by his desire to lay "chains of gold on the delicate wrists and encircle the white throat and shining hair with ropes and crowns of jewels" so that "she would follow him through life, till death." McClelland compares Redwood to disagreeable wild animals, his "eyes mottled like a snake's skin" and hair growing "straight from the scalp like the hair of an ape." Rebie Kennedy resists this northerner who secretly hunts for gold in the Kennedy family cemetery, where he is murdered by a freedman.[32]

Here, McClelland completely reshapes her northern man from the magnetic Nesbit Thorne of *Princess*. Unlike the desirable dark man of a decade earlier, Redwood appears as a blond predator, frenzied by the lust for gain. Male northerners of earlier novels simply possess wealth, but Redwood monomaniacally pursues it. Industriousness now appears as an obsession rather than a virtue, and northern male mastery has come to represent evil. McClelland also suggested southern superiority on the "race question." Redwood crudely repudiates his wartime sympathy for African Americans and shows greater racism than white southerners. Ultimately, he is murdered by an insane black man. By the 1890s, McClelland's writing had moved far closer to that of her kinsman Thomas Nelson Page, who trumpeted the superiority of white southerners.[33]

In the 1890s, Magruder also remodeled her northern men. In "Miss Ayr of Virginia," published in 1896, Magruder created a potential North-South romance focusing only on the southern woman. In this short story, Carter Ayr, a poor young Virginia woman visiting her wealthy, snobbish New York City cousins, receives but rejects a marriage proposal from one of New York's wealthiest and most eligible young men. He, however, remains a cipher, as Magruder keeps the spotlight on Carter's southern charm and know-how, which enables her to move a stalled team of oxen off a major city street, sing slave spirituals, and force an African American jockey to ride in a race by ordering him around with southern decisiveness. The story's end finds Carter back in Virginia with her equally impoverished but affectionate southern fiancé, whose character remains completely undeveloped.[34]

32. M. G. McClelland, *Broadoaks* (St. Paul, Minn., 1893), 214–17.

33. Ibid., 157, 261–65; Thomas Nelson Page, *Red Rock: A Chronicle of Reconstruction* (New York, 1898).

34. Julia Magruder, *Miss Ayr of Virginia and Other Stories* (Chicago, 1896), 1–59.

Magruder, despite the declarations of southern cultural superiority character-
izing "Miss Ayr of Virginia," continued to write North-South romances and
remained critical of elements of southern society. *A Sunny Southerner,* first published in 1899, also chronicled a romance between a northern man and a southern woman. The reconstruction of Chiltern Hall near Charlottesville, Virginia,
after a fire brings northern men into the South and kindles romance. Her heroine, the aptly named Honora Chiltern, a southern beauty, shows great vivacity
and restlessness as well as a skepticism about Virginian aristocratic origins. Yet
Magruder significantly changed the romantic rivalry. A decade earlier, her
northern hero of *Across the Chasm* bested three southern rivals; here, the only
possible romantic interests are two northerners. The first suitor pursuing Honora is a northern architect who is excessively proud of his appearance and his
family. Vanity, materialism, and social snobbery are apparently the besetting sins
of the North. Honora, however, finds another man of interest: a muscular,
darkly handsome, young northern workman, who not only is kind, gentle, and
knowledgeable about horses, but who seems to spend all his evenings reading
and writing. At his departure, they pledge to meet again, and do so in New York
when she becomes engaged to him and discovers that he is in actuality a wealthy
New Yorker and labor reformer.[35]

A Sunny Southerner shares more in tone and theme with the earlier *Across the
Chasm* than with the southern nationalism of "Miss Ayr of Virginia." Magruder
not only again presents a sensitive, intelligent, wealthy, sexy northern man as
her hero, but she also ridicules Virginian beliefs about the cavalier origins of
their elite families and caricatures Confederate veterans and their female votives.
Yet the failure to construct a North-South rivalry leaves ambiguous whether she
no longer saw the southern man as needing reconstruction or had despaired of
the project. Moreover, Magruder, in reshaping her discourse about labor, moves
her focus to problems that she presents as typically northern, leaving aside the
particularly southern ones. She emphasizes class distinctions and prejudices
without suggesting southern parallels; she never seems to consider that her
northern labor reformer might wish to organize African American laborers. Nor
do southern textile workers enter the consciousness of either hero or heroine. In
A Sunny Southerner, labor is industrial and male, never agricultural, female, or
African American.

By the 1890s, the postwar South was becoming a less rural, more industrial-
ized society with large numbers of landless whites and blacks. How did female
novelists from the old elite, given their privileged status, approach the topics of

35. Ibid., 60–62, 69, 98–110, 178, 194.

class and race, which were so important in their society? One of the major themes of southern history has concerned the extent to which the South was an organic society, with a unity among whites regardless of their economic position. Antebellum southern society, largely rural in nature, had various face-to-face interactions among different social groups. Yet historians of the South differ about the depth of tension among these have's and have-not's. Eugene D. Genovese has argued that the planters' hegemony produced a sort of cultural superiority that they used to justify and maintain political and social rule. Others, such as Bertram Wyatt-Brown, have suggested that the community itself was not so easily controlled and that aristocrats could exert only a limited amount of influence, especially during times of crisis.[36]

In the antebellum South, elite women were the group that interacted least with people of different economic standing. Because privileged women moved little in political and economic settings, their opportunities to meet people from other classes were limited. Whereas men of different social groups jostled in business dealings, court affairs, and political campaigns, women were likely to know the poor only through the rural neighborhood. Here church attendance, charitable endeavors, and exchanges of eggs, butter, and the like provided a few interactions.[37]

Some historians believe that the disruptions of the Civil War upset class relations while increasing contacts among people of different stations in life. The movements involved in fleeing an enemy army threw privileged women into contact with their poorer counterparts. Nursing and soldiers' relief also brought upper-class women into closer quarters with yeoman and landless white men. At least one historian has found upper-class women becoming more welcoming to fellow residents outside their circle during the war, but some of these encounters were unpleasant for both sides. The yeomanry resented the snobbery of the rich while the latter disdained the ignorance and dirtiness they believed was endemic among the poor. Although wealthy southerners had long emphasized the importance of being from a "good" family, this elitism would be intensified in the postwar South, where those accustomed to be counted in the aristocracy found their wealth much diminished. Members of the old elite found themselves faced

---

36. Eugene D. Genovese, *Roll, Jordan, Roll: The World the Slaves Made* (New York, 1975), and more recently, *The Slaveholders' Dilemma: Freedom and Progress in Southern Conservative Thought, 1820–1860* (Columbia, S.C., 1992); Bertram Wyatt-Brown, *Southern Honor: Ethics and Behavior in the Old South* (New York, 1982).

37. See, for example, John Hammond Moore, ed., *A Plantation Mistress on the Eve of the Civil War: The Diary of Keziah Goodwyn Hopkins, 1860–1861* (Columbia, S.C., 1993), 41, 48, 62.

with the problem of demarcating class while simultaneously downplaying the prominence of the marker of wealth.[38]

In keeping with their general lack of interest in late-nineteenth-century southern fiction, scholars have paid relatively little attention to the role of class. Literary historian Merrill Skaggs, who has written the most thorough treatment of the topic, emphasizes the lack of sympathy in portrayals of poor people. Local color stories reveal this class bias, with the upper classes gawking at the strangeness and otherness of the lower ones. Yet, in the fascination that the lower classes—black and white—held for female writers, the beginning of a more nuanced and sympathetic perception of the poorer whites is also apparent.[39]

Antebellum southern male novelists had dealt with poorer whites in several different ways. Those who wrote "southwestern humor," with its rough and tumble situations, tended to emphasize the violence of lower-class men. In the adventure novels of William Gilmore Simms, poorer whites often challenged the authority of male planters but always ended up put back firmly in their places. In addition, Simms and other writers of plantation novels, such as John Esten Cooke, offered yeoman "sidekicks," minor characters who aided the aristocratic male in his quest for social order. Southern women writers in the prewar period, such as Augusta Jane Evans, sometimes included the worthy destitute, but rarely dealt directly with any class divisions. The rise of local color writing, with its emphasis on the regional English and distinct accents, over time encouraged women authors first to describe and then to chronicle the lower classes, which these writers saw as a distinctive part of southern society. Some of the postwar novels by elite Upper South women sidestepped the question of class, either by chronicling only the upper classes or by blurring all divisions of status in their stories. For example, Frances Christine Fisher depicted some families in reduced circumstances, but generally ignored questions of class.[40]

38. Joan Cashin, "Into the Trackless Wilderness: The Refugee Experience in the Civil War," in *A Woman's War: Southern Women, Civil War, and the Confederate Legacy*, ed. Edward D. C. Campbell Jr. and Kym S. Rice (Richmond, Va., 1996), 48–53; Whites, *Civil War as Crisis*. Sheila Rae Phipps, " 'Their Desire to Visit the Southerners': Mary Greenhow Lee's Visiting 'Connexion,' " in *Negotiating Boundaries of Southern Womanhood: Dealing with the Powers That Be*, ed. Janet L. Coryell et al. (Columbia, Mo., 2000), 215–33, suggests that the Civil War diminished such prejudices among some genteel women.

39. Merrill Maguire Skaggs, *The Folk of Southern Fiction* (Athens, Ga., 1972), 5–6, 9–42, 189. See also Watson, *Yeoman versus Cavalier*, 127, which argues that the cavalier myth did not allow for an independent dissenting yeomanry.

40. On Simms, consult Susan J. Tracy, *In the Master's Eye: Representations of Women, Blacks, and Poor Whites in Antebellum Southern Literature* (Amherst, Mass., 1995), 180–96. See also John Esten Cooke, *Lord Fairfax; or, The Master of Greenway Court* (1868; reprint, New York, 1897);

Perhaps the most sympathetic treatment of nonelite whites and their religion came in the early 1880s, in Henrietta Hardy Hammond's *The Georgians*. In this tragic tale of love and sin, the hero, Mark Laurens, is a devout Methodist who neither drinks nor dances. The heroine, who was reared in France, attends church with him and is struck by the "wonderful earnestness and simplicity" with which he leads the prayers. Hammond describes the congregation as "fair representatives of the surrounding population, which was made up of plain, simple country-people, store-keepers, and farmers, and the families of men whose business was in the city." The heroine finds that she admires the genuine community of this congregation.[41]

In the 1880s, depictions of social mobility became more evident in southern women's publications. Amélie Rives, M. G. McClelland, and Julia Magruder all wrote stories and novels whose main protagonists came from a lower-class background. *A Magnificent Plebeian,* the title that Julia Magruder chose for one novel, indicated her own attitude toward social mobility. She had no trouble creating a "plebeian" with the taste and finer instincts of a patrician. Yet, significantly, she did not set her novel in the South; it is instead the story of Vivien Vernon, a small-town northern boy making good in the northern big city. As a lawyer in partnership with an aristocrat, Vernon is wary of entering high society because of his lower-class origins, even though he is well-educated and refined in his tastes. During an ocean cruise, he meets his partner's cousin, Helen Mayne, and they fall deeply in love. The question is not whether Vivien fits in with Helen's world; instead, it is whether his background and kinship ties can be harmonized with his newer role as a well-to-do lawyer. Insofar as any problem exists, it lies in perceptions, prejudices, and appearances. The hero's innate nobility is unquestionable—even his plebeian sister, though lacking in education and good taste, is a woman of good intentions and basic kindness. Still, Vivien must first convince both Helen and himself that his social origins form no bar to their happiness.[42]

M. G. McClelland showed much greater ambivalence toward social mobility and its place in the South. The title character of her novella "A Self Made Man," published in the February 1887 issue of *Lippincott's Monthly,* was Ned Anthony, a Virginian who had struck it rich with a mine in the West. Anthony returns to postwar Virginia and purchases almost one thousand acres of Repton, the estate

idem, *Out of the Foam, A Novel* (1872; reprint, New York, 1900); Augusta J. Evans, *Beulah,* ed. Elizabeth Fox-Genovese (1859; reprint, Baton Rouge, La., 1992).

41. Hammond, *Georgians,* 180, 170.

42. Julia Magruder, *A Magnificent Plebeian* (New York, 1888).

on which his father had served as overseer. Part of what brings Anthony back is his remembrance of the kindness and comradeship of little Mary Beverley, the daughter of the family for whom his father had worked. Because Anthony neither advertises nor hides his origins, it takes some time for the local folks to figure him out. A barely concealed feature of this story is the crisis in the succession of the aristocracy. The present inhabitant of Repton is Mary Beverley—not the young woman Anthony so fondly recalls, but the widow of one of the four deceased Beverley sons. McClelland has allowed death to cut a huge swath in this Tidewater Virginia community: Mr. Beverley and his four sons were killed in the war, as were Anthony's father and his three brothers; young Mary Beverley also died. The Beverely family's only hope for the future are two young grandsons, Hector and Randolph. Although Ned Anthony courts the widowed Mary Beverley, it is a courtship destined to go nowhere, given his rough edges.

For McClelland, what she calls the "overseer class" is a distinct group, and here she uses it to emphasize the race prejudice of less well-off whites in the Tidewater. This comes through in several ways in her characterization of Ned Anthony. In his childhood, he detested the imperious older sister of Mary Beverley, not only because she treated him much like she did the slaves but also because she was more willing to believe them than him. McClelland commented, "The race-prejudice between the poor whites and negroes of the South is a thing of wonderful strength, their mutual contempt immense; and to have a negro believed before him, and that, too, when he was speaking the truth and the negro was lying, was an insult that was likely to live and rankle." Such antipathy is as apparent in the present as it had been in the past. For example, Anthony intends to tear down some cabins of aged freedpeople on his land in order to build an elaborate new house for himself. His callous answer to the problem of where these elderly African Americans will live is simple: he will send them to the county poorhouse.[43]

Here McClelland again draws a contrast between the old aristocracy and less affluent whites. Mary Beverley is the protector of the aged ex-slaves—she protests the proposed destruction of their cabins and convinces Anthony to move the buildings onto her remaining land. Even Anthony's kindnesses are full of racial contempt and crudeness. When Mary Beverley thanks him for sending a basket of food to an old family retainer, he responds, "That old nigger hates me worse than a rattlesnake. He'll eat my flour and bacon, though, and my coffee will go down all right, even if he curses me between swallows." The New South

43. M. G. McClelland, "A Self Made Man," *Lippincott's Monthly* 39 (Feb. 1887): 223.

symbolized by Ned Anthony finds African Americans useless and hateful; only the old aristocracy retains a relationship with freedpeople.[44]

In the end, McClelland undercuts her presentation of Anthony as a shrewd, well-intentioned man by emphasizing his instinctive recognition of his betters: "He valued his money, and he valued himself—both more highly than either deserved, but he valued other things also. He liked to feel himself welcome and well received among the gentry that had always seemed to him the flower of the earth, because of its exclusiveness, its traditions, and the position of his own class in regard to it." Not only his lack of manners but his coarseness of feeling prevent Ned's marriage into the aristocracy. Mary Beverley, while admiring Anthony's forthrightness, finds distasteful his treatment of the ex-slaves and his laughing at a misstep of her querulous sister-in-law. Ned's lack of sensitivity and gentlemanly behavior ultimately makes him an unsuitable prospect. Mary Beverley marries his friend, an impoverished but well-mannered architect from Canada; Ned Anthony shows generosity by giving the lands he had bought to young Randolph and Hector Beverley, thus in a way rescuing one family that symbolizes the old Virginia aristocracy from the effects of war.[45]

The other common whites depicted by M. G. McClelland mainly were mountain folk, who became an attraction of novels and short stories in the 1870s and 1880s. *Burkett's Lock,* perhaps her best book, depicted the difficulties of women's life in the mountains west of Lynchburg. Hester Burkett, the heroine, lives an emotionally impoverished life with an uncommunicative father and brothers, although she does have a suitor. When her sister Delia returns from town pregnant and drowns herself in the canal, Hester helps to shield Delia's seducer. A more sympathetic depiction of mountaineers appeared in McClelland's first published book, *Oblivion.* This story centered about the transformative romance between Dick Corbyn, the "forest king," and an amnesiac beauty called "Lady" who, with her dead baby, washes up in the community after a flood. The experience of teaching and associating with Lady brings out Corbyn's instinctive nobility. To some extent, McClelland's depiction of mountain folk resembles that of other common whites: they are unlettered, uncultivated, and live in a rough society. Yet the geographical isolation of the mountain people seems an important difference to her. Thus, mountaineers are more different than inferior, unlike the common whites in plantation areas, who compare poorly to their wealthier, more aristocratic neighbors. McClelland drew clear lines between groups of southerners: one was from the overseer class, or the aris-

44. Ibid.
45. Ibid., 215.

tocracy, or the mountains, or was African American. For her, the differences between these groups were deeper than differences of culture. The crudeness of a Ned Anthony was more profound than his lack of social skills; there was a basic flaw in his essential being that he could not overcome.[46]

Far more than either Magruder or McClelland, Amélie Rives achieved a rich depiction of lower-class life that found beauty, strength, and even nobility among the poor. In contrast to Magruder and McClelland, Rives chose women from the lower classes as subjects, making them major characters in at least three of her early stories and novels. One example of this is her novella, *Virginia of Virginia.* Rather than the aristocratic, or at least middle-class, heroines of most stories, Virginia Herrick is the daughter of an overseer, possibly a man who has lost his land. Little interested in domestic matters, Virginia happily spends her time outside with the horses and dogs, riding and hiking on the farm. The English purchaser of the horse farm where Virginia lives finds her refreshingly different, though his class consciousness limits his appreciation of her as a woman. Virginia has an admirable naturalness and embodies strength, honesty, and pride in life. Even her jealousy of the Englishman's courtship of a young lady from a planter family emphasizes Virginia as a creature of flesh and blood. Amélie Rives, both in the name of her heroine and the title of her story, was suggesting that this poorly educated but honest and kind heroine embodied the "real" Old Dominion. In the rather melodramatic ending, Rives allows Virginia to redeem her act of jealousy with one of heroism. In distinction to McClelland, Rives did not suggest that lower-class whites were especially racist and antagonistic to African Americans. Despite her poverty, Virginia has an African American "mammy," a cook-factotum, who cares for her, and Rives also includes two young black boys, humorously named after volcanoes. Despite this bow to broad racial humor, Rives makes Virginia relatively unconscious of prejudice. When the Englishman offers her his coat on a blustery day, she, much to his chagrin, wraps one of the small boys in it, commenting that they feel the cold far more than she. Here it is the aristocratic Englishman who is offended at an African American boy wearing his coat, rather than the poor white woman, who is concerned only that the boy be warm. In such a scene, race prejudice is more the affliction of aristocrats than of the lower-class whites.[47]

Still, in the end, even when Rives depicted a Virginia Herrick, or McClelland

---

46. M. G. McClelland, *Burkett's Lock* (New York, c. 1888); idem, *Oblivion: An Episode,* 2nd ed. (New York, 1885).

47. Amélie Rives, *The Quick or the Dead? A Study* (Philadelphia, 1888); idem, *Virginia of Virginia* (New York, 1888). To be sure, Rives depicted some lower-class white southerners who were merely figures of fun. Parson Buzzy in *The Quick or the Dead?* is one such peculiar, vulgar character.

a Ned Corbyn, the good-hearted mountain man of *Oblivion,* these elite writers found difficulty ending their stories. Once such ordinary people were ennobled, where did they belong? Rives and McClelland resorted to melodrama, closing these stories with heroic actions that redeemed their characters but also ended their lives. McClelland did manage a stronger conclusion for "A Self Made Man." After Ned Anthony's futile attempt to win the aristocratic Mary Beverley, he leaves the Virginia Tidewater. One bystander speculates that Anthony may even end up in politics.

While the writings of southern white women included more nuanced non-aristocratic whites over time, some early attempts of writing race into the fiction of the postwar South worked in dualities. Mary Magill's story "Sis" used the name "Virginia" more conventionally for the aristocratic heroine who is nick-named "Lily" because, in the words of her black nurse, "she's so white." Lily was "petite, fairy-like, and fair as her name-flower," while her nursemaid, Sajane, nicknamed "Sis" was "elfish, grotesque, hump-shouldered, and black as the ace of spades." Nonetheless, "the two were as closely bound by ties of affection as if born of the same mother." While Magill attempted to indicate the devotion of black servants for their white charges, her story has its own peculiar angles. As an adult, Sajane convinces Lily to teach her to read: "She would do anything for a lesson; but after a while Lily found her pupil so apt that her own laurels were in danger; and then, too, she tired of her task: and so one day she announced she would not teach Sis any more." A contest of wills then ensues, which ends with Lily capitulating, so that Sajane becomes a "fluent reader." The story closes at Lily's wedding with Sajane, dressed in black silk, recalling their long attach-ment.[48]

Here Magill depicts the African American nurse who is ugly and deformed but still possesses a basic intellectual capability. Lily is devoted to Sajane because the latter is an excellent nurse. Sajane, despite her lack of opportunities, is deter-mined to read and pushes Lily to teach her. Moreover, Sajane reacts with justi-fiable anger when Lily tells her that she was created to serve. Although working from a position that assumed black inferiority and subjection, Magill conceded to blacks a basic humanity and depicted them as both seeking and capable of literacy. Of course, in this case, Sajane's search for literacy was linked to her desire to read the Bible—a conservative goal that perhaps helped to legitimate the quest.

Other novels and stories by female novelists from the old elite included fe-male African American domestic workers, but until the 1890s, these characters

48. Mary Tucker Magill, "Sis," *Harper's New Monthly* 72 (Jan. 1886): 257–63.

retained some individuality. Since at least the 1850s, some maternal nurses or cooks represented what white southerners saw as the most admirable aspects of African American womanhood. Although the devoted black nurse can be found in early postwar fiction, she had by no means evolved into the stock "mammy" that would populate so many novels at the turn of the century. In the 1870s Sherwood Bonner of Mississippi wrote her "gran'mammy tales" about her elderly nurse, who had been her mother's mammy. These stories feature a woman of great dignity and religious belief; she lives with her family, her husband, and a loving daughter. Even though Mary Magill's Sajane is a nurse, her youth, body type, and quest for knowledge all distinguish her from the stereotypical later mammies. What Sajane and Gran'mammy share with the stereotypes is loyalty, but it is not the self-abasing loyalties of later mammies.[49]

Other African American women in postwar fiction exhibit a range of personalities and personal attributes but generally have only small roles. For example, Nannie Tunstall's depiction of Aunt Chloe, a former Brown family slave, in *"No. 40"* suggests that Aunt Chloe cares about the heroine, Janet Brown. Yet Chloe is working at the Hygeia Hotel at Point Comfort; she has not worked for the Brown family since after the war. Amélie Rives's postwar settings include live-in African American servants who are individuals rather than humorous stereotypes. In Rives's *The Quick or the Dead?* (first published in 1887), the heroine's maid, Martha Ellen, seems in form and behavior a former playmate rather than a typical mammy. The heroine, Barbara Pomfret, calls Martha Ellen "Ramses" because her profile resembles an Egyptian ruler. Sleeping in the same room with Barbara, Martha Ellen witnesses her employer's attack of hysterical laughter, which chills the "blood in Martha Ellen's rigid, black body." Yet rather than comfort Barbara, Martha Ellen simply is shocked: "It did not occur to her to go to her mistress. She sat up on the pallet where she was sleeping for the night, folded herself in her own embrace, and muttered between her clacking teeth,— 'Miss Barb'ra done gone mad! she done gone mad! I dunno what tuh do!'" Martha Ellen's behavior, while indicating powerlessness, suggests a certain distance between her and Barbara rather than the all-embracing warmth of the mammy.[50]

Neither does Sarah Ann, the African American who comes to nurse Barbara as she nears nervous collapse, resemble the stereotype of a mammy. Sarah is a

49. See Anne Gowdy, ed., *A Sherwood Bonner Sampler* (Knoxville, Tenn., 2000); Magill, *Women*. Contrast this characterization with Catherine Clinton, *Tara Revisited: Women, War, and the Plantation Legend* (New York, 1995), 191–213.

50. Nannie Whitmell Tunstall, *"No. 40": A Romance of Fortress Monroe and the Hygeia*, 2nd ed. (Richmond, Va., 1884), 21–22; Rives, *Quick or the Dead?*, 439.

"little delicate thin woman of about forty, possessing a face as keen and sweet as it was plain. She wore her black wool in neat masses pinned close to her head, and her small figure in its close black gown resembled an exclamation point, so slight and decided was it." Sarah makes Barbara take a comforting bath and assures her that many people love her and that she will find happiness.

> "Think of how good you are darlin'. That ought tuh comfut you. Think of how ev'body loves you,—ev'ybody, Miss Barb'ra, down to my po' little girl, that you has done so much for. She thinks they ain' nobody like Miss Barb'ra. She says a little prayer for you ev'y night. . . . Come on, Miss Barb'ra. Let Sarah help you up. Think of how ev'ybody loves you,—th' farm-han's an' ev'ybody."
>
> "Do they really love me, Sarah?" asked the girl, in the childish tone and manner that always accompanies absolute misery. "It is good to be loved: isn't it, Sarah? It helped you that time for me to love you: didn't it? I'm glad they love me."

Here Rives, while depicting the maid's deferential manner of speaking to her mistress, changes the equation. Sarah's feelings are not apparent, and the rote nature of her assurances suggests that they may be only soothing words. The relationship between the two women is ambiguous, for it is obvious that Barbara depends on the affirmation of her servants. Moreover, Barbara hints at a time when she in turn has comforted Sarah.[51]

The early postwar fiction of elite female writers provided few views of the romanticized plantation that, to many critics, has seemed a distinguishing feature of nineteenth-century southern literature. Surprisingly, some of the most sentimental depictions of plantation life in the 1860s and 1870s flowed from the pens of northern authors. Former Union officer John W. De Forest and Constance Fenimore Woolson, a grandniece of James Fenimore Cooper, peopled their southern stories with aged ex-slaves who were devoted to their white families. The ex-slaves in De Forest's *The Bloody Chasm* worked to support their former owners, while those depicted by Woolson showed an equally strong commitment to the slaveholding family.[52]

Southern male authors played the largest role in producing sentimentalized depictions of faithful African American retainers. In 1869, John Esten Cooke published "The Last of the 'Mammies,'" which purported to describe the mammy of his "friend, Bob Blank." This elderly mammy, while tiny and wizened, otherwise set the essential characteristics for future mammies; Cooke as-

---

51. Rives, *Quick or the Dead?*, 487.

52. John W. De Forest, *The Bloody Chasm: A Novel* (New York, 1881); Constance F. Woolson, "Old Gardiston," in *Rodman the Keeper: Southern Sketches* (1880; reprint, New York, 1969).

serted that such mammies "owned their young masters and mistresses much more than anybody has owned them." He argued that the mammy cared more for her white charges than her own children. In the mid-1880s, Thomas Nelson Page provided an even more important development for racial characterizations. He took the popular market by storm with his stories narrated in dialect by aged ex-slaves, who remained on the old plantation and who totally identified with their masters. One such elderly black recalled the white family's prewar glory: "We wuz rich den, quarters on ev'y hill, an' niggers mo'n you could tell dee names."[53]

Female authors also used black characters who speak in dialect, but the interracial relationships in these stories appear less romanticized. African Americans remained servants, but they tended to be more individualistic and less emotionally dependent on the white folks. For many female authors, casting the speech of African Americans and mountain-dwelling or less wealthy whites in dialect was part of their attempt to participate fully in the local color movement that flourished from the 1870s to 1890s. To be sure, their dialogues for aristocratic white southerners or even northerners never deviated from standard English. Yet some authors, such as Amélie Rives, were fascinated by dialect; in addition to creating characters with African American and white Virginia accents, she also wrote in Elizabethan dialect. Using dialect writing did not necessarily conform to social and political conservatism. Rives and Mississippian Sherwood Bonner, while deeply interested in dialect, were socially daring, while Frances Christine Fisher, who was more politically conservative, virtually never used it.[54]

In the wake of Page's success, by the 1890s, white southern writers, male and female, specialized in colorful mammies like the mammy in Molly Elliot Seawell's *Throckmorton*, who scolds her husband, bullies the white folks, and loves the white children. These stereotypes obtained whether the cook or nurse was slave or free.[55]

Although the stereotype of the mammy as a stock character emerged only in the last decade of the nineteenth century, some postwar fiction by southern women in the 1870s and 1880s cast other black characters in an unflattering light. These portrayals might have had greater impact because as a general rule, the more closely female authors focused upon African Americans, the more likely they were to portray them negatively. Humor became a major vehicle dis-

53. John Esten Cooke, "The Last of the 'Mammies,'" *The Galaxy* 7 (Jan. 1869): 110–13; Page, "Meh Lady," 86.

54. Welford Dunaway Taylor, *Amélie Rives (Princess Troubetzkoy)* (New York, 1973), 25–31.

55. Seawell, *Throckmorton*.

seminating the most damaging stereotypes of black character and behavior. Jane Lathrop Stabler, a Lynchburg resident who wrote as Jennie Woodville, premised many of her short stories on the inferiority of African Americans. At least two stories focused on blacks as believers in magic and witchcraft. One, "Witched" (1874) featured elderly Aunt Cynthy, a former family slave and cook, who had a "terrible temper." Although the tale's narrator rehires Aunt Cynthy, bringing her back at double the wages and dropping the demand for laundry services, Aunt Cynthy believes herself to be bewitched. Elderly Uncle Jube, the conjurer, pronounces Aunt Cynthy's troubles to have sprung from having nine pieces of her clothing ironed "with a red hot iron" by a spiteful woman. Unless this woman can be found and made to "drink nine drops o' black cat's blood," Aunt Cynthy will die in nine weeks "nine hours by the sun." The narrator's attempt to have Aunt Cynthy treated by a white doctor comes to naught; the physician declares that "she had no organic disease whatever, but that she was surely dying from starvation and the influence of imagination." The mysterious spiteful woman never appears, but Aunt Cynthy expires at the appointed time. "Witched" emphasizes blacks' ignorance and unreliability, contrasting them with the rationalism of white medicine. The death of Aunt Cynthy also suggests the beliefs of some whites, North and South, that the ex-slaves could not bear the weight of freedom and would die out as a race.[56]

Dark undercurrents of fear and suspicion ran just below the vicious humor in Jane Stabler's fiction. Her "Down by the Gully" (1874) centers around a black woman's jealousy toward the rival who had "witched" her fiancé. In this story the white narrator recounts a recent discussion with her new servant Juliet, who asks her, "Did you ever want to kill anybody?" Juliet then relates how Satan tempted her to attack her rival Henrietta with a knife down by the gully. Full of charms and countercharms, the tale portrays African Americans not only as prone to "superficiality" but also to impulses of random violence. Believing that she has been bewitched by an elderly woman, Juliet suffers various ailments as well as the loss of her lover, Jerry. After Jerry marries Henrietta, he treats her badly. In the unsympathetic Juliet's words: "How he did beat her for what she did do an' what she didn't do! My lor! It done my heart good to hear her holler." This story's purpose is to illustrate the "otherness" of blacks, whose Christianity only thinly veils a pagan and violent core. Even their religion is riddled with superstition; Juliet claims that only the Holy Spirit's warning that murder would deprive her of a harp in heaven actually restrained her from killing Henrietta.

56. Jane Lathrop Stabler [pseud. Jennie Woodville], "Witched," *Southern Magazine* 15 (Dec. 1874): 571.

Yet a third story by Stabler, "A Perfect Treasure," concerns the narrator's prized maid, Caroline, and the recurring problem of "disappearing items." The narrator's husband arranges a trip to an African American church, where they observe Caroline, who has "borrowed" her mistress's best dress, finding religion and literally bursting out of her seams. The story ends rather anticlimactically with the narrator's husband firing this "treasure."[57]

Black men appeared less often and even less favorably than black women in the stories of female authors. Although Jane Stabler's stories of the 1870s centered on domestic servants and emphasized the failings of black women, black men also appeared in them as incompetent, dishonest, and violent, at least toward their wives and girlfriends. Uncle Jube, the conjure man, is an unscrupulous faker, and the ex-lover Jerry brutalizes his wife. M. G. McClelland veered toward Stabler's views. She never produced the individualized blacks of Julia Magruder and Amélie Rives and turned to more negative stereotypes in the 1890s, but her African American men are not sociopaths. In *Broadoaks* (1893), the violent black man, Patrick, who kills a northerner desecrating the white family's cemetery, is more pitiful than menacing. A man of low intelligence, Patrick is unhinged by the experience in the graveyard and is found months later wandering, deranged, in the woods. In comparison to the African American male monsters that Thomas Nelson Page was unleashing in the 1890s and that Thomas Dixon would create the following decade, the negative male characters produced by female writers are relatively tame. White women writers showed relatively little interest in black pathologies, especially more violent ones. Only as the rape complex gained greater acceptance at the turn of the century did some women writers join in the depiction of black "brutes." Eventually the stereotype of the "black beast rapist" that was beginning to fill the pages of southern newspapers and popular culture found a parallel in fictional writings.

This trend toward depicting black men as brutes might have had at least an oblique influence on Julia Magruder. The few African American characters in her fiction are kindly folk, some of whom had been wronged; but *A Sunny Southerner,* published in 1899, includes a tension-filled meeting in the countryside between the heroine, Honora, and an unknown male who is actually the hero. As a shadowy figure, this stranger frightens the heroine, who thinks that he may be a tramp. While Magruder ascribes no race to her menacing tramp, by 1899 many of her readers were likely to assume that he was African American. Moreover, to give her otherwise feisty heroine such fears shows the inroads that

57. Jane Lathrop Stabler [pseud. Jennie Woodville], "Down by the Gully," *Southern Magazine* 14 (April 1874): 379; idem, "A Perfect Treasure," *Southern Magazine* 16 (June 1875): 601–608.

the notion that women needed "protection" had made in the southern female psyche.

In the 1880s, at least a small number of southern women writers criticized slavery, although they were careful about how they condemned it. Julia Magruder created Uncle Mose, an aged family retainer in a filthy hovel who receives a basket of food from the heroine and relates proud stories about her family. He also recalls how both his first wife and daughter, belonging to other families, were on separate occasions sold away from him. To Magruder, slavery was a tragic institution that explained the backward state of the postwar South. Henrietta Hardy Hammond, in *The Georgians,* set up a dialogue to inform her European-educated heroine, Félise Orlanoff, about slavery and its abolition. When Félise ventures, "I suppose nobody lives now who is not glad that slavery is abolished," her Georgia suitor responds, "There are many who find it hard to be altogether glad of that." Félise then questions whether emancipation is better for both races. The answer to this: "While the results of emancipation have disappointed many abolitionists . . . many of us Southerners agree, at least, that it is a calamity to have slaves."[58]

Literary scholars have suggested that the late-nineteenth-century southern literary scene, with a couple of important male exceptions, consisted of those celebrating a Confederate past or writing humorous local color pieces. Yet some of the writing by women was more complicated. As Chapter One has indicated, their stories celebrated the independence and intelligence of southern women but were less sanguine about southern men. As the original Confederate memorialist movement was waning in the 1880s, southern women began to suggest that northern men embodied virtues that could usefully reconstruct white male Southerners. In these novels, Confederate veterans were wounded gentlemen at their best; others were simply incompetent or boastful bores. Ellen Glasgow's skepticism of Confederate memorials and Virginia's history has been seen as a decisive break with the past, but some Virginia women writers had voiced such sentiments decades earlier. In the novels of the 1880s, northern heroes usually outshone their southern rivals. Only in the 1890s did southern women writers begin to glorify the martial valor of Confederate soldiers.

Women authors also experimented with differences of class and race. Their novels written before 1880 generally took a patronizing view of the southern lower classes, but in the 1880s some southern women were depicting their poorer neighbors more sympathetically and considering the possibility of social mobility. African Americans tended to fare worse at the hands of elite women

---

58. Hammond, *Georgians,* 89–90.

authors, even though female authors usually were less sentimental about the slave past than southern male authors. Still, even those who dealt least in stereotypes, such as Amélie Rives, tended to give black characters small, subservient parts. And the writers who focused most on African Americans, such as Jane Stabler, tended to stress black difference, unreliability, and uncivilized behavior.

Despite their racist writings, southern white female authors did not pioneer either the plantation myth or the image of blacks as beast-rapists, notions that were gaining ground in the 1890s. For example, in 1871 Mary Magill had filled her stories of Virginia households with ungrateful slaves who left for freedom during the war. It was Thomas Nelson Page who did the most to set the myths in stone as he created the devoted, loving, and loyal slaves in his stories of the mid-1880s. In the following decade, his vision of Reconstruction unleashed debased black schemers and their unscrupulous northern allies in works such as *Red Rock*.

By the 1890s, southern women's stories were changing. Their novels of that period illustrate the growing southern critique of the North and the reemergence of the Confederate hero. Even a novelist such as Julia Magruder, who had been openly critical of southern men, now turned her attention elsewhere, finding problems and problematic people in the North as well as the South. And in the 1890s, some women writers would join in the construction of a kinder, gentler past for the South, one that must have seemed far from the turbulent political scene that included Populists, African Americans, and white supremacists.

EPILOGUE

The years after the Civil War reverberated with change throughout the United States, so it is little surprise that white southern women from the old elite found their lives greatly altered. Many of these changes were as unwelcome as unanticipated. At the war's end, these women faced a region devastated by numerous battles. The years after the Confederate defeat were busy ones for women as well as men. While a few older women simply tried to reject the new order, others attempted and some achieved different private and public lives.

Many women from the second and third generation responded vigorously to the world of work. While some second-generation women successfully became teachers and writers, the third generation more often forged long-term commitments to their teaching and writing. Third-generation women tended to be most serious about education and most devoted to their charges. They also might have been most enamored of the status they achieved through their work. In the South, which was unused to independent females outside the family, teachers most challenged the domestic ideal. To be sure, these teachers were not rebels; many felt it was their duty to inculcate religious and civic ideals, and they taught their pupils to respect authority of many sorts. Yet their very existence posited a role for women outside the family and expanded the possibilities of female education, autonomy, and authority. They would carry some of these possibilities into the twentieth century, even in the face of resurgent southern myths about the belle.

Some of these women also found a greater civic role. The second generation led the way in the creation of sanitized cemeteries for the fallen Confederate soldiers, many of whom had been their brothers, husbands, or suitors. While these women continued to be active in church organizations, some looked to new charities and new activism, as Kate Waller Barrett's work with unwed mothers reveals. The third generation reacted in polarized ways to the Confederate legacy. Some, like Julia Magruder and Ellen Glasgow, found commemorative organizations and activities oppressive and criticized them for holding the South back from the modern world. By the 1890s, others joined in the more celebratory vision of the Old South and Confederacy that was arising and even beginning to dominate the region. In the area of women's status, this youngest generation was also divided, playing prominent roles both as suffragists and as "anti's," those who belonged to antisuffrage organizations. While some second-generation women campaigned for women's rights, it was the third generation and their daughters and nieces who were particularly active on both sides of the issue.

In part, women were rethinking the kind of lives that they wanted for themselves and the younger generations, male and female. Continuing to value education, they found a new usefulness in it as well. Many of these women wanted to construct their own well-being; as well as avoiding dependence, they wished to help others, often close relatives. The war, which killed or physically and emotionally maimed many potential marriage partners, helped to create a large number of southern women who either never married or, once widowed, never remarried. Still, for some women, it was not a lack of suitors that determined their fate; ironically, the ideals of romantic love and companionate marriage were particularly important in influencing women to remain single. The kinds of marriages that were available in many cases did not approach the ideal; women sometimes deemed them not to be preferable to their lives with their families and their work. As unmarried women sought new possibilities for themselves, some accentuated the merely individualistic aspects of their enhanced autonomy. Owning property in their own right, they found in the postwar period a new freedom of movement. Some, like Nannie Tunstall, made trips to Europe; others, like schoolteacher Anna Cogswell Wood, traveled to places as remote and exotic as Russia and Egypt. Some, like Mary Lee, were almost peripatetic in their travels in America, using their extensive network of relatives and friends to provide lodgings. Those who pursued a husband as their best option for a comfortable life highlighted the materialistic side of women's participation in the marriage market. After the war, women had to think harder about their options.

In the renegotiation of household affairs and family work, women played an important part. Some older women were overwhelmed and unequal to the task, but the younger generations helped to rebuild their households, though few scrupled against making harsh demands on their African American servants and workers. Among the second and third generation, women brought a new emphasis to their role in the domestic sphere. In the late nineteenth century, women of the elite came to prize their ability to preside over clean, well-run households. Although they still preferred to compel other women, mostly African American ones, to do the hardest work of creating and maintaining these places of comfort and refinement, southern privileged women also became more skilled in the domestic arts. Some scholars have interpreted this entanglement with domesticity as lessening women's independence, but the women themselves saw their ability to master the new machinery of housekeeping as a marker of nondependence. To them, their creations, both indoors and outdoors, stood as tangible and worthy achievements.

The kind of activities that involved women from the old elite can be further interpreted as having played a crucial role in the forging of a new white southern middle class and in enunciating its ideals. In part, such work was self-centered; since many members of the old elite no longer had the same lands and material goods to define their status, they had to concentrate on alternate ways to celebrate their distinctiveness. Virginians and North Carolinians had long emphasized the importance of "good family" and this tradition continued, even in some ways that other Americans found easy to stereotype and lampoon. But it was southern women, and particularly women of the old elite, who looked to education and culture as markers of standing in society. The most reformist women of this group sought to create a larger, better educated, sober, respectable society in the South. In the new century their ideals of independence, self-control, temperance, and education gained many adherents among new town and urban dwellers and farmers alike. These ideals gained many opponents as well, who found that women's views posed too great a challenge to southern male prerogatives.

Even though the South has often been treated as unique, these postwar developments among southern elite women mirrored changes taking place elsewhere in the world. In the nineteenth century, the patriarchal family had become weakened in much of western society—from western Europe to the United States. Women clamored for expanded access to education, jobs, and the public sphere. That such a similar ferment existed in the South has perhaps been obscured by the fact that such agitation was greater in the North and by the South's early-twentieth-century history of repression and discrimination.

The experiences of defeat and its aftermath gave white women's achievements an equivocal and ambiguous cast, both for themselves and to the modern observer. Women created unprecedented roles for themselves. Though they could not overcome the racism of their region, at times they made detours from it. The women of the old elite measured their region and households, men, and plantations against changing ideals. In some ways northern and southern ideals might have been closest in the 1870s and 1880s; during these decades, some southern women found much to admire in the energetic, intelligent prosperity that northern men and cities seemed to promise. Moreover, in the 1880s, Confederate memorialism—at least as the Ladies Memorial Associations had conceived it—seemed to be weakening. That decade also saw a brief flurry of interracial cooperation in benevolent work. For example, elite women in Charlotte, North Carolina, despite their genteel racism, willingly collaborated with African American women in hospital work and campaigns for temperance.

Scholars of the late nineteenth century South have too seldom appreciated the role that women played in southern society. Most historians have assumed a basic continuity of social relations and cultural attitudes, measuring change primarily in terms of political efforts, such as agitation for women's suffrage. But women had significant nonpolitical achievements well beyond the home. The reverberations from women's new kinds of work, both paid and charitable, touched upon parts of life that discomfited many men and some women. Further, women came to exert a far greater influence in domestic life. Yet many historians have missed this development because they have concentrated on conventional politics. Although clergymen supported the women's efforts at temperance, southern male culture largely encouraged the exclusion of women from politics and from regulation of male behavior outside the house. A common male response of this period was to try to confine women's reforming proclivities to their own homes, churches, and children.

The peculiar nature of nineteenth-century southern politics influenced women's relative lack of interest in it. In part, formal politics was influenced by the general rowdiness that, to many southern males, symbolized a manly independence. This independence had always involved a good bit of touchiness, and the experience of defeat had done nothing to assuage male prickliness. Men did not believe that women belonged in politics; many of them did not want women to attend their political meetings. In particular, most men, both white and black, opposed the kinds of programs that women were most likely to pursue, such as temperance. Southern males perhaps most successfully dissuaded women from suffrage agitation by insistently associating it with northern radicalism. The antebellum link between woman's suffrage and abolitionism had made political action unacceptable to southern women before the Civil War; and while the continued connection of women's rights with a host of northern "isms" did not frighten all southern women, it continued to be a negative factor that pushed many of them toward nonpolitical forms of action as the best ways to accomplish their goals for society. This in turn has led historians to ignore the dynamic influence of women in teaching and reform activities.

Looking beyond the scope of this book, one finds white men in the South during the last decade of the nineteenth century who were in no mood to brook challenges to their political or social preeminence. Farmers, faced with falling prices for staple crops, rising prices for transportation, and an emerging world of large-scale industrial production, turned to third-party movements and agitated for political change. As conflict between the sections and between different social groups in the South worsened, the dominant ideology of the period became increasingly shrill, and it sharply critiqued outsiders and outside influences. Thus, while elite families in the postbellum South had needed and gained greater help from their womenfolk, frustrated southern men fought all the harder against expanded roles for women.

The 1890s marked the end of a period in postwar southern women's endeavors. Increasingly, the female ideal of nondependence and achievement was challenged by various revived notions of belledom. While many female educators of the third generation continued to work, their occupation was becoming more appealing to farmers' daughters than to younger women in higher social circles. As prosperity returned to the South, challenges to privileged women's working for pay increasingly arose. In benevolent work as well, the civic housekeeping and religiously oriented patriotism of the older generations was being replaced by the more dutiful image of "daughters" of the various revolutions, American or Confederate.

In the 1890s, southern women of all classes became more thoroughly enmeshed in the racial tragedy that came to characterize the twentieth-century South. The "great reaction" brought black disfranchisement, the spread of segregation, and terroristic measures such as lynching and whitecapping. Earlier in the postwar years, racialist ideas had suffused white women's writings, but women had rarely displayed the depths of contempt for blacks evident in southern white men's private and public utterances. By the end of the century, this had changed. Women were penning their share of the hate-filled articles and novels that characterized the period. A growing fear of blacks—especially black men—among white women was a critical factor in this development. The increased female autonomy of the postwar years had sparked a desire for greater freedom of movement and travel; racism compromised this freedom, with its constant warning that white women needed "protection" from black men, in the countryside or the city.

These developments emerged from certain elements of the immediate postwar past. While discarding the kinds of interracial cooperation that had appeared after Reconstruction, a majority of southerners from the old elite concentrated on celebrating their earlier history of slavery and the Confederacy. As they demanded and enforced white supremacy, these members of the old elite harkened back to an ideal, mythical antebellum regime in which racial hierarchy and harmony supposedly had prevailed. In this re-creation of a past South, the only women celebrated were the plantation mistress and belle, and they primarily for their ornamental functions. Not all women from elite families would agree with this vision of the world and their role in it. Some, like Amélie Rives, would come to pursue woman's suffrage and other "radical" measures for women's autonomy. Like Rives, some women would insist on more overt sexuality in their lives. But many women would accept the constricted world advocated for southern women as necessary for themselves and others.

Even the reaction of the 1890s could not totally erase the changes that had occurred since the Civil War. With aggressive notions of white male supremacy abroad, the minority of women who favored a more public role and expanded rights for their sex had to fight harder to ensure any hearing. Although the women involved in the Daughters of the Confederacy and antisuffrage activities had abandoned adventurous ideas, they were actually far more politically active and visible than the antebellum women they praised or than the ideal of womanhood they advocated. In their avid pursuit of pleasure and individualistic satisfaction, the revived belles of the turn-of-the-century South, though often apolitical or politically conservative, differed from the demure antebellum belle. Both they and female conservative activists indicated the extent of the changes that had occurred since the war, even as they channeled their activities into "accepted" forms.

BIBLIOGRAPHY

MANUSCRIPT COLLECTIONS

Colonial Williamsburg Foundation Library

Shirley Plantation Papers

Duke University Rare Book, Manuscript, and Special Collections Library

Samuel S. Biddle Papers
Amy Bradley Papers
Henry Selby Clark Papers
Clement C. Clay Papers
William W. Corcoran Papers
Edward A. Crudup Diary
Samuel S. Downey Papers
Paul Hamilton Hayne Papers
Julia Magruder Papers
Adelaide Savage Meares Papers
Thomas Nelson Page Papers
Presley C. Person Papers
Amélie Rives Papers
William Tarry Papers

Library of Congress

Willie Person Mangum Family Papers
William Cabell Rives Papers
John Tyler Papers

Library of Virginia

Ladies Memorial Association of Petersburg, Va., Records, 1866–1912. Association 24254, Organization records collection
"Reminiscences of Maria Gordon Pryor Rice" (unpub. typescript, c. 1920)

Southern Historical Collection, Wilson Library, University of North Carolina at Chapel Hill

Lucy Tunstall Alston Collection
Maria Taylor Beale Papers
Benbury-Haywood Papers
Elizabeth Amis Cameron (Hooper) Blanchard Papers
Mary Biddle Norcott Bryan Scrapbook
Burgwyn Family Papers
Cameron Family Papers
Maxwell Troax Clarke Papers
Anne Cameron Collins Papers
DeRosset Family Papers
George Hairston Papers
Peter W. Hairston Diary
Hairston-Wilson Papers
Charles E. Hamilton-John Bullock Papers
Hawkins Family Papers
John S. Henderson Papers
Hubard Family Papers
William B. Meares Papers
Meares-DeRosset Family Papers
Pettigrew Family Papers
Skinner Family Papers
Peter E. Smith Papers
John and William A. Williams Papers
Lucy Alston Williams Papers
Mrs. Bayard Wooten Papers

Special Collections Department, University of Virginia Library

Bondurant-Morrison Family Papers
Cabell Family Papers
Cabell-Ellet Family Papers
Latané Family Papers
Magruder Family Papers
Julia Magruder Collection, Clifton Waller Barrett Library of American Literature
Staples-Persinger Family Papers
Tayloe Family Papers

Virginia Historical Society

Appomattox [Va.] Ladies Memorial Association Minutes
Aylett Family Papers

Bailey Family Papers
Baskerville Family Papers
Battle Family Papers
Beverley Family Papers
Blanton Family Papers
Bruce Family Papers
Carrington Family Papers
Cocke Family Papers
Emily Dupuy Papers
J. D. Eggleston, ed. "Misses Carrington's Sunnyside School for Young Ladies, 1872–
    1908" (unpub. ms., c. 1930s)
Eppes Family Papers
Guerrant Family Papers
Guest Family Papers
Gwathmey Family Papers
Hankins Family Papers
Harvie Family Papers
Holladay Family Papers
Mason Family Papers
Preston Family Papers
Saunders Family Papers
Tarry Family Papers
Julia Tyler Papers
Watkins Family
Wickham Family Papers

PUBLIC RECORDS

Three repositories, the Hall of Records of the Fauquier County (Virginia) Circuit
Court, Library of Virginia, and the North Carolina Division of Archives and History hold the wills, deeds, and estates records utilized throughout this study. I also
relied on the federal manuscript censuses of population for these two states, 1850–
1880, available on microfilm from the National Archives and Records Service.

NEWSPAPERS

Atlanta Constitution
Warrenton (Va.) True Index

Contemporary Fiction

Cooke, John Esten. *Lord Fairfax; or, The Master of Greenway Court.* 1868. Reprint,
    New York, 1897.
———. *Out of the Foam. A Novel.* 1872. Reprint, New York, 1900.

De Forest, John William. *The Bloody Chasm: A Novel.* New York, 1881.

——. *Miss Ravenel's Conversion from Secession to Loyalty.* Ed. Gordon S. Haight. 1867. Reprint, New York, 1955.

Evans, Augusta J. *Beulah.* Ed. Elizabeth Fox-Genovese. 1859. Reprint, Baton Rouge, La., 1992.

——. *Macaria, or Altars of Sacrifice.* Ed. Drew Gilpin Faust. 1864. Reprint, Baton Rouge, La., 1992.

Gowdy, Anne, ed. *A Sherwood Bonner Sampler.* Knoxville, Tenn., 2000.

Hammond, Henrietta Hardy [pseud. Henri Daugé]. *A Fair Philosopher.* New York, 1882.

——. *The Georgians.* Boston, 1881.

——. "A Love Story." *Southern Magazine* 17 (July–Dec. 1875), 101–18, 143–66, 273–94, 395–412, 513–34, 641–62.

Haw, M. J. *The Beechwood Tragedy: A Tale of the Chickahominy.* Richmond, Va., 1889.

Jordan, Cornelia Jane Matthews. *Corinth and Other Poems of the War.* Lynchburg, Va., 1865.

——. *Flowers of Hope and Memory.* Richmond, Va., 1861.

McClelland, M. G. *Broadoaks.* St. Paul, Minn., 1893.

——. *Burkett's Lock.* New York, c. 1888.

——. *Oblivion: An Episode.* 2nd ed. New York, 1885.

——. *Princess.* New York, 1886.

——. "A Self Made Man." *Lippincott's Monthly* 39 (Feb. 1887): 195–284.

McDowell, Katharine Sherwood Bonner [pseud. Sherwood Bonner]. *Like unto Like.* Ed. Jane Turner Censer. 1878. Reprint, Columbia, S.C., 1998.

Magill, Mary Tucker. "Sis." *Harper's New Monthly* 72 (Jan. 1886): 257–63.

——. *Women, or Chronicles of the Late War.* Baltimore, 1871.

Magruder, Julia. *Across the Chasm.* New York, 1885.

——. *Dead Selves.* Philadelphia, 1898.

——. *A Magnificent Plebeian.* New York, 1888.

——. *Miss Ayr of Virginia and Other Stories.* Chicago, 1896.

——. *A Sunny Southerner.* 1899. Reprint, Boston, 1906.

Page, Thomas Nelson. *Bred in the Bone.* New York, 1904.

——. *In Ole Virginia, or Marse Chan and Other Stories.* New York, 1887.

——. *Red Rock: A Chronicle of Reconstruction.* New York, 1898.

Putnam, Sallie A. Brock. *Kenneth, My King.* New York, 1873.

Rives, Amélie. "Inja." *Harper's New Monthly* 76 (Nov. 1887): 31–50.

——. *The Quick or the Dead? A Study.* Philadelphia, 1888.

——. *Virginia of Virginia.* New York, 1888.

Robinson, Martha M. Harrison. *Helen Erskine.* Philadelphia, 1870.

Seawell, Molly Elliot. *Throckmorton: A Novel.* New York, 1890.

Stabler, Jane Lathrop [pseud. Jennie Woodville]. "Down by the Gully." *Southern Magazine* 14 (1874): 376–80.

———. *Left to Herself*. Philadelphia, 1871.

———. "A Perfect Treasure." *Southern Magazine* 16 (June 1875): 601–08.

Tiernan, Frances Christine Fisher [pseud. Christian Reid]. *After Many Days: A Novel*. New York, 1877.

———. *A Daughter of Bohemia: A Novel*. New York, 1874.

———. *Ebb Tide and Other Stories*. New York, 1872.

——— -. *Heart of Steel: A Novel*. New York, 1883.

———. *Hearts and Hands: A Story in Sixteen Chapters*. New York, 1875.

———. *"The Land of the Sky"; or, Adventures in Mountain By-Ways*. New York, 1875.

———. *Mabel Lee*. New York, 1872.

———. *Morton House: A Novel*. New York, 1872.

———. *Nina's Atonement and Other Stories*. New York, 1873.

Tunstall, Nannie Whitmell. *"No. 40": A Romance of Fortress Monroe and the Hygeia*. 2nd ed. Richmond, Va., 1884.

Woolson, Constance F. "Old Gardiston." In *Rodman the Keeper: Southern Sketches*. 1880. Reprint, New York, 1969.

PUBLISHED PRIMARY SOURCES

Andrews, Eliza Frances. *Journal of a Georgia Woman, 1870–1872*. Ed. S. Kittrell Rushing. Knoxville, Tenn., 2002.

Andrews, Marietta Minnigerode. *Memoirs of a Poor Relation: Being the Story of a Post-war Southern Girl and Her Battle with Destiny*. New York, 1927.

Ayers, Edward L., and Bradley C. Mittendorf, eds. *The Oxford Book of the American South: Testimony, Memory, Fiction*. New York, 1997.

Bleser, Carol K. Rothrock, ed. *The Hammonds of Redcliffe*. New York, 1981.

Brock, Sallie. *Richmond during the War: Four Years of Personal Observation*. 1867. Reprint, Lincoln, Neb., 1996.

Burr, Virginia Ingraham, ed. *The Secret Eye: The Journal of Ella Gertrude Clanton Thomas, 1848–1889*. Chapel Hill, N.C., 1990.

Cashin, Joan, ed. *Our Common Affairs: Texts from Women in the Old South*. Baltimore, 1996.

Clark, Emily. *Innocence Abroad*. New York, 1931.

Coleman, Charles. "The Recent Movement in Southern Literature." *Harper's New Monthly* 74 (May 1887): 837–55.

Confederated Southern Memorial Association. *History of the Confederated Memorial Associations of the South*. New Orleans, 1904.

Crabtree, Beth G., and James W. Patton, eds. *"Journal of a Secesh Lady": The Diary of Catherine Ann Devereux Edmondston, 1860–1866*. Raleigh, N.C., 1979.

Eggleston, George Cary. *A Rebel's Recollections*. 1905. Reprint, New York, 1969.

Fleet, Betsy, ed. *Green Mount after the War: The Correspondence of Maria Louisa Wacker Fleet and Her Family, 1865–1900*. Charlottesville, Va., 1978.

Gilbert, Sandra, and Susan Gubar, eds. *The Norton Anthology of Literature by Women: The Traditions in English.* 2nd ed. New York, 1996.

Glasgow, Ellen. *The Woman Within.* New York, 1954.

Hayne, Paul Hamilton. "Literature at the South." *Southern Magazine* 14 (June 1874): 651–55.

Herbert, Robert Beverley. *Life on a Virginia Farm: Stories and Recollections of Fauquier County.* Warrenton, Va., 1968.

Long, Mary Alves. *High Time to Tell It: "Ah, Distinctly I Remember."* Durham, N.C., 1950.

Moore, John Hammond, ed. *A Plantation Mistress on the Eve of the Civil War: The Diary of Keziah Goodwyn Hopkins, 1860–1861.* Columbia, S.C., 1993.

Moore, Rayburn S., ed. *A Man of Letters in the Nineteenth-Century South: Selected Letters of Paul Hamilton Hayne.* Baton Rouge, La., 1982.

National Florence Crittenton Mission. *Fourteen Years' Work among "Erring Girls."* Washington, D.C., [1897].

O'Brien, Michael, ed. *An Evening When Alone: Four Journals of Single Women in the South, 1827–1867.* Charlottesville, Va., 1993.

Raper, Julius Rowan, ed. *Ellen Glasgow's Reasonable Doubts: A Collection of Her Writings.* Baton Rouge, La., 1988.

Rice, John Andrew. *I Came out of the Eighteenth Century.* New York, 1942.

Robertson, Mary D., ed. *Lucy Breckinridge of Grove Hill: The Journal of a Virginia Girl, 1862–1864.* Columbia, S.C., 1994.

Smith, Presley A. L. *Boyhood Memories of Fauquier.* Richmond, Va., 1926.

"Some Days with Amélie Rives." *Lippincott's Magazine* 42 (April 1888): 531–33.

Tardy, Mary T. *The Living Female Writers of the South.* Philadelphia, 1870.

Terhune, Mary Virginia [pseud. Marion Harland]. *Marion Harland's Autobiography: The Story of a Long Life.* New York, 1910.

Vogtsberger, Margaret Ann. *The Dulanys of Welbourne: A Family in Mosby's Confederacy.* Berryville, Va., 1995.

Webb, Allie Bayne Windham, ed. *Mistress of Evergreen Plantation: Rachel O'Connor's Legacy of Letters, 1823–1845.* Albany, N.Y., 1983.

Wood, Anna Cogswell. *Idyls and Impressions of Travel.* New York, 1904.

———. *The Story of a Friendship: A Memoir.* New York, 1901.

Woodward, C. Vann, ed. *Mary Chesnut's Civil War.* New Haven, Conn., 1981.

SECONDARY SOURCES

Books

Aiken, Katherine G. *Harnessing the Power of Motherhood: The National Florence Crittenton Mission, 1883–1925.* Knoxville, Tenn., 1998.

Alderman, Edwin Anderson, et al., eds. *Library of Southern Literature.* 15 vols. New Orleans, 1907–10.

Alexander, Adele Logan. *Ambiguous Lives: Free Women of Color in Rural Georgia, 1789–1879*. Fayetteville, Ark., 1991.

Allmendinger, David F. *Ruffin: Family and Reform in the Old South*. New York, 1990.

Anderson, Jean Bradley. *The Kirklands of Ayr Mount*. Chapel Hill, N.C., 1991.

Avery, Mary Johnston. *She Heard with Her Heart*. Birmingham, Ala., 1944.

Ayers, Edward L. *The Promise of the New South: Life after Reconstruction*. New York, 1992.

Bain, Robert, and Joseph M. Flora, eds. *Fifty Southern Writers before 1900*. Westport, Conn., 1987.

Banta, Martha. *Imaging American Women: Idea and Ideals in Cultural History*. New York, 1987.

Bardaglio, Peter. *Reconstructing the Household: Families, Sex, and the Law in the Nineteenth-Century South*. Chapel Hill, N.C., 1995.

Baym, Nina. *Woman's Fiction: A Guide to Novels by and about Women in America, 1820–1870*. 2nd ed. Urbana, Ill., 1993.

Beard, Mary. *Woman as Force in History: A Study in Traditions and Realities*. New York, 1946.

Bordin, Ruth. *Woman and Temperance: The Quest for Power and Liberty, 1873–1900*. New Brunswick, N.J., 1981.

Boswell, Angela. *Her Act and Deed: Women's Lives in a Rural Southern County, 1837–1873*. College Station, Tex., 2001.

Brodie, Janet Farrell. *Contraception and Abortion in Nineteenth-Century America*. Ithaca, N.Y., 1994.

Brundage, W. Fitzhugh. *Lynching in the New South: Georgia and Virginia, 1880–1930*. Urbana, Ill., 1993.

Buck, Paul H. *The Road to Reunion, 1865–1900*. Boston, 1937.

Burton, Orville Vernon. *In My Father's House Are Many Mansions: Family and Community in Edgefield, South Carolina*. Chapel Hill, N.C., 1985.

Camp, Cornelia. *Some Pioneer Women Teachers of North Carolina*. N.p., 1955.

Cantrell, Gregg. *Kenneth and John B. Rayner and the Limits of Southern Dissent*. Urbana, Ill., 1993.

Carraway, Gertrude S. *Crown of Life: History of Christ Church, New Bern, N.C., 1715–1940*. New Bern, N.C., 1940.

Cashin, Joan E. *A Family Venture: Men and Women on the Southern Frontier*. New York, 1991.

Censer, Jane Turner. *North Carolina Planters and Their Children*. Baton Rouge, La., 1984.

Chudacoff, Howard P. *The Age of the Bachelor: Creating an American Subculture*. Princeton, N.J., 1999.

Clark-Lewis, Elizabeth. *Living In, Living Out: African American Domestics in Washington, D.C., 1910–1940*. Washington, D.C., 1994.

Clinton, Catherine. *The Plantation Mistress: Woman's World in the Old South*. New York, 1982.

————. *Tara Revisited: Women, War, and the Plantation Legend.* New York, 1995.

Cohen, Lucy. *Chinese in the Post–Civil War South: A People without a History.* Baton Rouge, La., 1984.

Coulling, Mary Price. *Margaret Junkin Preston: A Biography.* Winston-Salem, N.C., 1993.

Coultrap-McQuin, Susan. *Doing Literary Business: American Women Writers in the Nineteenth Century.* Chapel Hill, N.C., 1990.

Cowan, Ruth Schwartz. *More Work for Mother: The Ironies of Household Technology from the Open Hearth to the Microwave.* New York, 1983.

Cyganowski, Carol Klimick. *Magazine Editors and Professional Authors in Nineteenth-Century America: The Genteel Tradition and the American Dream.* New York, 1998.

Davidson, Cathy N., et al., eds. *The Oxford Companion to Women's Writing in the United States.* New York, 1995.

Dailey, Jane. *Before Jim Crow: The Politics of Race in Postemancipation Virginia.* Chapel Hill, N.C., 2000.

DeRosset, William Lord. *One Hundredth Anniversary Commemorating the Building of St. James Church, Wilmington, North Carolina, April 30th and May 1st, 1939: The Two Hundred and Tenth Year of the Parish.* Wilmington, 1939.

Diffley, Kathleen. *Where My Heart Is Turning Ever: Civil War Stories and Constitutional Reform, 1861–1876.* Athens, Ga., 1992.

Dublin, Thomas. *Transforming Women's Work: New England Lives in the Industrial Revolution.* Ithaca, N.Y., 1994.

Durrill, Wayne K. *War of Another Kind: A Southern Community in the Great Rebellion.* New York, 1990.

Dusinberre, William. *Them Dark Days: Slavery in the American Rice Swamps.* 1996. Reprint, Athens, Ga., 2000.

Edwards, Laura F. *Gendered Strife and Confusion: The Political Culture of Reconstruction.* Urbana, Ill., 1997.

————. *Scarlett Doesn't Live Here Anymore: Southern Women in the Civil War Era.* Urbana, Ill., 2000.

Enstam, Elizabeth. *Women and the Creation of Urban Life: Dallas, Texas, 1843–1920.* College Station, Tex., 1998.

Escott, Paul D. *Many Excellent People: Power and Privilege in North Carolina, 1850–1900.* Chapel Hill, N.C., 1985.

Farnham, Christie Ann. *The Education of the Southern Belle: Higher Education and Student Socialization in the Antebellum South.* New York, 1994.

Fauquier County Bicentennial Committee. *Fauquier County, Virginia, 1759–1959.* Warrenton, Va., 1959.

Faust, Drew Gilpin. *Mothers of Invention: Women of the Slaveholding South in the American Civil War.* Chapel Hill, N.C., 1996.

Fidler, William Perry. *Augusta Evans Wilson, 1835–1909: A Biography.* University, Ala., 1951.

Foner, Eric. *Reconstruction: America's Unfinished Revolution, 1863–1877*. New York, 1988.

Foster, Gaines. *Ghosts of the Confederacy: Defeat, the Lost Cause, and the Emergence of the New South*. New York, 1987.

Fox-Genovese, Elizabeth. *Within the Plantation Household: Black and White Women of the Old South*. Chapel Hill, N.C., 1988.

Frank, William L. *Sherwood Bonner (Catherine McDowell)*. New York, 1971.

Friedman, Jean E. *The Enclosed Garden: Women and Community in the Evangelical South, 1830–1900*. Chapel Hill, N.C., 1985.

Friedman, Lawrence J. *The White Savage: Racial Fantasies in the Postbellum South*. Englewood Cliffs, N.J., 1970.

Genovese, Eugene D. *Roll, Jordan, Roll: The World the Slaves Made*. New York, 1975.

———. *The Slaveholders' Dilemma: Freedom and Progress in Southern Conservative Thought, 1820–1860*. Columbia, S.C., 1992.

Gilmore, Glenda Elizabeth. *Gender and Jim Crow: Women and the Politics of White Supremacy in North Carolina, 1896–1920*. Chapel Hill, N.C., 1996.

Godbold, E. Stanly, Jr. *Ellen Glasgow and the Woman Within*. Baton Rouge, La., 1972.

Green, Elna C. *Southern Strategies: Southern Women and the Woman Suffrage Question*. Chapel Hill, N.C., 1997.

Greenwood, Janette Thomas. *Bittersweet Legacy: The Black and White "Better Classes" in Charlotte, 1850–1910*. Chapel Hill, N.C., 1994.

Hale, Grace Elizabeth. *Making Whiteness: The Culture of Segregation in the South, 1890–1940*. New York, 1998.

Hiatt, Mary. *Style and the "Scribbling Women": An Empirical Analysis of Nineteenth-Century American Fiction*. Westport, Conn., 1993.

Hofheimer, Jo Ann Mervis. *Annie Wood, a Portrait: The Life and Times of the Founder of the Irene Leache Memorial*. Norfolk, Va., 1996.

Hunter, Tera. *To 'Joy My Freedom: Southern Black Women's Lives and Labors after the Civil War*. Cambridge, Mass., 1997.

Jabour, Anya. *Marriage in the Early Republic: Elizabeth and William Wirt and the Companionate Ideal*. Baltimore, 1998.

James, Edward T., et al., eds. *Notable American Women, 1607–1950: A Biographical Dictionary*. 3 vols. Cambridge, Mass., 1971.

Jones, Anne Goodwyn. *Tomorrow Is Another Day: The Woman Writer in the South, 1859–1936*. Baton Rouge, La., 1981.

Kelley, Mary. *Private Woman, Public Stage: Literary Domesticity in Nineteenth-Century America*. New York, 1984.

Kennard, Jean. *Victims of Convention*. Hamden, Conn., 1978.

Kerr-Ritchie, Jeffrey R. *Freedpeople in the Tobacco South: Virginia, 1860–1900*. Chapel Hill, N.C., 1999.

Kneebone, John, et al., eds. *Dictionary of Virginia Biography*. Richmond, Va., 1998–.

Knight, Edgar Wallace. *Public School Education in North Carolina*. 1916. Reprint, New York, 1969.

Kunzel, Regina. *Fallen Women, Problem Girls: Unmarried Mothers and the Professionalization of Social Work, 1890–1945.* New Haven, Conn., 1993.

Lankford, Nelson D. *The Last American Aristocrat: The Biography of David K. E. Bruce,
   1898–1977.* Boston, 1996.

Lebsock, Suzanne. *The Free Women of Petersburg: Status and Culture in a Southern Town,
   1784–1860.* New York, 1984.

———. *"A Share of Honour": Virginia Women, 1600–1945.* Richmond, Va., 1984.

Lewis, Henry W. *Northampton Parishes.* Jackson, N.C., 1951.

Link, William A. *A Hard Country and a Lonely Place: Schooling, Society, and Reform in
   Rural Virginia, 1870–1920.* Chapel Hill, N.C., 1986.

Litwack, Leon F. *Been in the Storm So Long: The Aftermath of Slavery.* New York, 1980.

Longest, George C. *Three Virginia Writers: Mary Johnston, Thomas Nelson Page and
   Amélie Rives Troubetzkoy.* Boston, 1978.

McAlexander, Hubert Horton. *The Prodigal Daughter: A Biography of Sherwood Bonner.*
   2nd ed. Knoxville, Tenn., 1999.

McArthur, Judith N. *Creating the New Woman: The Rise of Southern Women's Progressive
   Culture in Texas, 1893–1918.* Urbana, Ill., 1998.

McCandless, Amy Thompson. *The Past in the Present: Women's Higher Education in the
   Twentieth-Century American South.* Tuscaloosa, Ala., 1999.

McDowell, John Patrick. *The Social Gospel in the South: The Woman's Home Mission
   Movement in the Methodist Episcopal Church South, 1886–1939.* Baton Rouge, La.,
   1982.

McGraw, Marie Tyler. *At the Falls: Richmond, Virginia, and Its People.* Chapel Hill,
   N.C., 1994.

MacKethan, Lucinda H. *Daughters of Time: Creating Woman's Voice in Southern Story.*
   Athens, Ga., 1990.

Marchalonis, Shirley, ed. *Patrons and Protégées: Gender, Friendship, and Writing in Nineteenth-Century America.* New Brunswick, N.J., 1988.

Matthews, Pamela R. *Ellen Glasgow and a Woman's Traditions.* Charlottesville, Va., 1994.

Maza, Sarah. *Servants and Masters in Eighteenth-Century France: The Uses of Loyalty.*
   Princeton, N.J., 1983.

Meagher, Margaret. *History of Education in Richmond.* Richmond, Va., 1939.

Mixon, Wayne. *Southern Writers and the New South Movement, 1865–1913.* Chapel
   Hill, N.C., 1980.

Moore, James Tice. *Two Paths to the New South: The Virginia Debt Controversy, 1870–
   1883.* Lexington, Ky., 1974.

Morgan, Lynda. *Emancipation in Virginia's Tobacco Belt, 1850–1870.* Athens, Ga.,
   1992.

Morris, Christopher. *Becoming Southern: The Evolution of a Way of Life, Warren County
   and Vicksburg, Mississippi, 1770–1860.* New York, 1995.

Moss, Elisabeth. *Domestic Novelists in the Old South: Defenders of Southern Culture.*
   Baton Rouge, La., 1992.

Muhlenfeld, Elisabeth. *Mary Boykin Chesnut: A Biography.* Baton Rouge, La., 1981.

Nagel, Paul C. *The Lees of Virginia: Seven Generations of an American Family.* New York, 1990.

O'Brien, Gail Williams. *The Legal Fraternity and the Making of a New South Community, 1848–1882.* Athens, Ga., 1986.

Orgain, Kate. *Southern Authors in Poetry and Prose.* New York, 1908.

Ownby, Ted. *Subduing Satan: Religion, Recreation, and Manhood in the Rural South, 1865–1920.* Chapel Hill, N.C., 1990.

Pattee, Fred Lewis. *A History of American Literature since 1870.* 1915. Reprint, New York, 1968.

Pease, Jane H., and William H. Pease. *A Family of Women: The Carolina Petigrus in Peace and War.* Chapel Hill, N.C., 1999.

Perlmann, Joel, and Robert A. Margo. *Women's Work? American Schoolteachers, 1650–1920.* Chicago, 2001.

Perry, Carolyn, and Mary Louise Weeks, eds. *The History of Southern Women's Literature.* Baton Rouge, La., 2002.

Powell, William S., ed. *Dictionary of North Carolina Biography.* 8 vols. Chapel Hill, N.C., 1979.

Pulley, Raymond H. *Old Virginia Restored: An Interpretation of the Progressive Impulse, 1870–1930.* Charlottesville, Va., 1968.

Rable, George. *Civil Wars: Women and the Crisis of Southern Nationalism.* Urbana, Ill.,1989.

Ramey, Emily, and John K. Gott, eds. *The Years of Anguish: Fauquier County, Virginia, 1861–1865.* Warrenton, Va., 1965.

Ransom, Roger, and Richard Sutch. *One Kind of Freedom: The Economic Consequences of Emancipation.* Cambridge, Eng., 1977.

Raper, J. R. *Without Shelter: The Early Career of Ellen Glasgow.* Baton Rouge, La., 1971.

Roark, James. *Masters without Slaves: Southern Planters in the Civil War and Reconstruction.* New York, 1977.

Roediger, David. *The Wages of Whiteness: Race and the Making of the American Working Class.* London, 1991.

Rowe, Anne. *The Enchanted Country: Northern Writers in the South, 1865–1910.* Baton Rouge, La., 1978.

Rubin, Louis, ed. *The History of Southern Literature.* Baton Rouge, La., 1985.

———. *The Writer in the South: Studies in a Literary Community.* Athens, Ga., 1972.

Rutherford, Mildred Lewis. *The South in History and Literature: A Hand-book of Southern Authors from the Settlement of Jamestown 1607 to Living Writers.* Atlanta, 1906.

Savage, Kirk. *Standing Soldiers, Kneeling Slaves: Race, War, and Monument in Nineteenth-Century America.* Princeton, N.J., 1997.

Scott, Anne Firor. *Natural Allies: Women's Associations in American History.* Urbana, Ill., 1993.

———. *The Southern Lady: From Pedestal to Politics, 1830–1930.* Chicago, 1970.

Shammas, Carole, Marylynn Salmon, and Michel Dahlin. *Inheritance in America: From Colonial Times to the Present.* New Brunswick, N.J., 1987.

Silber, Nina. *The Romance of Reunion: Northerners and the South, 1865–1900.* Chapel Hill, N.C., 1993.

Sims, Anastatia. *The Power of Femininity in the New South: Women's Organizations and Politics in North Carolina, 1880–1930.* Columbia, S.C., 1997.

Sizer, Lyde Cullen. *The Political Work of Northern Women Writers and the Civil War, 1850–1872.* Chapel Hill, N.C., 2000.

Skaggs, Merrill Maguire. *The Folk of Southern Fiction.* Athens, Ga., 1972.

Smith, Claiborne Thweatt, Jr. *Smith of Scotland Neck: Planters on the Roanoke.* Baltimore, 1976.

Smith, Page. *Daughters of the Promised Land: Women in American History.* Boston, 1970.

Sprunt, James. *Chronicles of the Cape Fear River, 1660–1906.* 2nd ed. Raleigh, N.C., 1916.

Stowe, Steven. *Intimacy and Power in the Old South: Ritual in the Lives of the Planters.* Baltimore, 1987.

Strasser, Susan. *Never Done: A History of American Housework.* 1982. Reprint, New York, 2000.

Taylor, Helen. *Gender, Race, and Region in the Writings of Grace King, Ruth McEnery Stuart, and Kate Chopin.* Baton Rouge, La., 1989.

Taylor, Welford Dunaway. *Amélie Rives (Princess Troubetzkoy).* New York, 1973.

———. *Virginia Authors Past and Present.* N.p., 1972.

Thomas, Emory M. *Robert E. Lee: A Biography.* New York, 1995.

Tolbert, Lisa C. *Constructing Townscapes: Space and Society in Antebellum Tennessee.* Chapel Hill, N.C., 1999.

Tracy, Susan J. *In the Master's Eye: Representations of Women, Blacks, and Poor Whites in Antebellum Southern Literature.* Amherst, Mass., 1995.

Treadway, Sandra Gioia. *Women of Mark: A History of the Woman's Club of Richmond, Virginia, 1894–1994.* Richmond, Va., 1995.

Tuchman, Gayle. *Edging Women Out: Victorian Novelists, Publishers, and Social Change.* New Haven, Conn., 1989.

Turner, Elizabeth Hayes. *Women, Culture, and Community: Religion and Reform in Galveston, 1880–1920.* New York, 1997.

Ulrich, Laurel Thatcher. *Good Wives: Image and Reality in the Lives of Women in Northern New England, 1650–1750.* New York, 1987.

Varon, Elizabeth R. *We Mean To Be Counted: White Women and Politics in Antebellum Virginia.* Chapel Hill, N.C., 1998.

Walsh, Richard. *Literary North Carolina: A Brief Historical Survey.* Raleigh, N.C., 1970.

Watson, Ritchie Devon, Jr. *Yeoman versus Cavalier: The Old Southwest's Fictional Road to Rebellion.* Baton Rouge, La., 1993.

Weaver, Richard. *The Southern Tradition at Bay: A History of Postbellum Thought.* New Rochelle, N.Y., 1968.

BIBLIOGRAPHY   293

Wedell, Marsha. *Elite Women and the Reform Impulse in Memphis, 1875–1915.* Knoxville, Tenn., 1991.

Wheeler, Marjorie Spruill. *New Women of the New South: The Leaders of the Woman Suffrage Movement in the Southern States.* New York, 1993.

Whitener, Daniel J. *Prohibition in North Carolina, 1715–1945.* Chapel Hill, N.C., 1945.

Whites, LeeAnn. *The Civil War as a Crisis in Gender: Augusta, Georgia, 1860–1890.* Athens, Ga., 1995.

Wiencek, Henry. *The Hairstons: An American Family in Black and White.* New York, 1999.

Williamson, Joel. *The Crucible of Race: Black-White Relations in the American South since Emancipation.* New York, 1984.

Wright, Gavin. *Old South, New South: Revolutions in the Southern Economy since the Civil War.* New York, 1986.

Wyatt-Brown, Bertram. *The House of Percy.* New York, 1994.

———. *The Literary Percys: Family History, Gender and and Southern Imagination.* Athens, Ga., 1994.

———. *Southern Honor: Ethics and Behavior in the Old South.* New York, 1982.

Articles

Appleby, Joyce. "Reconciliation and the Northern Novelist, 1865–1880." *Civil War History* 10 (June 1964): 117–29.

Barber, E. Susan. "Anxious Care and Constant Struggle: The Female Humane Association and Richmond's White Civil War Orphans." In *Before the New Deal: Social Welfare in the South, 1830–1930,* ed. Elna C. Green, 120–37. Athens, Ga., 1999.

Baron, Ava, and Susan E. Klepp. "'If I Didn't Have My Sewing Machine . . .': Women and Sewing Machine Technology." In *A Needle, a Bobbin, a Strike: Women Needleworkers in America,* ed. Joan M. Jensen and Sue Davidson, 20–59. Philadelphia, 1984.

Bishir, Catherine W. "Landmarks of Power: Building a Southern Past in Raleigh and Wilmington, North Carolina, 1885–1915." In *Where These Memories Grow: History, Memory, and Southern Identity,* ed. W. Fitzhugh Brundage,139–68. Chapel Hill, N.C., 2000.

———. "'A Strong Force of Ladies': Women, Politics, and Confederate Memorial Associations in Nineteenth-Century Raleigh." *North Carolina Historical Review* 77 (Oct. 2000): 455–91.

Boucher, Ann Williams. "The Plantation Mistress: A Perspective on Antebellum Alabama." In *Stepping out of the Shadows: Alabama Women, 1819–1990,* ed. Mary Martha Thomas, 28–42. Tuscaloosa, Ala., 1995.

Brown, Alexis Girardin. "The Women Left Behind: Transformation of the Southern Belle, 1840–1880." *The Historian* (summer 2000): 759–78.

Campbell, Randolph. "Population Persistence and Social Change in Nineteenth-

Century Texas: Harrison County, 1850–1860." *Journal of Southern History* 48 (May 1982): 185–204.

Carter, Christine Jacobson. "Indispensable Spinsters: Maiden Aunts in the Elite Families of Savannah and Charleston." In *Negotiating Boundaries of Southern Womanhood: Dealing with the Powers That Be,* ed. Janet L. Coryell et al., 110–34. Columbia, Mo., 2000.

Cashin, Joan E. "According to His Wish and Desire: Female Kin and Female Slaves in Planter Wills." In *Women of the American South: A Multicultural Reader,* ed. Christie Anne Farnham, 90–199. New York, 1997.

———. "Households, Kinfolk, and Absent Teenagers: The Demographic Transition in the Old South." *Journal of Family History* 25 (April 2000): 141–57.

———. "Into the Trackless Wilderness: The Refugee Experience in the Civil War." In *A Woman's War: Southern Women, Civil War, and the Confederate Legacy,* ed. Edward D. C. Campbell Jr. and Kym S. Rice, 29–53. Richmond, Va., 1996.

———. "The Structure of Planter Families: 'The Ties that Bound Us Was Strong.'" *Journal of Southern History* 56 (Jan. 1990): 55–70.

Censer, Jane Turner. "A Changing World of Work: North Carolina Elite Women, 1865–1895." *North Carolina Historical Review* 73 (Jan. 1996): 28–55.

———. "Reimagining the North-South Reunion: Southern Women Novelists and the Intersectional Romance, 1876–1900." *Southern Cultures* (summer 1999): 64–91.

———. "Southwestern Migration among North Carolina Planter Families: 'The Disposition to Migrate'." *Journal of Southern History* 57 (August 1991): 407–26.

Cook, Cita. "Women's Role in the Transformation of Winnie Davis into the Daughter of the Confederacy." In *Searching for Their Places: Women in the South across Centuries,* ed. Thomas Appleton and Angela Boswell. Columbia, Mo., forthcoming 2003.

Coulter, E. Merton. "The Confederate Monument in Athens, Georgia." *Georgia Historical Review* 40 (Sept. 1956): 230–47.

Dean, Pamela. "Learning to Be New Women: Campus Culture at the North Carolina Normal and Industrial College." *North Carolina Historical Review* 68 (July 1991): 286–306.

Effland, Anne B. W., Denise M. Rogers, and Valerie Grim. "Women as Agricultural Landowners: What Do We Know About Them?" *Agricultural History* 67 (spring 1993): 235–61.

Falk, Stanley L. "The Warrenton Female Academy of Jacob Mordecai, 1809–1818." *North Carolina Historical Review* 35 (July 1958): 281–98.

Faust, Drew Gilpin. "'Trying to Do a Man's Business': Slavery, Violence, and Gender in the American Civil War." *Gender and History* 4 (summer 1992): 197–214.

Garrison, Dee. "Immoral Fiction in the Late Victorian Library." In *Victorian America,* ed. Daniel Walker Howe, 142–59. Philadelphia, 1976.

Hamburger, Susan. "We Take Care of Our Womanfolk: The Home for Needy Confederate Women in Richmond, Virginia, 1898–1990." In *Before the New Deal: Social Welfare in the South, 1830–1930,* ed. Elna C. Green, 61–77. Athens, Ga., 1999.

Holman, Harriet R. "Mary Greenway McClelland, 1853–1895." *Virginia Magazine of History and Biography* 56 (July 1948): 294–98.

Jabour, Anya. "Albums of Affection: Female Friendship and Coming of Age in Antebellum Virginia." *Virginia Magazine of History and Biography* 107 (spring 1999): 125–58.

———. "'It Will Never Do for Me to Be Married': The Life of Laura Wirt Randall, 1803–1833." *Journal of the Early Republic* 17 (summer 1997): 193–236.

Jones, Anne Goodwyn. "The Work of Gender in the Southern Renaissance." In *Southern Writers and Their Worlds,* ed. Christopher Morris and Steven G. Reinhardt, 41–56. College Station, Tex., 1996.

Kenzer, Robert. "'The Uncertainty of Life': A Profile of Virginia's Civil War Widows." In *The War Was You and Me: Civilians in the American Civil War,* ed. Joan E. Cashin, 112–35. Princeton, N.J., 2002.

Lebsock, Suzanne. "Radical Reconstruction and the Property Rights of Southern Women." *Journal of Southern History* 43 (May 1977): 195–216.

———. "Woman Suffrage and White Supremacy: A Virginia Case Study." In *Taking Off the White Gloves: Southern Women and Women Historians,* ed. Michele Gillespie and Catherine Clinton, 28–42. Columbia, Mo., 1998.

Lewis, Jan, and Kenneth A. Lockridge. "'Sally Has Been Sick': Pregnancy and Family Limitation among Virginia Gentry Women, 1780–1830." *Journal of Social History* 22 (1988): 5–20.

Manning, Carol S. "The Real Beginnings of the Southern Renaissance." In *The Female Tradition in Southern Literature,* 37–56. Urbana, Ill., 1993.

Matthews, Pamela R. "Between Ellen and Louise: Female Friendship, Glasgow's Letters to Louise Chandler Moulton, and *The Wheel of Life.*" In *Ellen Glasgow: New Perspectives,* ed. Dorothy Scura, 106–23. Knoxville, Tenn., 1995.

Mixon, Wayne. "'A Great, Pure Fire': Sexual Passion in the Virginia Fiction of Amélie Rives." In *Looking South: Chapters in the Story of an American Region,* ed. Winfred B. Moore Jr. and Joseph F. Tripp, 207–16. Westport, Conn., 1989.

Moore, Rayburn S. "Paul Hamilton Hayne and Northern Magazines, 1866–1886." In *Essays Mostly on Periodical Publishing in America: A Collection in Honor of Clarence Gohdes,* ed. James Woodress, 134–47. Durham, N.C., 1973.

Parrott, Angie. "'Love Makes Memory Eternal': The United Daughters of the Confederacy in Richmond, Virginia, 1897–1920." In *The Edge of the South: Life in Nineteenth-Century Virginia,* ed. Edward Ayers and John C. Willis, 219–38. Charlottesville, Va., 1991.

Phipps, Sheila Rae. "'Their Desire to Visit the Southerners': Mary Greenhow Lee's Visiting 'Connexion.'" In *Negotiating Boundaries of Southern Womanhood: Dealing with the Powers That Be,* ed. Janet L. Coryell et al., 215–33. Columbia, Mo., 2000.

Pugh, Evelyn L. "Women and Slavery: Julia Gardiner Tyler and the Duchess of Sutherland." *Virginia Magazine of History and Biography* 88 (April 1980): 186–202.

Rachal, William M. E. "Walled Fortress and Resort Hotels." *Virginia Cavalcade* 2 (summer 1952): 20–27.

Rury, John L. "Who Became Teachers? The Social Characteristics of Teachers in American History." In *American Teachers: Histories of a Profession at Work,* ed. Donald Warren, 9–33. New York, 1989.

Schuman, Howard, and Jacqueline Scott. "Generations and Collective Memories." *American Sociological Review* 54 (June 1989): 359–81.

Scott, Anne Firor. "Women in the South: History as Fiction, Fiction as History." In *Rewriting the South: History and Fiction,* ed. Lothar Hönnighausen and Valeria Gennaro Lerda, 22–34. Tübingen, 1993.

Shammas, Carole. "Re-assessing the Married Women's Property Acts." *Journal of Women's History* 6 (1994): 9–30.

Shugg, Roger. "The Survival of the Plantation System in Louisiana." *Journal of Southern History* 3 (Aug. 1937): 311–25.

Sicherman, Barbara. "Sense and Sensibility: A Case Study of Women's Reading in Late-Victorian America." In *Reading in America: Literature and Social History,* ed. Cathy N. Davidson, 201–25. Baltimore, 1989.

Smith, Daniel Scott. "Family Limitation, Sexual Control, and Domestic Feminism in Victorian America." *Feminist Studies* 1 (winter–spring 1972): 40–57.

Steelman, Lala Carr. "The Life-Style of an Eastern North Carolina Planter: Elias Carr of Bracebridge Hall." *North Carolina Historical Review* 57 (winter 1980): 32–33.

Stowe, Steven M. "City, Country, and the Feminine Voice." In *Intellectual Life in Antebellum Charleston,* ed. Michael O'Brien and David Moltke-Hansen, 295–334. Knoxville, Tenn., 1986.

Tonkovich, Nicole. "Writing in Circles: Harriet Beecher Stowe, the Semi-Colon Club, and the Construction of Women's Authorship." In *Nineteenth-Century Women Learn to Write,* ed. Catherine Hobbs, 145–75. Charlottesville, Va., 1995.

Toth, Susan Allen. "'The Rarest and Most Peculiar Grape': Versions of the New England Woman in Nineteenth-Century Local Color Literature." In *Regionalism and the Female Imagination: A Collection of Essays,* ed. Emily Toth, 15–28. New York, 1985.

Townes, A. Jane. "The Effect of Emancipation on Large Landholdings, Nelson and Goochland Counties, Virginia." *Journal of Southern History* 45 (Aug. 1979): 403–12.

Treadway, Sandra Gioia. "A Most Brilliant Woman: Anna Whitehead Bodeker and the First Woman Suffrage Association in Virginia." *Virginia Cavalcade* 43 (spring 1994): 166–77.

Van Zelm, Antoinette G. "Virginia Women as Public Citizens: Emancipation Day Celebrations and Lost Cause Commemorations, 1863–1890." In *Negotiating Boundaries of Southern Womanhood: Dealing with the Powers That Be,* ed. Janet L. Coryell et al., 71–88. Columbia, Mo., 2000.

Wagner, Linda W. "Ellen Glasgow: Daughter as Justified." In *The Lost Tradition: Mothers and Daughters in Literature,* ed. Cathy N. Davidson and E. M. Broner, 139–46. New York, 1980.

Walker, Nancy. "The Romance of Self-Representation: Glasgow and *The Woman Within.*" In *Ellen Glasgow: New Perspectives,* ed. Dorothy Scura, 33–41. Knoxville, Tenn., 1995.

Whites, LeeAnn. "The Charitable and the Poor: The Emergence of Domestic Politics in Augusta, Georgia, 1860–1880." *Journal of Social History* 17 (1984): 601–13.

———. "The Degraffenried Controversy: Race, Class, and Gender in the New South." *Journal of Southern History* 54 (Aug. 1988): 449–78.

———. "'Stand By Your Man': The Ladies Memorial Association and the Reconstruction of Southern White Manhood." In *Women of the American South: A Multicultural Reader,* ed. Christie Anne Farnham, 133–49. New York, 1997.

Wiener, Jonathan. "Female Planters and Planters' Wives in Civil War and Reconstruction: Alabama, 1850–1870." *Alabama Review* 30 (April 1977): 135–49.

———. "Planter Persistence and Social Change: Alabama, 1850–1870." *Journal of Interdisciplinary History* 7 (autumn 1976): 235–60.

Williamson, Eleanor Ramsay. "Exceptional Attainments and Constructive Force: Women, Education, and the Arts in Norfolk, 1871–1933." *Virginia Cavalcade* 47 (spring 1998): 64–75.

Williamson, Joel. "How Black Was Rhett Butler?" In *The Evolution of Southern Culture,* ed. Numan Bartley, 87–107. Athens, Ga., 1988.

Wood, Ann Douglas. "The Literature of Impoverishment: The Women Local Colorists in America, 1865–1914." *Women's Studies* 1 (1972): 3–45.

Wood, Kirsten E. "'The Strongest Ties That Bind Poor Mortals Together': Slaveholding Widows and Family in the Old Southeast." In *Negotiating Boundaries of Southern Womanhood: Dealing with the Powers That Be,* ed. Janet L. Coryell et al., 110–34. Columbia, Mo., 2000.

Dissertations and Unpublished Papers

Brewer, Priscilla. "Home Fires: Cultural Responses to the Introduction of the Cookstove, 1815–1900." Ph.D. diss., Brown University, 1987.

Burton, Orville Vernon. "On the Confederate Home Front: The Transformation of Values from Community to Nation in Edgefield, South Carolina." Unpub. paper, Woodrow Wilson International Center for Scholars, 1989.

Dean, Pamela Evelyn. "Covert Curriculum: Class, Gender, and Student Culture at a New South Woman's College, 1892–1910." Ph.D. diss., University of North Carolina at Chapel Hill, 1995.

Kurtinitis, Sandra Lee. "Sally Alston Mangum Leach, A Profile of the Family of a Plantation Mistress: An Analytical Study of the Correspondence of the Family of Willie P. Mangum." Ph.D. diss., George Washington University, 1986.

Rubin, Anne Sarah. "Redefining the South: Confederates, Southerners, and Americans, 1863–1868." Ph.D. diss., University of Virginia, 1999.

Thomas, Percival Moses. "Plantations in Transition: A Study of Four Virginia Plantations, 1860–1870." Ph.D. diss., University of Virginia, 1979.

Wilkerson-Freeman, Sarah. "Women and the Transformation of American Politics: North Carolina, 1898–1940." Ph.D. diss., University of North Carolina at Chapel Hill, 1995.

INDEX